Perilous and Fair:

Women in the Works and Life of J. R. R. Tolkien

Other Titles from the Mythopoeic Press

Chad Walsh Reviews C. S. Lewis
by Chad Walsh
preface and bibliography by Joe R. Christopher
with a memoir by Damaris Walsh McGuire

The Masques of Amen House
by Charles Williams
introduction by Bernadette Bosky
edited and annotated by David Bratman

The Pedant and the Shuffly
by John Bellairs
illustrated by Marilyn Fitschen
foreword by Brad Strickland

Sayers on Holmes: Essays and Fiction on Sherlock Holmes
by Dorothy L. Sayers
introduction by Alzina Stone Dale
bibliography by Joe R. Christopher

Tolkien on Film: Essays on Peter Jackson's The Lord of the Rings
edited by Janet Brennan Croft

The Travelling Rug
by Dorothy L. Sayers
introduction and bibliography by Joe R. Christopher
annotations by Janet Brennan Croft

Past Watchful Dragons: Fantasy and Faith in the World of C. S. Lewis
edited by Amy H. Sturgis

Intersection of Fantasy & Native America:
From H. P. Lovecraft to Leslie Marmon Silko
edited by Amy H. Sturgis and David D. Oberhelman

Mythlore Index Plus
edited by Edith Crowe and Janet Brennan Croft

Perilous and Fair:
Women in the Works and Life of J. R. R. Tolkien

Edited by
Janet Brennan Croft
and Leslie A. Donovan

Mythopoeic Press
Altadena, CA • 2015

Mythopoeic Press is an imprint of the Mythopoeic Society (www.mythsoc.org). Orders may be placed through our website at www.mythsoc.org/press. For general inquiries or requests to reprint material from our publications, contact:

Editor, Mythopoeic Press
c/o Mythopoeic Society
P.O. Box 6707
Altadena, CA 91003
USA
press@mythsoc.org

Copyright 2015 by the Mythopoeic Press
All rights reserved

ISBN: 978-1-887726-01-6

LCCN: 2014959965

Published in the United States of America

Cover illustration: *Yavanna Kementári* by Ulla Thynell
Cover design by Ulla Thynell
Internal layout by Leslie A. Donovan; set in Palatino Linotype
Index by Janet Brennan Croft

Printed and produced by CreateSpace, a division of Amazon.com

Contents

Introduction: Perilous and Fair, Ancient and Modern, Luminous and Powerful 1
Janet Brennan Croft and Leslie A. Donovan

Acknowledgments 8

Abbreviations and Conventions 9

Historical Perspectives

The History of Scholarship on Female Characters in J. R. R. Tolkien's Legendarium: A Feminist Bibliographic Essay 13
Robin Anne Reid

The Missing Women: J. R. R. Tolkien's Lifelong Support for Women's Higher Education 41
John D. Rateliff

She-who-must-not-be-ignored: Gender and Genre in *The Lord of the Rings* and the Victorian Boys' Book 70
Sharin Schroeder

Power of Gender

The Feminine Principle in Tolkien 99
Melanie A. Rawls

Tolkien's Females and the Defining of Power 118
Nancy Enright

Power in Arda: Sources, Uses and Misuses 136
Edith L. Crowe

Specific Characters

The Fall and Repentance of Galadriel 153
Romuald I. Lakowski

Lúthien Tinúviel and Bodily Desire in the Lay of Leithian 168
Cami D. Agan

The Power of Pity and Tears: The Evolution of Nienna in the Legendarium 189
Kristine Larsen

At Home and Abroad: Éowyn's Two-fold Figuring as War Bride in *The Lord of the Rings* 204
Melissa A. Smith

Earlier Literary Contexts

The Valkyrie Reflex in J. R. R. Tolkien's *The Lord of the Rings*: Galadriel, Shelob, Éowyn, and Arwen — 221
Leslie A. Donovan

Speech and Silence in *The Lord of the Rings*: Medieval Romance and the Transitions of Éowyn — 258
Phoebe C. Linton

Hidden in Plain View: Strategizing Unconventionality in Shakespeare's and Tolkien's Portraits of Women — 281
Maureen Thum

Women Readers

Finding Ourselves in the (Un)Mapped Lands: Women's Reparative Readings of *The Lord of the Rings* — 309
Una McCormack

Contributors — 327
Index — 331

Introduction:
Perilous and Fair, Ancient and Modern, Luminous and Powerful

Janet Brennan Croft and Leslie A. Donovan

> "The Lady of Lórien! Galadriel!" cried Sam. "[...] Beautiful she is, sir! Lovely! Sometimes like a great tree in flower [...]. Hard as di'monds, soft as moonlight. Warm as sunlight, cold as frost in the stars. Proud and far-off as a snow-mountain [...]."
>
> "Then she must be lovely indeed," said Faramir. "Perilously fair."
>
> "I don't know about perilous," said Sam. "It strikes me that folk takes their peril with them into Lórien, and finds it there because they've brought it. But perhaps you could call her perilous, because she's so strong in herself. You, you could dash yourself to pieces on her, like a ship on a rock[...]." (*LotR* IV.5.679–80)

> Still she did not blench: maiden of the Rohirrim, child of kings, slender but as a steel-blade, fair yet terrible. A swift stroke she dealt, skilled and deadly. The outstretched neck she clove asunder, and the hewn head fell like a stone. (*LotR* V.6.841)

Critical interest in J. R. R. Tolkien's treatment of female characters dates back to the beginnings of serious scholarship on his works. As early as 1971, Doris T. Myers published "Brave New World: The Status of Women According to Tolkien, Lewis, and Williams" in the *Cimarron Review*. Works like Myers's grew out of philosophies central to the United States civil rights movements of the 1960s and 1970s that inspired interest in marginalized fiction, such as Tolkien's fantasy, as well as new investigations of those works from feminist perspectives. Yet, because the topic of women in Tolkien's works and life has been troublesome for some readers and scholars, criticism generally has focused on how his major works seem either to ignore women or to place them on unattainable pedestals. Most often, readers and critics have discussed his Middle-earth narratives as lacking in women, preserving cultural stereotypes of female roles, and reflecting antifeminist tendencies. Laura Michel sums up such views when she writes that:

> For years, Tolkien has been criticized, attacked, explained, forgiven, and mainly misunderstood when it comes to the matter of

> women. Criticism on this topic has ranged from mild attempts to excuse Tolkien's point of view to truly violent accusations of misogyny and chauvinism. (56)

At the same time, other researchers have produced detailed, innovative scholarship that recognizes myriad positive contexts for Tolkien's female characters and argues more nuanced understandings of Middle-earth's women. Although these scholars usually agree that the historical context of Tolkien's life prevents him from being considered a feminist of any sort, radical or otherwise, published discussion frequently interprets female characters in *The Lord of the Rings* and *The Silmarillion* as imbued with unconventional power. In the twenty-first century, scholars note increasingly that, where other works of modern fantasy or mythopoeic literature still offer fairly traditional presentations of female characters, Tolkien's women highlight less common and more affirming positions of power.

Despite such active attention to the subject of women in Tolkien's world, some recent works still echo views from earlier periods of Tolkien scholarship. For instance, *A Companion to J. R. R. Tolkien*, published in 2014 and intended to serve as an essential resource for Tolkien specialists and students alike, includes a chapter titled "Women" that insists "enforced female passivity is present in all three of the main female characters of *The Lord of the Rings*" (Roberts 476). The editors of the present volume find perspectives such as that of Roberts troubling after so much research effort and printer's ink has gone to correct similarly ill-informed positions.

With this in mind, *Perilous and Fair: Women in the Works and Life of J. R. R. Tolkien* is motivated by the editors' observation that Roberts's chapter is not an isolated example. Rather, for us, his comments represent a continuing and alarming tendency among some current Tolkien scholars to remain unfamiliar with or to disregard outright the more positive readings of Tolkien's female characters and gender politics found easily in both classic and recent research.

Our collection aims in part to remedy perceptions that Tolkien's works are bereft of female characters, are colored by anti-feminist tendencies, and have yielded little serious academic work on women's issues. We selected these fourteen articles for their use of diverse forms of evidence to examine the relevance of women to Tolkien's works, life, and literary sources. Central to these articles is a consistent recognition that, although Tolkien's fiction undeniably contains many more male than female characters, women fulfill essential, rather than merely supportive, roles in Middle-earth and in his life.

Certainly, Tolkien's primary female characters are fair in ways identical to those of earlier fantasy heroines: they are beautiful, unblemished, courteous, and kind. Nevertheless, many of his women are also perilous in ways earlier literature generally attributes to villainous or evil women. Two examples of female characters who are clearly perilous, but not villains are: Éowyn, who is a warrior trained to wield a sword, and destined to slay the Witch-king of Angmar; and Lúthien, who rescues Beren from Sauron's prison and uses her magic to help him wrest a Silmaril from the Iron Crown of Morgoth. Although such female characters typically require the aid of male heroes, it is equally significant that the male heroes require the efforts of these women to achieve their victories. Unifying the concepts of *perilous* and *fair* in our title lends a metaphor for the issues of female power examined throughout this collection.

The fourteen articles collected here include seven first published in various sources between 1984 and 2007; these represent strong and textually sound readings that have contributed significantly to the evolution of scholarship on women in Tolkien's fiction. We balance these classic explorations with seven new essays that build on past studies and point to future directions for the topic. Since many additional fine articles might have been included, this collection is best considered a representative sample, rather than a definitive canon, for women in Tolkien's works and life. We have restricted contributions to studies exclusively on Tolkien and have avoided works that overlap each other considerably in material or approach.

This collection opens with a section on "Historical Perspectives" that consists of three new articles. "The History of Scholarship on Female Characters in J. R. R. Tolkien's Legendarium: A Feminist Bibliographic Essay," by Robin Anne Reid, establishes a long-needed critical context for studying women in Tolkien's works and life. Along with the entire collection, her essay clarifies the breadth of Tolkien scholarship on the subject of women. By summarizing the historical development of scholarship on women in Tolkien's works, Reid documents the increase in the number of works focusing on his female characters as well as the variety of critical theories and approaches applied to them.

John D. Rateliff's study "The Missing Women: J. R. R. Tolkien's Lifelong Support for Women's Higher Education" corrects perceptions that Tolkien's professional and personal interests were focused largely on men. Rateliff provides a variety of compelling historical evidence to analyze the ways in which Tolkien's female family members, students, and colleagues informed his views on women as well as his writing. Rather than teasing tiny, ambiguous fragments from the fabric of Tolkien's biography, Rateliff examines several clear and often overlooked instances of strong women in Tolkien's life. His article highlights Tolkien's commitment to higher education for women as proof that he understood and empathized with women's concerns.

With "She-who-must-not-be-ignored: Gender and Genre in *The Lord of the Rings* and the Victorian Boys' Book," Sharin Schroeder concludes the section by identifying relationships between Tolkien's novel and adventure-romances such as H. Rider Haggard's *She: A History of an Adventure,* which Tolkien enjoyed as a young reader and which influenced his writing. Through close comparisons of Galadriel and Haggard's She, as well as of genre differences and expectations, Schroeder corrects some chief misconceptions about the portrayal of women and gender in *The Lord of the Rings*. However, where others seek to make Haggard's central female character a model upon which Tolkien drew when creating Galadriel, Schroeder argues that other elements of Haggard's work had a more crucial impact on Tolkien's writing.

In the section "Power of Gender," we present three classic articles that serve as a foundation for the development of scholarship on women in Tolkien's fiction. "The Feminine Principle in Tolkien," by Melanie A. Rawls (1984), explores the interaction of masculine and feminine principles, gender as opposed to sex, in Middle-earth. An essential work for refuting claims that Tolkien rejects the feminine, Rawls's essay demonstrates how the balance of feminine and masculine principles factors into a character's place in Middle-earth's struggle between good and evil.

Expanding the conversation on Tolkien's women to incorporate issues of gender from a spiritual vantage, Nancy Enright's "Tolkien's Females and the Defining of Power" (2007) evaluates how characters critique traditional and worldly power as it is typically embodied in masculine imagery. Enright establishes Tolkien's female characters as reflective of biblical teachings that promote the choice of love over pride as a more powerful alternative to domination by force.

Edith L. Crowe's "Power in Arda: Sources, Uses and Misuses" (1996) analyzes issues of power and their renunciation in Tolkien's works. She pays particular attention to dichotomous models of power relations, such as dominator vs. partnership and power *within* vs. power *over*. Crowe considers spiritual, political, and physical sources of authority and how various peoples and individuals in Middle-earth wield such control.

The "Specific Characters" section deals with individual characters in *The Silmarillion* and *The Lord of the Rings*. "The Fall and Repentance of Galadriel" (2007), by Romuald I. Lakowski, examines material from the development of Tolkien's legendarium regarding Tolkien's depiction of his elven queen. Focusing particularly on Tolkien's evolving views of Galadriel's rebellion and redemption, Lakowski suggests that his ongoing efforts to rethink Galadriel's place in his mythology until the end of his life indicate the importance of this character in his works.

Cami D. Agan's new article, "Lúthien Tinúviel and Bodily Desire in the Lay of Leithian," positions and emphasizes the role of the female body as a fundamental source of women's power. Agan reads Lúthien as taking on the authority to challenge male figures by enacting a sexual agency centered in her own desire. For Agan, Lúthien's feminine attributes, grounded specifically in her gendered body, make her an active, potent force in Middle-earth's mythology and history in contrast to the passive and ineffectual maiden other scholars perceive.

"The Power of Pity and Tears: The Evolution of Nienna in the Legendarium," a new article by Kristine Larsen, describes the character's development from her earliest iterations as a one-dimensional goddess of death and doom to a complex and key figure in Middle-earth's mythology. Larsen contradicts views that Nienna's primary mode is to weep passively. She argues that Tolkien ultimately empowers her with mercy and mourning as participatory actions echoing those in which the Christian faith perceives the Virgin Mary to interact with humanity.

Closing this section is Melissa A. Smith's "At Home and Abroad: Éowyn's Two-fold Figuring as War Bride in *The Lord of the Rings*" (2007), which compares Tolkien's shieldmaiden with World War I war brides to provide striking insights about her psychology. Situating

Tolkien's works within this historical context, Smith analyzes Éowyn's relationships with Aragorn and Faramir as fictional analogues to the lived experiences of women who were cast in the roles of left-behind or foreign war brides during the war.

Any study of Tolkien's works and life would be seriously flawed without discussion of his medieval and Renaissance literary sources. In "Earlier Literary Contexts," we include Leslie A. Donovan's "The Valkyrie Reflex in J. R. R. Tolkien's *The Lord of the Rings*: Galadriel, Shelob, Éowyn, and Arwen" (2003) to highlight the ways in which his medieval Old Norse and Anglo-Saxon sources express female power. Donovan traces Tolkien's adaptation of materials from heroic Germanic literatures to construct his more modern vision. Her analysis of characteristics traditionally attributed to valkyries argues that Galadriel, Shelob, Éowyn, and Arwen exhibit, subvert, or transform the legacy they inherit from these mythological women.

In contrast, Phoebe C. Linton explores Éowyn as modeled on medieval romance and quest conventions in her new article "Speech and Silence in *The Lord of the Rings*: Medieval Romance and the Transitions of Éowyn." Linton examines Tolkien's use of traditional patterns associated with medieval female knights to inspire his more modernly motivated war-maid. She describes Éowyn's character as constructed on alternating moments of silence and speech that go beyond Tolkien's medieval sources as she evolves from a passive and vulnerable court lady to a powerfully effective wife and healer.

Bringing us into the Renaissance, Maureen Thum's "Hidden in Plain View: Strategizing Unconventionality in Shakespeare's and Tolkien's Portraits of Women" (2006) challenges us to look closely at the disguises of women in *The Lord of the Rings* and *Twelfth Night* to discover alternative styles of power and gender. Thum urges readers to recognize that both Tolkien and Shakespeare adapt traditional stereotypes of women in similar ways to advance gender roles beyond the normal limitations of their societies.

The final article stands by itself in its own category, "Women Readers," to point toward directions for future studies of women both within Tolkien's life and works and as these may inhabit other fiction. Una McCormack's "Finding Ourselves in the (Un)Mapped Lands: Women's Reparative Readings of *The Lord of the Rings*" explores fanfiction by women as a creative-critical response to Tolkien's text. McCormack investigates a representative sample of works that inserts new female figures into Middle-earth or expands previously marginalized female characters in order to dialogue with the canonic text about issues of gender and power.

What directions might scholarship on Tolkien's women take from here? Possibilities include close examinations of female characters in media adaptations of Tolkien's works—artwork, movies, television, and games. What do such adaptors draw from Tolkien, and what aspects of his works do they omit or alter? What do adaptations have to say about their creators' own readings of Tolkien? The tools of digital humanities also offer intriguing new ways to study Tolkien's texts at a granular level, revealing gendered patterns of vocabulary and frequency of speech, for example, and enabling evidence-based comparisons with other authors.

Our central aim in *Perilous and Fair* is to refute simplistic claims that Tolkien has nothing useful, relevant, or modern to say about women. We also intend to confirm that critics have engaged fruitfully with issues surrounding the feminine and female power since the early days of Tolkien scholarship and that they continue to do so. We hope this body of work will spark further discussion and criticism about the roles of women in Tolkien's works and life and establish clearly the continuing importance of this topic to future scholarship.

Works Cited

Michel, Laura. "Politically Incorrect: Tolkien, Women, and Feminism." *Tolkien and Modernity* 1. Eds. Frank Weinreich and Thomas Honegger. Zollikofen, Switzerland: Walking Tree, 2006. 55–76. Print.

Myers, Doris T. "Brave New World: The Status of Women According to Tolkien, Lewis, and Williams." *Cimarron Review* 17 (1971): 13–19. Print.

Roberts, Adam. "Women." *A Companion to J. R. R. Tolkien*. Blackwell Companions to Literature and Culture 147. Ed. Stuart D. Lee. Chichester, West Sussex, UK: Wiley-Blackwell, 2014. 473–86. Print.

Acknowledgments

First, the editors wish to express our most sincere appreciation to our contributors for their past and present care and attention to scholarship on the subject of women in the field of Tolkien studies, a subject dear to both of us personally, professionally, and politically.

In addition, we thank Megan Abrahamson and Sarah Croft for proofreading and citation checking. We are also especially grateful to Zachary N. Watkins for a host of wide-ranging copyediting tasks and editorial assistance. Any errors that remain are, of course, our responsibility and no fault of theirs.

The various present and past members of the Mythopoeic Press Editorial Board and the Mythopoeic Society Council of Stewards deserve special acknowledgment for their abiding support of this project and mythopoeic scholarship in general.

Finally, we bow to the many strong women who enriched Tolkien's personal and professional lives in ways that empower both his fiction and the lives and careers of so many of us later authors, scholars and readers. Among these, we honor particularly Edith Bratt Tolkien, Mabel Suffield Tolkien, Priscilla Tolkien, Jane Suffield Neave, Simone d'Ardenne, Stella Mills, Elizabeth Wright, and Dorothy L. Sayers.

Conventions and Abbreviations

Each article includes its own Works Cited list in an effort keep individual articles as self-contained as possible. However, to maintain consistency in references, citations to works by Tolkien that appear in several articles have been standardized throughout and not repeated in Works Cited lists for individual articles. Abbreviations for Tolkien's works commonly used in this volume are listed below.

Along with corrections to obvious errors in the original publication, references appearing in the seven classic articles have been silently emended to the editions we determined as our standards.

- *H* — *The Annotated Hobbit*. Ed. Douglas A. Anderson. Second edition, revised. Boston: Houghton Mifflin, 2002.
- *Jewels* — *The War of the Jewels*. Ed. Christopher Tolkien. Boston: Houghton Mifflin, 1994. Vol. 11: *The History of Middle-earth.*
- *Letters* — *The Letters of J. R. R. Tolkien*. Ed. Humphrey Carpenter, with the assistance of Christopher Tolkien. Boston: Houghton Mifflin, 1981.
- *LotR* — *The Lord of the Rings*. 50th anniversary ed. One volume. Boston: Houghton Mifflin Harcourt, 2005.
- *Lost Tales I* — *The Book of Lost Tales, Part One*. Ed. Christopher Tolkien. Boston: Houghton Mifflin, 1984. Vol. 1: *The History of Middle-earth.*
- *Lost Tales II* — *The Book of Lost Tales, Part Two*. Ed. Christopher Tolkien. Boston: Houghton Mifflin, 1984. Vol. 2: *The History of Middle-earth.*
- *OED* — *Oxford English Dictionary*
- *OFS* — *On Fairy-stories*. Various editions cited by authors.
- *Peoples* — *The Peoples of Middle-earth*. Ed. Christopher Tolkien. Boston: Houghton Mifflin, 1996. Vol. 12: *The History of Middle-earth.*
- *S* — *The Silmarillion*. Ed. Christopher Tolkien. Second edition. Boston: Houghton Mifflin, 2001.
- *Treason* — *The Treason of Isengard*. Ed. Christopher Tolkien. Boston: Houghton Mifflin, 1989. Vol. 7: *The History of Middle-earth.*
- *UT* — *Unfinished Tales of Númenor and Middle-earth*. Ed. Christopher Tolkien. Boston: Houghton Mifflin, 1980.

Historical Perspectives

The History of Scholarship on Female Characters in J. R. R. Tolkien's Legendarium:
A Feminist Bibliographic Essay[1]

Robin Anne Reid

The purpose of this bibliographic essay is to provide an historical overview of fan, independent, and academic scholarship on female characters in J. R. R. Tolkien's legendarium. The element that makes this essay feminist is not that the scholarship is defined as feminist, or written by self-identified feminists (although some is), or is even limited to authors who identify as women. Instead, as a feminist academic trained in cultural studies, I have identified articles and book chapters that primarily focus on Tolkien's female characters.[2] The organization of the essay is chronological to show the development of scholarship on female characters over time, including not only the increasing attention paid to these characters, but also a growing application of newer critical theories and methods. Another change in criticism over time is that publications shift from fanzines to peer-reviewed journals and academic collections. The first five sections cover a decade, while the sixth considers works from 2010–2013. The classic essays reprinted in *Perilous and Fair* are identified and discussed in the sections on the decade in which they were first published. Besides the primary focus on literary scholarship, two essays on female characters in Peter Jackson's films are included because of

---

1. I am grateful to Texas A&M University-Commerce for a Spring 2014 faculty development leave to develop my Tolkien project which included this essay; to Jacob Pichnarcik, Interlibrary Loan Specialist, for aid in securing materials; and to Wilma Shires who volunteered to help copyedit the final draft.

2. There are no monographs primarily or completely focused on the female characters although some mention them briefly or in passing. Rather than deal with the handful of references that are not particularly developed, I have chosen not to include them. I have tried to be as complete as possible in assembling information on articles and book chapters, but gaps in databases and difficulties in acquiring early publications resulted in having to leave some publications out.

their discussion on Tolkien's female characters. Also included are one dissertation and a discussion of relevant sections from the *J. R. R. Tolkien Encyclopedia* edited by Michael D. C. Drout.

In 2000, Drout and Hilary Wynne published a comprehensive bibliographic essay on Tolkien scholarship since 1982 that suggests needs for future Tolkien criticism; their essay begins where Richard C. West's second edition of *Tolkien Criticism: An Annotated Bibliography* ends.[3] They make a number of excellent points, but most pertinent for this project is the need for contemporary scholars to familiarize themselves with existing Tolkien scholarship. Related to that need is the production of a "complete, up-to-date, annotated and evaluative bibliography of Tolkien scholarship" (104). While the lack of awareness of past scholarship on Tolkien is a general problem, it may be more apparent with regard to the topic of women and Tolkien.[4] I agree with Drout and Wynne, and would highlight also work by Douglas Anderson in constructing checklists on specific scholars' work as well as that of David Bratman and Merlin DeTardo in compiling "The Year's Work in Tolkien Studies" and Drout, Rebecca Epstein, Laura Kalafarski, Stefanie Olsen, Kathryn Paar, and Jason Rea in compiling the annual "Bibliography (in English)" as important contributions to that goal.

However, the sheer amount of extant scholarship is daunting.[5] Given the increase in scholarship, thoroughness, rather than completeness, has been my goal in presenting this annotated and evaluative bibliography.[6] Additionally, the field of Tolkien studies is no longer limited to literary studies, but includes scholars in disciplines across and outside the humanities who increasingly draw on inter-, multi-, and transdisciplinary methodologies to publish scholarship on films, games, fan

---

3. Johnson's *J. R. R. Tolkien: Six Decades of Criticism*, published in 1986, covers a wide range of publications from the 1920s to the 1980s.

4. Croft notes that, as editor of *Mythlore*, "I still get papers reinventing the wheel on a regular basis. [...] nowhere is this more evident than on the topic of women in *The Lord of the Rings*."

5. A June 12, 2014, search ("Tolkien: Subjects" "not: film") in the *MLA International Bibliography* resulted in a total of 1,897 sources: 1,268 Academic Journal Articles; 457 Book Articles; 83 Books; 47 Dissertation Abstracts; 37 Book Collections; four editions; and one website. Even so, good evidence suggests that not all published scholarship on Tolkien's work is indexed in MLA.

6. The *MLA International Bibliography* indexes 249 publications from January 1960–December 1980. From January 2000 to December 2013 (excluding the film citations), the MLA indexes 909 publications (as of June 12, 2014).

culture, tourism, and marketing. Such scholarship may ignore Tolkien's primary works entirely or may include them as a focus for discussion to varying degrees. The growth of professional outlets for scholarship in Tolkien studies, shown in the recent announcement of a new online open-access journal, *The Journal of Tolkien Research*, as well the debut of a Tolkien Studies Area at the 2014 National Popular and American Culture Association Conference, is likely to result in more scholarship in all areas of the field. I suspect that in the future, bibliographic work will have to acknowledge a specific focus and purpose, as this essay does, rather than attempting comprehensive coverage.

From the perspective of a scholar trained in critical theories rather than in national or period literary specializations, I am interested in reading beyond the "best" literary Tolkien criticism from peer-reviewed journals (or monographs published by university presses). That is, I read publications in addition to those works Drout and Wynne identify as necessary for anyone interested in Tolkien criticism. As a feminist, I am interested in the reception of Tolkien's work in the twentieth and now twenty-first centuries, as it speaks to a cultural context shaped by the period in which women in the United Kingdom and the United States won the right to vote and demanded access to education and professions that had been previously denied them. During recent decades of activism, the development of feminist, women, and gender studies programs at universities has changed the circumstances of production and the content of academic scholarship, including Tolkien studies.[7] Thus, unlike Drout and Wynne, I recognize that the Modern Language Association's International Bibliography attempts to index earlier work on Tolkien, published in what were then fanzines, specifically *Mythlore* and *Mallorn*.[8]

---

7. Similar changes relating to critical race and anti-racist initiatives have also occurred. The effect of Marxist and other class-related theories is perhaps greater in the U. K. than in the U. S., but these changes are both incredibly complex and outside the scope of this essay. I do not claim that feminism is the cause of foundational changes in higher education, only that women, if primarily white and middle-class, have had increasingly greater access to and success in academic settings such as humanities programs and scholarly publishing. Additionally, scholarship on female characters need not utilize feminist theories to have been considered for this essay.

8. Drout and Wynne themselves note that it is not easy to "separate out the scholarly from the non-scholarly. [...] While it does not appear that *Mallorn* is a refereed journal, and while *Mythlore*, at least since its recent format change, is, using

The 1970s

Myers, Doris T. "Brave New World: The Status of Women According to Tolkien, Lewis, and Williams." *Cimarron Review* 17 (1971): 13–19. Print.

Goselin, Peter Damien. "Two Faces of Eve: Galadriel and Shelob as Anima Figures." *Mythlore* 6.3 (#21) (1979): 3–4. Print.

At least two essays on female characters were published during the 1970s; the first appears in what was a new literary journal and was the first work I found to consider Tolkien's work in the context of women's liberation. The second, published in *Mythlore,* is a Jungian analysis.[9] Doris T. Myers's essay is the second *Cimarron Review* published on Tolkien. She looked at the status of women in the three "Oxford Christian" authors' fiction. Tolkien's work is set in the past; Lewis's in "outer space [...] peopled by spiritual beings," and Williams's in an "unseen world" that connects with the material world. Noting that fantastic genres allow creators to create any type of gender system, Myers asks what "the women's liberationist," a hypothetical and distanced phrase, would find in these authors' new and fantastic worlds (13–14). She argues that Tolkien's and Lewis's works reproduce the characterization of women found in medieval and Renaissance literature but that Williams's work does not. Myers concludes that none of the three authors considered showing any change in the "present social system" (which Myers sees as outdated and sexist), but that Williams's characters, male and female, are different enough from those of the other two authors that she considers his created world "better for women—for people—than the worlds of Tolkien and Lewis" (19).

Peter Damien Goselin's three-page essay opens with quotes from *Sir Gawain and the Green Knight* and Jung before presenting an analysis of anima and shadow figures in Tolkien's work. The majority of the piece is spent on major characters from *The Lord of the Rings* although

---

(note continued)

this distinction to separate *Mallorn* from *Mythlore* on purely formal terms was unsatisfactory, since there are articles in *Mallorn* that are easily of as high quality as the best in *Mythlore* (and likewise the earlier issues of *Mythlore* are just as full of non-scholarly work as is *Mallorn*)" (136).

9. At this time, *Mythlore* was a fanzine produced by the Mythopoeic Society. It became a peer-reviewed academic journal in 1999.

female figures from *The Silmarillion* are mentioned. Goselin identifies Jungian characteristics shared by Galadriel and Shelob (antiquity, beauty or ugliness, wisdom or conceit) and argues that Tolkien constructs them as opposing aspects of the feminine principle, with the bright anima being more powerful.

The 1980s

Johnson, Janice. "The Celeblain of Celeborn and Galadriel." *Mythlore* 9.2 (#32) (1982): 11–19. Print.

Partridge, Brenda. "No Sex Please–We're Hobbits: The Construction of Female Sexuality in *The Lord of the Rings*." *J. R. R. Tolkien: This Far Land*. Ed. Robert Giddings. Critical Studies Series. Totowa, NJ: Barnes and Noble, 1983. 179–97. Print.

Rawls, Melanie. "The Feminine Principle in Tolkien." *Mythlore* 10.4 (#38) (1984): 5–13. Print.

Ryan, J. S. "Another Warrior Woman Who Gave Up Thoughts of Battle and Heroism: Greta the Strong." *Minas Tirith Evening-Star* 16.2 (1987): 4–7. Print.

Startzman, L. Eugene. "Goldberry and Galadriel: The Quality of Joy." *Mythlore* 16.2 (#60) (1989): 5–13. Print.

Four of these five publications were printed in Tolkien fan publications (*Mythlore* and the *Minas Tirith Evening-Star*): Johnson, Rawls, Ryan, and Startzman. Partridge's chapter appears in the first academic collection of essays on Tolkien published in the United Kingdom. I would argue that Partridge and Rawls have a feminist purpose, although they make different arguments on Tolkien's work.

Johnson's essay traces Galadriel and Celeborn's lives and relationship through the different versions, drawing on Christopher Tolkien's publications and archival research at Marquette University. At eight pages, this article is longer than many in *Mythlore* at the time and cites secondary as well as primary and archival sources. Johnson's is the first publication I found on Galadriel, and her use of archival materials sets it apart from most early scholarship on Tolkien's work in general, and especially scholarship on the female characters.

The next two essays (Partridge and Rawls) move away from a specific focus on female characters to larger thematic issues of female sexuality and the feminine principle, respectively, by drawing on Freudian and Jungian psychoanalytic theories. These pieces differ in tone, focus, and methodology: Partridge is more critical of the construction of female characters in *The Lord of the Rings,* while Rawls analyzes paired male and female characters in *The Silmarillion* and *The Lord of the Rings* to argue the complementarity of feminine and masculine characteristics in a more positive evaluation of Tolkien's work. Partridge's evidence includes biographical as well as textual explication, whereas Rawls focuses solely on a close reading of the texts. Thus, Partridge's argument extends beyond the scope of the fictional texts to claim the existence of sexism "in the conventions and symbolism of literary and religious tradition. [...] which reflect conscious and subconscious conflicting attitudes to sexuality and the definition of the economic and political role of men and women in society" (195).[10] Despite their differences, the essays share a common psychoanalytic approach. Rawls's essay is one of the classic articles selected to be included in this anthology.

J. S. Ryan's essay is a short descriptive article about a 1970 novel by Donald Sobol, *Greta the Strong*. The novel, set in Arthurian Britain after the King's death, focuses on an eighteen-year-old farm girl who is honorable enough to survive chivalric tests but rejects Excalibur and chooses marriage and peace. Ryan's purpose in discussing this novel is to address "feminist criticism" (not feminist critics) that he characterizes as being not "pleased" by Éowyn's marriage to Faramir (5). His conclusion is that the two authors' "heroines" are similar and "nearer our time than the older Germanic tales of legendary women warriors" and that the narratives have "pleasing elements of moral fable, of exemplum, and of proto-Christian qualities of meekness, service and love of all" (6). Ryan's introduction constructs "feminist criticism" as expressing a negative emotion about Éowyn's decision which he defends with an

10. I have heard slighting references to Partridge's essay in conversation with a number of Tolkienists at conferences, primarily to the section presenting the Freudian reading of Shelob and Sam's battle, and to her accusations of Tolkien's sexism as a typical example of a feminist reading. Having revisited the Giddings collection for this project, I might note that a number of its essays are critical of Tolkien in ways commonly not seen in American criticism while a number of Partridge's other points have been developed in later Tolkien criticism—the closeness of the homosocial male friendships in Tolkien's life, the patterns of chivalric and modern warfare, and the relationship of Sam and Frodo relating to Tolkien's World War I experiences among them. I have been guilty of dismissing this essay in the past myself because of its Freudian elements and was surprised to see it contained more nuance than I had remembered.

appeal not only to another fantasy novel but also to a Christian theme of spirituality, a defense that will appear again in the scholarship covered in this essay.

L. Eugene Startzman contextualizes an argument about Goldberry's and Galadriel's narrative functions through Tolkien's discussion of consolation and joy in "On Fairy-stories," an early example of drawing on Tolkien's theory as a tool for analyzing his legendarium, a now common-practice in Tolkien criticism. Startzman focuses on the encounters the hobbits have with Goldberry and Galadriel and contrasts the two types of joy through analysis of the settings, the relative power of the two characters, the imagery associated with them, and the nature of the sanctuaries they offer to the hobbits. His essay is not solely focused on the female characters; Startzman analyzes them primarily in the context of their help and impact on the quest, as "archetypal, feminine image[s] of goodness and light" (12).

The 1990s

Crowe, Edith L. "Power in Arda: Sources, Uses and Misuses." *Mythlore* 21.2 (#80) (1996): 272–77. Print.

Fenwick, Mac. "Breastplates of Silk: Homeric Women in *The Lord of the Rings*." *Mythlore* 21.3 (#80) (1996): 17–23; 50. Print.

Hopkins, Lisa. "Female Authority Figures in the Works of Tolkien, C. S. Lewis and Charles Williams." *Mythlore* 21.2 (#80) (1996): 364–66. Print.

All three of the essays on female characters in Tolkien published in the late 1990s appeared in *Mythlore*. Two of them, although disagreeing in their interpretation of Tolkien's work, present feminist perspectives. Edith Crowe's article is the first academic essay to foreground itself as a feminist analysis rooted in feminist scholarship, written by a self-identified feminist. While three earlier publications have feminist perspectives, none identify the feminist issues to the extent Crowe's does, and two of the three (Partridge and Myers) are negative in their evaluation of Tolkien's work. Partridge's and Rawls's are feminist psychoanalytic essays, but they, unlike Crowe, never use the word "feminist" and cite no feminist scholarship.[11]

One of the classic essays reprinted in this anthology, Crowe's article provides an historical context for feminist reception of Tolkien's work, noting that readers in the 1990s have access to many more works involving feminist themes than did readers in the 1960s. Her article also identifies two different feminist theories: social constructionism and essentialism. Crowe presents a short history of feminist activism, from early attempts to increase women's access to and participation in education and professions to later questioning of social values. The latter place, she argues, is where feminists and Tolkien come together on concerns about power. Crowe's final argument is not that Tolkien, or his world as developed in *The Silmarillion* and *The Lord of the Rings*, is feminist; instead, she argues that the works share similar values with those of many feminists.

Mac Fenwick's article draws on scholarship about classical literature as well as earlier essays from *Mythlore*. Addressing the split between Germanic and Classical mythologies, and acknowledging Tolkien's primary interest in the Germanic, Fenwick argues for the influence of classical texts Tolkien studied at Oxford. Citing essays on the structural influences of the *Aeneid* and *Odyssey* on Tolkien's work, Fenwick's argument is that the "conflict between Galadriel and Shelob, as mediated by Frodo" is "highly reminiscent of the conflict between Circe/Calypso and the female monsters of the *Odyssey* as mediated by Odysseus" (17). Detailed explication of the episodes involving the characters supports his claim, similar to Startzman's, that the two female characters are only significant in their narrative function in regard to the male hero, Frodo.

Although she does not cite Myers in her essay on powerful female characters in Tolkien, Lewis, and Williams, Lisa Hopkins has a similar focus despite her different conclusion. She argues that female authority figures in William and Lewis are presented as "at best a contradiction in terms, at worst a fear of nightmare proportions" (364). She covers one character from Williams's work (Damaris in *The Place of the Lion*) and several from Lewis's (the White Witch, Lady of the Green Kirtle,

11. While feminist psychoanalytic theories exist, the male founders of major schools of psychology and psychoanalysis are not known for feminist work.

Fairy Hardcastle, the Lady of Perelandra, Jane, Lucy, and Susan), arguing that Lewis's books show that although young "girls [...] may be likeable and even admirable characters, the translation into womanhood invariably turns females into something much more worrying" (365). Approximately two-thirds of the essay focuses on Tolkien's work, acknowledging the small number of female characters among the main characters and among entire species. Hopkins's argument has become commonplace in Tolkien studies: even though the actual number of female characters is small, they "have a range of parts to play whose importance is remarkably disproportionate to their numbers. Their very scarcity seems to invest them with an [...] almost talismanic status, and in some cases their very femininity [... is] the very source of their strength" (365). Hopkins is able to draw on the female characters of *The Silmarillion,* which Myers was not, to discuss Melian, Lúthien, Idril, Gilraen, and Morwen. She concludes that Tolkien's work, in spite of showing traditional attitudes about women, differs from Lewis's in constructing female characters who show "a powerful clarity and novelty, unhampered by that crippling fear of femininity which besets the works of his fellow Inklings" (366).

The 2000s

Clark, George, and Daniel Timmons, eds. *J. R. R. Tolkien and His Literary Resonances: Views of Middle-earth*. Contributions to the Study of Science Fiction and Fantasy 89. Westport, CT: Greenwood, 2000. Print.

Ringel, Faye. "Women Fantasists: In the Shadow of the Ring." Clark and Timmons 159–71.

Sly, Debbie. "Weaving Nets of Gloom: 'Darkness Profound' in Tolkien and Milton." Clark and Timmons 108–19.

Pretorius, David. "Binary Issues and Feminist Issues in *LOTR*." *Mallorn* 40 (2002): 32–38. Print.

Chance, Jane, ed. *Tolkien the Medievalist*. Routledge Studies in Medieval Religion and Culture 3. London: Routledge, 2003. Print.

Donovan, Leslie A. "The Valkyrie Reflex in J. R. R. Tolkien's *The Lord of the Rings*: Galadriel, Shelob, Éowyn, and Arwen." Chance 106–32.

Maher, Michael W. " 'A Land without Stain': Medieval Images of Mary and Their Use in the Characterization of Galadriel." Chance 225–36.

West, Richard C. "Real-World Myth in a Secondary World: Mythological Aspects in the Story of Beren and Lúthien." Chance 259–67.

Croft, Janet Brennan, ed. *Tolkien on Film: Essays on Peter Jackson's* The Lord of the Rings. Altadena, CA: Mythopoeic Press, 2004. Print.

Akers-Jordan, Cathy. "Fairy Princess or Tragic Heroine? The Metamorphosis of Arwen Undómiel in Peter Jackson's *The Lord of the Rings* Film." Croft 195–213.

Thum, Maureen. "The 'Sub-Subcreation' of Galadriel, Arwen, and Éowyn: Women of Power in Tolkien's and Jackson's *The Lord of the Rings.*" Croft 231–56.

Fife, Ernelle. "Wise Warriors in Tolkien, Lewis, and Rowling." *Mythlore* 25.1/2 (#95/96) (2006): 147–62. Print.

Neville, Jennifer. "Women." *Reading* The Lord of the Rings*: New Writings on Tolkien's Classic*. Ed. Robert Eaglestone. London: Continuum, 2006. 101–10. Print.

Weinreich, Frank, and Thomas Honegger, eds. *Tolkien and Modernity 1.* Cormarë Series 9. Zollikofen, Switzerland: Walking Tree, 2006. Print.

Benvenuto, Maria Raffaella. "Against Stereotype: Éowyn and Lúthien as 20th-Century Women." Weinreich and Honegger 31–54.

Michel, Laura. "Politically Incorrect: Tolkien, Women, and Feminism." Weinreich and Honegger 55–76.

Carter, Susan. "Galadriel and Morgan Le Fey: Tolkien's Redemption of the Lady of the Lacuna." *Mythlore* 25.3/4 (#97/98) (2007): 71–89. Print.

Croft, Janet Brennan, ed. *Tolkien and Shakespeare: Essays on Shared Themes and Language.* Critical Explorations in Science Fiction and Fantasy 2. Jefferson, NC: McFarland, 2007. Print.

Lakowski, Romuald I. " 'Perilously Fair': Titania, Galadriel, and the Fairy Queen of Medieval Romance." Croft 60–78.

Thum, Maureen. "Hidden in Plain View: Strategizing Unconventionality in Shakespeare's and Tolkien's Portraits of Women." Croft 229–50.

Drout, Michael D. C., ed. *J. R. R. Tolkien Encyclopedia: Scholarship and Critical Assessment*. New York: Routledge, 2007. Print.
Armstrong, Helen. "Arwen." Drout 38–39.
Dickerson, Matthew. "Finwë and Míriel." Drout 212–13.
Fisher, Jason. "Galadriel." Drout 227–28.
Hesser, Katherine. "Éowyn." Drout 168–69.
---. "Goldberry." Drout 244–46.
---. "Melian." Drout 412–13.
Houghton, John Wm. "Ungoliant." Drout 687.
Leibeger, Carol A. "Women in Tolkien's Work." Drout 710–12.
Ripley, Aline. "Feminist Readings of Tolkien." Drout 202–03.
Seaman, Gerald. "Lúthien." Drout 396–97.
Smol, Anna. "Gender in Tolkien's Works." Drout 233–35.
Tubbs, Patricia. "*Juliana*." Drout 313–17.
Zettersten, Arne. "*Ancrene Wisse*." Drout 15–16.

Enright, Nancy. "Tolkien's Females and the Defining of Power." *Renascence: Essays on Values in Literature* 59.2 (2007): 93–108. Print.

Fredrick, Candice, and Sam McBride. "Battling the Woman Warrior: Females and Combat in Tolkien and Lewis." *Mythlore* 25.3/4 (#97/98) (2007): 29–42. Print.

Hatcher, Melissa McCrory. "Finding Woman's Role in *The Lord of the Rings*." *Mythlore* 25.3/4 (#97/87) (2007): 43–54. Print.

Lakowski, Romuald I. "The Fall and Repentance of Galadriel." *Mythlore* 25.3/4 (#97/98) (2007): 91–116. Print.

Smith, Melissa. "At Home and Abroad: Éowyn's Two-Fold Figuring as a War Bride in *The Lord of the Rings*." *Mythlore* 26.1/2 (#99/100) (2007): 161–72. Print.

Basso, Ann McCauley. "Fair Lady Goldberry, Daughter of the River." *Mythlore* 27.1/2 (#103/104) (2008): 137–46.

Doughan, David. "Women, Oxford and Tolkien." *Mallorn* 45 (2008): 16–20. Print.

Taylor, Taryne Jade. "Investigating the Role and Origin of Goldberry in Tolkien's Mythology." *Mythlore* 27.1/2 (#103/104) (2008): 147–56.

During the first decade of the twenty-first century, twenty-three articles and book chapters were published on Tolkien's female characters: thirteen in themed academic collections, eight in *Mythlore* (now a peer-reviewed journal), and two in *Mallorn*. Also published during this decade was the first encyclopedia devoted to Tolkien's work. The number and scope of theories and methodologies in this body of work supports Dimitra Fimi's observation in her 2009 monograph that "Tolkien scholarship has started afresh during the last few years" (200). She speculates that one reason for the growing recognition of Tolkien's work in academic circles is "the boundary between 'high' literature and fiction that appeals to mass audiences has become blurred, especially with the advent of 'theory' and cultural studies. [...] In this context, Tolkien can be re-discovered and re-analysed in a serious way, a process that has already started during the last few years" (201).

Two essays in *J. R. R. Tolkien and His Literary Resonances: Views of Middle-earth* deal with women and Tolkien. Faye Ringel's essay is not directly concerned with Tolkien's female characters but is worth noting because it is the only essay to analyze the impact of Tolkien's work on women authors. Ringel interviews Rosemary Edghill, Greer Ilene Gilman, Patricia McKillip, and Delia Sherman, adapting Harold Bloom's theory of the "anxiety of influence" to discuss how the authors have "swerved" from Tolkien's work. She concludes that the American women fantasists acknowledge "their debt to Tolkien's authentic Secondary World," but also experience "uneasiness with what they see as certain of Tolkien's premises: his acceptance of limitations on women's roles as well as traditional hierarchies of class" (159).

Debbie Sly's essay, comparing religious elements in Tolkien's and Milton's work, covers Varda, Galadriel, and Ungoliant, as well as the extent to which the Valar's gender is symbolic of their powers rather than biological. One important aspect of Sly's essay is her claim that Tolkien's description of Ungoliant "comes close to making her power of negation so strong it is in danger of becoming a positive force," her "Darkness" nearly being a creation with its own power (116–17). Sly also notes that Tolkien made only one short reference to Ungoliant in letters in which he discusses how he presents evil in his work. Sly establishes that this character, as well as others, shows the conflict between the theological and the aesthetic in Tolkien's work (117).

David Pretorius's essay is one of only two publications I have found by a male author that incorporates feminist issues (as opposed to focusing on female characters). His essay has three sections, the first on whether *The Lord of the Rings* is a novel or a romance, and the second on binary oppositions in the text. The third section on "Feminist issues" is a page and a half of the six-page article. Pretorius covers mythic elements, Christian imagery, Tolkien's portrayal of nature as sacred, Galadriel (as a Marian figure), and Shelob. Feminist issues arise in his inclusion of quotes from Sandra Gilbert and Susan Gubar's 1979 work, *The Madwoman in the Attic: The Woman Writer and the Nineteenth-Century Literary Imagination*, considered one of the originating works of Anglo-American feminist literary criticism. Pretorius then reads Shelob as embodying a negative space of female power. In this last section, he also discusses the symbolism of caves, Moria, and the dwarven mining that roused the Balrog using language that mirrors Partridge's Freudian analysis of Shelob and Sam's battle (the sword as phallic symbol) and describes Frodo, without any elaboration, as the "champion of the Age and its accompanying patriarchal order" (38). The "feminist issues" are Gilbert and Gubar's analysis of the binary of the "angel" and "monster" in Victorian literature by male and female writers that attempt to subvert that binary, along with one reference to the patriarchy.

Three essays from *Tolkien the Medievalist* focus on female characters: Donovan, Maher, and West. Leslie A. Donovan's essay, reprinted as one of the classics in this anthology, analyzes connections between Tolkien's major female characters and light, and the extent to which the physical and spiritual aspects of light are associated with their characterization. Some gain power from light (Galadriel, Arwen, Éowyn), while others are weakened by it. Donovan explores the influence of heroic literature on Tolkien's work, but emphasizes the extent to which Tolkien adapted the material, as he adapted other medieval models, to serve his modern Christian vision of his epic. The balance of competing cultures of medievalism and modernity is a strong aspect of Donovan's essay, as is the review of relevant scholarship on Tolkien's female characters with which she begins the essay.

Michael W. Maher complicates the standard comparison of Galadriel as a Marian figure. He cites Tolkien's letter about Galadriel leading a rebellion and notes that her pride is very different from the portrayal of the Virgin Mary in Catholic iconography: her rebellion is similar to Lucifer's. Maher considers Catholic elements that might have influenced Galadriel, settling on the Loreto Litany, a popular rather than scholarly source. His primary interests are the Catholic elements since his cited scholarship includes only one Tolkien citation among a number of theological works.

Taking a different approach than Donovan or Maher, Richard C. West traces the development of the story of Beren and Lúthien through Tolkien's different versions of it and analyzes the extent to which their story becomes an important element in *The Lord of the Rings*. West frames his discussion of the texts in the biographical context of Tolkien's letter to Christopher about a memory of walks in the woods when Edith Bratt Tolkien sang and danced for him. While his essay does not focus solely on the female character, it is a highly developed and strong reading of the importance of Lúthien not only in the subcreated mythology but as a reflection of the influence of Edith Bratt Tolkien on Tolkien's legendarium.

While the present essay focuses on scholarship about Tolkien's written work, the 2001-03 release of the live-action films directed by Peter Jackson not only has generated wider popular interest in Tolkien's work, but also has inspired more scholarship in multiple disciplines (film and literary studies as well as gender, media, and tourism studies). Such scholarship has led to more extensive consideration of female characters, gender, and feminist issues in general in Tolkien studies. A significant amount of scholarship on the film has been written by literary scholars. As film scholar Kristin Thompson notes in "Gollum Talks to Himself: Problems and Solutions in Peter Jackson's Film Adaptation of *The Lord of the Rings*," "numerous essays written by Tolkien scholars have decried the changes made in the adaptation of the novel into the film. It's an interesting phenomenon, since numerous literary works get adapted as films without such essays being published, let alone in such quantity as to become a genre unto itself" (25). Thompson's claim has some merit: of the 228 entries in the *MLA International Bibliography* for "The Lord of the Rings" and "film," 195 are about Jackson's film and only 33 are about other adaptations. Of course, not all these essays "decry" the changes. This area of research will only grow following the release of Jackson's *Hobbit* trilogy, with its inclusion of Galadriel and an original female character, Tauriel. Of interest to this essay, however, are essays that, in dealing with the film, also develop an original analysis of female characters in Tolkien's text to the extent that the discussion includes new and relevant approaches to them.

Four of the fourteen essays in the first collection on the film, *Tolkien on Film: Essays on Peter Jackson's* The Lord of the Rings, deal with female characters, more than on any of the other topics in the collection. Since no literary anthologies on Tolkien's work have a large percentage of essays on the female characters, this number is worth noting.[12] While the essays as a group are well worth reading, only two, Cathy Akers-Jordan's and Maureen Thum's, devote significant textual attention to the analysis of female characters in Tolkien's work. Akers-Jordan compares Tolkien's characterization of Arwen to Jackson's, including substantive quotes and explication from the films and book. By the end of her essay, she argues that Jackson's film remains "true to the spirit of the books" (212). Thum focuses on Galadriel, Arwen, and Éowyn, using Tolkien's concept of subcreation as a way of describing the film. Her argument about the book and films resonate well with Crowe's and Donovan's arguments about the book. She acknowledges that some viewers might see the film's changes in all three female characters as so "radical" as to prove that Jackson took "considerable license in his translation from text to film." Yet, Thum counters that view by arguing that the powerful figures created in the film better represent the complexity of Tolkien's "vision of women [...] than many [literary] critics have allowed" and that Jackson's adaptation "accurately represents the positive view of unconventional and powerful women throughout Tolkien's writing" (232). A significant portion of Thum's essay presents a stand-alone analysis of female characters in Tolkien's legendarium, while sections devoted to each character provide additional evidence from Tolkien's work.

Ernelle Fife, in "Wise Warriors," defines "wise warriors" as characters who exemplify the concept of the just war by fighting to protect rather than to conquer, and compares those characters to Athena. Her essay covers wise warriors, including some "female wise warriors," in Tolkien's, Lewis's, and Rowling's fiction. In her discussion of Tolkien's works, she discusses Éowyn, the Entwives, Sam, and Faramir, but also the narrative strategy Tolkien creates through his characters' point of view, especially in the masking of Dernhelm's identity from Merry, and thus from readers.

---

12. In the first endnote for "Light (noun, 1) or Light (adjective, 14b)?: Female Bodies and Femininities in Tolkien's *The Lord of the Rings*" (discussed later), I present a quantitative analysis of the percentages of essays written by women in major Tolkien anthologies. But, of course, not all the women scholars write about the female characters.

Jennifer Neville, in a chapter in *Reading* The Lord of the Rings*: New Writings on Tolkien's Classic,* offers not only an oppositional view to the commonplace claim about sexism in Tolkien's work, whether attributed to medieval culture or to his own, but also a useful reminder of the difficulty of making such generalized claims about any historical period. She focuses on the Rohirrim since the general critical assumption is that, like the culture of the Anglo Saxons portrayed in *Beowulf,* the culture of the Mark is "a society in which women have traditionally been seen as decorative but ultimately powerless, as pawns in a man's world" (101). Neville cites a 1990 article on stereotypes in Old English literature, allowing her to emphasize a vital point: our ideas about the "past" are mediated, always, by what is known at any given time. Thus, Neville's point that the "best nineteenth- and early twentieth-century scholars left no room for active women in Old English poetry, and late twentieth- and early twenty-first-century feminist criticism of Old English literature continues to create an image of the powerless, voiceless, and hopeless woman who can do no more than weep" (101). She argues that the image of the helpless woman is thus a construct originating in Victorian scholarship: "female helplessness and passivity are easier to find in scholarship about Old English poetry than in Old English poetry itself. The traditional passive female of Old English poetry is not as old as we might think. She is Victorian, not Anglo-Saxon" (102–03).[13] Neville's bibliography is an excellent resource. She crafts a counter-argument to the interpretation of the queen in *Beowulf* as passive and explores how Tolkien adapted similar readings in his own work. Neville acknowledges that Tolkien's work does "not destroy, invert, or even question the patriarchal system [...] as modern feminist readers may have wished," but argues that his work in a modern context may not be as "disempowering as has been thought," given that modern

13. Drout, in a 1996 note in *The Medieval Feminist Newsletter,* discusses how his experiences teaching Old English literature indicate that "[b]ecause many students inherit their perceptions of medieval literature through Tolkien's interpretations, they are often surprised to find women in the literature they read in their classes," and may "resent the 'intrusion' of gender [...] into their comfortable fantasy world. It seems to me that the challenge for educators concerned with gender is to complicate productively the world view inherited from Tolkien without completely destroying students' familiarity with and love for their idealized (and ideologized) view of the Middle Ages" (27).

men cannot normally achieve the status of either a Beowulf or an Aragorn (110).

In one of two essays on female characters in the collection *Tolkien and Modernity 1,* Maria Raffaella Benvenuto argues that female characters, while few in number, are powerful and important in the legendarium and that changes in women's rights that occurred during Tolkien's lifetime appear in his characterizations. Benevenuto focuses her argument on the two characters whom she considers most closely fit contemporary ideas of women's roles: Éowyn and Lúthien.

In the second essay from *Tolkien and Modernity 1,* Laura Michel incorporates information on different types of feminist belief systems as well as information about important women in Tolkien's life into her discussion of Jackson's film adaptations. The two characters Michel discusses are Éowyn and Erendis (*Unfinished Tales*), and she argues that Tolkien's view of women is one of equality although not one some feminists (undefined) would acknowledge.

A major milestone for Tolkien criticism was the publication of the *J. R. R. Tolkien Encyclopedia: Scholarship and Critical Assessment,* edited by Michael D. C. Drout. It contains a number of entries relevant to the focus of this essay as well as entries on the women in Tolkien's life. The entries most relevant to this essay are: *Ancrene Wisse*, Arwen, Éowyn, Feminist Readings of Tolkien, Finwë and Míriel, Galadriel, Gender in Tolkien's Works, Goldberry, *Juliana,* Lúthien, Melian, Ungoliant, and Women in Tolkien's Works. *Ancrene Wisse* is one of Tolkien's scholarly works, and is of relevance because it is a Middle English "guide for female recluses." Tolkien's edition is part of an ongoing study of a text which survives in seventeen manuscripts. In addition, Tolkien's studies of the Old English poem *Juliana* led to him working closely with one of his students (Simonne d'Ardenne) on an edition of a Middle English version of the same saint's life for her dissertation, which she later published and dedicated to Tolkien. The *Encyclopedia* entry concludes that evidence suggests the Old English poem may have influenced Tolkien's female characters.

A number of Tolkien's major female characters receive their own *Encyclopedia* entries. Most of these entries cover the relevant scholarship and provide useful cross references; unfortunately, that is not true for several other entries. While little scholarship exists on some characters (Goldberry and Melian), the lack of cross-references is a problem, and existing scholarship should have been listed in the entry on Éowyn. The entry on Feminist Readings of Tolkien provides a good overview and summary of a range of feminist interpretations, from "Christian feminism, to Jungian interpretations, to literary-historical interpretations generally," and notes areas that could be developed in future work (203). The Gender in Tolkien's Works entry acknowledges the topic's complexities, covering Tolkien's essentialist belief about gender, that belief's influences on his fiction, the "interdependence of masculinity and femininity," and the importance of the feminine. The "Further Reading" and cross-references in this entry are excellent (234). The same is true of the entry on Women in Tolkien's Works, which contextualizes Tolkien's work, summarizes critical disagreements concerning the characters in his legendarium, and includes a strong list of "Further Readings."

Two essays in *Mythlore* consider female characters from a feminist perspective but with different arguments. Susan Carter develops a strong and comparative analysis of the similarities between Galadriel and Morgan Le Fey. It draws on previous scholarship for the two characters to present an argument based on reading the gaps in the text, the "lacuna," as integral to the construction of their powers, which are heightened by "a sense of enigma [...] generated by the silence surrounding the women's ability to influence events and characters" (71). Acknowledging both are female characters in heroic epics, Carter presents close and detailed readings of the text, supported by existing scholarship, to propose that the textual absences of both characters are "productive," and the lacunae are "a trope in [their] own right" (73).

Candice Fredrick and Sam McBride consider the issue of women and war in both Tolkien and Lewis. They frame their argument with reference to Father Christmas's warning to the Pevensies in Narnia about the ugliness of war when women fight, arguing for the importance of further consideration of the question of what Tolkien's and Lewis's constructions of women and war mean. Their overall conclusion is that Tolkien's "depictions of females in combat suggest women simply are not suited for the task of warfare. Both their natures and their thought processes prevent them from fighting effectively," though they also note the reason is not that women are essentially good (citing Shelob as the counter-example and the only female enemy in *The Lord of the Rings*) (36).

Nancy Enright's essay, one of the classics reprinted in this volume, focuses on the extent to which female characters are essential to the theme of power in Tolkien's work, especially the extent to which epic heroic masculinity is limited by the characters' and narratives' respect for moral and spiritual power. In this reading, the number of female characters and their lack of physical or material powers supports Enright's claim that they offer "the choice of love over pride, reflective of the Christ-like inversion of power rooted in Scripture, and ultimately more powerful than any domination by use of force" (93). Countering feminist and negative criticism of Tolkien's female characters with an analysis of the characters' "religious depth," Enright's essay situates Tolkien's work within a religious tradition that associates Christ's sacrifice with femininity. Feminine self-sacrifice is shown by both major male and female characters in the text.

Melissa McCrory Hatcher argues that Tolkien's presentation of female characters and the roles they play, specifically the narrative arc of Éowyn, has been criticized by feminists who "[overlook] much of the importance of his vast and compelling work" (43). The primary feminist critics Hatcher (and Enright) identify as interpreting Tolkien's work in this way are Candice Fredrick and Sam McBride in their monograph, *Women Among the Inklings*. Hatcher joins Enright and others in arguing against claims that, by marrying Faramir, Éowyn becomes an example of "conventional female submissiveness." Instead, Hatcher argues that Éowyn not only "embodies the full-blooded subjectivity that Tolkien posits as essential for peace," but is the most complete example of that ideal (43). Hatcher foregrounds the historical context of Tolkien's time as one of social changes, noting that Virginia Woolf and Gertrude Stein were contemporaries of Tolkien, that he worked with important female scholars at Oxford, and that he saw women taking over the jobs of men during World War II. She concludes that Éowyn "embodies the persistent struggle of women in the West to assert their voices and presence, to avoid erasures, and to figure in history (and fiction) as they do in life" (45).

In a classic essay reprinted in this collection, Romuald I. Lakowski analyzes various versions of Galadriel's story that Tolkien developed outside *The Lord of the Rings*, some of them after its publication, as well as the early drafts in five volumes of *The History of Middle-earth* (6–9, 12). Beginning with Tolkien's letters concerning Galadriel's rebellion,

Lakowski notes that substantial contradictions appear when the different versions, notes, and letters are examined, complicating any chance at a simple narrative pattern concerning a fall and a later redemption. Lakowski's careful assemblage of texts would be useful for any scholars wishing to consider the construction of Galadriel's character and narrative arc, and Lakowski concludes that the time and attention given to the character over time, until the end of Tolkien's life, shows her importance to him.

A second essay by Lakowski, published in *Tolkien and Shakespeare*, is a well-developed, extended analysis of how Shakespeare and Tolkien adapted the medieval traditions of the Fairy Queen, with Tolkien "re-envisioning" Shakespeare's Queen Titania (60). Acknowledging Tolkien's negative commentary about Shakespeare's and Drayton's impact on popular perceptions of "fairy," and that Galadriel appears to be more different than similar to Titania, Lakowski nonetheless explores a number of striking similarities between the two characters: the setting in a woodland, the fear of the "fair and perilous" world of fairy (a phrase coming from Aragorn's warning to Boromir), the singing, the effect meeting the Fairy Queen has on mortals, and the gift of prophecy. One important difference is that Galadriel herself faces a test when Frodo offers her the Ring, rather than only herself testing mortals.

Melissa Smith's essay, another classic work reprinted in this anthology, takes a different approach to the characterization of Éowyn: Smith contextualizes her through the concept of "war-bride," a term that gained popularity during World War I. Smith's work is part of a movement in Tolkien studies to situate Tolkien's work within the context of World War I. Smith argues that through the relationships Éowyn has with Aragorn and then with Faramir, she fits into the "dual roles of war bride-left-behind and foreign war bride, and while comparison of her experiences with the courtship, marriage and assimilation experiences of women in the war-torn twentieth century reveal her to be a negative example of the former, she is clearly, for Tolkien, a positive exemplar of the latter" (161).

Rather than concerning herself with Shakespeare as a source or influence on Tolkien's world, Maureen Thum's essay in *Tolkien and Shakespeare* examines the complex reception both authors' work has received. Both have been accused of supporting the patriarchal status quo by some critics, while others argue that their works subvert the "dominant patriarchal codes of their respective times" (229). Drawing on Mikhail Bakhtin's theory of Carnival, Thum identifies Shakespeare's *Twelfth Night* and Tolkien's *The Lord of the Rings* as literature set in alternate worlds involving "fantasy, dream, or vision" which allows subversion of gender hierarchies through role reversal and masquerade (230). She notes the extent to which Shakespeare's and Tolkien's works offer sites of major cultural debates over the status of women because important historical challenges to patriarchal order were occurring (Queen Elizabeth's lengthy rule without marriage and the education of upper-class women in Shakespeare's time, and the high profile women's movements of Tolkien's time that demanded the right to vote and access to education and professions). After establishing the "experimental fantasticality" of the worlds of both texts, Thum presents a striking analysis of role reversal and masquerade in *Twelfth Night* and *The Lord of the Rings*: specifically, the role reversal of Éowyn. Thum notes that Éowyn not only goes into battle as Dernhelm, but resists Wormtongue's manipulations and is not punished for her defiant actions. After analyzing masquerade in both texts, Thum then focuses on Éowyn's and Galadriel's masks and actions during the novel, ending by noting the lack of any [female] witches in Tolkien's work, and the existence only of a "Witch-King" (247). She concludes that being "cloaked in conventionality" allows Galadriel "to expand gender roles even while her unconventionality remains hidden in plain view" (248).

Ann McCauley Basso's analysis of the character of Goldberry is well grounded in previous scholarship on female characters. Building on that scholarship, Basso argues that except for Goldberry, the female characters are divided into two categories (noble and rustic), and analyzes the extent to which Goldberry "[bridges] the gap between the Anglo-Saxon, noble women and the rustic women of the Shire providing an Eve figure who parallels the Mary figure Galadriel" (137). Basso's explication of the characterization of Goldberry is supplemented with additional evidence from Tolkien's letters, *The Adventures of Tom Bombadil*, and strong summaries of relevant scholarship. She analyzes the extent to which the plot events in the first part of the narrative mirror later events in ways that contribute to the rising action of the narrative and show Goldberry's parallels to Galadriel.

David Doughan's four-page commentary, published in *Mallorn*, is included here because it is the second publication I found by a male author dealing with issues relating to feminism and because of the background it provides on the history of women's colleges at Oxford. While he begins by summarizing the common argument about Tolkien's sexism, by the end Doughan concludes that Tolkien's attitude toward women was both more complex than many have assumed and that his ideas changed over the years (as Oxford has changed). Doughan covers some of the history of British women's campaigns for education and the colleges for women before World War I, the impact of World War I, and Oxford's admission of women to membership and degrees.

Taryne Jade Taylor's source study of Goldberry takes a different approach than Basso's; besides analyzing parallels with classical and Celtic mythologies, Taylor also considers the extent to which Goldberry's origins could lie in *The Silmarillion*, arguing that she "was created in the first united music of the Ainur before Melkor tainted the music," before the creation of Elves and Men (which came with the third theme). She is associated with water which still contains "the echo of the Music of the Ainur more than in any substance else that is in this earth" (*S* 19), as Basso notes with support from *The Silmarillion*. While Taylor's exploration of the various mythic and classical sources of the character (well supported by secondary scholarship) is a strong foundation, the move to considering the connections with *The Silmarillion* also creates an original and provocative reading.

2010–2013

Whitaker, Lynn. "Corrupting Beauty: Rape Narrative in *The Silmarillion*." *Mythlore* 29.1/2 (#111/112) (2010): 51–68. Print.

Downey, Sarah. "Cordial Dislike: Reinventing the Celestial Ladies of *Pearl* and *Purgatorio* in Tolkien's Galadriel." *Mythlore* 29.3/4 (#113/114) (2011): 101–17. Print.

Ray, Stella M. "Constructions of Gender and Sexualities in J. R. R. Tolkien's *The Silmarillion* and *The Lord of the Rings*." Diss. Texas A&M University-Commerce, 2011. Print.

Kowalik, Barbara, ed. *'O, What a Tangled Web': Tolkien and Medieval Literature, a View from Poland.* Cormarë Series 29. Zürich, Switzerland: Walking Tree, 2013. Print.

Błaszkiewicz, Maria. "Tolkien's Queen-Women in *The Lord of the Rings*." Kowalik 69–91.

Kowalik, Barbara. "Elbereth the Star-Queen Seen in the Light of Medieval Marian Devotion." Kowalik 93–113.

Vaccaro, Christopher, ed. *The Body in Tolkien's Legendarium: Essays on Middle-earth Corporeality.* Jefferson, NC: McFarland, 2013. Print.

Reid, Robin Anne. "Light (Noun, 1) or Light (Adjective, 14b)? Female Bodies and Femininities in *The Lord of the Rings.*" Vaccaro 98–118.

Williamson, James T. "Emblematic Bodies: Tolkien and the Depiction of Female Physical Presence." Vaccaro 134–56.

This section covers four essays published in academic collections, two in *Mythlore,* and one dissertation. Drawing on feminist theoretical work on the complexities of representing rape in art without "creating a vicarious [and misogynistic] pleasure in sexual violence," Lynn Whitaker analyzes the literary techniques Tolkien uses in *The Silmarillion,* focusing on the tales of Aredhel and Lúthien. Arguing that Tolkien avoids a misogynistic representation of rape, Whitaker concludes that the trope of showing how the beauty of female characters operates "as the catalyst for violent seduction or unrestrained lust remain[s] problematic other than as understood in mythic mode" (51). Analyzing and deconstructing the myth that female beauty is an "inevitable trigger of male sexual aggression" has been one of the major goals of feminist activism. She incorporates feminist definitions and discussion of the complexity of consent and non-consent in the context of genre conventions that have acted to "normalize or naturalize the element of sexual violence," especially in plots dealing with a "rescue/romance trajectory" (52). Whitaker's close readings of the narratives of Aredhel and Lúthien and narrative techniques (description, focalization, imagery, plot structure, diction, and syntax) show how Tolkien uses the mythic mode to avoid a "literal representation of rape while still maximizing the narrative and symbolic impact of the crime," allowing his work to "successfully [negotiate] the demands of using rape narrative in a non-misogynist and meaningful manner" (67).

Sarah Downey considers the importance of the allegorical mode to Tolkien's medieval sources as well as his familiarity with it to argue that while *The Lord of the Rings* is not an allegory "in the same way that some of its medieval influences" are, the work includes elements which may have a "resonance with the medieval allegorical tradition" (101). The focus of Downey's essay is the "image of an authoritative female character encountered in an earthly paradise," i.e. Galadriel. The phrasing is important because Downey does not claim Galadriel is an allegorical figure in the sense of a "static and abstract female personification," but a "fully realized character" (101). Noting that the scholarship on Galadriel has analyzed the character as influenced by a number of sources, Germanic, Celtic, Arthurian, Shakespearean, and Catholic, Downey contributes to the rich web of associations an analysis of the Christian dream-vision, considering Beatrice in the *Divine Comedy* and the pearl-maiden in *Pearl*. Downey concludes that Tolkien could have taken what he most liked about these specific characters to adapt for his own work while keeping the symbolism of "earthly paradise, light and water, the encircling stream and the stars, and the consolatory lady herself" (115).

Dissertations are not usually cited in reviews of literature, but Stella M. Ray's "Constructions of Gender and Sexualities in J. R. R. Tolkien's *The Silmarillion* and *The Lord of the Rings*" is the first (and so far only) of 47 dissertations indexed in the *MLA International Bibliography* that focuses entirely on female characters in Tolkien's legendarium; it draws on contemporary gender theories to develop approaches to Varda, Ungoliant, Galadriel, and Shelob. Ray analyzes the characters in the contexts of gender roles in medieval literature and the changing constructions of gender in post-World War I Britain, and then moves to a resistant reading of constructions of masculinity by female characters.[14]

Two essays in a collection by Polish medievalists focus on female characters (Błaszkiewicz and Kowalik). Maria Błaszkiewicz argues against interpreting the scarcity of female characters in Tolkien's work as a sign of sexism or lack of authorial skill; instead, she argues that Tolkien's choice is "a conscious design which aims not to diminish the importance of the female element but, on the contrary to glorify it" (70). Błaszkiewicz argues that Tolkien's careful construction of female char-

---

14. I directed Ray's thesis and include it here for two reasons: first, it is the only work so far to deal in such depth with these four characters; second, the summer after she graduated, before she could begin the full-time tenure track job she had been offered, Ray was murdered by her ex-husband, who is now sentenced to death. As a result, plans she had for publishing articles from her dissertation will not occur, although I still hope to edit and publish a posthumous version of her work, with the copyright still held by her family.

acters associated with one specific type of sanctuary, places safe from evil (as opposed to resting places where characters may still be at risk), is an important thematic element. These "omphalic spaces" associated with female characters range from Farmer Maggot's house to Lórien and are contrasted with dying and wasted lands in areas where no female characters are present. She concludes that "Tolkien's design in *The Lord of the Rings* has been to highlight the exceptional and royal function of a woman, a source of life in all its senses" (88).

Kowalik's essay analyzes the figure of Varda/Elbereth in medieval contexts of devotion to the Virgin Mary; earlier scholarship (Pretorius, Maher) has discussed the Marian elements of Galadriel, but this essay is the first I have found focusing on Varda in this context. Kowalik identifies an important difference between Galadriel and Varda: that Varda is not present in the material world, as Galadriel is, and thus is closer to the medieval perception of Mary, who is outside the world but "accessible to its inhabitants through stories, icons, relics, prayers, and songs" (95). Tolkien's introduction of Varda/Elbereth to the hobbits through songs, Galadriel's phial, Sam's calling upon Elbereth during his battle with Shelob, and his choice to use her name as a password in the Tower resonate with medieval Marian devotional elements.

Two essays in *The Body in Tolkien's Legendarium: Essays on Middle-earth Corporeality* focus on female bodies and materialities (Reid and Williamson). My essay blends an applied linguistic approach (the functional grammar developed by M. A. K. Halliday) with queer theory to analyze the grammar of female bodies. I contextualize my work on the scholarship of female characters, foreground a feminist approach, and note the lack of queer or gender scholarship on female characters by women scholars. I analyze the agency of female characters through quantitative analysis of the subjects of clauses and the types of processes (verbs) associated with the characters of Arwen, Galadriel, Goldberry, Shelob, and Éowyn in their introductory text, and then consider how light imagery is grammatically constructed (through nouns, adjectives, or processes associated with the characters). Drawing on Judith Halberstam's theory of female masculinity, I conclude by presenting a queer and resistant reading of Éowyn.

James T. Williamson discusses the "emblematic, rather than biological," nature of female bodies in *The Lord of the Rings*, focusing on Goldberry, Arwen, Galadriel, and Éowyn to suggest that this method of characterization is similar to Tolkien's earlier works and provides a "notable stylistic continuity between the Legendarium and *The Lord of the Rings*, in many respects notable for their divergences of style and narrative approach" (134). Williamson identifies this emblematic approach as typical to the northern literatures Tolkien studied. For Williamson, female bodies in Tolkien's work are "conventional and figural, tied to thematic associations with [...] earth, plants, and waters, as well as with the heavens—and with cyclic time" (134). He references the extent to which emblematic and poetic constructions of female bodies exist in the text with one exception, that of Shelob, whom he presents as a possible Freudian type of repression. He ends by arguing that the "consistency and apparent deliberateness with which the imagery is deployed" suggests Tolkien is interested not in romantic and sexual elements, but in the style of heroic saga and medieval romances (153).

Looking Ahead

If the current anthology is any indication, scholarship on female characters is likely to continue to develop in the future, building on the past 43 years of work. In the present collection, the seven classic essays on female characters and feminist issues in Tolkien's legendarium are accompanied here by seven new critical works written specifically for this project, including this bibliographic essay. The new essays fall broadly into the categories of cultural studies, genre studies, gender studies and feminist studies, medieval studies, and fan or reception studies. While I summarize the reprinted essays earlier to establish their connections to Tolkien scholarship at the time they were published, the essays newly published here may act as guides to future scholarship in which the consideration of Tolkien's female characters, and their intersections with feminisms, will not seem so perilous in the growing body of work on Tolkien's legendarium and its reception.

As Drout and Wynne point out, "the 'defense' of Tolkien's works has become rather tired," noting that both Dan Timmons and Tom Shippey argue effectively that Tolkien's work is not only popular, which is unlikely to change, but that the literary canon has changed sufficiently to allow Tolkien in. Fimi not only agrees with that position, citing Shippey, but argues that one reason for the change in the canon is the advent of cultural studies and critical theories in the field (200). Additionally, the need for literary scholars to distance themselves from the fandom, especially by making fun of it, is no longer necessary. Drout and Wynne accurately point to the fallacy in such a position, calling it an "appeal, by insecure critics, to the literary establishment" (125).

I agree with these suggestions for future scholarship in Tolkien studies and would like to highlight an additional suggestion signaled by this collection. I would argue that it is time for Tolkien studies to move beyond the perceived need to defend Tolkien (whether the author, the body of work, or the human being) from the outdated stereotype of "feminist critics" who exist only to rend and destroy. As this essay and the collection overall prove, both classic and recent scholarship show that more than enough space exists for a growing range of approaches to female characters in Tolkien's legendarium. Expanding the range of theories and methods used by medievalists as well as postmodernists and everyone in between to incorporate cultural studies and critical theories that deal with gender, race, class and the intersections between them in the context of the twentieth- and twenty-first centuries can only enhance Tolkien studies.

Works Cited

Anderson, Douglas A. "Brian Rosebury on J. R. R. Tolkien: A Checklist." *Tolkien Studies: An Annual Scholarly Review* 5 (2008): 21–21. Print.

---. "Carl F. Hostetter: A Checklist." *Tolkien Studies: An Annual Scholarly Review* 4 (2007): 47–50. Print.

---. "John D. Rateliff: A Checklist." *Tolkien Studies: An Annual Scholarly Review* 6 (2009): 22–26. Print.

---. "Richard C. West: A Checklist." *Tolkien Studies: An Annual Scholarly Review* 2.1 (2005): 11–14. Print.

---. "Tom Shippey on J. R. R. Tolkien: A Checklist." *Tolkien Studies: An Annual Scholarly Review* 1.1 (2004): 17–20. Print.

Bratman, David. "The Year's Work in Tolkien Studies 2006." *Tolkien Studies: An Annual Scholarly Review* 6 (2009): 315–44. Print.

---. "The Year's Work in Tolkien Studies 2007." *Tolkien Studies: An Annual Scholarly Review* 7 (2010): 347–78. Print.

Bratman, David, and Merlin DeTardo. "The Year's Work in Tolkien Studies 2008." *Tolkien Studies: An Annual Scholarly Review* 8 (2011): 243–95. Print.

Croft, Janet Brennan. "Where are the Women?: Criticism, *The Lord of the Rings,* and the Feminine." Academia.edu, 10 June 2014. Web.

DeTardo, Merlin. "The Year's Work in Tolkien Studies 2010." *Tolkien Studies: An Annual Scholarly Review* 10 (2013): 253–89. Print.

Drout, Michael D. C., and Hilary Wynne. "Tom Shippey's *J. R. R. Tolkien: Author of the Century* and a Look Back at Tolkien Criticism Since 1982." *Envoi* 9.2 (2000): 101–67. Print.

Drout, Michael D. C., Rebecca Epstein, and Kathryn Paar. "Bibliography (in English) for 2005." *Tolkien Studies: An Annual Scholarly Review* 4 (2007): 355–65. Print.

Drout, Michael D. C., Laura Kalafarski, and Stefanie Olsen. "Bibliography (in English) for 2001–2002." *Tolkien Studies: An Annual Scholarly Review* 1.1 (2004): 183–89. Print.

Drout, Michael D. C., et al. "Bibliography (in English) for 2006." *Tolkien Studies: An Annual Scholarly Review* 5 (2008): 299–308. Print.

Drout, Michael D. C. "The Influence of J. R. R. Tolkien's Masculinity Medievalism." *The Medieval Feminist Newsletter* 22 (1996): 26–27.

Epstein, Rebecca, David Bratman, and Merlin DeTardo. "Bibliography (in English) for 2011." *Tolkien Studies: An Annual Scholarly Review* 10 (2013): 291–307. Print.

Epstein, Rebecca, et al. "Bibliography (in English) for 2009." *Tolkien Studies: An Annual Scholarly Review* 8 (2011): 297–307. Print.

Epstein, Rebecca, Michael D. C. Drout, and David Bratman. "Bibliography (in English) for 2008." *Tolkien Studies: An Annual Scholarly Review* 7 (2010): 379–98. Print.

Epstein, Rebecca, et al. "Bibliography (in English) for 2010." *Tolkien Studies: An Annual Scholarly Review* 9 (2012): 141–52. Print.

Fimi, Dimitra. *Tolkien, Race and Cultural History: From Fairies to Hobbits*. Houndsmills, Basingstoke, Hampshire: Palgrave Macmillan. 2009. Print.

Fredrick, Candice and Sam McBride. *Women Among the Inklings, Gender, C. S. Lewis, J. R. R. Tolkien, and Charles Williams*. Greenwood Professional Guides in School Librarianship 91. Westport, CT: Praeger: 2001. Print.

Johnson, Judith A. *J. R. R. Tolkien: Six Decades of Criticism*. Westport, CT: Greenwood, 1986. Print.

Rea, Jason, Kathryn Paar, and Michael D. C. Drout. "Bibliography (in English) for 2007." *Tolkien Studies: An Annual Scholarly Review* 6 (2009): 345–60. Print.

Ripp, Joseph. "Middle America Meets Middle-earth: American Discussion and Readership of J. R. R. Tolkien's *The Lord of the Rings*, 1965–1969." *Book History* 8 (2005): 356–86. Print.

Thompson, Kristin. "Gollum Talks to Himself: Problems and Solutions in Peter Jackson's Film Adaptation of *The Lord of the Rings*." *Picturing Tolkien: Essays on Peter Jackson's* The Lord of the Rings *Film Trilogy*. Eds. Janice M. Bogstad and Philip E. Kaveny. Jefferson, NC: McFarland, 2011. 25–45. Print.

West, Richard. C. *Tolkien Criticism: An Annotated Checklist*. 2nd ed. Kent, OH: Kent State UP, 1981. Print.

The Missing Women:
J. R. R. Tolkien's Lifelong Support for Women's Higher Education

John D. Rateliff

In his authorized and still iconic biography, Humphrey Carpenter goes to great lengths to portray J. R. R. Tolkien as a man who, by choice, spent most of his time, most of his life, in exclusively male company. Carpenter's biography and those accounts derived from it certainly acknowledge the early "idyllic" days of young Tolkien living with his mother in a remote cottage and also the great romance of his life: his courtship, separation from, and reunion with Edith Bratt. And yet, outside these two episodes, the focus is heavily on the masculine: raised by a priest, serving as altar boy in the Oratory, playing by the old mill with his brother, attending a boys' school, the all-male experience of Oxford, among the troops at the front, plunging into the male world of tutorials and lectures and committee meetings.

It is important, I think, to note that this is not at all how his life seemed to Tolkien himself. When questioned about the scarcity of female characters in *The Lord of the Rings*, Tolkien replied first by comparing his story to tales of polar exploration: "after all, these are *wars* and [...] a terrible expedition to the North Pole, so to speak" (Gueroult), which suggests he saw the Fellowship as analogous to Amundsen's or Peary's, or even Scott's and Shackleton's, (all male) expeditions. He then continued:

> How do you explain it? [...] I know how one reviewer[1] explained it. He says it's written by a man who's never reached puberty, and knows nothing about women [...] except [as] a schoolboy. And all [...] the good characters come home like happy boys safe from the War.
>
> I thought it was very rude, from a man who so far as I know is childless, writing about a man surrounded by children—wife, daughter, grandchildren.

---

1. The reviewer in question was poet and translator Edwin Muir, whose review of *The Return of the King* was titled "A Boy's World." Muir praises Tolkien for world-building but hammers *The Lord of the Rings* for essentially being a boy's story stretched out to inordinate length.

> Still, it isn't that. [...] It's equally untrue, isn't it? That it's a happy story. One friend of mine said he only read it in Lent because it was so hard and bitter. (Gueroult)

Tolkien's self-description as "a man surrounded by [...] wife, daughter, grandchildren" may contrast our mental image of Tolkien built up from the standard biography, but it matches closely the way Simonne d'Ardenne and Icelandic *au pair* girl Arndís Þorbjarnardóttir remembered him in their memoirs: Tolkien as family man, or *paterfamilias* (d'Ardenne; Þorbjarnardóttir). In this paper, I'd like to draw attention to an aspect of Tolkien's life and career that I think has been overlooked and provide an overview of his involvement in higher education for women.

Tolkien was unusual for dons of his era in his support for women taking degrees and pursuing academic careers.[2] Examples abound: his pride in his Aunt Jane's science degree and academic accomplishments (she was at one time headmistress of a women's college); his mentoring by Joseph Wright (a noted advocate of women's education, much admired by Virginia Woolf for his enlightened stance); his welcoming women to his tutorials from the time he was a fledgling don onward; his encouragement of his female students' subsequent academic careers. In contrast with the starkly dismissive attitude of C. S. Lewis, which was more representative of the Oxford of his time (upon joining the English School in 1925, Lewis was dismayed to find it seemed to consist mainly of "Women, Indians, and Americans" [Carpenter, *Inklings* 14]),[3] Tolkien was consistently supportive of women in academia. It is entirely fitting that the endowed "J. R. R. Tolkien Professor of English Language and Literature" (established in 1981, eight years after Tolkien's death) is attached to one of Oxford's traditionally women's colleges (Lady Margaret Hall); it's a legacy I think Tolkien would be proud of.

---

2. For examples of the long, hard struggle for acceptance women faced at Oxford, see Doughan; Brittain. I am grateful to David Doughan for providing me with a copy of his speech, originally delivered at Somerset College during the 2006 Oxonmoot.

3. To see how deeply Lewis's disdain for women in academia ran, see the Appendix at the end of the present essay: C. S. Lewis's letter to E. R. Eddison.

Mabel Suffield

Like many of us, Tolkien's initial experience with women and education came in the form of being educated by women: specifically his mother Mabel Suffield Tolkien and, to a lesser extent, his aunt Jane Suffield.[4] Both seem to have been unusually well educated for the time; Mabel knew not just French and German but also Latin (Carpenter, *Biography* 17) in addition to what used to be called "accomplishments" such as drawing, painting, and playing piano (the last of these being the only one of these gifts that did not pass down to her son). She apparently taught Tolkien how to read at an early age (by the time he was four) (21), as well as how to write (despite having an eccentric calligraphic hand herself, with the letters full of odd curls and loops) (Tolkien and Tolkien 17). She certainly tutored him in Latin and French, and (rather unusually) botany (Carpenter, *Biography* 22); all this when he was between the ages of four and eight, at the end of which he began at King Edward's School. He briefly transferred to a Catholic school, St. Philip's, in 1902 at age ten, but was pulled from the school shortly afterwards for doing too well (27), having gotten ahead of his classmates. She then tutored him herself again until he won a scholarship and returned to King Edward's in the fall of 1903. Here he thrived; by the end of 1903, one of his teachers was reporting that young Tolkien, not yet twelve, "has read *too* much, everything fit for a boy under fifteen" among the classics (28; emphasis in original).

So here in his schoolboy days, Tolkien was already demonstrating academic excellence, and showing that he thrived in classrooms and in private tutorials, at home and at school. As far as we can tell from surviving evidence, nothing suggests Tolkien compartmentalized the instruction he got from the various masters at his school and that from his mother or prized one above the other.

Aunt Jane

For all that he idolized his mother in later life (for which we can hardly fault him), it is his aunt, Jane Suffield (later Jane Suffield Neave),

---

4. The third of old John Suffield's daughters, May Incledon, contributed nothing to Tolkien's education, so far as we know, but it was from her two daughters, Tolkien's cousins Marjorie and Mary, that he first got the idea of creating his own languages.

who provided Tolkien with the nearest thing he had to a role model within his own family.[5] Among the Suffields and Tolkiens, she was the only one before Tolkien himself to enter academia, to become a teacher and administrator, having taught science at King Edward's Foundation Bath Row School from 1892, when she was just twenty, till her marriage in 1905 (Morton and Hayes 12). She also served on the Birmingham School Board from 1901 until she moved from the area following her marriage (12). She was the only prior member of his family to earn a university degree (Morton and Hayes 13; Morton 28): a B.Sc. from Birmingham's Mason College (now Birmingham University) in 1895, at age 23.

Although she tutored young John Ronald, age ten, in geometry,[6] her professional specialties were botany, geology, and physiology (Morton and Hayes 13). Following her husband's death in 1909, she resumed her academic career and became the Warden of University Hall at the University of St. Andrew's (16). But unlike Tolkien, she did not remain in academia; instead, she abandoned her academic career in 1911 when not quite forty to become a farmer (16), like Tolkien's brother Hilary. (Indeed, she was much closer to her younger nephew than his famous brother). Even after retiring from farming some twenty years later (in 1931, when nearing sixty)[7] and having formed two

---

5. It is perhaps worth reflecting that, in an age when sons were more likely to follow in their fathers' footsteps than is now the case, Tolkien did not become a banker, like his father, nor own an iron foundry like his grandfather Suffield, nor make pianos like his grandfather Tolkien. Nor did he become a farmer like his brother Hilary, though he idealized his brother's profession in *The Lord of the Rings*. Nor, despite his obvious piety, do we have any indication that he ever seriously considered entering the priesthood, like Fr. Francis (his guardian, whom Tolkien considered a foster-father). Instead, he broke with family tradition and became a teacher, like his aunt.

6. As Tolkien wrote in a letter to Charlotte and Denis Plimmer, 8 Feb. 1967:

> My interest in languages was derived solely from my mother, a Suffield [...] She knew German, and gave me my first lessons in it. She was also interested in etymology, and aroused my interest in this; and also in alphabets and handwriting [...] Two years before her death I had with her sole tuition* gained a scholarship to King Edward VI School in Birmingham.
>
> *except in geometry which I was taught by her sister. (*Letters* 377)

7. Her biographer, Andrew Morton, believes her retirement and move to Chelmsford was at least in part motivated by a desire to be near a religious community of Christian mystics founded by Evelyn Underhill; for more on Jane Neave's interest in Christian mysticism, particularly Julian of Norwich and Hildegard of Bingen, see Morton and Hayes 21–22.

women-owned farming partnerships, she remained, in the words of her biographer, "a great leader and organizer," helping organize the local Women's Institute, of which she became president (Morton 32)

We know Tolkien was proud of his aunt's career choice and achievements from his description of her in a 1961 letter:

> The professional aunt is a fairly recent experience, perhaps; but *I was fortunate* in having an early example: one of the first women to take a science degree. She is now ninety, but only a few years ago went botanizing in Switzerland. (*Letters* 308; emphasis mine)

Nor were her interests limited to scientific subjects; Morton notes that she was "widely read and knowledgeable" about poetry (Morton and Hayes 53). Jane Neave's love of poetry is testified to by a little booklet she put together at the time she sold her Worcestershire farm, "Bag End," in 1931,[8] in which she includes three passages of poetry among descriptions of the Tudor farm buildings and their history: two from poems by Rupert Brooke ("The Old Vicarage, Grantchester" [1912] and "Town & Country" [circa 1911], respectively) and one by Tennyson ("Come Down, O Maid" from *The Princess* [1847]).

Finally, Morton quotes from her obituary as it appeared in a St. Andrews alumni chronicle decades after her brief tenure there: "Her vivid mental life knew no boundaries, her knowledge of English Literature was so vast that one felt *she should have been a professor* [...] *a scholar, and the author of many books*" (Morton and Hayes 17; emphasis mine).

Aunt Beatrice, Mrs. Faulkner, and Mrs. MacSherry

Leaving aside the theme of women in academia for a moment to look at that of women in Tolkien's life outside academia, I'd like to point out that even during the period when Tolkien was attending an all-male school (King Edward's) and experiencing what he would long after-

---

8. Reproduced in facsimile by Morton; see 45, 47, and 51 (pages 5, 7, and 12, respectively, of the original booklet). We also know she cherished a book of Chaucer and Spenser's poetry, a gift from her brother John (Morton and Hayes 17), and that Tolkien gave her a detailed description of the verse-form of *Pearl* "as these things interest you" (*Letters* 317). He also, of course, put together the poetry collection *The Adventures of Tom Bombadil* [1962] at her specific request (Carpenter, *Biography* 243–44). That a love of literature ran in the family is also suggested by her owning a copy of Sterne's *A Sentimental Journey* that had been in her family since 1786 (Morton and Hayes 17; note that this is only sixteen years after that remarkable work's first publication).

wards portray as an almost monastic existence, describing himself as having been "virtually a junior inmate of the Oratory house" (*Letters* 395), he was in fact living with his Aunt Beatrice down the road. That is, although under the guardianship of a priest (whom he saw as a father-figure), after his mother's death Tolkien remained in a household dominated by a woman. The biographers have been harsh to Beatrice Suffield,[9] who failed to provide emotional warmth for her young charges over the three years they lived with her (from early 1905 until early 1908) (Scull and Hammond, *Chronology* 10, 13). Certainly it would have been better if their new caregiver, who had recently been widowed, had bonded with her two young orphaned nephews (a la "Hallmark Hall of Fame," or indeed the final act of *Shadowlands*). But sometimes tragedy drives people apart, rather than drawing them together (a good example being C. S. Lewis and his brother's estrangement from their father after their mother's death, vividly described in *Surprised by Joy* [19]). For all her shortcomings, I confess to some sympathy for a thirty-year-old woman, recently widowed and apparently without prospects, suddenly made responsible for the upbringing of two boys aged ten and thirteen; her failure was that of passivity, of taking care of their needs but not providing them with a loving home. But what does it say of Fr. Francis's acumen (or lack of it) that he left the Tolkien brothers in such unsatisfactory accommodations for three years? Or, having taken them out of Aunt Beatrice's home, that he in turn placed them in a boarding house that failed to provide for a basic need, by not feeding them enough to keep the two brothers (now sixteen and thirteen going on fourteen) from going hungry?

After leaving Aunt Beatrice's, the brothers lived for the next two years at Mrs. Faulkner's boarding house,[10] from early 1908 to January 1910 (Scull and Hammond, *Chronology* 13, 17). Mrs. Faulkner's housekeeping was described by Priscilla Tolkien, based no doubt on her parents' memories, as "both genteel and incompetent," with the result

---

9. Part of this is no doubt because Beatrice Suffield destroyed Mabel Tolkien's papers, thus depriving future biographers of much material. More significantly, this act probably turned Tolkien into a hoarder, whose own papers ultimately preserved vast quantities of drafts for many projects.

10. There was a Mr. Faulkner, but he is mentioned just in passing (e.g. Scull and Hammond, *Chronology* 13); it is his wife who dominates all stories about the house.

that the youths were "perpetually hungry" (Bonsor). It seems that Tolkien's friendship with Edith Bratt, another boarder in the house, began out of sympathy for the brothers' predicament, leading her to conspire with the maid, Annie Gollins, to smuggle them extra food at night (Bonsor; Scull and Hammond, *Chronology* 13). Not until the summer of 1909, when Tolkien was seventeen and Edith twenty, did their friendship deepen into a love affair (Scull and Hammond, *Chronology* 14), which peaked toward the end of the year before being broken off by a series of increasingly incensed interventions on the part of Father Francis between December 1909 (17) and February 1910 (18). In the midst of this crisis, when Tolkien had just turned eighteen, he moved to Mrs. MacSherry's, another boarding house, where he stayed from January 1910 until going up to Oxford in October 1911 (17, 28).

It was probably during this period that an incident occurred which was shared with me by Christopher Wiseman when I was fortunate enough to meet him in the summer of 1981. Wiseman recalled how a cousin of his had come on a visit, along with a friend her own age, and that Tolkien had dropped by. After an afternoon spent pleasantly together, Tolkien took his leave. Whereupon the cousin and her friend turned to Wiseman and asked "who was that *charming* man?" I think we may take from this that, while Carpenter relates that Tolkien had no virtually no experience with women (i.e., of his own age) when he arrived at Mrs. Faulkner's (*Biography* 39), this was not true of Tolkien by the time he was ready to go off to college, being then nearly twenty.[11]

Undergraduate days at Oxford

In describing Tolkien's student days at Oxford, Carpenter stresses the degree to which it was exclusively masculine:

---

11. In light of this, we might need to revisit and modify Carpenter's statement that, after separation from Edith, Tolkien withdrew both from the oratory and ordinary social interaction as typified by life in a boarding house, so that "school [i.e., King Edward's] now became the centre of [his] life. [...] [I]t was into an all-male society that he now threw himself. At the age when many young men were discovering the charms of female company he was endeavouring to forget them and to push romance into the back of his mind. All the pleasures and discoveries of the next three years [...] were to be shared not with Edith but with others of his sex, so that he came to associate male company with much that was good in life" (*Biography* 45).

> Tolkien was at his happiest in groups of cronies where there was good talk, plenty of tobacco [...], and male company.
>
> At Oxford the company had to be male. Admittedly there were a number of women students attending lectures, but they lived in ladies' colleges, grim enclaves on the outskirts of the city; and they had to be severely chaperoned whenever they approached a young man. In any case the men really preferred each other's company. The majority of them were fresh from the male preserves of the public school and they gladly accepted the masculine tone of Oxford. (*Biography* 54)

All this seems straightforward enough. And yet, just two pages later Carpenter writes of Tolkien's weekly visits to Joseph Wright—not just his lectures and classes, though Tolkien certainly attended these (55), but tutorials, which were given at Wright's home in north Oxford. Furthermore, he describes as the highlight of Tolkien's week "the huge Yorkshire teas given by the Wrights on Sunday afternoons" (56).[12] Carpenter notes in passing that Wright, a self-made man, had "married a former pupil" (56), but this breezy description tends to obscure the fact that Elizabeth Mary Wright was a scholar in her own right, who arrived in Oxford in 1887, a year before Wright himself, as a student at the newly established Lady Margaret Hall, earning a First in 1890 (Brittain 71–72) and publishing a book-length *Old Northumbrian Grammar* (1894). After her marriage, she co-authored a number of her husband's books: e.g., *An Old English Grammar* (1908), *An Elementary Middle English Grammar* (1923), and *An Elementary Historical New English Grammar* (1924). In her own right she published the book *Rustic Speech and Folk-lore* (1913), and a number of philological essays on cruxes in *Beowulf* (1901), *Sir Gawain and the Green Knight* (1906, 1935–36), and so on. That Tolkien took her seriously as a fellow scholar is shown by a 1923 letter thanking her for an offprint and congratulating her on solving a crux in *Sir Gawain and the Green Knight* (which Tolkien was currently editing) (*Letters* 11).[13] Furthermore, Tolkien re-

12. These teas, which Wright sometimes characterized as "our P.S.A. [i.e., Pleasant Sunday Afternoon] Society," are described in greater detail in Wright 586–89.

13. Thanks to Wayne Hammond (personal communication), we can now identify the specific article Elizabeth Wright sent Tolkien in 1923 as "The Word 'Abloy' in 'Sir Gawayne and the Green Knight,' l.1174" (Wright, "Abloy"). We are thus able to see that Tolkien and Gordon did indeed accept her suggestion, entering a note to line 1174 crediting that reading as follows: "explained by Mrs.

mained in contact with her long after Wright himself died; as late as 1957, more than a quarter-century after Professor Wright's death, Tolkien was still corresponding with Mrs. Wright and conducting business on her behalf as executor of her husband's estate (*Letters* 74; Scull and Hammond, *Chronology* 513).

Not only did Wright set an example Tolkien followed, of holding his tutorials at his home rather than in his rooms in college[14]— C. S. Lewis, by contrast, always tutored at his rooms in Magdalen and was careful never to invite his pupils to his home at the Kilns—but like Wright, Tolkien began his teaching career at Oxford tutoring women, as we will see. In Wright's case, he came to Oxford in 1888 to teach for

---

(note continued)
Wright, *Mod.Lang.Rev.*, xviii. 86" (Tolkien and Gordon 101–02). Like Tolkien, Elizabeth Wright made a special study of *Gawain*. She had published one significant piece on the poem back in 1907 ("Notes") and was to publish another in two parts in *The Journal of English and Germanic Philology* in 1934–35 ("Gawain"), with a follow-up article published in the same journal the next year; amusingly enough, the *JEGP* pieces largely chronicle her dissent from Tolkien and Gordon over various details of interpretation. I am grateful to Wayne Hammond for locating Elizabeth Wright's 1923 piece and sharing a copy with me.

14. Or so we may infer from Tolkien's *Valedictory Address*, which he closes by recalling a half-dozen vignettes from his early days at Oxford, what he calls "salient moments in my academic past," the first of which describes "[t]he vastness of Joe Wright's dining-room table (when I sat alone at one end learning the elements of Greek philology from glinting glasses in the further gloom)" (31). Since here Tolkien recalls studying Greek rather than Gothic or Old High German, this memory must date from his first year at Oxford (1911–12), when he was a Classicist, before he switched his major to the Germanic languages. And since it's unlikely Wright would have a huge dining table in his rooms in college, it seems safe to infer that the tutorials Tolkien is remembering took place at Wright's home, Thackley, on the Banbury Road in northern Oxford (Wright, *Life* 582ff; at that time, all professors were required by statute to live within a mile and a half of Carfax, the city center; Wright's home was just within the prescribed limit [582]). In choosing to give his own tutorials from home, Tolkien was departing from common custom and following his mentor's example.

Tolkien also followed Wright's example in that both men graded exams out of term-time to earn extra money (120). The two men differed in that while Tolkien found work outside tutoring at the Oxford English Dictionary, Wright tutored for the Taylorian Institute in addition to the Association for the Higher Education of Women (117). And, of course, having once arrived, Wright stayed in Oxford the remainder of his long career (1888 to his death in 1930, having become Professor Emeritus following his retirement in 1925; Wright, *Life* 651), while Tolkien departed to Leeds to advance his career and enable him to qualify as a serious candidate for the Oxford professorship much sooner than would have been the case had he stayed in Oxford (as the example of C. S. Lewis shows).

the A.E.W., or Association for the Higher Education of Women (what later became known as the Society of Home-Students, and later still St. Anne's College), and for a time (1889–91) even taught at the Oxford High School for Girls (Wright, *Life* 119) before becoming "Deputy-Professor" to Max Muller (he of "mythology is a disease of language" infamy) in 1891, succeeding Muller as Professor of Comparative Philology a decade later, in 1901 (121).

Wright was an early advocate of women's degrees (Wright, *Life* 599), arguing that "if women did the same work as the men, they should be equally rewarded by having the B.A. Degree" (600). In fact, Wright's enlightened views so impressed Virginia Woolf when she read Elizabeth Wright's biography of her husband, *The Life of Joseph Wright* (1932), that she worked a fictionalized version of a visit with the Wrights for tea into *The Years*, her penultimate novel (1937), where they appear under the name "the Robsons" (*Years* 66–73).[15] In her draft version of this passage as it appears in *The Pargiters: The Novel-Essay Portion of "The Years,"* (1932; publ. 1977), where the Wright-analogues are successively called the Gabbit, Hughes, and Brook family, Woolf depicts this visit as a high point of one of her point-of-view characters' life, an eye-opening revelation of a professor who treated women as equals, as fellow human beings (*Pargiters* 127), and she immediately follows the scene with a discussion of Wright himself, making the linkage explicit (154–58).

We know Wright influenced Tolkien profoundly as a philologist, and there is good evidence that Tolkien at least to some degree modeled his career upon that of his mentor. What we do not know is whether Wright's ideas regarding equality for women were shared by his most famous disciple.

---

15. See also Woolf's diary entry for Wednesday, July 13, 1932, in which she sets down her admiration for the Wrights, based on reading Volume I of the *Life*: "Old Joseph Wright & Lizzie Wright are people I respect [...] Odd how rare it is to meet people who say things that we ourselves could have said [...] [it] is a testimony to Joe & Lizzy that I've been thinking how I should have liked to see them—would now like to write to her" (Woolf, *Diary* IV 115–16). Woolf did in fact write a letter of appreciation to Elizabeth Wright, which unfortunately is not included in her collected letters. It should also be noted that "progressive" is a relative measure; while Wright firmly believed in equality between husband and wife in a marriage, and supported women's degrees, he did not support their becoming "voting members of the University" (Wright, *Life* 600).

For my part, I find it suggestive that both Joseph Wright, Tolkien's mentor as an academic, and William Morris, the author who most deeply and directly influenced him as a writer, were renowned for their advocacy of equality for women.

The War

There was indeed one period of Tolkien's life in which he found himself in all-male surroundings for weeks and months at a time, but it was most emphatically not by choice: his days as a soldier during the Great War. I'll pass briefly over this, since it's clear Tolkien joined the army as late as he decently could in 1915, a full year into World War I (Scull and Hammond, *Chronology* 69), and left it as early as possible, returning to Oxford in October 1918, a few weeks before the Armistice (106). The one point I'd like to make here is that while Tolkien's time in barracks and at the front perforce found him in all-male company, once he had been invalided out this was no longer the case. Not only did the newly married Edith Tolkien move repeatedly to be near where he was hospitalized, but as soon as he was out of the hospital and assigned to invalid duties he joined her in a little household along with their infant son John and Edith's cousin Jennie Grove, who was more or less the little family's honorary aunt.

Even within the military hospital, we can catch a glimpse of a break in the supposedly all-male environs; I have a letter Tolkien wrote decades later, in 1949, in which he asks a reader (Miss R. Turnbull) who enjoyed *The Hobbit* to do him a favor:

> I have a very dear old friend, one of the Sisters of Mercy of Hull (who have also a house in Whitby). I have known her since she befriended me in hospital as a lonely soldier in 1917. She is now very old, and is going to celebrate her Diamond Jubilee as a nun (60 years!) on 15 March. I last saw her a few years ago in Whitby [...] she has had a partial stroke and is bed-ridden [...] Few things would give her more pleasure than some special remembrance from me. I wonder could you arrange for some flowers to be sent in for the morning of that date (Tuesday next)? [...] It would be so kind of you. The old darling (Mother Mary Michael) would be much mystified how I had arranged it. The card, if any, should say "Mother Mary Michael with love from Ronald Tolkien."

Such were the complexities of sending flowers cross country in the days before FTD (or indeed the internet).[16] A minor episode, certainly, but I think worth including to make the point that even in wartime there were some exceptions to the all-male life.

Tutoring Women: Early Days at Oxford

It is with Tolkien's return to Oxford after the war that we begin to have direct evidence of Tolkien's work tutoring women and hints and suggestions about his attitude toward such work, and toward the women he tutored. Long afterwards he described himself at this time in his life as "a jobless soldier" ("Valedictory" 31), but he did not remain one long, pursuing a double-track career as both on-staff researcher for the *Oxford English Dictionary* (*OED*) and as a tutor. As both Carpenter and Scull and Hammond note, as a tutor he was particularly associated with the four women's colleges: Somerville, Lady Margaret Hall, St. Hugh's, and St. Hilda's (*Biography* 101–02; *Chronology* 107)—and, so we may assume from later evidence, the Society of Home-Students, which arranged for tutorials for students who lived off-campus. Within a year and a half, his work as a tutor had prospered to the extent that he gave up his post at the *OED* (where one suspects he might otherwise have happily spent his whole career engaged in the highly congenial work of etymology) to devote himself to tutoring and scholarly work; by this time (May 1920) he was already teaching his first class (on *Sir Gawain and the Green Knight*) and already working on what would be his first major academic publication: *A Middle-English Vocabulary* [1922] (Scull and Hammond, *Chronology* 108). We have relatively little information about Tolkien's pupils at this period, but what we have is suggestive: Scull and Hammond record that two months earlier, in March 1920, Tolkien was asked by one student, Miss Duncan of Somerville, "for guidance on questions that she might face in the Old English paper of her examination. He [sent] her fifty possible questions, many taken

16. Scull and Hammond, *Chronology* adds some details to help flesh out the picture: that the hospital in question was the Brooklands hospital in Hull, to which Tolkien was transferred in August 1917 (101); that she later became Michael Tolkien's godmother (114); and that Tolkien may have visited with her during a visit to Hull in September 1945 (293). John Garth adds the additional information that Brooklands, a hospital for officers, was overseen by a Mrs. Strickland Constable (239), and that Tolkien stayed there on and off until as late as October 11, 1918 (242, 246–48).

from past papers" and regrets not yet having time to compile "a select bibliography" as well (*Chronology* 112). Such a detailed reply, and the time it must have taken him to draw it up, strongly implies that he took her question, and her commitment, seriously and responded in kind; I see no sign here that he took her request any less seriously than he would have any male student's.

The date May 1920 is important, because that is the month in which Oxford amended its statutes to allow women to become full members of the university for the first time (Brittain 150–52, 154). That fall came the momentous event where women who had attended Oxford in the preceding forty years and passed their course of studies by the examiners were finally granted their degrees (155): among those who took part in that ceremony was Dorothy L. Sayers (who had been a contemporary of Tolkien's at Oxford, both their work appearing together for the first of two times in *Oxford Poetry 1915*).[17] Elizabeth Wright would have been eligible as well, though I can find no proof as to whether she took part. Tolkien himself would have missed this event, since he began teaching at Leeds that same month.

Leeds

Here, we venture into a period of Tolkien's life about which we know far too little: his years at Leeds. Christopher Tolkien has carefully dated all that can be dated of Tolkien's imaginative work (poetry, fiction, invented languages, and invented scripts), and Scull and Hammond have scoured Leeds University records to assemble a framework of which classes Tolkien taught and when, but reading through the twenty-four page section they devote to these five or six years turns up virtually no mention of any women at all besides Edith, a landlady, and a felonious maid or two (*Chronology* 123): none at all connected with his teaching or tutoring.

And yet we know Tolkien had female students at Leeds, some of whom he maintained ties with for decades. Even in his 1941 letter memorializing George Gordon, he makes mention of how serious the Yorkshire students were about their studies, and stresses that this applied to men and women alike (*Letters* 57). For example, there was Stella Mills—described by Priscilla Tolkien as "one of my father's outstanding

17. The other being *Essays Presented to Charles Williams* (1947).

students" from the Leeds period (P. Tolkien 9) —who became a lifelong friend of the family, keeping in touch with Priscilla even after Tolkien's death. Mills is one of eleven medieval scholars to whom Tolkien sent author's copies of *The Hobbit* when it was first published in September 1937 (Rateliff, *History* 887–88).[18] Like Tolkien, she worked for a time at the *OED*; her major scholarly publication was a translation of *The Saga of Hrolf Kraki* (1933), dedicated to E. V. Gordon, Tolkien, and *OED* editor C. T. Onions. We know less about another name on the author's copies list, K. M. (Katharine) Kilbride, except that she was one of his students at Leeds and retained fond memories of "the old English House" at Leeds, and that Tolkien over the years sent her not just *The Hobbit* but also "Beowulf: The Monsters and the Critics" and *The Lord of the Rings.* Another student from this period was Mother M. [Mary?] Agnes: in an unpublished 1948 letter to Tolkien she reminisces of Leeds days and stresses Tolkien's "courteous kindness":

> If you think back as far as 1920 when you were our lecturer at Leeds for Middle English you may possibly recall two of us sitting in the front row working through Sir Gawayne and the Green Knight. Many years have gone since then but never have I forgotten your courteous kindness to me always. (Agnes)

Given the date of 1920, this must have been during Tolkien's first term at Leeds, and Mother Agnes's description of "courteous kindness" is strikingly reminiscent of John Lawlor's encounter with Tolkien a quarter-century later when meeting his newly assigned thesis supervisor in 1946: "My first and abiding impression was one of immediate kindness. Tutored by Lewis I had expected to be tested with a few falls, so to speak. But the gentle creature who sucked his pipe and

---

18. Thirteen, if you include copies of the American edition sent to Francis Magoun and Kemp Malone the next year. The others from Tolkien's 1937 list included E. V. Gordon, K. M. Kilbride, A. H. Smith, and George Gordon (all four being students and/or colleagues of Tolkien's from Leeds, like Mills; another Leeds associate included in Tolkien's list was W. R. Childe, but he was a poet, not a medievalist); Oxford associates such as C. S. Lewis, C. L. Wrenn, Helen Buckhurst, Simonne d'Ardenne, and Elaine Griffiths; and also R. W. Chambers (never a colleague, but a medievalist Tolkien greatly admired—he considered that Chambers had produced the single best essay ever written on *Beowulf*—and with whom he kept in close touch).

gazed meditatively along its stem seemed interested only in what he could do to help" (Lawlor 31).[19]

Again, I suggest that no distinction can be seen here between the way Tolkien treats his female students and his male ones.

I can add one new anecdote regarding Tolkien's Leeds days, told to me in 1981 when I was researching the origins of *Songs for the Philologists*, that reflects the easygoing camaraderie he had with his students, male and female alike. While the moving spirit behind the little booklet's publication, A. H. (Hugh) Smith—one of Tolkien's most illustrious students from Leeds—had died some years before, in 1967, I did get to meet with his son, who told me that his mother (Helen Smith, née Tomlinson) had herself been a student of Tolkien's during those now-distant Leeds days. She declined to meet with me, being a person, her son said, who lived in the present and didn't like to dwell on the past. However, she did pass along one little story about Tolkien and his students from those days I think worth sharing. She mentioned that Tolkien's classes were often followed by discussion sessions, which could stretch on so long that Tolkien would invite the group of students back to his house for tea, so they could continue the discussion. They would go to Tolkien's house, and the tea would very pointedly not arrive—the implication being that Mrs. Tolkien did not approve of students in the house, at least outside scheduled tutorial times. Carpenter says Edith was much happier at Leeds than she had been at Oxford,[20] but the evidence suggests this was not because there she had more contact with Tolkien's students, but that Leeds was less

19. This kindness, Lawlor notes, was practical as well: "Tolkien was directly instrumental in my first appointment [...] Meditating on the salary I was very ready to accept, he said pensively that a married man with two young children really needed a thousand pounds. Dazzling prospect (not to be realised for many a year!) but entirely typical coming from a man with a thriving family—and utterly unlike anything that would remotely occur to any others among the dons of that day, where decent reticence at all costs kept its distance" (37).

20. "Edith found the atmosphere in the university [i.e., Leeds] refreshingly informal, and she made friends with other wives" (Carpenter, *Biography* 105). Carpenter continues: "[T]he Tolkiens moved to Leeds, and Edith found that things were different there. People occupied ordinary modest houses [. . .]. Another university wife lived a few doors down [. . .] and often called for a chat. Edith also began to see a good deal of Ronald's pupils who came in for tutorials or tea, and she liked many of them very much. Many of these pupils became family friends who kept in touch with her in later years and often came to visit" (155).

of a university town and thus she had a wider circle beyond her husband's associates.

Oxford

With Tolkien's return to Oxford, we have a long period that is relatively well-documented, particularly from the time of *The Hobbit*'s submission to Allen & Unwin onward (i.e., starting around the end of 1936). Out of that mass of material, there are so many examples of him teaching and mentoring women that here we can only pick and choose a few examples to focus upon.

It might be argued that Tolkien began tutoring women immediately after the war because that is the sort of student the low man on the totem pole might be assigned or able to attract. But that argument cannot apply to Tolkien in the twenties and thirties, when he was an eminent scholar (listed in *Who's Who* from 1925 onward, holder of one of the most prestigious Old English chairs in the world). Several sources suggest that his not needing a chaperon when tutoring young single women, being a married man, accounts for Tolkien's getting so many women as students in those early days immediately following the War. But Tolkien continued to be closely associated with the teaching of women long after chaperons were dispensed with, and long after he shifted from tutoring to lecturing and overseeing theses upon his return to Oxford in 1925–26.

Significantly, Tolkien had no sooner taken up his new post as Anglo-Saxon professor at Oxford on October 1, 1925 (Scull and Hammond, *Chronology* 132), than he was assigned to supervise the thesis of Julia Maud Keays-Young of the Society of Home-Students on October 30 (133), and also appointed the supervisor of M. G. Last, also of the Society of Home-Students and therefore almost certainly another female student. He was similarly appointed the supervisor of Ruth A. Crook of Somerville in November 1926 (138, 140), E. Olszewska of Lady Margaret Hall in November 1927 (142), Helen Buckhurst of St. Hugh's a month later (143), and, in November 1928, R. Tuve of Somerville (147); during the same period he supervises two men as well, A. C. Corlett of St. Edmund Hall in February 1927 (140) and Daniel Ferguson Aitkin of Balliol in June 1927 (141). And this is only a very partial list: Scull and Hammond record that almost half of the advanced degree students

Tolkien oversaw during his thirty-five year career were women (*Reader* 1111), which seems a remarkably high proportion for the era.

A vivid glimpse into Tolkien as a teacher of women can be found in the biography of Mary Challans, better known by her pen name, Mary Renault. Renault's biographer notes that Tolkien had tutored women from St. Hugh's while working at the *OED* and describes the impact of Tolkien's return from Leeds on Renault and her fellow students at St. Hugh's in these terms:

> the women at St. Hugh's [...] had every reason to be grateful for his return. He was a conscientious lecturer, offering almost double the statutory hours in order to ensure that his students, female as well as male, covered the entire subject. Indeed, he was unusual in being notably sympathetic to women undergraduates. (Sweetman 29)

We don't have any contemporary references by Challans to Tolkien during her undergraduate days (1925–28), although we know she was obsessed with all things medieval at the time and that long afterward her letters exchanged with her old college roommate, Kasia Abbott, make "frequent references to their old teacher Tolkien" (Sweetman 28, 264). And that, when asked about him more than sixty years later, Kasia described him to Renault's biographer as "*darling* Tolkien" (29, emphasis in original). We don't have any correspondence between Tolkien and Renault, unfortunately, but we know that Tolkien and Renault admired each other's fiction; he singles out *The King Must Die* and *The Bull from the Sea* for special praise (*Letters* 377) and mentions receiving "a card of appreciation" from Renault, describing it as the piece of fan mail that had pleased him the most (377).

Lest we think Tolkien only appealed to the serious linguistically minded student, here are a few diary entries from 1933 by Barbara Pym, who devoted her time at St. Hilda's to chasing boys and thus gathering copy for her future novels:

> July 29th. I worked at Old English for about 1 1/2 hours after breakfast—Wulfstan's address to the English. Really it gave me the pip! After lunch I started to make a summer frock (deep orangey-pink and white check gingham [...]) I think it should be rather nice. (Pym 25)
>
> October 10th. An amusing lecture in the morning—Professor Tolkien on Beowulf. I bought [...] some Amami Henna application—but doubt whether I shall have the nerve to use it strongly! (28)

If Tolkien was able to amuse and capture (at least briefly) the attention of non-specialist students uninterested in philology such as Pym, it shows he had greater skill as a lecturer than is generally acknowledged.

One student who was so deeply interested forms a link between Tolkien and Renault: Helen Buckhurst, who became a tutor at St. Hugh's in 1926 and began her thesis, under Tolkien's supervision, in 1927. Renault's biography mentions that Buckhurst delivered the inaugural lecture to the college's newly formed English Club in December 1926; a contemporary report describes it as "an amusing paper on Icelandic folklore" (Sweetman 29). This may have been the same lecture Buckhurst delivered to the Viking Society earlier that year (February 1926), or redacted from it. Buckhurst is another of those to whom Tolkien gave a presentation copy of *The Hobbit,* and her letter of thanks (now in the Bodleian; MS. Tolkien 21, folio 117) shows she considered him more a colleague than a teacher, referring to him as "Dear Ronald." In addition to becoming Priscilla Tolkien's godmother, Buckhurst is unusual among Tolkien's students in that she may have influenced his Middle-earth stories in one small, significant way: a good case can be made for her Viking Society lecture as having been the direct source of Tolkien's scene in *The Hobbit* where the trolls turn to stone.

An even greater influence on Tolkien's imaginative work came through Elaine Griffiths of the Society of Home-Students, whose thesis he had been appointed to oversee in late 1933, not long after he had finished drafting *The Hobbit*. Griffiths never completed her B.Litt on the *Ancrene Wisse,* nor the revision of the Clark-Hall *Beowulf* (for which Tolkien provided an extensive preface on the poem's alliterative metre), despite working closely with Tolkien on both projects (Scull and Hammond go so far as to call her "his *de facto* assistant") (Scull and Hammond, *Reader* 354, 353). But she was responsible for putting Tolkien in contact with another former Home-School student, Susan Dagnall, who borrowed *The Hobbit* and soon recommended it to her employers, Allen & Unwin; it is thus appropriate that Griffiths is another of those medievalists who received a presentation copy. Griffiths herself failed to publish any scholarship of note, instead devoting herself to tutoring. She became a fellow of the Society of Home-Students in 1938; Scull and Hammond note that by the time of her retirement she had held "at one time or another, nearly every office" in what was successively known as the Society of Home-Students, St. Anne's Society, and finally St. Anne's College (*Reader* 354).

By far the most successful of all Tolkien's women students, and the one he worked closest with, was Simonne d'Ardenne, yet another of the names that appear on the author's copies list. Tolkien was appointed her supervisor in early 1932 (Scull and Hammond, *Chronology* 163), a relationship that evolved into a full collaboration; d'Ardenne's thesis, an edition of *Þe Liflade ant te Passiun of Seinte Iulienen*, was in fact a joint work by d'Ardenne and Tolkien, although published under her name alone, thus earning her her doctorate (Tolkien having no need to "publish or perish").[21] They also become personally close, with d'Ardenne living with the Tolkiens as a sort of honorary member of the family for a year, beginning in October 1932 (Scull and Hammond, *Chronology* 165).

D'Ardenne is unusual among Tolkien's female students in that she quickly published her thesis (1936), gained her doctorate, became a professor (at the University of Liege, 1938), and had a long, productive career in academia, while so many of Tolkien's talented female students drifted out of academia, or wound up teaching at grammar school level, or failed to produce any significant publications. And this phenomenon, which seems to have puzzled and disappointed Tolkien, I think leads directly to the Letter to Michael.

The Letter to Michael

I think it's fair to say that one of the most notorious things J. R. R. Tolkien ever wrote comes in a letter to his son Michael, offering him advice on women on the eve of his marriage—although we should note that Tolkien's intention in this letter is actually to talk his son *out* of marrying. The whole letter is essentially a version of a father and son having "The Talk," except that by chance in this case it was written down and thus survives to bemuse and perhaps horrify us in a

21. Carpenter puts it discreetly: "Tolkien contributed much to her edition [. . .]. Indeed, [it] paradoxically contains more of his views on early Middle English than anything he ever published under his own name" (*Biography* 140). Scull and Hammond are more blunt, stating that "Tolkien was a silent joint editor" (*Chronology* 820) and explaining that it "bears d'Ardenne's name alone [...] because it was her thesis. But for that it would have appeared as her joint work with Tolkien, as she referred to it in correspondence" (*Reader* 202).

changed world several generations later. I pass by Tolkien's statement that *men are polygamous; women are monogamous* (*Letters* 51, emphasis added) as one of those things men tell themselves in self-justification of their more reprehensible impulses, to concentrate on a passage I think relevant to Tolkien's attitude toward his students, particularly his female students, when he writes:

> they can in fact often achieve very remarkable insight and understanding, even of things outside their natural range: for it is their gift to be [...] stimulated [...] by the male. Every teacher knows that. How quickly an intelligent woman can be taught, grasp his ideas, see his point—and how (with rare exceptions) they can go no further, when they leave his hand, or when they cease to take a *personal* interest in *him*. (*Letters* 49; emphasis Tolkien's)

Now, this is remarkably similar to something his old mentor, Joseph Wright, had said half a century earlier: As Elizabeth Wright notes, "His first pupils in Oxford were the women students," whom he praised as "very good workers" who "worked fearfully hard" (*Life* 130). Yet, Wright went on to say "The thing that bothers me most is that they are not men and therefore I have no direct proof that they will propagate the subject further when they leave here" (*Life* 117).

I think here Tolkien is wrestling with a phenomenon he would have seen throughout his career: why did his male students do so much better, after they had left his supervision, than his female students did? Consider E. V. Gordon, who succeeded to Tolkien's Leeds professorship at age thirty and had already amassed an impressive list of scholarly publications before his early death twelve years later, even having been knighted by the King of Denmark for services to Scandinavian studies (Anderson 18). Or A. H. Smith, another Leeds student, who succeeded R. W. Chambers as Quain Professor of English at University College London and became the driving force behind the English Place Name Society. Or Robert Burchfield, who never completed his thesis (a Tolkien-supervised edition of *Ormulum*) but nonetheless became Chief Editor of the *OED*. Or Arthurian scholar Brian Woledge.[22] Or Meredith

22. Woledge, another of Tolkien's Leeds students, became an expert on the medieval French Arthurian cycle, publishing a 1936 critical edition of the thirteenth-century Gawain adventure *L'Atre Périlleux* ("The Perilous Graveyard") and three years later becoming Professor of French at University College London (the first Englishman to hold the Fielden Chair of French) (Day).

Thompson. Or Norman Davis. Or A. J. Bliss. Or Gabriel Turville-Petre. Or any of a dozen others who might be named.

Against this can be set d'Ardenne, one of only two of Tolkien's female students whom I have been able so far to confirm became full professors (albeit at foreign universities).[23] Elaine Griffiths held a fellowship (at St. Anne's) as did Ursula Dronke, the great *Edda* scholar, at Linacre College. Many of those discussed above, however, failed either to gain a professorship or other prestigious academic post or to produce more than a handful of publications. Stella Mills was teaching at St. Joseph's Catholic Primary School in Oxford at the time Tolkien sent her a presentation copy of *The Hobbit*; we know that Tolkien felt Mills was "far too well qualified" for such a job, and that he was pleased when she eventually found a post at the Maria Assumpta Teacher Training College in Kensington; however, most of the time that she might otherwise have devoted to scholarly research was taken up tending to an elderly and demanding mother (P. Tolkien 9). Helen Buckhurst, whose early publications had shown such promise, by 1937 was out of the university system altogether, teaching at a Catholic school for girls in St. Albans, Loreto College (Scull and Hammond, "Addenda"; Rateliff, *History* 885).

Faced with such a discrepancy, Tolkien, who had seen how skilled these women were when he worked closely with them and knew how smart and dedicated they were, in the Letter to Michael is, I think, reaching for some sort of explanation of why they failed to continue as they had begun and faltered once they'd graduated with their degrees. Looking back now from well into the twenty-first century, I think the key factor he failed to take into account was that he underestimated the glass ceiling. There were precious few professorial chairs to go

23. I have since learned of another: Auvo Kurvinen of St. Anne's, a Finnish scholar whose B.Litt (published in 1951 as *Sir Gawain and the Carl of Carlisle*) Tolkien supervised from 1947 to 1949 (Scull and Hammond, *Chronology* 324, 328, 348). He also oversaw her D.Phil from 1954 through 1962, well after his retirement (442, 542)—a long process perhaps made longer by its overlap with her teaching at the University of Helsinki from 1955 on, passing from Assistant Professor (1958) through Associate Professor (1963) to finally full Professor in 1972, the year before Tolkien's death. However, not to diminish Kurvinen's achievement, by this point the glass ceiling already had significant cracks in it: both Oxford and Cambridge by that point had women in full professorships. I am grateful to Christina Scull for calling Kurvinen to my attention.

around—even noted scholars like Lord David Cecil (1948), C. S. Lewis (1954), and Nevill Coghill (1957) had to wait years to gain one—and inertia and institutional bias was against their going to a woman, however gifted. I would suggest that when Tolkien wrote "they can go no further, when they leave his hand" he was observing a very real phenomenon but completely missing the factors that caused it.

Lewis's Professorship

Following up the thread of professorships, it's worthy of note that Tolkien himself gained the status of professor—roughly the equivalent in the U.S. university system of being named department chairman—at the remarkably early age of thirty-two, and gained his first Oxford chair just a year later; each of his three professorial chairs was more prestigious than the last. By contrast, Lewis, who began tutoring at Oxford in autumn 1925 at about the time Tolkien returned there, had to wait almost thirty years to gain his professorship, after repeated failures, and then only became Professor of Medieval and Renaissance Literature at Cambridge because of Tolkien's direct and repeated intervention. The story of Lewis's Cambridge chair, and Tolkien's role in it, is now well-known:[24] the post being specifically created with Lewis in mind, his being the unanimous choice of the selection committee (whose eight all-male members included Tolkien) although he never bothered to apply; Lewis's two peremptory and comprehensive refusals, only to reverse himself and accept the chair after it had already been offered to the committee's second choice, Helen Gardner. I'd like to change the focus a bit and look at events from Gardner's point of view.

In the first place, let's not overlook the fact that, while Lewis was the committee's first choice, they had selected Gardner as their second choice, and thus as also being worthy of the chair. (Tolkien himself had been a second choice for the Rawlinson and Bosworth chair back in 1925, only gaining the appointment after it had been offered to, and turned down by, R. W. Chambers [Scull and Hammond, *Companion* 131].) Had she accepted, she would, as far as I

24. The definitive account can be found in Barbour, particularly the section "Lewis at Cambridge: The Chair" (459–65). My thanks to Morgan Thomsen for drawing this article to my attention and providing me with a copy.

have been able to discover, have become the first woman to hold a chair in English Language or Literature at Oxford or Cambridge: a significant achievement. We do not know details about who on the committee voted for whom, and thus how Tolkien voted in regards to Gardner's appointment, nor who any of the other candidates might have been, which has led to considerable speculation.[25] What is certain is that Lewis's belated change of mind placed Gardner in an unenviable position.[26] If she declined, it might mean missing out on the chance of a lifetime. If she went ahead and accepted, it would be with the knowledge that word would inevitably get out and many would view the position as having rightfully been Lewis's. In the end she declined, and thus had to wait another twelve years to gain her own professorship (succeeding to Nevill Coghill's chair as Merton Professor of English Literature in 1966), by which time Dorothy Whitelock had already (in 1957) become Elrington and Bosworth Professor of Anglo-Saxon at Cambridge.[27]

And yet, today Lewis's Cambridge chair is held by Helen Cooper.[28] And Tolkien's Merton Professorship is held by Suzanne Romaine. Sometimes half a century does not pass in vain.

---

25. A. N. Wilson in his biography of Lewis spreads some malicious gossip to the effect that Gardner was never really offered the post at all (245), which we now know to be entirely untrue. William Griffin goes so far as to imply that Tolkien used the threat of Gardner's getting the position to successfully persuade Lewis to reconsider (Griffin 352; Barbour 462, note 55). Neither offers any evidence for these claims.

26. That Gardner was well aware of Lewis's change of mind is shown by a passage in her obituary of him: "When first approached he was unwilling to leave Oxford, and the Chair was indeed offered to someone else. Fortunately the 'second string' declined, *partly on account of having heard that Lewis was changing his mind,* for it was obvious that this ought to be Lewis's chair" (427–28; emphasis mine). She gives no indication that here she is speaking of herself. The other reason usually given as also weighing on her decision was her having just been offered a Readership in Renaissance Literature, a promotion that would allow her to stay at her own college (St. Hilda's) and in Oxford.

27. Whitelock had earlier tried and failed to succeed Tolkien as Rawlinson and Bosworth Professor at Oxford in 1945, the chair instead going to C. L. Wrenn. Her *Dictionary of National Biography* entry stresses her "bitter disappointment" over this defeat, and the degree to which the difficulty of female scholars to gain posts almost drove her from academia in the mid-forties (Keynes 692–93).

28. In addition, we might note that Cooper is the sixth person to hold this chair (Lewis having been the first), and that among her predecessors was Chauceri-

And there's a J. R. R. Tolkien Professor of English Language and Literature, created in 1981, which has been held successively by Douglas Gray (1981–97), Paul Strohm (1998–2003), and now Vincent Gillespie (2004ff.). Rather than being attached to one of the centuries-old colleges like Pembroke or Merton or Exeter, it has been accompanied by a fellowship to Lady Margaret Hall (Gray), then St. Anne's (Strohm), and now Lady Margaret Hall again (Gillespie), with St. Hilda's said to be next in the queue.[29]

I think this legacy would have pleased Tolkien greatly. His daughter Priscilla Tolkien (herself a graduate of Lady Margaret Hall) wrote upon her father's centenary:

> [My father believed completely] in higher education for girls; never at any time in my early life or since did I feel that any difference was made between me and my brothers, so far as our education needs and opportunities were concerned [...] It was [...] a source of pride and pleasure to him that he had a daughter as well as sons at the University, which was his scholarly and academic home for much of his working life. (qtd. in Scull and Hammond, *Reader* 1111)

As for the larger legacy of Tolkien outside academia, the final proof that Tolkien understood and empathized with women can be found in the simple fact that a large percentage of Tolkien's audience have been women, who thus do not find his world unwelcoming. These women obviously have not been put off by *The Lord of the Rings'* mostly male world.

Envoy

Finally, I'd like to leave you with a thought. When I described my paper's thesis to my wife, she made two points I think worth sharing:

> The reason Éowyn resonates with so many women is because he's writing about how women, who were capable, could do the job, but, because they were women, were not allowed to do the job.

(note continued)
an scholar Jill Mann (the fourth to hold this post, from 1988–99). Thus a third of those holding this chair during its sixty-year existence have been women.

29. I am grateful to Elizabeth Solopova, and through her to Professor Anne Hudson, formerly of Lady Margaret Hall, for information regarding the J. R. R. Tolkien Professorship.

> Sometimes, they might be the only person who could do the job—i.e., defeat the Witch-king—and they had to defy everybody to do the job.
>
> How did Tolkien, who'd never been told *you can't do that, you're a girl,* come to understand that so well?
>
> And, a second question: Who taught Éowyn to fight?
>
> Whoever it was, that person is analogous to Tolkien teaching a talented young woman something she wanted to learn, but which there was very little chance of her ever being able to use.

Appendix: C. S. Lewis's letter to E. R. Eddison

To appreciate how unusual Tolkien's support for women seeking advanced degrees was in the Oxford of his time, it's useful to contrast him with his friend and colleague C. S. Lewis. When writing his first letter to E. R. Eddison in mock-medieval English, Lewis described the person responsible for introducing him to Eddison's works through

> a foolish book (on the *novello*) that came lately to my hands, made by som seely wench that seeketh a B.Litt or a D.Phil, when God knows shad a better bestowed her tyme makynge sport for some goodman in his bed and bearing children for the stablishment of this reaulme or els to be at her beads in a religyous house [...] comparing of youre eloquent stile to Swinburne [this wench] made plain discoverie of her own follie and her ignorance. (*Collected* 535)

Oddly enough, when Eddison wrote back, asking the author and title of the book that discussed his work, Lewis professed being unable to recall either:[30]

> Now to trete of yo~ hono~'s question concerning the house woman that wrote of your stile, the name, with the book, is goon from me;

---

30. This is curious, given the assertions frequently made for Lewis's possessing an almost photographic memory when it came to books and their contents. Obviously, his ability here was less than legend makes it, particularly if Lewis truly had forgotten everything about the book except that it had been written by a woman, mentioned Eddison's book, and at one point compared his style to that of Swinburne. Even the latter detail is distorted by being taken out of context: the full passage in which this line occurs is quite different in its thrust, saying of *The Worm Ouroboros* that "There is throughout a sweeping, changing luxuriance of language, sometimes of Swinburnian rhythm, sometimes vigorous Elizabethan, lordly or plebeian, sometimes Romanesque, sometimes echoing the cadences of Greece; and an atmosphere of magical enchantment, like a shining, iridescent bubble, is beautifully sustained" (Haines 204).

> but she saide it not, as you conceyued me, of evil intent, being rather of those who then most disable an auctour when they most go about to commend him amici hostibus infestiores ['friends more deadly than enemies']. (*Collected* 542)

Thanks to the research of Eddison scholar Paul Thomas, we now know that the book in question was *What's in a Novel* by Helen E. Haines (1942), a work whose main purpose is to recommend good books for libraries. Rather surprisingly, Haines devotes a whole chapter to fantasy, devoting special attention to James Branch Cabell, Eddison (discussing all three of his novels published to date) (203–05), and Robert Nathan; she also includes a warm recommendation of Tolkien's recently published *Hobbit*: "it fuses legend, tradition, and the dim beginnings of history into a robust imaginative creation that mingles homely simplicity, humor, drama, pictorial beauty, and a truly epic quality" (217).

As for Haines herself: far from being a student, she was seventy at the time, a distinguished figure who had helped develop the discipline of library science in the late 1890s and early 1900s. A protégée of Charles Cutter, Haines had been granted an annual pension by Andrew Carnegie "for her service to librarianship." A tireless advocate of books and public libraries, she would later suffer from blacklisting during the McCarthy era for her refusal to censor books. Throughout her career, she tirelessly championed popular fiction as deserving a place alongside more literary works and exercised a huge influence on which books smaller libraries, with limited budgets and shelf-space, chose to buy and put on those shelves—which makes her devoting an entire chapter to fantasy all the more significant.

Given that Lewis assumes Haines is a research student, and his condemnation of her on that basis—i.e., for pursuing an academic degree rather than taking on a traditional female role—it is interesting to note that he's similarly harsh on two fictional female research students, one in *The Place of the Lion*, his favorite novel by Charles Williams, and the other in his own *That Hideous Strength*.

Of the first, Lewis calls Damaris Tighe a "research-beetle" and delights in the negative depiction of her as "an extreme example of the complacent researcher" ("Novels" 24). In his private correspondence he was much less polite, calling her "a perfect [expletive] of a female researcher" (*Collected* 245); in both he asserts that she is glibly writing on a subject with no hint of an idea of its significance. Similarly, he describes Jane Studdock, the lead female character in the final volume of his Ransom trilogy, as someone "who follows an *imagined* vocation at the expense of a real one [...] her thesis on Donne was all derivative bilge" (*Collected* 670, emphasis in original)—her true vocation being that of housewife and future mother to Mark Studdock's children.

From this, I would argue that the evidence is limited (three examples) but all points to the same conclusion: that Lewis had a distaste for female research students that led him to denigrate them both in public and in private. By contrast, Tolkien was deeply supportive of his female research students and did all he could to further their researches and subsequent careers. Lewis's words to Eddison are shocking but accord with similarly negative depictions of women in his works (e.g., the short story "The Shoddy Lands" and the unfinished *The Dark Tower*), while there are no such characterizations of female characters in any of Tolkien's works, making it almost impossible to imagine Tolkien talking about one of his students like that.

Works Cited

Agnes, Mother M. Letter to JRRT, 5 January 1948. Bodleian Library, Department of Western Manuscripts, Tolkien papers. MS Tolkien 21, folio 6. MS.

Anderson, Douglas A. " 'An Industrious Little Devil': E. V. Gordon as Friend and Collaborator with Tolkien." *Tolkien the Medievalist.* Ed. Jane Chance. New York: Routledge, 2003. 15–25. Print.

d'Ardenne, Simonne. "The Man and the Scholar." *J. R. R. Tolkien, Scholar and Storyteller: Essays in Memoriam.* Ed. Mary Salu and Robert T. Farrell. Ithaca: Cornell University Press, 1979. 33–37. Print.

---, ed. [and J. R. R. Tolkien].*Þe Liflade ant te Passiun of Seinte Iulienen.* 1936. Rpt. Early English Text Society, vol. 248. London: Oxford UP, 1961. Print.

Barbour, Brian. "Lewis and Cambridge." *Modern Philology* 96.4 (May 1999): 439–84. Print.

Bonsor, Ann. *J. R. R. Tolkien.* Radio Oxford, 1974. Audiocassette.

Brittain, Vera. *The Women at Oxford: A Fragment of History*. New York: Macmillan, 1960. Print.

Buckhurst, Helen. Letter to J. R. R. Tolkien. 23 September 1937. Tolkien papers, Tolkien 21, folio 117. Department of Western Manuscripts, Bodleian Library, Oxford. MS.

Carpenter, Humphrey. *The Inklings: C. S. Lewis, J. R. R. Tolkien, Charles Williams, and Their Friends*. Boston: Houghton Mifflin, 1979. Print.

---. *Tolkien: A Biography*. London: Allen and Unwin, 1977. Print.

Day, Shirley. "Brian Woledge: French Scholar Who Put Literature Back in Context." obit. *The Guardian* 4 June 2002. Web. 2 May 2013.

Dickins, Bruce. "Elizabeth Mary Wright: A Bibliography." *Leeds Studies in English* 3 (1934): 1. Print.

Doughan, David. "Women, Oxford, and Tolkien." *Mallorn* 45 (2008): 16–20. Print.

Gardner. Helen. "Clive Staples Lewis 1898–1963." *Proceedings of the British Academy*. Vol. LI. [1965]. London: Oxford UP, 1966. 417–28. Print.

Garth, John. *Tolkien and the Great War: The Threshold of Middle-earth*. London: HarperCollins, 2003. Print.

Griffin, William. *C. S. Lewis: A Dramatic Life*. San Francisco: Harper and Row, 1986. Print.

Gueroult, Denis. BBC radio interview with JRRT, 1965. Re-released by Audio-Forum. Guilford, CN: 1980. Audiocassette.

Haines, Helen E. *What's in a Novel*. New York: Columbia UP, 1942. Print.

Keynes, Simon. "Whitelock, Dorothy." *Dictionary of National Biography*. Vol. 58. Oxford and New York: Oxford UP, 2004. 692–94. Print.

Lawlor, John. *C. S. Lewis: Memories and Reflections*. Dallas: Spence Publishing, 1998. Print.

Lewis, C. S. *The Collected Letters of C. S. Lewis, Vol. II: Books, Broadcasts, and the War 1931–1949*. Ed. Walter Hooper. San Francisco: HarperSanFrancisco, 2004. Print.

---. "The Novels of Charles Williams." *On Stories and Other Essays on Literature*. Ed. Walter Hooper. New York: Harcourt Brace Jovanovich, 1982. 21–27. Print.

---. *Surprised by Joy: The Shape of My Early Life*. San Diego: Harvest/Harcourt Brace Jovanovich, 1956. Print.

Morton, Andrew. *Tolkien's Bag End: Threshold to Adventure*. Studley, Warwickshire: Brewin Books, 2009. Print.

---. and John Hayes. *Tolkien's Gedling 1914: The Birth of a Legend*. Studley, Warwickshire: Brewin Books, 2008. Print.

Muir, Edwin. "A Boy's World." *Sunday Observer* [London] (27 Nov.1955): 11. Print.

Pym, Barbara. *A Very Private Eye*. London: Macmillan, 1984. Print.

Rateliff, John D. *The History of The Hobbit*. Revised one-volume edition. London: HarperCollins, 2011. Print.

Scull, Christina and Wayne G. Hammond. *The J. R. R. Tolkien Companion and Guide*. Vol. I: *Chronology*. London: HarperCollins, 2006. Print.

---. *The J. R. R. Tolkien Companion and Guide*. Vol. II: *Reader's Guide*. London: HarperCollins, 2006. Print.

Scull, Christina and Wayne G. Hammond. *Addenda and Corrigenda*. Entry for p. 142. April 2013. Web. 29 May 2013.

Solopova, Elizabeth. Letter to John D. Rateliff. 18 Sept 2012. E-mail.

Sweetman, David. *Mary Renault: A Biography*. London: Chatto and Windus, 1993. Print.

Tolkien, J. R. R. *Letters of J. R. R. Tolkien*. Ed. Humphrey Carpenter, with the assistance of Christopher Tolkien. Boston: Houghton Mifflin, 1981. Print.

---. Letter to Miss R. Turnbull. 11 March 1949. Privately owned. MS.

---. "Valedictory Address to the University of Oxford." *J. R. R. Tolkien, Scholar and Storyteller: Essays in Memoriam*. Ed. Mary Salu and Robert T. Farrell. Ithaca: Cornell UP, 1979. 16–32. Print.

--- and E. V. Gordon, ed. *Sir Gawain and The Green Knight*. First edition. Oxford: Clarendon Press, 1925. Print.

Tolkien, John, and Tolkien, Priscilla. *The Tolkien Family Album*. Boston: Houghton Mifflin, 1992. Print.

Tolkien, Priscilla. "Foreword." *The Saga of Hrolf Kraki*. Trans. Stella M. Mills. 1933. Marcellus, MI: Nodens Books, 2012. 9–11. Print.

Þorbjarnardóttir, Arndís. "Barnfóstran frá Íslandi og Tolkien-fjölskyldan." Interviewed by Lindu Ásdísardóttur. *Morganbladid* (February 28, 1999): Section A, 26. Web. 23 August 2013.

Wilson, A. N. *C. S. Lewis: A Biography*. New York: W. W. Norton, 1990. Print.

Woolf, Virginia. *The Diary of Virginia Woolf*. Volume IV: 1931–1935. Ed. Anne Olivier Bell, with the assistance of Andrew McNeillie. London: Hogarth Press, 1982. Print.

---. *The Pargiters: The Novel-Essay Portion of 'The Years'*. Ed. Mitchell A. Leaska. New York and London: Harcourt Brace Jovanovich, 1977. Print.

---. *The Years*. New York: Harcourt, Brace and Company, 1937. Print.

Wright, Elizabeth Mary. *The Life of Joseph Wright*. Two Volumes.London: Oxford University Press, 1932. Print.

---. "Notes on 'Sir Gawayne and the Green Knight'." *Englische Studien* 36 (1907): 209–27. Print.

---. "Sir Gawain and the Green Knight." *JEGP* 34.2 (April 1935): 157–179; *JEGP* 34.3 (July 1935): 339–50; and *JEGP* 35.3 (July 1936): 313–20. Print.

---. "The Word 'Abloy' in 'Sir Gawayne and the Green Knight', l. 1174." *The Modern Language Review* 18.1 (January 1923): 86–87. Print.

She-who-must-not-be-ignored: Gender and Genre in *The Lord of the Rings* and the Victorian Boys' Book

Sharin Schroeder

> I suppose as a boy *She* interested me as much as anything.
> —J. R. R. Tolkien (Resnik, "Interview" 40)

> Personally, I prefer [Robert Louis Stevenson's and H. Rider Haggard's] boys' books to their novels. They seem happier in their dealings with men than with women. [...] Mr. Haggard's savage ladies are better than his civilized fair ones, while there is not a petticoat in *Kidnapped* or *Treasure Island*.
> —Andrew Lang ("Realism" 690)

> If the critic is a woman she will put down *She* with the remark that it is impossible—almost all women have this feeling towards the marvelous.
> —Sir Walter Besant (Haggard, *Days* 193)

When *The Lord of the Rings* was published, a major challenge for critics was to determine its genre. Was it the descendant of Malory's *Morte d'Arthur* and Spenser's *The Faerie Queene*? Was it an epic? A heroic romance? Some reviewers professed to having never seen its like before. But reviewers who disliked *The Lord of the Rings* had a genre label ready—as Tolkien scholars and fans know well. Tolkien's work was a boys' book, or as those critical male reviewers put it, "an infantilist invasion," "A Boy's World," and "juvenile trash" (Richardson 835; Muir, "Boy's" 11; Wilson 314).[1] Edwin Muir was perhaps the first to identify the work with the boys' book genre. In response to the overwhelming

---

1. Alfred Leo Duggan's anonymous reviews in *The Times Literary Supplement* focus on the boyish nature of the hobbits in *The Fellowship of the Ring*, calling Bilbo "the hero of this happy community of elderly schoolboys" ("Heroic" 541). In response to *The Two Towers*, which he praises, he adds several qualifications, including this: "Large sectors of this mythic world are completely omitted: women play no part" ("Epic" 817). By *The Return of the King*, he labels the work as a boys' book: "This is not a work that many adults will read right through more than once" ("Saga" 704). Although Duggan believes that "even a single reading will not be quickly forgotten," he also claims that the book's popularity will be among youth: "In the schoolroom it will be read more avidly, perhaps again and again. If that comes to pass its influence will be immeasurable" (704).

accolades of C. S. Lewis, Naomi Mitchison, and Richard Hughes, Muir professed disappointment with *The Fellowship*, particularly with its style which, he claimed, alternated "between the popular novel and the boys' adventure story" ("Strange" 7). Maurice Richardson, after reading *The Two Towers* (and only *The Two Towers*), called the book "an allegorical adventure story for very leisured boys" with "prep school slang for hobbits and orcs" who "all speak with the same flat, castrated voice" (835). While Muir had more or less approved of *The Two Towers*, calling it "not a story for boys but for everyone" ("Ring" 9), by *The Return of the King*, he would change his mind again, writing one of the reviews that annoyed Tolkien most:

> For the astonishing thing is that all the characters, except a few old men who are apt to be wizards, are boys masquerading as adult heroes. The hobbits, or halflings, are ordinary boys; the fully human heroes have reached the fifth form; but hardly one of them knows anything about women, except by hearsay. Even the elves and the dwarfs and the ents are boys, irretrievably, and will never come to puberty. ("Boy's" 11)

"Blast Edwin Muir and his delayed adolescence," wrote Tolkien to Rayner Unwin on 8 Dec. 1955: "He is old enough to know better. It might do him good to hear what women think of his 'knowing about women', especially as a sign of being mentally adult" (*Letters* 230).

Tolkien's objection to Muir is based on a disagreement about who better understood women, a question that, as Tolkien maintains above, could only be decided by women—though he believed they would decide in his favor.[2] However, both in the nineteenth century, when the boys' book genre emerged, and in the twentieth, when male critics identified *The Lord of the Rings* with that genre, critical rhetoric (and nineteenth-century marketing strategies) created boys' books; the label did not always match up with the books' actual readership. In the mid-twentieth century, associating Tolkien's work with boys was a form of insult against its supposed predominately male adult readers.

---

2. For more of Tolkien's reaction to Muir's review, see John Rateliff's "The Missing Women" earlier in this collection and the Gueroult interview from which he quotes. Gueroult's first name appears as "Denis" on the audiocassette Rateliff cites and as "Denys" on the 2008 BBC reissue of parts of the interview, *The Spoken Word*, and in obituaries. Readers should note that the pertinent sections on Muir and women in *The Lord of the Rings* are not in *The Spoken Word* reissue.

In the late nineteenth century, on the other hand, a vociferous and influential group of male writers glorified the boy, intentionally wrote for youthful male readership, and were more concerned with disassociating their work from a reading audience of women. In both cases, the boys' book label determined readers' understanding of the books' audiences and perpetuated a cycle of marketing the books to boys or young men (Ripp); for *The Lord of the Rings*, the label also colored readers' understanding of the book's portrayal of gender.

Tolkien never saw *The Lord of the Rings* as a work for boys. Words that Tolkien most frequently used to describe *The Lord of the Rings* genre are *fairy-story*, *romance*, and *myth*. The popular connotations of the first two words, however, would likely have displeased Tolkien. The first was associated with children, and the second with boys. Although Tolkien had accepted the association between fairy-stories and children when he wrote *The Hobbit*, he rejected it by the time he wrote *The Lord of the Rings*, cogently arguing against the association in his 1939 Andrew Lang lecture (*Letters* 296–99). Tolkien seemed less prepared for the reviewers' charge of boys' book, even though it was mainly Andrew Lang himself who, in his many reviews of Robert Louis Stevenson and H. Rider Haggard, made the late nineteenth-century boys' book and the romance synonymous.

Although Tolkien, as a medievalist, would have been less likely to think of the romance as a late nineteenth-century genre, neither was he entirely unaware of the romance/boys' books conflation. In addition to his obvious familiarity with Lang, he had read and liked Haggard's stories as a boy. Indeed, he bought *King Solomon's Mines* for some boys in his care in 1913 (Scull and Hammond 355), and John Rateliff makes the case that Tolkien had read even Haggard's lesser-known fiction ("Revisited" 147). More significantly, when asked to name two or three of his favorite books in a 1966 telephone interview with Henry Resnik, Tolkien volunteered *She* (eventually). Because Tolkien so rarely named works he liked, his allusion to *She* deserves and is beginning to receive much critical examination.[3] Even without Tolkien's statement, any

3. John Rateliff ("*She* and Tolkien") and Jared Lobdell (*England and Always*) wrote the first short studies of Tolkien and Haggard, both published in 1981. Rateliff points out the many parallels between *The Lord of the Rings* and *She*, and Lobdell argues more broadly that in *The Lord of the Rings* Tolkien was writing "an

reader of *The Lord of the Rings* who picks up *She* will see that the former has a distinct Haggardian influence. As detailed in excellent articles elsewhere, the similarities between Galadriel and Ayesha are striking enough that no reader of Tolkien could miss them.[4] Both She and Galadriel are beautiful, immortal women (who are capable of death). Both ask their guests to look into pools of water that show the guest scenes from far away. Both explain that these pools are not magic. Both can inspire fear but also undying loyalty in the men who meet them. But She is evil, and Galadriel, without the Ring, is good.

In fact, the boys' book genre of Haggard's fiction, as defined by Andrew Lang, had more of an effect on how critics thought about *The Lord of the Rings* and gender than did Haggard's already demonstrably significant female character. While Tolkien's adventure had many commonalities with romances written for boys, the pronounced differences, particularly those between Tolkien's Galadriel and Haggard's female characters, suggest that Tolkien's construction of gender did not, as early negative reviewers assumed, participate in the same constructions of gender as the boys' books with which it was linked.

Tolkien, in writing a romance, inherited all of the baggage of the quest romance genre, in which women are rare. Nineteenth-century romances/boys' books had two particular approaches to women. On the one hand, the male characters in these romances might approach with awe the powerful, nearly supernatural, and definitely-not-English women they meet in their travels. In some Victorian boys' books such as Haggard's *She: The History of an Adventure* and Lang's and Haggard's *The World's Desire*, women play major, dangerous, and archetypal roles. She-who-must-be-obeyed foreshadows both C. S. Lewis's Jadis in *The Magician's Nephew* and, more positively, Galadriel in *The Lord of the Rings*. On the other hand, when women in this genre are not placed in positions of supernatural power, they are often ex-

---

(note continued)

adventure story in what may be called the Edwardian mode" (15). Many of Lobdell's examples, however (such as *She*, Sherlock Holmes, and *Dracula*), are actually late-Victorian (genre popularity seldom coincides with a monarch's reign) and were written at the height of Andrew Lang's popularity as a journalist, folklorist, and critic.

4. See Rateliff, "*She*"; Rateliff, "Revisited"; also the chapter "Spiders and Evil Red Eyes: The Shadow Sides of Gandalf and Galadriel" in Burns.

cluded entirely. Lang would more than once write approvingly of women's absence in his favorite boys' books, calling *Kidnapped* "probably [Stevenson's] best novel (and without a woman in it)" and praising *Treasure Island* because "there are no interfering petticoats in the story" (*History* 640, "Stevenson's" 30; Orel 145, 148).[5] Lang's formulation of the romance as a youthful and masculine genre stuck, and twentieth-century male critics who read romance as *de facto* boys' books found the label convenient for Tolkien's work.

The Nineteenth-Century Romance (for Boys)

The reasons for the late nineteenth-century return of the romance, renamed the "boys' book," are various. To some extent, they merely reflect the weariness of readers with a long-dominant school of fiction, the three-volume novel popular with circulating libraries. As Tolkien would say to Resnik regarding the popularity of his own books: "I think it is [...] a partly reactionary influence. I think it's part of the fun after so much rather more dreary stuff, isn't it?" ("Interview" 38).

Tolkien's and Haggard's romances both represented a clear shift in what the novel was doing from what predecessors thought the novel should do, and, though with different motivations and different ideas of audience (Haggard intended to write for boys), it was the same shift—a shift toward plot rather than introspection.[6] Even William Watson's thoroughly negative 1888 review of Haggard began by stating that Haggard's work functioned as a counterweight to the modern novel, which was "distinguished by an elaborate triviality which no amount of cleverness can render other than vapid. [...] Those miracles of inexhaustible nothingness, in which the tiniest rivulet of incident just trickles across a continent of dialogue, cannot long be interesting" (324).

5. In Haggard's *King Solomon's Mines*, to which Lang is alluding, the narrator Allan Quatermain also focuses on the missing petticoats. He at first records that he has written a story without a woman, but he quickly discovers that he actually means he has written a story without a young white heroine. Quatermain only thinks to mention women at all because he tells the reader his tale is strange—and a strange story *ought* to involve women (10).

6. Haggard and Tolkien's action-filled narratives often inspired nearly identical reactions. Particularly fascinating is Lang's defense of *She*, which reads almost exactly like Auden's defense of *The Lord of the Rings* ("She" 35–36, Auden 226). Both Lang and Auden were criticized for their consistent championing of their favorite authors.

In his 1905 preface to *The Red Romance Book,* written for an assumed boy audience, Lang summarizes his thoughts on novels popular for his day: "Here is the beginning of a celebrated novel: 'Comedy is a game played to throw reflections upon social life, and it deals with human nature in the drawing rooms of civilised men and women.' "[7] He continues, "You do not want to read any more of that novel. It is not at all like a good old romance of knights and dragons and enchanted princesses and strong wars. The knights and ladies would not have looked at such a book, all about drawing-rooms" (vii).

Lang's statement is part of a movement in late nineteenth-century fiction that saw the three-volume problem novel as effete and emasculated. Elaine Showalter claims that "after 1880, women novelists, while ever more numerous in the marketplace, entered a period of critical decline. After George Eliot's death in 1880, male professional jealousies erupted in critical abuse of women's emasculating effect on the English novel" (17). As Laurence Millman brusquely stated, "The male novel is in fact a conservative backlash to an overwhelming association of the Victorian novel with women, often made by people who neither liked novels or women" (qtd. in Kestner 7). Nevertheless, Lang's interactions with women and women writers are more complex than a blunt statement like Millman's expresses. Lang loved Jane Austen novels (*History* 536–40). He was a great admirer of Margaret Oliphant's supernatural tale *A Beleaguered City* and praised her for being as good a historian as the more famous James Anthony Froude, even though she was one of Lang's biggest rivals as a journalist. He was also disappointed never to have written a successful novel himself (Lang, *Academy* 36; Lang, Letter; Green 117). Lang also furthered the career of many women such as Graham R. Thomson (Rosamund Marriott Watson) and May Kendall (L. Hughes 137). However, Lang's prejudices are clear in his prefaces, journalism, and other writings, in which he frequently make asides and jokes at women's expense. Lang consistently rates boys and their taste in books higher than the tastes of either women or overly cultured men ("Realism" 689; "Stevenson's" 30).

For Lang, the boy, unlike the overly refined man or the novel-reading woman, is able to maintain the taste for the romances of the

7. The line is from George Meredith's *The Egoist* (1879).

past. As a folklorist (who believed in savage survivals within modern culture) and a man steeped in the ideas of his age, Lang accepted the common metaphor of the infancy of nations, in which the lifespan of a man (not a woman) is seen as akin to the progress of civilization as a whole.[8] Thus the child's credulity and lawlessness equate him with the savage, the boy's desire for adventure equates him with the fighting-filled but chivalrous Middle Ages, and the full-grown nineteenth-century man represents the civilized and cultured present. In "Realism and Romance," Lang posits that continued growth will only lead to senility: "The Coming Man may be bald, toothless, highly 'cultured,' and addicted to tales of introspective analysis. [...] I don't envy him the novels he will admire" (689).

Like many of his nineteenth-century contemporaries, Lang firmly identified the genre of romance with the "boys' book." Lang does not maintain that the romance was always a male genre. In the past, women (the ladies) and the knights might have had a taste for romance for, according to Lang, "romances were the novels of the people of the Middle Ages" (*Red* vii). However, in Lang's time, women readers with different tastes were dominating the circulating library: "[Medieval Romances] were not much like the novels which come from the library for your dear mothers and aunts." These, Lang claims, have "not much fighting [...] though there is any amount of love-making, and there are no giants; and if there is a knight, he is usually a grocer or a doctor, quite the wrong sort of knight" (vii).

To counteract the wrong tastes, Lang praised the fiction of H. Rider Haggard and Robert Louis Stevenson in review after review in weekly and monthly periodicals. Lang's "Realism and Romance" anticipates many of the arguments of J. R. R. Tolkien and C. S. Lewis. For example, he staunchly supports readers' rights to their own taste, particularly if their taste leans toward "the catawampus of Romance" (693). However, unlike Tolkien and Lewis, Lang is determined to claim, not that romance appeals to certain individuals regardless of their age, but rather that humans' boyish (and savage) nature cannot be completely wiped out: "The flutter in the dovecoats of culture caused by three or four boys' books is amazing. Culture is saddened

8. For more on the infancy of nations, see Forbes 21–23.

at discovering that not only boys and illiterate people, but even critics not wholly illiterate, can be moved by a tale of adventure" (690).

Haggard, too, complained of the feminized fiction of his day. In "About Fiction," an article that would provoke a flurry of indignant responses, Haggard disapproved of nineteenth-century English fiction because of its supposedly feminized nature:

> Why do *men* hardly ever read a novel? Because, in ninety-nine cases out of a hundred, it is utterly false as a picture of life; and, failing in that, it certainly does not take ground as a work of high imagination. The ordinary popular English novel represents life as it is considered desirable that schoolgirls should suppose it to be. (177)

Haggard found it "hard that all fiction should be judged by the test as to whether or not it is suitable reading for a girl of sixteen" (177). As for the American school of fiction, he wrote that it was full of "heroines [...] of silk and cambric, who soliloquize and dissect their petty feelings" and, as for the "men—well, they are emasculated specimens of an overwrought age, and, with culture on their lips, and emptiness in their hearts, they dangle round the heroines till their three-volumed fate is accomplished" (175).

The boys' book was not, however, merely a reactionary influence to George Eliot, Henry James, and Mrs. Humphrey Ward. It also had much to do with fiction's expanding market and increased literacy among the young. As Jeffrey Richards notes in *Imperialism and Juvenile Literature*, the Forster 1870 Education Act, which mandated that elementary education be available to children between the ages of five and twelve, provided a new audience for reading material (4).[9] One of the easiest ways to provide material, of course, was to remarket books originally for adults to boys, who were reading them anyway. The first boys' books were hand-me-downs, the nursery furniture that Tolkien mentions in "On Fairy-stories," "relegated to the play-room, primarily because the adults do not want it, and do not mind if it is misused" (*OFS* 50). Actually, however, in the case of the boys' book, the adults *did* mind if it was misused—though they had different ideas than Tolkien of what misuse meant. *Robinson Crusoe* and *Ivanhoe* were adult books particularly recommended

9. Education before age twelve was not compulsory until 1880. See also Ferrall and Jackson 6–7.

for boys because of the morals such fiction would teach. In their goal of providing healthy reading for boys, a contingent of mid- to late-nineteenth-century writers and publishers eventually redefined the entire romance genre as the province of young male readers.[10]

Who Read Rider Haggard?

Haggard's *King Solomon's Mines* and *Allan Quatermain,* at least, were books written intentionally for boys in a much more marked way than was *The Hobbit.* While Tolkien's sons (but not his daughter) report hearing the story as boys, most of *The Hobbit*'s known pre-publication readers were women, and Tolkien was not marketing the book to anyone.[11] *King Solomon's Mines,* on the other hand, was written with an eye to publication, as the result of a bet that Haggard could write something as good as Stevenson's *Treasure Island* (Cohen 85). *King Solomon's Mines* is dedicated by its main character, Allan Quatermain, "to all the big and little boys who read it."

Not only was Haggard writing for boys, he intended his works to be good for them. The sequel to *King Solomon's Mines, Allan Quatermain* (1887), is dedicated by Haggard (rather than his character):

> To my Son Arthur John Rider Haggard in the hope that he, and many other boys whom I shall never know, may, in the acts and thoughts of Allan Quatermain and his companions, as herein recorded, find something to help him and them to reach to what, with

---

10. A combination of authorial intent, Victorian marketing and education, and reader taste determined what became a boys' book. Beiderwell and McCormick note that the 1870 Education Act mandated that "every schoolchild [...] have two reading books," one of which was sometimes an edition of *Ivanhoe* (170). They also outline how, once *Ivanhoe's* audience changed from predominately adult to predominately child readers, academic critics began either to discount Scott or to worry about Scott's association with the young (175). When we read surveys of the favorite books of nineteenth-century boys, the list includes titles that were classics, popular among all demographics, and titles that were explicitly marketed to boys. In 1888, the year after *She* was published, a "survey of 790 boys in different kinds of schools [...] revealed that the favourite authors were Charles Dickens (223), W. H. G. Kingston (179), Walter Scott (128), Jules Verne (114), Captain Marryat (102), R. M. Ballantyne (67) and W. Harrison Ainsworth (61). The favourite individual titles were *Robinson Crusoe* (43), *Swiss Family Robinson* (24), *The Pickwick Papers* (22), and *Ivanhoe* (20)" (Richards 9).

11. For *The Hobbit*'s known pre-publication readers, see Rateliff, *History* xxxviii. On the dating of *The Hobbit* and on Tolkien's boys hearing it, see Rateliff, *History* xvii; Burns 196, note 1.

> Sir Henry Curtis, I hold to be the highest rank whereto we can attain—the state and dignity of English Gentleman. (5)

Various reviewers balked at Haggard's claim that such a work was fit to teach gentlemanly behavior. Margaret Oliphant, one of the few *identified* women reviewers of Haggard (her August 1887 discussion of *Allan Quatermain* was, as usual, unsigned in *Blackwood's*) remarks that the dedication

> somewhat takes away one's breath: we have no desire to detract from the claims of Sir Henry Curtis and the rest to be considered gentlemen. They are fine fellows in their way. They will not accept the sacrifice, for example, of a little girl's life to save their own, though they consent to place both on the issue of a battle [...]. If boys are to be taught that the love of adventure is justification enough for any unreasonable enterprise, and that killing savages is the leading duty of man, then nothing could be better adapted for their instruction than the adventures of Allan Quatermain and his companions. (262)

The anonymous September 1888 *Fortnightly* writer, William Watson, sarcastically claimed, "It may really be that [Haggard's books] are, as their author evidently believes, a school of great sentiments and noble manners. We would merely observe that this is not exactly the light in which we have hitherto been accustomed to regard them" (325). Watson explains that perhaps the *Fortnightly* had "been misled by an erroneous conception of the nature of true gentility," thinking it involved, among other things, "modesty" and the lack of "a gloating delight in details of carnage and horror and ferocity for their own ghastly sake. But with a sigh we resign these cherished delusions" (325). And James Barrie's pseudonymous review in the *British Weekly* would have been the most biting of all; he emasculated the most masculine of Haggard's fiction: "So far as I can see 'Allan Quatermain' is more likely to make boys bloodthirsty blackguards. However, it is ladies chiefly who read these books, and when they finish them they go shopping" (Oglivy 218).

Barrie's remark is of interest because Lang and Haggard were so adamant that Haggard's and Stevenson's work were written for boys; they were meant for boys, and they certainly have been influential as boys' books. Haggard's fiction is usually cited for the impression it left on famous men such as Sigmund Freud, Carl Jung, King Edward VII,

D. H. Lawrence, C. S. Lewis, Gilbert Murray, and Winston Churchill (Etherington xxxi; Cohen 230–31; Higgins 117).[12]

But even though Haggard intended his work for an exclusively boy market, he soon found that his works were read by many who were not boys—or even male. Lang had explained away the interest of men in Haggard's work by claiming it reawakened the eternal boy in them. He accounted for critical dislike by questioning (literally) the critics' manhood. After receiving Haggard's 1905 sequel to *She*, *Ayesha: The Return of She*, Lang wrote to Haggard that he was worried he was too old now to enjoy it: "I am almost afraid to read 'She,' as at 61,00000 [*sic*] one no longer has the joyous credulity of forty, and even *your* imagination is out of the fifth form. However, plenty of boys are about, and I hope they will be victims of the enchantress" (qtd. in Haggard, *Days* 390).[13] Haggard writes in his autobiography of his relief when Lang wrote again the next day, saying, "It is all right: I am Thrilled: so much obliged. I thought I was too Old, but the Eternal Boy is still on the job. Unluckily I think the dam[n] reviewers never were boys—most of them the Editor's nieces" (qtd. in *Days* 391).[14]

Margaret Oliphant, definitely *not* the niece of her editor, had reviewed and disliked *She*, calling it "a sham, and not a pleasant one" (305).[15] However, neither did she identify *She* as a boys' book like *King Solomon's Mines*. Oliphant wrote in her review of *She* in "The Old Saloon," *Blackwood's* more polished monthly competitor to Lang's "At the Sign of the Ship" in *Longman's*, that " 'King Solomon's Mines' was a

12. Haggard's influence on Freud is particularly interesting. In *On the Interpretation of Dreams*, Freud recounts how Louise N. mocked him after he recommended *She* to her, telling him she knew the book already and asking Freud when he would publish his own work (Freud 317). Her ridicule led Freud to have a disturbing dream.

13. Lang was sixty-one when *Ayesha* was published in 1905. In early 1887, when *She* was published, he was forty-two.

14. Lang is a misogynist, but, in his defense, he would likely not have wanted this line to have become public. According to Roger Lancelyn Green, Lang, after reading a letter about him published in Margaret Oliphant's autobiography, indignantly requested that his own letters be destroyed and no biography be published: "Think what letters are: hasty, indiscreet, inaccurate!" (qtd. in Green ix).

15. Lang and Walter Besant both felt compelled to blame negative critical reactions on women's inability to understand *She*. In the epigraph, Besant claimed that women were by nature opposed to the marvelous. Such a claim obviously couldn't explain Oliphant's reaction. She was a writer of marvelous tales herself, tales that both Stevenson and Lang admired (Williams vii; Lang, "She" 36).

strong pull upon the wholesome curiosity of the race [...] but 'She' is a stronger. We were half disposed to account for our excitement over the former book by a half-apologetic inference that it was intended for 'the boys,' and therefore required to be inspected with a benevolent anxiety to know whether it was good for them" (302). *She*, apparently, was not written for boys, and *King Solomon's Mines* could intrigue an adult reader, even if that reader felt it necessary to explain away her interest.

Despite the fact that Oliphant's negative response to *She* was not an outlier, those who knew her authorship might have construed her response as gendered. Indeed, her negative response to *She* was misogynistically foretold by Holly himself in the manuscript, when he confessed his love for the character:

> I am in love with Ayesha myself to this day, and I would rather have been the object of her affection for one short week than that of any other woman in the world for a whole lifetime. And let me add that, if anybody who doubts this statement, and thinks me foolish for making it, could have seen Ayesha draw her veil and flash out in beauty on his gaze, his view would exactly coincide with my own. Of course, I am speaking of any *man*. We never had the advantage of a lady's opinion of Ayesha, but I think it quite possible that she would have regarded the Queen with dislike, would have expressed her disapproval in some more or less pointed manner, and ultimately have got herself blasted. (162, emphasis in original)

Whether they would have gotten themselves blasted or not, numerous female readers were Haggard fans. Elaine Showalter notes, "*She* had interested many women writers, from Willa Cather to Margaret Atwood" and Elizabeth Bowen, who "read *She*, dreamed *She*, lived *She* for a year and a half" (88). And, as Cohen writes about *King Solomon's Mines*,

> Not only did the book establish itself firmly in boys' schools, public and otherwise, but in the girls' schools as well, as Haggard knew from his post that included a letter from a group of girls congratulating him "with great earnestness" in having produced in *King Solomon's Mines* "a thrilling book without a heroine." (96)

Meanwhile, the same Mudie's circulating library that received significant criticism from male writers as being too prudish and feminine bought thousands of copies of *King Solomon's Mines*, all of which seemed to have been in demand.

When *Allan Quatermain* was published, Barrie lamented the fate of, in his mind, better English authors, for "In the great circulating library of which the hasty ones among us are so proud, 2,000 copies of 'Allan Quatermain,' Mr. Haggard's latest romance, are in circulation, and not a single copy of Mr. Hardy's 'A Pair of Blue Eyes' " (Oglivy 218). Barrie blamed both women novel readers and male literary critics, such as Lang, for their poor taste:

> It is not difficult to see why [Thomas Hardy's, Grant Allen's, and Robert Louis Stevenson's] works should find small favour with the ladies of the libraries, nor why Mr. Haggard's horrors should be so popular with the same persons; but that critics of repute should weave countless reviews in glorification of "She," makes one hesitate to trust his own judgment. (218)

The Resnik Interview and She

Tolkien's admiration for *She* was not nearly so pronounced as Lang's (and other male "critics of repute"). Rather than countless accolades of the novel, we have one brief reference in a little-known telephone interview. However, it is significant that the reference occurs at all. Others before me have asked why Tolkien would mention his interest in *She* in 1966 when he was so keen, at this point in his life, to reject other works as formative (Rateliff, "Revisited" 146). Tolkien was notoriously cagey when asked about questions of influence, and in the Resnik interview he is more so than usual; he rejects the influence of Williams, Lewis, and MacDonald shortly after admitting his boyhood interest in *She* (Resnik, "Interview" 40–41). But in eliciting Tolkien's brief allusion to Haggard, Resnik had the good luck to ask his question in a way that required a direct answer: "Could you name two or three of your favorite books? Do you have favorite books, either at the moment, or books that have endured over your span of reading?" Resnik's question also avoided the use of the word *influence.*

Even so, Tolkien's first reaction to Resnik's question was not particularly encouraging: "No, I don't think so." However, Tolkien went on to elaborate:

> I think I was born with what you might call an inventive mind, and the books that have remained in my mind remain as those things which I acquired and don't really seem much like the book itself. For instance, I now find that I can't stand George MacDonald's books at any price at all. [...] The same with most books that I've read. I suppose as a boy *She* interested me as much as any-

> thing—like the Greek shard of Amynatas [*sic*], which was the kind of machine by which everything got moving. (40)

Note that Tolkien is speaking about his boyhood interest in a book, rather than claiming *She* as an influence for *The Lord of the Rings*. Instead, parts of *She* function as one of many details in his mind that went into his soup of story. As remembered, Tolkien's *She* might be very different than "the book itself."[16]

This view of sources as mines of details that may be used by a new storyteller is consistent with Tolkien's views on how story works, as detailed in "On Fairy-stories." There are bones (sources and material) in the soup of story, but researchers and folklorists should beware of that "misleading 'shorthand' " which leads them sometimes "to say that any two stories that are built round the same folk-lore motive, or are made up of a generally similar combination of such motives, are 'the same stories' " (*OFS* 40, 38). This same method of thinking would make Tolkien averse to the idea of allegory. *The Lord of the Rings* is not the same story as the Gospel or World War II or the Cold War. Nor is it a retelling of *She*, despite similarities between Galadriel and that long-lived lady.

When Tolkien's reference to *She* in the Resnik interview is quoted at length, it seems that Tolkien's interest in *She: A History of an Adventure* is not, as it was for Haggard and Lang, a love affair with a fascinating, dangerous, and undying fictional woman but an interest in the way this tale of the marvelous was told. Haggard, like Tolkien, was extremely interested in creating verisimilitude for his fantasy. Significantly, Tolkien's memory of *She* is of the Greek Sherd of Amenartas, which Haggard painstakingly reproduced and placed in facsimile opposite the title page.[17] In the text, Haggard included transcriptions of

---

16. See also Rateliff, "Revisited" 147–48.

17. Like Tolkien, Haggard provided maps, documents, and artifacts for his reader—though, as is clear from the reviews and letters to the editor that criticize Haggard's mathematics and his astronomy, Haggard's lack of erudition and hasty writing (*She* was written in a little more than six weeks) led to frequent mistakes, errors which he always corrected in subsequent editions ("That Quite" 79; M.B.B. 81; Evans 144). However, for *King Solomon's Mines*, Haggard "personally prepared a map and went to great lengths to make it appear authentic" (Etherington 214), insisting, for instance, that it be written in blood (Cohen 91). "In the case of the Sherd of Amenartas he took more extreme measures. Besides commissioning scholars to concoct translations, he and his sister-in-law made up a sherd, which he claimed was good enough to fool experts" (Etherington 214).

the Greek in uncial and cursive scripts and translations of the Greek into Latin and English. Haggard went on for pages with transcriptions from the back of the sherd, which "was covered from top to bottom with notes and signatures in Greek, Latin, and English" by Leo's ancestors, all of whom explained why they failed to do as Amenartas asked: go to Africa to avenge the death of her husband, Kallikrates, caused by a Queen "who is a magician having a knowledge of all things, and life and loveliness that does not die" (26, 22).

All of Haggard's historical and linguistic information would have appealed to Tolkien, who liked to study languages not only for themselves but for the stories they created. As Tolkien discussed with Resnik, the seed of Middle-earth came out of Tolkien's linguistic interests: "I eventually made the discovery that language can't exist in a void and if you invent a language yourself you can't cut it in half. It has to come alive—so really the languages came first and the country after" ("Interview" 41). In Haggard's *She*, quite literally, the languages come first and the quest and the country (an unknown African kingdom) after.

But Haggard's tale not only has the excitement of exploring new territory (as had *King Solomon's Mines*), but it also, like *The Lord of the Rings*, evokes one of Tolkien's most enduring interests: the "old [...] [A]ntiquity has an appeal in itself" (*OFS* 48). In "On Fairy-stories," Tolkien discusses the fairy tale *The Juniper Tree*, stating that "always the chief flavour of that tale lingering in the memory was not beauty or horror, but distance and a great abyss of time, not measurable even by *twe tusend Johr*" (48). In *She*, Holly is also confronted with that abyss of time. A little over two thousand years is the amount of time in She's memory. When Ayesha takes Leo and Holly to see Leo's double (his embalmed ancestor Kallikrates, whom She had murdered), Holly notices that the "steps were worn in the centre to such an extent that some of them had been reduced from seven and a half inches, at which I guessed their original height, to about three and a half" (156). She notices his wonder and informs him that the "feet that have worn away the rock [...] are mine":

> "I can remember when these stairs were fresh and level, but for two thousand years and more have I gone down hither day by day, and see, my sandals have worn out the solid rock!"
>
> I made not answer, but I do not think that anything that I had heard or seen brought home to my limited understanding so clear a sense of this being's overwhelming antiquity as that hard rock

> hollowed out by her soft white feet. How many hundreds of thousands of times must she have passed up and down that stair to bring about such a result? (156)

Neither *She* nor *The Lord of the Rings* can boast the antiquity of *The Juniper Tree,* but both are striving after its effect: "a mythical or total (unanalysable) effect, an effect quite independent of the findings of Comparative Folk-lore, and one which it cannot spoil or explain; they open a door on Other Time, and if we pass through, though only for a moment, we stand outside our own time, outside Time itself, maybe" (*OFS* 48). Thus, Tolkien's interest in *She* may have had less to do with his views on women than with his views on language, time, and myth.

To say, however, that the influence of *She* on Tolkien was about language and time rather than about Tolkien's fascination with She herself does not negate the importance of gender to the *She*/*Lord of the Rings* question. It shows, instead, that gender was a part of the genre question. Tolkien's genre problem, the association of the romance with the boys' book, gave critics certain expectations. Critics thought of *The Lord of the Rings* and the nineteenth-century boys' book as being similar genres. That thinking was influenced by the dominant critical framework: Lang had identified the romance as a boys' book, and Lang's critical opponents identified boys' books (most of them) with the kind of unliterary fiction that they did not respect (James 243; Oglivy 218).[18] Thus, in the twentieth century, when Tolkien's critics defined *The Lord of the Rings* as a boys' book, they were to a certain extent merely saying that they recognized the work as a quest romance. But once they had identified it thus far, they also assumed it would fit their other assumptions about the boys' book genre; *The Lord of the Rings* would conform to certain unliterary genre conventions and treat women in the same way they were treated in books like *King Solomon's Mines* and *She*. Of course, non-boys'-book romances had existed before Haggard, and those who liked Tolkien might be content to associate his work with those earlier authors. However, if a critic wished to label the work a boys' book, not a romance, it was enough to demonstrate one point of difference between *The Lord of the Rings* and *The Faerie Queene* or Tolkien and Malory. Indeed, Muir seems to go as

---

18. In "The Future of the Novel," Henry James wrote, "Great fortunes, if not great reputations, are made [...] by writing for schoolboys" (243).

far as to claim that *because* Tolkien does not have a Lancelot or Tristram—noble but adulterous men who broke their vows—his work *therefore* is like Haggard's boys' adventure story. Muir writes, "The story, then, is not at all like Malory, but it does have a resemblance to Rider Haggard" ("Boy's" 11).[19] Muir demands unfaithful men and a tragic ending and claims that Tolkien's characters "with a boy's idea of heroism, romance, women, good and evil, are not fully human."

Muir is unfair, particularly in his assumption that unfaithful sexualized love is what makes for serious, non-schoolboy reading; if it did, Leo's crawling over his lover Ustane's dead body and into She's arms would make Haggard's novel an ideal adult choice. However, it cannot be denied that surface similarities exist between Haggard's women (or lack of women) and Tolkien's. Although none of the critics explicitly mention Ayesha in their discussions of Galadriel, they had surely read their Haggard and would know of the commonalities. And, while Duggan's and Muir's statements that "women play no part" and "hardly one of [the characters] knows anything about women" is overstating the case, women *do* appear infrequently in *The Lord of the Rings* ("Epic" 817; "Boy's" 11).

Nonetheless, when Galadriel is compared to Haggard's Ayesha, her most fascinating aspects are not in her surface similarities but her differences. The fact that *The Lord of the Rings* was identified by critics as a boys' book only serves to highlight the distinction. When contrasted with her predecessor She, Galadriel's strength as a female character becomes apparent. Haggard toys with giving power to his women characters but ultimately denies it to them. Galadriel, on the other hand, represents the powerful woman at her best. She rules because of a clear superiority of wisdom rather than, like Ayesha, through pretended wisdom, sensuality, manipulation, and cruelty.

Galadriel and She: What Tolkien's Characterization Says About Gender

> "But here is a strange thing," said Ayesha in astonishment, "a queen whom her people love!" (Haggard, *She* 169)

---

19. Muir is perfectly willing to grant "respectability" to Tolkien provided *The Lord of the Rings* be considered a boys' book and not a high romance ("Boy's" 11).

Although Tolkien's and Haggard's main female characters share many surface-level characteristics, the themes of the books as a whole separate them. Intriguingly, though Tolkien's theme is not women and gender relations, as Haggard's claims to be, Galadriel becomes a superior, more multifaceted character. While Galadriel considers the fate of her own and other peoples in Middle-earth, Ayesha becomes trapped by her own inward-looking passions and considers nothing else. When Haggard describes his process of writing *She* in his autobiography, he writes that "the only clear notion that I had in my head was that of an immortal woman inspired by an immortal love" (*Days* 251). Although Haggard's novel appears to have smatterings of feminism in the power he gives to both Ayesha and the women among the Amahagger people over whom She rules, Haggard consistently takes away with one hand the power he gives with the other.

Among the Amahagger, the tribe who lead Holly, Leo, and Job to Ayesha, women are given pretended power but then ultimately denied it. Women chose their partners in marriage, indicating their choice by embracing a man and waiting to see if their embrace is returned. As Norman Etherington notes, "[Holly] appears to endorse simultaneously the feminist proposition that women should be given more choice in romance and the conventional man's desire for women who will fulfill his sexual fantasies without prompting" (xxx). Etherington explains that "Haggard's narrative proceeds in similar fashion to undercut each apparent mark of women's power among the Amahagger" (xxx). Holly is initially impressed with Billali's remark that the women in their country "do as they please. We worship them, and give them their way, because without them the world could not go on; they are the source of life" (78). But Billali goes on to explain that his worship only goes so far: when the women become "unbearable," "we rise, and kill the old ones as an example to the young ones, and to show them that we are the strongest' " (78).

Even when the Amahagger are excluded from consideration of gender relations in *She*, Ayesha herself perpetuates the idea that females in power are willful, capricious, emotion-driven, and fear-inducing. Haggard is handicapped by his theme, Ayesha's obsessive love, the more painfully so because he does not realize his theme is limited but rather believes it great and glorious.

In "About Fiction," Haggard claims that "sexual passion is the most powerful lever with which to stir the mind of man, for it lies at the root of all things human," and his novel *She* certainly represents both Ayesha and the men who adore her as unable to focus on any other goal than the fulfillment of their own personal desires.[20] Fully aware that Ayesha is evil, Holly yet asserts, "I do not believe that either of us would really have left Ayesha even if some superior power had suddenly offered to convey us from these gloomy caves and set us down in Cambridge" (*She* 160). Holly compares himself and Leo to moths around a flame and confirmed opium eaters. Ayesha is akin to the One Ring, addictive and evil, possible only to destroy in the fire in which she gained her power. Once seen, she cannot be given up.

But Holly's assertions both of the shame and the addiction of She are undercut by his simultaneous belief that She was the wisest of all beings and that being her lover would be a man's highest wish:

> No man who once had seen *She* unveiled, and heard the music of her voice, and drunk in the bitter wisdom of her words, would willingly give up the sight for a whole sea of placid joys. [...] No doubt she was a wicked person, but then she was very faithful, and by a law of nature man is apt to think but lightly of a woman's crimes, especially if that woman be beautiful, and the crime be committed for the love of him. (161)

By allowing Ayesha this easy forgiveness, Holly represents men as the ultimate judges of good and evil, but judges who are highly flawed and apt to decide right and wrong based on their own myopic admiration of the evil but beautiful women who admire them. Ayesha is no better. All moral choices that lead to her goal of obtaining Leo as her lover, including her murder of Leo's previous lover, Ustane, are acceptable. Provided She obtains him, she claims she will become virtuous. Until he is hers, all is fair in love and war.

Haggard unsuccessfully attempts to give She a change of heart, trying to make her a teacher about the dangers of power. Even as Ayesha takes Leo to the fire that will make him immortal, she claims to warn him against its perils:

---

20. Strangely enough, Haggard makes this point about sexual passion in order to argue against the naturalistic school of writing. He wants neither the French unrestrained eroticism nor the English school, which he claims is "at the mercy of the Young Person, and a dreadful nuisance most of us find her" ("About Fiction" 177).

> Be careful when power comes to thee also, lest thou too shouldst smite in thine anger or thy jealousy, for unconquerable strength is a sore weapon in the hands of erring man. Yea, I have sinned—out of bitterness born of a great love have I sinned—but yet do I know the good from the evil, nor is my heart altogether hardened. (187)

She then humbles herself to Leo, telling him to take her hand and lift her veil "with no more fear than though I were some peasant girl, and not the wisest and most beauteous woman in this wide world, and look me in the eyes, and tell me that thou dost forgive me [...] and that with all thine heart thou dost worship me" (187). Leo does both, and Holly remarks that he is no longer "fascinated against his better judgment, something as a bird is fascinated by a snake, but [...] he realized that he really loved this strange and glorious creature, as, alas! I loved her also" (187). Haggard and Leo grant Ayesha forgiveness despite her lack of remorse for the murders she has committed—and despite the fact that her crimes are not really theirs to forgive.

In fact, Ayesha continues to believe that she has the power to decide good and evil in order to reach her ends; when she submits to Leo, what she is really doing is granting that same power of deciding good and evil to him. She has never repented.

Haggard did not concede that She's inability to feel remorse and her unwillingness to give Leo up eliminated the possibility of her future virtue. After reading the *Spectator*'s review, which objected to Ayesha's unbelievable change of heart, Haggard wrote the *Spectator* a letter, in which he maintained not only that Ayesha had been redeemed, but that her unrequited love for Kallikrates, whom she murdered, was "true and holy":

> Therefore, when Ayesha in the course of ages grows hard, cynical, and regardless of that which stands between her and her ends, her love yet endures, true and holy, changeless amidst change. Therefore, too, when at last the reward is in her sight, and passion utterly possesses her, it gives her strength to cast away the evil, and (what your reviewer considers inconsistent with her nature) even to do homage to "the majesty of virtue." ("She" 111)

Haggard forgets that Ayesha had been quite as willing to use any means to reach her aims when faced with the original Kallikrates, two thousand years ago. He claims, without evidence, that Ayesha's love is "a saving grace and a gate of redemption [...] through the sacred agency of love, she once more became (or at the moment imagined that she would become) what she had been before disillusion, disappointment, and two thousand years had turned her heart to stone" (111).

Like his characters, because he is in love with Ayesha, Haggard wishes to make her good. But Ayesha never feels actual remorse for her actions as long as she can satisfy her obsessive love for Leo, a man quite average in everything but his Apollo-like looks. Haggard shows weak characters who confuse beauty with wisdom and fall into the trap of believing that good and evil can be decided by what seems most advantageous to any powerful individual at the time.

What Tolkien has done in his creation of Galadriel, on the other hand, is to create a woman who actually is "the wisest and most beauteous woman in this wide world" but who does not ask for worship or seek to satisfy her own desires to the detriment of others.

When Holly looks on Ayesha, he immediately knows she is evil (and falls in love with her anyway), but Aragorn knows of Galadriel: "There is in her and in this land no evil, unless a man bring it hither himself" (*LotR* II.7.358). When Gimli looks on Galadriel, he falls quite as much in love with her as Holly does with She, but his feelings are in no way sensual. After Celeborn blames the dwarves for stirring up the Balrog, it is Galadriel's generosity and empathy that excite Gimli's admiration: he "looked up and met her eyes; and it seemed to him that he looked suddenly into the heart of an enemy and saw there love and understanding" (II.7.356).

Like She, Galadriel may be seen as a threat to male power.[21] Galadriel is more wise and powerful than any of the eight remaining fellowship members who stand before her for judgment. But, unlike with She, the men, if following their quest, have no need to fear Galadriel's power and what it will do to them. Indeed, Galadriel's threat to male power is the opposite of Ayesha's: Ayesha uses her power, her irresistible beauty, and male desire for that beauty to force those around her to submit to her wishes; Galadriel uses men's (non-

---

21. No one in her realm, however, including her husband Celeborn, feels threatened, and, as "on the land of Lórien no shadow lay," it can be assumed that gender relations are also intended to be included in that praise. Although Celeborn rules with Galadriel and usually speaks first, no one seems to mind that the elves of Lothlórien almost always refer to "the Lady" alone.

sexual) desire as a test of their loyalty to the quest itself. Then, with Frodo's help, she tests herself.

When Galadriel looks at each member of the Fellowship, "none save Legolas and Aragorn could long endure her glance" (*LotR* II.7.357). Sam tells Pippin that he blushed because, "If you want to know, I felt as if I hadn't got nothing on, and I didn't like it. She seemed to be looking inside me and asking me what I would do if she gave me the chance of flying back home to the Shire to a nice little hole with—with a bit of garden of my own" (II.7.357). Tolkien writes, "each had felt that he was offered a choice between a shadow full of fear that lay ahead, and something he greatly desired [...]. 'And it seemed to me, too,' said Gimli, 'that my choice would be secret and known only to myself' " (II.7.357-58).

Galadriel, however, knows the limits even of her own wisdom. She is good, but no less capable of falling than any member of the Fellowship. Thus, when Frodo offers Galadriel the Ring, she laughs,

> "Gently are you revenged for my testing of your heart at our first meeting. You begin to see with a keen eye. I do not deny that my heart has greatly desired to ask what you offer. For many long years I had pondered what I might do, should the Great Ring come into my hands, and behold! it was brought within my grasp. The evil that was devised long ago works on in many ways, whether Sauron himself stands or falls. Would not that have been a noble deed to set to the credit of his Ring, if I had taken it by force or fear from my guest?"(II.7.365)

With her own ring (and without Sauron's), it is impossible to imagine Galadriel ruling her people by force or "blast[ing] them for very sport" as Ayesha desires to do (Haggard, *She* 298). With the Ring, Galadriel becomes Ayesha, " 'a Queen [...] beautiful and terrible as the Morning and the Night! [...] Stronger than the foundations of the earth.' [...] She stood before Frodo seeming now tall beyond measurement, and beautiful beyond enduring, terrible and worshipful" (*LotR* II.7.366). But, unlike Ayesha, Galadriel does not revel in her beauty beyond endurance or demand worship for worship's sake. Ayesha quite unintentionally diminishes at the end of Haggard's book when her second trip into the fire that made her immortal goes terribly wrong. Galadriel chooses to diminish and remain Galadriel.

While Galadriel is, like She, a token powerful (and stationary) female surrounded by mobile males, the men's interactions with her do not resemble those found in *She* nor in other Victorian male quest romances such as *Treasure Island* or *King Solomon's Mines*. In these boys' books, the men are attempting to get away from "petticoats" in order to participate in masculine adventures. They go for the adventure's sake and seek to gain experience and wealth. Tolkien's quest does not seek to gain treasure and glory but to lose it. Nor does Galadriel act like She, who tempts Holly with her beauty for her own caprice because she enjoys male admiration. In Lothlórien, women and men are not in competition for power but are both striving toward what is good. Goodness, however, is not confused with safety. Although Galadriel tests the Fellowship members, for their benefit and because of the consequences if one of them should be disloyal, she knows that she is as fallible as they and that she also requires (and receives) this testing.

As a romance clearly enjoyed by adolescents that certainly lacks as many female characters as it has males, *The Lord of the Rings'* identification with the boys' book has led to misconceptions about the work's portrayal of women and gender relations. Although Muir believed "hardly one of [the Fellowship] knows anything about women," in fact the Fellowship members' understandings of gender relations surpass those portrayed in *She* and in *Morte d' Arthur*, Muir's arbitrarily chosen non-boys'-book high romance. Muir demands from Tolkien the pessimistic realism he sees in Malory; he admires Malory's characters *because* they can't maintain their ideals. They were "sometimes unfaithful to their vows, or torn between opposing claims of love and duty" ("Boy's" 11). But Malory's characters find that if vows are broken and men are unfaithful, the kingdom will fall. Tolkien's characters know that too. Sometimes, as in Boromir's and Frodo's failure, personal desires take precedence over everyone else's good. However, *The Lord of the Rings* highlights the virtues of sublimating or deferring individual desires in order to create a society in which all live without fear.

Epilogue

Not long after the Resnik interview, Tolkien was asked again about his adolescent taste in books, this time for a project started in New York City's Elizabeth Barrett Browning Junior High School, where school administrators hoped to "increase and improve the reading habits of the girls" by asking famous authors to recommend their favorite books (Byrne and Penzler xi–xii). Entitled *Attacks of Taste* (1971), the resulting book quotes Archibald MacLeish to claim that the young "have attacks of taste like attacks of measles" (frontispiece). The editors note that

> after displaying the authors' letters and printing them in the school newspaper, a marked change was noticed in the girls' reading tastes. The improvement, both quantitatively and qualitatively, was nothing short of astonishing. [...] Suddenly, the girls read Dickens and the Brontes for pleasure [...]. Mark Twain, Robert Louis Stevenson and the Sherlock Holmes series, normally preferred by boys, were constantly off the shelves. A few adventurous souls even tried Tolstoy and Dostoevsky. (xii)

Encouraged by the result, the book editors wrote additional letters to authors to achieve "a better balance, appealing to all literary and philosophical tastes" (xii).

This project proves Tolkien right that young people's "lack of critical experience and vocabulary" causes them to "like or try to like what is given to them" and is one more indicator of the obvious point that marketing affects the demographics of books' audiences (*OFS* 53). When it came to improving the students' reading tastes, however, Tolkien was not particularly helpful to the Elizabeth Barrett Browning Junior High School's endeavor. In his very brief response, he does not mention *She* or any work of "literature," a subject which he states did not interest him "[d]uring most of this period" (Byrne and Penzler 43). Instead, he notes that the teenage years represent quite a long time: "there is a vast gap between one's thirteenth birthday and one's twentieth. I can name no book that influenced me deeply as a book. I found certain elements in books I liked and stored away in memory." He goes on to state, "In the early part of this period things I read with most pleasure were mostly scientific in reference, especially botany and astronomy. My most treasured volume was Johns' *Flowers of the Field,* an account of the flora of the British Isles" (43).

Perhaps some adolescent girl in New York was inspired to take up botany?

At any rate, *Flowers of the Field* was the very opposite of a boys' adventure story. Lang would not have approved of the recommendation. As he recounts in his preface to *The Olive Fairy Book* (1907), "At a very early age I read a number of advertisements of books, and wept because I could not buy dozens of them, and somebody gave me a book on Botany! It looked all right, nicely bound in green cloth, but within it was full of all manner of tediousness" (viii).

Works Cited

Auden, W. H. "At the End of the Quest, Victory." Rev. of *The Return of the King*, by J. R. R. Tolkien. *New York Times* 22 Jan. 1956: 226. *ProQuest*. Web. 21 Apr. 2008.

Beiderwell, Bruce, and Anita Hemphill McCormick. "The Making and Unmaking of a Children's Classic: The Case of Scott's *Ivanhoe*." *Culturing the Child, 1690-1914: Essays in Memory of Mitzi Myers*. Ed. Donelle Ruwe. Lanham, MD: Scarecrow Press, 2005. 165-77. Print.

Burns, Marjorie. *Perilous Realms: Celtic and Norse in Tolkien's Middle-earth*. Toronto: U of Toronto P, 2005. Print.

Byrne, Evelyn B., and Otto M. Penzler, eds. *Attacks of Taste*. New York: Gotham Book Market, 1971. Print.

Cohen, Morton N. *Rider Haggard*. New York: Walker, 1960. Print.

[Duggan, Alfred Leo]. "The Epic of Westernesse." Rev. of *The Two Towers*, by J. R. R. Tolkien. *Times Literary Supplement* 17 Dec. 1954: 817. *Times Literary Supplement Centenary Archive*. Web. 23 May 2008.

[---]. "Heroic Endeavour." Rev. of *The Fellowship of the Ring*, by J. R. R. Tolkien. *Times Literary Supplement* 27 Aug. 1954: 541. *Times Literary Supplement Centenary Archive*. Web. 23 May 2008.

[---]. "The Saga of Middle Earth." Rev. of *The Return of the King*, by J. R. R. Tolkien. *Times Literary Supplement* 25 Nov. 1955: 704. *Times Literary Supplement Centenary Archive*. Web. 23 May 2008.

Etherington, Norman. "Critical Introduction." Haggard, *Annotated* xv-xliii. Print.

Evans, John W. "Fact and Fiction." Letter [On Astronomical Errors in *King Solomon's Mines*]. *The Athenæum* 31 July 1886: 144. Print.

Ferrall, Charles, and Anna Jackson. *Juvenile Literature and British Society, 1850–1950: The Age of Adolescence*. New York: Routledge, 2010. *Taylor and Francis*. PDF file.

Forbes, Duncan. *The Liberal Anglican Idea of History*. Cambridge, UK: Cambridge UP, 1952. Print.

Freud, Sigmund. *The Interpretation of Dreams*. Trans. A. A. Brill. New York: The Modern Library, 1994. Print.

Green, Roger Lancelyn. *Andrew Lang: A Critical Biography*. Leicester: Edmund Ward, 1946. Print.

Gueroult, Denis. BBC radio interview with JRRT, 1965. Re-released by Audio-Forum. Guilford, CN: 1980. Audiocassette.

--- [Denys]. "J. R. R. Tolkien." Interview with J. R. R. Tolkien. 20 Jan. 1965. *The Spoken Word: British Writers*. BBC, 2008. CD.

Haggard, H. Rider. "About Fiction." *The Contemporary Review* 51 (Feb. 1887): 172–80. *British Periodicals*. Web. 31 Aug. 2013.

---. *Allan Quatermain*. Leipzig: B. Tauchnitz, 1887. *HathiTrust*. Web. 15 Dec. 2013.

---. *The Annotated* She: *A Critical Edition of H. Rider Haggard's Victorian Romance*. Ed. Norman Etherington. Bloomington, IN: Indiana UP, 1991. Print.

---. *The Days of My Life*. 1926. Ed. C. J. Longman. Gloucester: Dodo Press, 2008. PDF file.

---. *King Solomon's Mines*. Oxford: Oxford UP, 2008. Print.

---. "She." *The Spectator* 60 (22 Jan. 1887): 110–11. *ProQuest*. Web. 18 July 2013.

Higgins, D. S. *Rider Haggard: A Biography*. New York: Stein and Day, 1981. Print.

Hughes, Linda K. "A Woman Poet Angling For Notice: Rosamund Marriott Watson." *Marketing the Author: Authorial Personae, Narrative Selves and Self-Fashioning, 1880–1930*. Ed. Marysa Demoor. New York: Palgrave Macmillan, 2004. 134–55. Print.

Hughes, Richard. "The Lord of the Rings." Rev. of *The Fellowship of the Ring*, by J. R. R. Tolkien. *The Spectator* 1 Oct. 1954: 408–09. Print.

James, Henry. "The Future of the Novel." *The Art of Criticism: Henry James on the Theory and Practice of Fiction*. Eds. William Veeder and Susan M. Griffin. Chicago: U of Chicago P, 1986. Print.

Kestner, Joseph. *Masculinities in British Adventure Fiction, 1880-1915*. Burlington, VT: Ashgate, 2010. Print.

Lang, Andrew. "At the Sign of the Ship [Some Novels]." *Longman's Magazine* 18 (July 1891): 329–35. *British Periodicals*. Web. 6 April 2013.

---. *History of English Literature from "Beowulf" to Swinburne*. 1912. London: Longmans, Green and Co., 1914. *HathiTrust*. Web. 18 May 2013.

---. Letter to William Blackwood III. 20 Dec. 1905. MS. Blackwood Papers. National Library of Scotland, Edinburgh. 2013.

---. "Mr. Stevenson's Work." *Essays in Little*. New York: Scribner, 1897. 24-35. *Hathi Trust*. Web. 8 May 2013.

---. Preface to *The Olive Fairy Book*. 1907. New York: Dover, 1968. v–ix. Print.

---. Preface to *The Red Romance Book*. London: Longman's, 1905. v–viii. Print.

---. "Realism and Romance." *The Contemporary Review* 52 (Nov. 1887): 683–93. *British Periodicals*. Web. 31 Jan. 2013.

---. "She." *The Academy* 31.767 (15 Jan. 1887): 35–36. Print.

Lewis, C. S. "The Gods Return to Earth." Rev. of *The Fellowship of the Ring*, by J. R. R. Tolkien. *Time and Tide* 35 (1954): 1082–83. Print.

Lobdell, Jared. *England and Always: Tolkien's World of the Rings*. Grand Rapids, MI: Eerdmans, 1981. Print.

M. B. B. "Fact and Fiction." Letter [On Astronomical Errors in *King Solomon's Mines*]. *Athenæum* 17 July 1886: 81. Print.

Mitchison, Naomi. "One Ring to Bind Them." Rev. of *The Fellowship of the Ring*, by J. R. R. Tolkien. *The New Statesman and Nation* 18 Sep. 1954: 331. Print.

Muir, Edwin. "A Boy's World." Rev. of *The Return of the King*, by J. R. R. Tolkien. *The Observer* 27 Nov. 1955: 11. Print.

---. "The Ring." Rev. of *The Two Towers*, by J. R. R. Tolkien. *The Observer* 21 Nov. 1954: 9. Print.

---. "Strange Epic." Rev. of *The Fellowship of the Ring*, by J. R. R. Tolkien. *The Observer* 22 Aug. 1954: 7. Print.

Oglivy, Gavin [James Barrie]. "Mr. H. Rider Haggard." *The British Weekly* 5 Aug. 1887: 218. Print.

[Oliphant, Margaret]. "The Old Saloon." *Blackwood's Magazine* 141 (February 1887): 291–315. *British Periodicals*. Web. 15 July 2014.

[---]. "The Old Saloon." *Blackwood's Magazine* 142 (August 1887): 235–63. *British Periodicals*. Web. 15 July 2014.

Orel, Harold. *Victorian Literary Critics: George Henry Lewes, Walter Bagehot, Richard Hold Hutton, Leslie Stephen, Andrew Lang, George Saintsbury, and Edmund Gosse*. London: Macmillan, 1984. Print.

Rateliff, John D. *The History of The Hobbit*. Rev. ed. London: HarperCollins, 2011. Print.

---. "*She* and Tolkien." *Mythlore* 8.2 (#28) (Summer 1981): 6–8. Print.

---. "*She* and Tolkien, Revisited." *Tolkien and the Study of His Sources: Critical Essays*. Ed. Jason Fisher. Jefferson, NC: McFarland, 2011. 145–61. Print.

Resnik, Henry. "The Hobbit-Forming World of J. R. R. Tolkien." *Saturday Evening Post* 2 July 1966: 90–94. Web. 5 Sep. 2013.

---. "An Interview with Tolkien." *Niekas* 18 (Spring 1967): 37–47. Print.

Richards, Jeffrey, ed. *Imperialism and Juvenile Literature*. Manchester: Manchester UP, 1989. Print.

Richardson, Maurice. "New Novels." Rev. of *The Two Towers*, by J. R. R. Tolkien. *New Statesman and Nation* 48 (18 Dec. 1954): 835–36. Print.

Ripp, Joseph. "Middle America Meets Middle-earth: American Discussion and Readership of J. R. R. Tolkien's *The Lord of the Rings*, 1965–1969." *Book History* 8 (2005): 235–86. *JSTOR*. Web. 7 Feb. 2014.

Scull, Christina, and Wayne G. Hammond. *The J. R. R. Tolkien Companion and Guide*. Vol. I: *Chronology*. Boston: Houghton Mifflin, 2006. Print.

Showalter, Elaine. *Sexual Anarchy: Gender and Culture at the Fin de Siècle*. New York: Viking, 1990. Print.

"That Quite Impossible 'She.' " *The Spectator* (15 Jan. 1887): 78-79. Print.

Tolkien, J. R. R. *The Letters of J. R. R. Tolkien*. Ed. Humphrey Carpenter with the assistance of Christopher Tolkien. Boston: Houghton Mifflin, 1981. Print.

---. *Tolkien On Fairy-stories*. Eds. Verlyn Flieger and Douglas A. Anderson. London: HarperCollins, 2008. Print.

[Watson, Sir John William]. "The Fall of Fiction." *Fortnightly Review* 44 (1 Sep. 1888): 324–36. Print.

Williams, Merryn. Introduction. *A Beleaguered City and Other Stories*. Margaret Oliphant. Oxford: Oxford UP, 1988. vii–xxii. Print.

Wilson, Edmund. "Oo, Those Awful Orcs!" *Nation* 182 (1956): 312–14. Print.

Power of Gender

The Feminine Principle in Tolkien

Melanie A. Rawls

One cannot acquire much insight into Tolkien's view of women from *The Hobbit* or *The Lord of the Rings*—too few women appear in these books, and none are pivotal characters. Of the women who appear in *The Lord of the Rings*, only Éowyn of Rohan is depicted in any detail of character, desire, motivation, and activity. Arwen, Elrond's daughter, is a half-glimpsed dream. Galadriel is a mighty Elven ruler, and we learn something of her thought and powers; but she is peripheral to the action and we learn little of her history and relationships. There are no female counterparts for Gandalf or Sauron, Aragorn or Saruman, Frodo or Gollum.

But open *The Silmarillion*. The feminine presence abounds and in such a manner as should satisfy any inquirer into the nature of the Feminine Principle as presented by J. R. R. Tolkien.

From the opening pages of *The Silmarillion*, it is clear that Tolkien believes that *gender* and *sex* are not one and the same; and that gender, or Masculine and Feminine, is a condition of the universe that goes deeper, higher, and wider than sex, mere male and female and the necessities of reproduction. Through *The Silmarillion* runs this theme: in Arda and in the Heavens, the Feminine and the Masculine are present; when they are in equilibrium and in harmony, there is Good, but Evil is the result of an insufficiency or a disharmony of the attributes of one or the other of the genders. Concepts of Feminine and Masculine and their attributes and roles are thus tied to concepts of Good and Evil, and are therefore near the center of Tolkien's tale which is, after all, a tale of the struggle between Good and Evil.

Tolkien makes an explicit statement on gender early in *The Silmarillion*. He writes: "But when they clothe themselves the Valar take upon them forms of male and some as of female; for that difference of temper they had even from the beginning, and it is but bodied forth in the choice of each, not made by the choice" (*S* 21).

According to Tolkien, Feminine and Masculine possess different characteristics that are meant to complement and augment one another.

Attributes of the gender are not necessarily confined to the sex of the same gender, i.e. feminine attributes are not confined to females nor masculine attributes to males. The Macho Man, with his paucity of finer feeling and his neglect of thought in favor of action, is not admired in Middle-earth or Valinor. Neither is the Total Woman, with her wiles and dependence on males. Those beings in Arda who are able to achieve good either embody both Feminine and Masculine within themselves or have access to the nature of the other gender, usually in the form of a spouse, a sibling, or a mentor.

And it is an intricate dance, this complementarily—in the words of Mark M. Hennelly, Jr., a "rhythmic modulation of polar extremes, each of which [...] can realize itself only through interaction with its complement" (4). This interaction is often simply stated, as in Tolkien's description of the relationship between the Valar spouses Manwë and Varda: "if Varda [demiurge of light, the medium of sight] is beside him he sees further than all other eyes [...] And if Manwë [lord of air, the medium of sound] is with her, Varda hears more clearly than all other ears the sound of voices that cry from east to west" (*S* 26). Or this interaction is stated more subtly, as it is in the development of Aragorn. In order to prove his fitness to reign, Aragorn must display characteristics feminine and masculine—the feminine power of healing, the masculine skill of wise and just rule.

What are these Feminine and Masculine traits or characteristics? Though, as I said earlier, characteristics of the gender are not necessarily confined to the sex of that gender, for the most part, males display masculine traits and females display feminine traits. Careful attention to the personalities and activities of the inhabitants of Valinor and Middle-earth reveals a list of complementary masculine and feminine characteristics.

In Arda, the prime feminine characteristic is *understanding*. The prime masculine characteristic is *power*. Out of their understanding of the nature of beings and things, feminines give counsel; out of their power, masculines act. Action without understanding is rashness; understanding without action is impotence.

FEMININE (understanding)	MASCULINE (power)
Positive	
love	law
counsel	action
intuition (insight and foresight)[1]	reason
mercy and compassion	justice
Forms of Creativity	
song, dance, healing	fine arts, crafts
weaving	technology
Negative	
impotence	rashness
passivity	aggression
consuming or devouring	self-aggrandizement

The various positive traits derive, in general, from the prime characteristic. If understanding often results in mercy and compassion, the proper use of power results in justice. Justice, however, works best when tempered by mercy and compassion, and vice versa. Thus the dance of complementarity.

How does it come about, then, that few feminines, elf or woman, play prominent roles in the histories of Middle-earth?

The answer lies in a difference of modes of activity or influence, derived from the feminine attribute of understanding and the masculine tendency to action. This difference leads feminines to influence history in one manner while masculines influence history in another.

1. The intuition of which Tolkien so often speaks would be termed *clairvoyance*, literally clear sight, in our primary world. The best of the people of Middle-earth and Valinor display this talent—Frodo, Aragorn, Elrond, Galadriel, Gandalf, and Faramir, for example. Visions of past and future events or events occurring somewhere else in the present come to Frodo and Faramir in dreams. Aragorn, Elrond, and Gandalf foretell the future. They express this ability in terms of what their hearts tell them, and not their reasoning minds. Aragorn, for example, warms Gandalf that to pass the doors of Moria may be fatal for him, and Gandalf tells Frodo that "My heart tells me that he [Gollum] has some part to play yet, for good or ill, before the end" (*LotR* I.2.59).

As Paul Kocher observes in his book *Master of Middle-earth,* Sauron and Shelob are both evil, yet are not allies but competitors. Observe the difference in their methods.

Shelob is totally self-involved. She has no interest in what happens outside her cave. Her goal in life is to devour all light and life that have the misfortune to wander into her lair. Unlike Sauron, she waits for her victims to come to her; she does not weave webs up and down the countryside or cast spells to lure travelers from a distance. She takes as little action as is possible. Gollum seems to be the only bait she ever uses, presumably because he is such an unappetizing meal himself and because he promises to bring her a better dish. Shelob is what happens when the feminine concern with the individual and the inner life is taken to its extreme.

Sauron, on the other hand, is completely outer-directed. With a disastrous lack of self-understanding or respect for the natures of other beings, he seeks to make the world over in his own image. Consequently, he is very active in the world, affecting many lives, all of history. Sauron is what happens when the masculine predilection toward outer-directed activity is taken to the extreme.

Shelob is utterly private. Sauron is utterly public.

Thus the difference. The concerns of the Feminine Principle tend to derive from intuition: they are personal, specific, and inner-directed. The effect in history tends to be subtle, discernible in the variations of personality in individuals and not in the kind of action which is written in history books.

The Masculine Principle, being active and outer-directed, tends to be general and public, affecting the affairs of groups rather than just individuals. Certainly this is what is written about in history books.

Another, more subtle, example of this difference in modes of action and effect can be seen in the fates of the brothers Boromir and Faramir in *The Lord of the Rings*. Boromir, the favorite of their father, is overbalanced on the masculine side: "Rather he was a man after the sort of King Eärnur of old, *taking no wife* and delighting chiefly in arms; fearless and strong, but *caring little for lore,* save the tales of old battles" (*LotR* Appendix A.I.iv.1056, emphasis added). Boromir tragically lacks the feminine attributes of insight and understanding. It is no wonder that he is easy prey for the self-inflationary spell of the Ring.

Faramir, on the other hand, is his mother's son and is described as follows:

> He read the hearts of men as shrewdly as his father, but what he read moved him sooner to pity than scorn. He was gentle in bearing, and a lover of lore and music, and therefore by many in those days his courage was judged less than his brother's. But it was not so, except that he did not seek glory in danger without a purpose. (*LotR* App.A.I.iv.1056, emphasis added)

Faramir's personality has a better balance of positive feminine and masculine qualities than does Boromir's, and he understands himself and the false promises of the Ring. The fates of Frodo and Samwise and the possible outcome of the War of the Ring would surely have been different if Faramir had been as rash as his brother or if he had been over-feminine, unable to take action when necessary.

In attributing the balance of Faramir's personality to the influence of his mother, we see how Finduilas of Dol Amroth affected history almost as profoundly as did her husband Denethor, last Ruling Steward of Gondor—but not as publicly.

We should note here that the "Tookish part" of Mr. Bilbo Baggins, Esquire, that brave, adventurous part of him that supported him through his trials, was said to be inherited from his *mother*, Belladonna. Curious—that a hobbit should be propelled from a creature-comfortable, self-involved inactive existence into an outer-directed rash life by the prompting of impulses inherited not from his father but from his mother!

Insight—self-knowledge and the ability to understand others—is a crucial trait for good. Melkor the Morgoth lacks it: "He had gone often alone into the void places seeking the Imperishable Flame [...] Yet he found not the Fire for it is with Ilúvatar (God)" (*S* 16). But that Ilúvatar is also found within, Tolkien states elsewhere in the book: "Manwë sat long in thought [...] and he sought the counsel of Ilúvatar. [...] Then Manwë said to the Valar: 'This is the counsel of Ilúvatar in my heart' " (*S* 50). Morgoth, self-aggrandizing and outer-directed, seeks the power of creation—and power *over* creation—precisely where it is *not*: outside of himself.

Tolkien states that of all the Valar, Melkor feared and hated Varda most, presumably because of the clarity of her understanding of him, of his envy and possessive desire for all creation: "Out of the deeps of

Eä she came to the aid of Manwë; for Melkor she knew from before the making of the music and rejected him, and he hated her" (*S* 26).

Ages after, Galadriel displays the same ability to "see" into herself and into other persons. Her magic mirror of water "shows things that were, and things that are, and things that yet may be" (*LotR* II.7.362). She is able to see into Sauron's mind, though he is not able to divine her thought:

> "I say to you, Frodo, that even as I speak to you, I perceive the Dark Lord and know his mind, or all of his mind that concerns the Elves. And he gropes ever to see me and my thought. But still the door is closed!" (*LotR* II.7.364–65)

She tests all the members of the Fellowship with her glance, offering each his heart's desire should he relinquish the quest—and how could she do this if she had not the skill of instant and true perception into the natures of her fellow beings? When Frodo offers to surrender to her the One Ring, she answers him with great passion and a clear perception of the nature of the One Ring and the one who wrought it; and with wise self-understanding:

> "I do not deny that my heart has greatly desired to ask what you offer. For many long years I had pondered what I might do, should the Great Ring come into my hands, and behold! it is brought within my grasp. The evil that was devised long ago works on in many ways, whether Sauron himself stands or falls. Would not that have been a noble deed to set to the credit of his Ring, if I had taken it by force or fear from my guest?
>
> "And now at last it comes. You will give me the Ring freely! In place of the Dark Lord you will set up a Queen. And I shall not be dark, but beautiful and terrible as the Morning and the Night! Fair as the Sea and the Sun and the Snow upon the Mountain! Dreadful as the Storm and the Lightning! Stronger than the foundations of the earth. All shall love me and despair!
>
> "[...] I pass the test [...] I will diminish and go into the West, and remain Galadriel." (*LotR* II.7.365–66)

The wise counselors of Arda are often feminines or proteges of feminines. Melian, Galadriel and Idril all function as counselors, though they are sparing in their advice: "advice is a dangerous gift, even from the wise to the wise, and all courses may run ill," says the elf Gildor Inglorian, when Frodo asks for his counsel (*LotR* I.3.84). All are careful to avoid coercing the will of other persons. One of the signs that Boromir is falling under the spell of the Ring is his increased airing of his opinions and his presumption in offering advice.

Gandalf, who was Olorin in Valinor, is a student of the feminine Vala Nienna of whom, it is said, he learned pity and patience.

Healing, song, dance, and weaving are the feminine modes of creativity and power. The Vala Estë is known as the Healer. Nessa, spouse of Tulkas and sister of Oromë the Hunter, is said to delight in dancing. Vairë, spouse to Mandos, is known as the Weaver, and she weaves "all things that have been in Time into her storied webs" (*S* 28). Míriel, Fëanor's tragic mother, is also renowned for her weaving. The great singers of Valinor and Middle-earth are feminines of great power: Yavanna, the personification of nature, who sang the Two Trees into existence; Melian, who sang for the Valar during the mingling of the light of the Two Trees before departing to Middle-earth; and Melian's daughter Lúthien, whose song of power brought down the walls of Sauron's stronghold, whose song of enchantment overcame Morgoth even in the heart of his realm, and whose song of grief moved the heart of Mandos to pity, doomspeaker of the Valar "who never before was so moved, nor has been since" (*S* 187). Lúthien is also a great healer, and often heals by means of song.

All creation comes into being because of the power of song, as is told in the "Ainulindalë," the creation tale. That God, Eru Ilúvatar, uses song as His primary mode of creation signals that the Feminine Principle lies at the heart of all creation and has done so from the beginning. Eru is both feminine and masculine: omniscient—all-knowing—and omnipotent—all powerful.

Note that with the exception of weaving, all the forms of creativity of the Feminine Principle involve action of the body or the Self, rather than manipulation of objects. Tolkien seems to be saying that the Feminine Principle finds creative expression in activities of the body—no bad description of childbirth.

The best of the males of Arda display these feminine traits. Beren and Tuor, heroes of the First Age, are singers. That the young dwarves Fili and Kili are less susceptible to hoard-lust is demonstrated by their preference for gold and silver harps rather than jewels in Smaug's hoard. Later on in the story, Tolkien says that they alone may have stood on principle against Thorin's refusal to share the prize with the elves and the Lake-men: they are of superior character, and a clue to this may be their love of music.

Elrond is both healer and counselor—in fact, the peculiar passivity of his daughter Arwen, the near invisibility of his sons and the absence of his wife may be attributed to the femininity of his nature. Elrond has no need of a complementary feminine, for his nature embodies those traits most feminine.

Rivendell bears all the marks of a place of the Great Mother archetype. It is Hearth-centered, and all travelers find within song, rest, healing, understanding, and those creature-comforts provided by the best of mothers. It is situated in a hidden valley through which runs water, a common description for paradisiacal or mother-archetypical spots.

Elrond's sons represent what action he does take in the world beyond Rivendell—and that appears to be very little. Elrond is the best example that attributes of the gender are not necessarily confined to members of the sex of that gender.

Contrast Arwen's relationship with her father, Elrond, to Idril Celebrindal's relationship to *her* father Turgon. Turgon has also lost his wife, but Turgon is very masculine and in need of a feminine counterpart. His daughter Idril plays this part. While Turgon rules Gondolin, making laws, dispensing justice, preparing for war, all outer-directed, masculine activities, Idril sits at his right hand and counsels him. Idril, too, is noted for her intuition: she senses from the beginning that something is not quite right about her cousin Maeglin. Idril is also capable of taking action (masculine trait) after achieving understanding. Because of her suspicions of Maeglin, she causes a secret route out of Gondolin to be constructed, which, during the sack of Gondolin, saves many lives. Idril is a well-balanced personality, and Tuor, who also combines masculine and feminine traits as a counselor and a warrior, matches her well.

It should be noted that by the Third Age, the most powerful Elves are not warriors but are conservationists and counselors. The most influential Noldorin and Sindarin Elves of the First and Second Ages are very masculine: rulers, warriors, and makers. Fëanor, Fingolfin, Finrod, Glorfindel, Thingol, and Turgon are among the great names of the First Age. Celebrimbor and Círdan, artists and technicians, and Gil-galad, king and warrior, are the Elven heroes of the Second Age. In the Second Age, even Elrond goes to war, though by then he is also acting as a wise counselor. Galadriel, in her earlier days, is both outer-directed and rather masculine. She takes part in the rebellion of the Noldor not for love of Fëanor but because "she yearned to see the wide unguarded lands and to rule there a realm at her own will" (*S* 84). The following is written of her in *Unfinished Tales*: "Her mother-name was Nerwen ('man-maiden') and she grew to be tall beyond the measure even of the women of the Noldor; she was strong of body and mind and will, a match for both the loremasters and athletes of the Eldar in the days of their youth" (*UT* 229). The histories of the First and Second Ages indicate a strongly masculine bent among the Noldorin Elves of Middle-earth—perhaps even an overdose of the masculine principle. By the Third Age, the race of Elves has swung to the polar principle and has become, overall, much more introverted and less active in the public affairs of Middle-earth. Thus Arwen of the Third Age has less of a role to play than does Idril, who is a very much needed feminine counterweight during the tumultuous First Age.

Elrond, of course is not wholly feminine. The center of his house is the Hall of Fire—and fire is a masculine element. At the heart of all creation is a flame, Eru's Imperishable Flame; and this Fire achieved all creation through the medium of Song. In Elrond's Hall of Fire, Frodo succumbs to the enchantment of fire and song and walks in dreams made real. Again Tolkien reiterates the interplay of the Masculine and Feminine Principles.

Sauron is a horrible parody of this masculine/feminine interplay. By the Third Age, all that is visible of Sauron is a Hand and an Eye. According to Mark Hennelly and Marion Perret,[2] the hand and the

---

2. In his essay "The Road and the Ring: Solid Geometry in Tolkien's Middle-earth," Mark Hennelly discusses the dialectic of the Road and the Ring, recurring motifs in *The Lord of the Rings*. He makes reference to the essay by Marion Perret entitled "Rings Off Their Fingers: Hands in *The Lord of the Rings*." To their observations, I add my dialectic of the Feminine and Masculine Principles. The Ring, and other rings, are Feminine and the Road is Masculine.

> [...] The Road provides action, the Ring provides contemplation. The Road is an aggressive offense; the Ring is a protective defense, a posture of rest and recovery [...] The Road focuses its attention on the present, the Ring on understanding and remembering the lessons of the past and planning for the future (Hennelly 5).

eye are part of the Tolkien dialectic and interplay for good or evil, as when "the hand and eye of Legolas" (*LotR* II.9.387) guide the arrow that destroys a Nazgûl's steed; or as with Gollum, who seems to be all bulging, gleaming eyes and strangling hands. It is simple to deduce that the eye motif is feminine and that the hand is masculine. Eyes perceive, hands act.

But Sauron's feminine Eye is entirely outer-directed (masculine) and behind is nothing:

> But suddenly the Mirror went altogether dark [...] and Frodo looked into emptiness. In the black abyss there appeared a single Eye that slowly grew, until it filled nearly all the mirror [...] The Eye was rimmed with fire, but was itself glazed, yellow as a cat's, watchful and intent, and the black slit of its pupil opened on a pit, a window into nothing. (*LotR* II.7.364)

Sauron's black hand is entirely occupied with possessive clutching of the world. In the end, when the One Ring is destroyed, Middle-earth is treated to a last view of Sauron:

> And as the Captains gazed south to the Land of Mordor, it seemed to them that, black against the pall of cloud, there rose a huge shape of shadow, impenetrable, lightning-crowned, filling all the sky. Enormous it reared over the world, and stretched out towards them a vast, threatening hand, terrible but impotent. (*LotR* VI.4.949)

Impotence is one of the negative-feminine traits.

Impotence is a peculiarly feminine failing. Most of the weak or wicked feminines do not so much as actively participate in evil deeds as they are powerless to initiate *any* deed, much less halt an evil act. Two examples of this failing are Tar-Míriel, last queen of Númenor, and Aredhel, Turgon of Gondolin's sister.

Tar-Míriel is unable to prevent her cousin Ar-Pharazôn from usurping her throne. She is unable to prevent him from forcibly marrying her. Her end is the ultimate in impotence for she is overwhelmed by the great power of the sea and drowns. Tolkien gives us a

---

(note continued)

> [...] Each is a necessary complement to the other; and someone falls to evil, like Sauron and Saruman, only if he selfishly seeks to destroy the dialectic itself (4).

picture of a very beautiful yet ineffectual female, and if we pity her fate, we are also, perhaps, impatient of her helplessness.

Aredhel's fate is somewhat more complicated, but still involves an interplay of masculine and feminine traits that, nevertheless, end in impotence.

To begin with, Aredhel is rash (masculine)—she takes action without understanding. Against good counsel, she leaves Gondolin, then rashly decides to change her road and ride in perilous country. (It is, perhaps, understandable that she has grown tired of her confinement in Gondolin, however beautiful the city, and has developed a wanderlust. But her desire for freedom endangers many others, and she seems not to care.) She is then ensnared by Eöl, the Dark Elf, who more or less coerces her consent to marriage. She manages to corrupt her son Maeglin with her dissatisfaction, which leads directly to his fatal covetousness of Turgon's kingdom and Turgon's daughter. She dies trying to protect her son from his father's jealous assault with a javelin; her brother Turgon then executes her husband in revenge. She has helped create a set of circumstances that generates actions both harmful and evil. In the end, she is powerless to achieve any of her desires or to protect those she loves.

Aredhel's unbalanced masculinity leads to a negative-feminine end—impotence. Totally outer-directed Sauron also ends in a negative-feminine manner, becoming "a mere spirit of malice that gnaws itself in the shadows" (*LotR* V.9.879). He, like Ungoliant, is self-consuming: "Yet some have said that she ended long ago, when in her uttermost famine she devoured herself at last" (*S* 81).

We may accept that Ungoliant is the inverse of Melkor: he totally outer-directed, she completely inward-oriented. According to the speculations of the Eldar, when Melkor first looked down on Creation with his outer-directed envy to possess and rule, down clambered Ungoliant from the outer darkness with her inner-directed compulsion to consume all existence (*S* 73).

Now, Éowyn of Rohan is a female character of masculine habit. How, then, does she escape the fate of Aredhel?

Éowyn escapes Aredhel's fate primarily because Éowyn's life has been shaped by *events* over which she has little control. She is trapped in a web of negative-feminine circumstances: confined to the house and tied to an uncle who has given over his masculine prerogatives.

How significant that Théoden has put away his sword, that phallic symbol, and has sunk in *impotence* and *inactivity* upon his throne. His ears are filled with the whispers of Wormtongue, servant of that hypermasculine personality, Saruman. Éowyn is denied her place as her uncle's counselor and is forced to stand by powerless. Théoden's negative-feminine behavior nearly consumes her life.

To achieve equilibrium, she must take a positive masculine action. Being only human, she overcompensates, disguises herself as a man, and rides off to that preeminently male activity, war. However, on the battlefield, it is love, a feminine attribute, which motivates her and gives her the power to act—again, an interplay of positive masculine and feminine attributes.

She falls in love with Faramir, who wins her through feminine tenderness and understanding, and *not* through his masculine prowess as a warrior. Wise and kind Aragorn knows that this is what she needs; he is aware all along that she is originally drawn to him for all the wrong reasons—for his warrior magnificence and worldly position. Faramir embodies, in a male, those positive feminine characteristics lacking in her life. For Éowyn to have wed a warrior, a Boromir-type for example, would have settled her permanently in an overly masculine environment, which would not have made her whole. She would then probably have lived out her life as a "wild shieldmaiden of the North" (*LotR* VI.5.965) or been thrust back into a confined, inactive life—it is difficult to imagine Boromir (a noble but not particularly sensitive or insightful man) accepting counsel or assistance from a wife or allowing her to live a life as much more than his appendage. Nor is it likely that proud and independent Éowyn would have sought or tolerated such a role in those circumstances.

On the walls of Minas Tirith, intuitive Faramir helps Éowyn to new self-understanding:

> And she said: "I do not wish to play at riddles. Speak plainer!"
>
> "Then if you will have it so, lady," he said, "you do not go because only your brother called for you, and to look on the Lord Aragorn, Elendil's heir, in his triumph would now bring you no joy. Or because I do not go, and you desire still to be near me. And maybe for both these reasons, and you yourself cannot choose between them. Éowyn, do you not love me, or will you not?" [...]

> Then the heart of Éowyn was changed, or else at last she understood it. And suddenly her winter passed, and the sun shone on her.
>
> "I stand in Minas Anor, the Tower of the Sun," she said; "and behold! the Shadow is departed. I will be a shieldmaiden no longer, nor vie with the great Riders, nor take joy only in the songs of slaying. I will be a healer, and love all things that grow, and are not barren." (*LotR* VI.5.964–65)

Éowyn elects to remain in the Houses of Healing until time to return to Rohan. Obviously she has embraced the feminine principle in its positive aspects, including healing and the bearing of children, and has laid aside the frenetic activity of masculine warriors. She is no longer driven to rash acts; nor will she be consumed.[3]

I think it is significant that Éowyn announces that she stands "in Minas Anor, the Tower of the Sun" (*LotR* VI.5.964) rather than in Minas Tirith, the Tower of Guard. Rather than refer to the current warlike title, she refers to the city's earlier title—and the Sun, in Valinor and Middle-earth, is feminine. Her choice of title for the city in which she makes her statement about how she will live her life is a step away from the masculine activity of war and toward the feminine principle as exemplified by the Sun.

The Feminine Principle shapes individuals. The Masculine Principle shapes events. But as individuals are shaped by events, so are events determined by individuals: there is no escape from the complementarity of these polar principles.

Fëanor is another example of how the imbalance of one of the gender principles leads to a fate which typifies an imbalance of the

---

3. "The Mariner's Wife," the tale of the Númenórean couple Aldarion and Erendis, as told in *Unfinished Tales*, depicts another example of the interplay of masculine and feminine characteristics within a relationship, though in the case of this couple, the marriage fails. Aldarion, who becomes a king in Númenor, is very masculine: a wandering sailor and a builder of ships. Erendis is very feminine in her attachment to her home. Though their love is great, they never reach a balance or a blend of masculine and feminine characteristics. They become estranged. Significantly, Aldarion becomes more outer-directed, voyaging further and longer, often behaving rashly, and ever more resistant to any moderating influences of counsel. Erendis withdraws into her own home and creates an all-female household wherein she attempts to confine their daughter. She turns inward, nursing her grievances and pride.

polar principle, a leading, as Carl Jung says, to *enantiodromia*—"conversion to its opposite" (152).

From the beginning, Fëanor was *consuming*, a negative-feminine trait, rather than *giving*, a positive, outer-directed hence masculine trait. His mother Míriel dies of his birth, telling her husband as she expires, "Never again shall I bear child; for strength that would have nourished the life of many has gone forth in Fëanor" (*S* 63). It is as if, having consumed the Feminine Principle in the form of his mother, Fëanor overbalances into the masculine. Fëanor is preeminently a Maker: artist and technician. At first, he heeds the counsels of his wise wife Nerdanel who, writes Tolkien, desires to "understand minds rather than master them" (*S* 64). His masculine hand and feminine eye augment one another. The *palantíri* are an example of this: round shapes created by the hand to aid the eye in seeing.

But Fëanor grows progressively more masculine. He becomes estranged from his wife. He becomes possessive of his father and jealous of his public place and prerogatives as the son of the king of the Noldor. His feminine eye is made subservient to his masculine hand and he becomes more outer-directed and less introspective. He loses the ability to read accurately the intentions of his half-brothers.

His greatest work, however, reflects his essentially consuming nature. For the Silmarils, significantly, *imprison* the light of the Two Trees, that is, keep inward the light that the Trees radiated outward.

The basically negative-feminine Fëanor suffers a negative-masculine end. Rashness on the battlefield results in a sorry death in the very first battle with Morgoth:

> For Fëanor in his wrath against the Enemy would not halt, but pressed on [...] he was fey, *consumed* by the flame of his own wrath [...] he drew far ahead of the van of his host [...] Fëanor was surrounded [...] but at the last was smitten to the ground. (*S* 107, emphasis added)

The notion that wives, sisters, and mothers influence society by influencing their spouses, siblings and offspring is a Victorian notion generally rejected these days because it is employed as a pretext for denying women power in the public sector. Tolkien appears to view the situation from a different perspective. His feminines wield power within their sphere and the masculines wield power within their own. The societies of Arda are patriarchal, but Tolkien appears to desire this arrangement to be attributed to the masculine talent for public affairs, rather than to general masculine superiority coupled with feminine weakness and incompetence, or the inappropriateness of females in public roles, the rationales given for male dominance in our public arenas. The treatment of feminines with anything less than respect and a notion of equality in diversity is, in Arda, a signal of things going wrong.

Thus we may interpret Aredhel's flouting of her brother Turgon's authority as the improper use of a blood relationship to obtain a privilege denied others, rather than the rebellion of an undisciplined female against proper male authority.

Tolkien frowns upon forced marriages, an arrangement wherein an alliance between the masculine and the feminine is coerced, usually for reasons of public policy. The "Akallabêth," the tale of the downfall of Númenor, tells of the Lady Inzilbêth who is compelled to wed the Númenórean king Ar-Gimilzôr. Her eldest son and the one she influences becomes Tar-Palantir, the wise, far-seeing king (positive feminine traits) who attempts to redress some of the harmful acts of the rebellious Númenóreans. But her second son, most like his father, is the discontented rebel Gimilkhad. Gimilkhad's son is Ar-Pharazôn, who also forces marriage on an unwilling woman, then usurps the throne and brings about the ruin of Númenor. Great evil usually comes from these forced marriages, as Eöl, Aredhel's reluctantly taken husband, learns to his cost.

Tolkien's treatment of wives also differs from the all-too-common Western treatment in which a wedding ring converts a woman from a highly desirable individual (or love object) to a household fixture. The great lovers of Arda marry and maintain beautiful romances ever after.

The romance of Elwing and Eärendil is an example of this. *The Silmarillion* contains this Tennysonian passage:

> [...] but Elwing with the Silmaril upon her breast had cast herself into the sea.
>
> [...] Ulmo bore Elwing out of the waves, and he gave her the likeness of a great white bird, and upon her breast there shone as a star the Silmaril, as she flew over the water to seek Eärendil her beloved. On a time of night Eärendil at the helm of his ship saw her come towards him, as a white cloud exceedingly swift beneath the moon, as a star over the sea moving in strange course, a pale flame on wings of storm. And it is sung that she fell from the air upon

> the timbers of Vingilot, in a swoon, nigh unto death for the urgency of her speed, and Eärendil took her to his bosom; but in the morning with marveling eyes he beheld his wife in her own form beside him with her hair upon his face, and she slept. (*S* 248)

Further on in the tale, their devotion to each other is again expressed:

> Then Eärendil, first of living Men, landed on the immortal shores; and he spoke there to Elwing and to those that were with him [...] And Eärendil said to them: "here none but myself shall set foot lest you fall under the wrath of the Valar. But that peril I will take on myself alone." [...]
>
> But Elwing answered: "Then would our paths be sundered for ever; but all thy perils I will take on myself also." And she leaped into the white foam and ran towards him. (*S* 248)

Other devoted couples are Húrin and Morwen, Gorlim and Eilenel, and Melian and Thingol.

In terms of power and creativity, the feminines of Arda are the equals of the masculines and sometimes surpass them. Two of the greatest works of Eä are the creations of feminines: Varda's stars and Yavanna's Two Trees. Among several couples, the wives surpass their husbands in lineage and power: Melian and Thingol, Lúthien and Beren, and Galadriel and Celeborn. In the cases of Melian and Lúthien, however, their power is intimately bound with their lovers:

> For Melian was of the divine race of the Valar, and she was a Maia of great power and wisdom; but for love of Elwë Singollo she took upon herself the form of the Elder Children of Ilúvatar, and in that union she became bound by the chain and trammels of the flesh of Arda. In that form she bore to him Lúthien Tinúviel; and in that form she gained power over the substance of Arda, and by the Girdle of Melian was Doriath defended [...] But now Thingol lay dead, and his spirit had passed to the halls of Mandos; and with his death a change came also upon Melian. (*S* 234)

Lúthien achieves feats of greatness for love of Beren, just as he is inspired to deeds far beyond the power of mortal men for love of her. Both escape the Curse of the Silmarils because they are prompted in their actions by love for one another, rather than hoard-desire for the Silmarils.

The curious history of the creation of the Dwarf and Ent races demonstrates what happens when the masculine and feminine creative powers, while not in opposition, are, nevertheless, not quite in step. It is also, of course, a tale of the uneasy relationship between nature and technology.

Aulë created the dwarf race without the knowledge or aid of his spouse Yavanna. Consequently, dwarves are very masculine: absorbed by handicrafts, war-like, sometimes just, but not particularly compassionate. They also suffer a shortage of females, as if Aulë forgot that a race needs mothers as well as fathers! They are possessive, a negative-masculine trait.

When Yavanna discovers Aulë's secretive activity, she is not pleased. She observes that his creations will have little love for hers because no thought of hers went into their making. She then seeks out Manwë with a request that some protection be provided for the plants and animals that are her contribution to Arda. Ents are the result.

Ents, like dwarves, are somewhat one-sided. They remain in their forests and have little to do with other races—rather self-involved, as Treebeard admits to Merry and Pippin. They practice few of the masculine crafts of making—fine arts, handicrafts, and technology. In fact, their only crafts appear to be the brewing of special draughts for consumption and the making of their homes. A bad Ent or huorn is like Old Man Willow or Shelob: rooted in one place, voracious, and contenting himself with corrupting the immediate environment and luring individuals to destruction. "Don't be hasty," is a motto of the Ents, a warning against the masculine fault of rashness.

Ents also have a sexual dysfunction within the race. The males are wandering herders while the females are settled gardeners, and the two genders go their separate ways, pursuing their different interests (echoes of Aulë and Yavanna!). Neither sexual attraction nor the necessities of procreation are sufficient to arrest this gradual drift apart. Nature devises a unique method for the continuation of the Ent race, a method which does not involve sexual congress between males and females.

Note that throughout the entire incident, Yavanna's work is considered as important as is Aulë's.

All in all, Tolkien's treatment of women and the Feminine Principle is much more flattering and satisfying, in my opinion, than the treatment commonly accorded them. In all too many fantasy and science fiction tales, women are cast in subordinate or antagonistic roles. Recently, this situation has changed, due to the influence of the feminist movement and to the influx of women writers into the field. Yet all too often the heroines of modern fantasy and science fiction are simply males in drag. They are given swords and guns, phallic implements of the hand, and sent out on warrior-sagas. They are little different in motivation, activity, reaction and basic character from the male warriors.

The sexual activity of these "liberated" Amazons—meaning liberated from the direct control of men—has taken on some of the more unappealing aspects of our macho male characters: unrelated to bonding or procreation, and exploitative, self-indulgent, serial, and random. This is enantiodromia with a vengeance.

In short, too many writers appear unable to conceive of how women can be distinct from men without also being a version of, subordinate to, an appendage of, or in competition with men. The presence of women raises serious questions: Who is woman? What is woman?

The easiest way to avoid these questions is to avoid the presence of women altogether. The "heroes in drag" maintain the perspective and stance that masculinity is the norm and the standard, that all things of value belong to the masculine sphere, and that we shall all be equal once we are all converted to men.

Thus is the Feminine Principle denied, and women are invalidated.

But such an arrangement diminishes men as well. This is the monochromatic world sought by Sauron, the "clamorous unison" (*S* 17) of Morgoth's music. The negation of the harmony arising from cooperative diversity leaves us with one-dimensional, repetitive, stereotypical characters and situations.

We may look to Tolkien for *one* answer to the question of "Who and what is feminine?" For his Feminine Principle is *not* the negative of the Masculine Principle, but is another kind of being, equal yet other in stature and power. This diversity adds dimension and complexity to his characters, as they dance the dance of complementarity. Compare your Conans and Conans-with-bosoms to Beren and Lúthien or Aragorn and Éowyn. Who stirs the heart most or holds the imagination longest?

Is Lúthien mannish? No. Without recourse to such masculine appurtenances as swords or rayguns, she nevertheless outperforms in courage, daring, resourcefulness, adventure, and sheer power most of our weapon-brandishing heroes and heroines. Her deeds are masculine—active and outer-directed—but her methods are not, and she has not been turned into an imitation male.

Is Elrond effeminate? No. He embodies characteristics we most often associate with women, for he is hearth-centered, intuitive, caring, and introspective. But we know that Elrond is a match for any he-man type who comes along, for he is neither dependent and passive, nor ineffectual, characteristics also commonly associated with femininity. He is a powerful, respected figure in Middle-earth histories.

There is no war between the sexes in Tolkien's subcreation. Complementary and mutually augmenting positive feminine and masculine qualities are set against enantiodromic, negative feminine and masculine qualities. Feminine and Masculine are diverse—not subordinate nor antagonistic to one another. Tolkien shows how this is to the greater glory of each.

This article was published originally in Mythlore *10.4 (#38) (1984): 5–13. The version here has been slightly revised by the author. It is reprinted here with permission.*

Works Cited

Hennelly, Mark M., Jr. "The Road and the Ring: Solid Geometry in Tolkien's Middle-earth." *Mythlore* 9.3 (#33) (Autumn 1982): 1–13. Print.

Jung, C. G. *Four Archetypes*. Princeton, NJ: Princeton UP, 1970. Print.

Kocher, Paul H. *Master of Middle-earth*. Boston: Houghton Mifflin, 1972. Print.

Perret, Marion. "Rings Off Their Fingers: Hands in *The Lord of the Rings*." *ARIEL: A Review of International English Literature* 6.4 (1975): 52–66. Print.

Tolkien's Females and the Defining of Power

Nancy Enright

In *The Lord of the Rings,* J. R. R. Tolkien's female characters, though few in number, are very important in the defining of power, a central thematic concern of the text. In fact, in *The Lord of the Rings,* power, when presented in the traditional male-oriented way, is undercut as often as it is asserted. Even typically "heroic" characters like Aragorn and Faramir use traditional masculine power in a manner tempered with an awareness of its limitations and a respect for another, deeper kind of power. Aragorn shows this recognition of an alternative kind of power in his reverence for the Elves, who though brave fighters, are not known for their physical prowess. The stereotypical and purely masculine kind of power, as represented by Boromir for instance, is shown to be weaker morally and spiritually than its nontraditional counterparts, thus allowing Boromir to fall, while less typically heroic characters, including all the major female characters, stand. In the context of these depictions of power, both asserted and subverted, the female characters interact with the males in a much more complex world than might at first be assumed when reading *The Lord of the Rings*. The general lack of a female presence in battle scenes (with the important exception of Éowyn's contest with the Nazgûl) or even among the members of the Fellowship does not imply that female power and presence are unimportant. On the contrary, Tolkien's female characters epitomize his critique of traditional, masculine, and worldly power, offering an alternative that can be summed up as the choice of love over pride, reflective of the Christ-like inversion of power rooted in Scripture, and ultimately more powerful than any domination by use of force.

Jane Chance, in her insightful study *The Lord of the Rings: The Mythology of Power,* explores the development of the theme of power throughout *The Hobbit* and *The Lord of the Rings,* coming to the very accurate conclusion that "the ability to understand the necessity for locating a 'paradise' within" turns out to be "the greatest power of all" (138). She explores how Tolkien, whom she links with philosopher

Michel Foucault and C. S. Lewis in this regard, "questioned the validity of the human sciences to represent the rationality of the age" (20), arguing that, for Tolkien, "true power emerges from wise and healing service to the community" (24). In another study concerned with the issue of power, Anne C. Petty argues that power, as depicted in *The Lord of the Rings*, can be divided into two varieties—internal (as in power, such as magic, intrinsic to someone, as in the case of the Elves) and external (power contained in a thing, such as the Ring)—but goes on to argue that this distinction is far less important than how power is used—or abused (138–39, and elsewhere). In light of these insights into Tolkien's depiction of power, it is important to consider how this thematic concern connects with Tolkien's Christian beliefs *and* his depiction of gender, linking them in a meaningful way.

J. R. R. Tolkien has been criticized for creating too few female characters in *The Lord of the Rings* and, of those few, having them fill supposedly traditionally feminine and, therefore, stereotypical roles. As a member of the Inklings, the famous group of writers and thinkers including C. S. Lewis and Charles Williams, Tolkien was included in an all-male community, and, according to Candice Fredrick and Sam McBride, this community was blatantly sexist. Specifically referring to Tolkien's works, they argue that the "males operate within a system that is overtly patriarchal. Men are the doers, workers, thinkers, and leaders. Women are homemakers, nurses, and distant love interests" (109). Fredrick's and McBride's book, *Women Among the Inklings: Gender, C. S. Lewis, J. R. R. Tolkien, and Charles Williams*, offers a chapter including a summary of other feminist critiques of the works of the Inklings with regard to lack of female characters and/or the way they are depicted (Chapter 5, "Mere Feminism: Gender, Reading, and the Inklings" 163–70). The range of these critical responses goes from some who feel there is no problem with gender in the Inklings' writings to Fredrick's and McBride's own suggestion that gender bias is a very serious failing in these works. In a collection of essays on Tolkien written by other writers of fantasy, Terri Windling, while crediting Tolkien for inspiring her own works of fantasy, remembers feeling as a child that "there was no place for me, a girl, on Frodo's quest" (226). And, though his article basically challenges the negative criticism of Tolkien for lack of female characters, William H. Green says that "there is certainly a bias here, an emotional charge pushing the women to margins of stories or deep into their symbolic cores" (190), referring not only to *The Hobbit* (though his article focuses on that text), but on what he calls "the marginalization" of women characters in Tolkien's other writings.[1] Along these same lines, Jes Battis claims, "women are not given easy identities to inhabit within *The Lord of the Rings*, and many are stereotyped to the point of excess" (913).[2]

Other critics have attempted to justify the small number of females in *The Lord of the Rings* by pointing out the powerful roles they play or the fact that these roles are important as archetypes or as mythologically resonant images. Jessica Yates argues that Tolkien's style of epic fantasy necessitates the placing of all major characters into archetypal roles, "[a]nd so we have Aragorn the Hero, Arwen the Princess, Éowyn the Amazon, Galadriel the Enchantress, and Gandalf the Wizard"; Yates claims that it renders them less "developed" than characters in a more typical twentieth-century novel. Another critic connecting Tolkien's female characters with myth is Leslie A. Donovan, who points out many symbolic associations from Norse legend apparently attached to Galadriel, Arwen, and Éowyn, as well as the evil spider Shelob (106–07 and elsewhere). However, I would disagree with Donovan when she argues that "applications of Christian typology [with the exception of the connection between Galadriel and the Virgin Mary] hold little promise for explaining the authority of other women in Tolkien's trilogy" (107). Furthermore, the view of Tolkien's depiction of females as being a mere reflection of traditional or archetypal gender roles does not account for the religious depth of these characters, nor does their scarcity in number lead to an explanation such as the overly simplified argument that Tolkien is, in fact, "sexist." On the contrary, I would argue that it is only through a careful examination of Tolkien's depiction of power that the role of his female characters can be fully understood. In *The Lord of the Rings*, the female

---

1. W. Green qualifies his remarks, saying that he is not going so far as Catherine Stimpson, whom he quotes as referring to Tolkien's "subtle contempt and hostility toward women" (Stimpson 19; qtd. by W. Green 190).

2. W. Green and Battis go on to argue that Tolkien's *apparent* limitation with regard to female characters is at least somewhat redeemed through a certain "feminization" (in Battis's article, the homosexual resonance) attached to key male characters. Green attributes the absence of women characters to Tolkien's supposed "fear of sex."

characters, in their inversion of power, exhibit a virtue that, in Tolkien's view, is crucial to salvation—the choice of love over pride—a message central to the novel and one that transcends all gender roles.

The prototype for other, more significant female characters in *The Lord of the Rings* (such as Arwen, Éowyn, and Galadriel) is Goldberry, the wife of Tom Bombadil, in *The Fellowship of the Ring*. This character offers an interesting introduction to the kinds of female power important in the story. Prior to the forming of the "Fellowship of the Ring" at the Council of Elrond, the four hobbits travel through the Old Forest on their way to Bree, where they hope to meet Gandalf. In this chapter, the four previously sheltered hobbits, along with the reader, are being introduced to the world of danger and beauty outside the Shire. The Old Forest, evocatively linked with hobbits' lore but, for the most part, left unexplored by them, is a place of ancient beauty and grave dangers. One of these dangers is Old Man Willow, a humanized and wicked tree, who captures Merry and Pippin in its roots. As Frodo runs off, calling for help, he comes across an odd character, a personification of nature, called Tom Bombadil. Tom knows the proper song to calm Old Man Willow, causing him to release the two hobbits. At Tom's home, the hobbits are introduced to Bombadil's wife, Goldberry, the "River daughter." Physically resembling Galadriel, who appears later, Goldberry is golden-haired, slender, and exquisitely beautiful, but she is more "natural," less ethereal than her Elven counterpart. Goldberry is, in fact, mythologically similar to a water nymph or a dryad. Her clothing, like her husband's, suggests a link with nature, as Jane Chance points out (*Mythology* 41); for instance, in one scene, Goldberry "was clothed all in silver with a white girdle, and her shoes were like fishes' mail" (*LotR* I.7.132). Seeing Goldberry, the hobbits experience a kind of awe, abashed at her beauty and appreciative of her kindness (123 and elsewhere). While Tom Bombadil is called "Master," it is clear that both husband and wife are equally in command of their little household, though their roles differ from each other. The hobbits watch the dance-like movements of Tom and Goldberry as they set the table, hers defined by grace and beauty, his both merry and whimsical. They respect each other most deeply, and, together, offer the hobbits what they need on this resting place of their journey. As the hobbits look at Goldberry upon their leaving, she stands "small and slender like a sunlit flower against the sky" (I.8.136). Despite her lack of overt physical strength, she represents the power of nature, ancient and renewing. However, more significant female representations of power follow, the first of these being Arwen, daughter of Elrond.

When the hobbits first meet Arwen, she has already met, fallen in love with, and pledged her troth to Aragorn, a love story told in the appendix to *The Return of the King*. Arwen is descended from Lúthien, another Elven princess[3] who falls in love with a mortal man. In fact, when Aragorn meets Arwen in Lothlórien, where she is visiting her grandparents, Galadriel and Celeborn, he is "singing a part of the Lay of Lúthien, which tells of the meeting of Lúthien and Beren in the forest of Neldoreth. And behold! there Lúthien walked before his eyes in Rivendell" (*LotR* App.A.I.v.1058). Lúthien was, according to the legend told by Aragorn to the hobbits on Weathertop, "the fairest maiden that has ever been among all the children of this world. As the stars above the Northern lands was her loveliness, and in her face was a shining light" (II.1.193). When Aragorn himself first sees Arwen, he is enchanted by her beauty just as Beren was by Lúthien's, as Arwen appears to him "clad in a mantle of silver and blue, fair as the twilight in Elven-home; her dark hair strayed in a sudden wind, and her brows were bound with gems like stars" (App.A.I.v.1058). Her beauty is of a kind so high that the one viewing it is abashed, as Frodo feels when he first sees Arwen at the dinner preceding the Council of Elrond. A key component of Arwen's beauty, like Lúthien's, is the fact that it is not simply physical; her intellectual and spiritual essence is conveyed through it: "Young she was and yet not so. The braids of her dark hair were touched by no frost; her white arms and clear face were flawless and smooth, and the light of stars was in her bright eyes, grey as a cloudless night; yet queenly she looked, and thought and knowledge were in her glance, as of one who has known many things that the years bring [...] Such loveliness in living thing Frodo had never seen nor imagined in his mind" (II.1.227).

3. Arwen lives the life of an Elf, and I refer to her as "Elven" here, but strictly speaking she is one of the Half-Elven. Her father, Elrond, child of a mortal and an Elf and given the choice of Elven immortality or human mortality, chose the former. His brother, Elros, chose the latter.

The inner power of Arwen is subtly conveyed, but present throughout *The Lord of the Rings*. Arwen does not ride out "on errantry," as do her brothers; instead, like her father, she remains at Rivendell, inspiring events through her relationship with Aragorn from afar. It is the thought of Arwen that comes to Aragorn at moments offering him a release from the burdens he must carry and allowing him to seem to the eyes of Frodo "clothed in white, a young lord tall and fair," speaking words in Elvish to Arwen, though she is not physically present (II.6.352). Lynnette R. Porter calls Arwen a "hero" for offering this kind of inspiration (118–25), and truly there is a heroic quality to the length and depth of her devotion to Aragorn. At a crucial moment, she sends him the banner she has woven for him, with the words, "The days now are short. Either our hope cometh, or all hopes end. Therefore I send thee what I have made for thee. Fare well, Elfstone" (*LotR* I.2.775). But what is most crucial about Arwen is her renunciation of Elven immortality for love. Like Lúthien, she must become mortal if she marries a mortal, a choice she willingly makes when she and Aragorn plight their troth on Cerin Amroth (App.A.I.v.1060). As Elrond sadly says to Aragorn, "Maybe it has been appointed so, that by my loss [i.e. of Arwen] the kingship of Men may be restored" (App.A.I.v.1060).

Even more so than Elrond's, Arwen's loss is personal and profound. She herself must suffer separation from all her kindred and experience personal mortality. Of all the characters in *The Lord of the Rings*, Arwen is the one who makes the Christ-like choice of taking on mortality out of love. And her decision, though rooted in her love of Aragorn, becomes part of the "*eucatastrophe*,"[4] as Tolkien calls it, the "good catastrophe" that saves Middle-earth. This paradoxical *power through the abdication of power* echoes the *kenosis* of Jesus, as described by St. Paul:

> Have this attitude in yourselves which was also in Christ Jesus, who, although He existed in the form of God, did not regard equality with God a thing to be grasped, but emptied Himself, taking the form of a bond-servant, and being made in the likeness of men. And being found in appearance as a man, He humbled Himself by becoming obedient to the point of death, even death on a cross. (Phil. 2.5–8)

---

4. For a detailed definition of this term, see *OFS*.

Arwen, while certainly never "in the form of God," does exist in a form higher than human, and her renunciation of her Elven immortality suggests the humility of Christ in laying aside the privileges of divinity (while retaining His divine nature), enjoined by St. Paul on all believers. Tolkien is not writing an allegory, so Arwen cannot be looked at as an allegorical representation of Jesus; no character in *The Lord of the Rings* has that role. However, Arwen's Christ-like renunciation of power leads to her role in the healing of Frodo from the results of his bearing of the Ring. Referring to the end of *The Return of the King*, where Arwen offers her jewel and her passage to the West to Frodo, Tolkien wrote in a letter: "Arwen was the first to observe the disquiet growing in him, and gave him her jewel for comfort, and thought of a way of healing him" (*Letters* 327). Therefore, her loss—freely chosen out of love for Aragorn—becomes yet another means of salvation for someone else, in fact, the very person (i.e. Frodo) who has helped to bring about the *eucatastrophe* which has saved Middle-earth and in which Arwen's and Aragorn's love has become entwined.

The appendix of *The Return of the King* tells the end of her story. Though experiencing years of happiness with Aragorn, Arwen eventually has to face both the loss of her beloved husband, first, and then her own death. Dying, Aragorn acknowledges to Arwen the pain of death: "I speak no comfort to you, for there is no comfort for such pain within the circles of the world" (*LotR* App.A.I.v.1062). Linda Greenwood argues that this story "involves an element of sacrifice, a sacrifice that does not belong solely to the lives of Aragorn and Arwen, but also to those who give their lives as a gift for the salvation of others" (187), her phrasing certainly connecting this story implicitly to the sacrificial death of Jesus. Greenwood approaches the entire text in terms of what she calls the "deconstruction" allowed by love, which literally turns evil into good, death into life (171); she uses the term "deconstruction" apparently to mean an overturning of a usual evil result, a kind of *eucatastrophe*. However, this transformation of evil into good does not take away the reality of suffering for those willing to undergo it for the sake of others. Greenwood says, "Instead of giving up mortality for immortality, Arwen does the exact opposite. As with Lúthien, Arwen surrenders immortality and takes on mortality as a gift to Aragorn" (188). Watching Aragorn die, "[Arwen] tasted the bitterness of the mortality that she had taken upon her" (*LotR*

App.A.I.v.1062). After Aragorn's death, Arwen leaves Minas Tirith and faces her own death in the fading woods of Lothlórien, where her Elven relatives no longer live. Her story ends thus: "with the passing of Evenstar no more is said in this book of the days of old" (App.A.I.v.1063). As an Elf-Human, Arwen provides a bridge between the Third Age and the Fourth, and in renouncing her Elven heritage, she embodies in her loss the sacrifice the Elves, in general, willingly endure in accepting with the destruction of the Ring, the end not only of Sauron's evil, but of all that belongs to "the days of old," the world of Elves and Dwarves, as well as Orcs and Nazgûl, a world that is being turned over to human beings.

No Elf sees more clearly the nature of this loss than Galadriel, Lady of the Galadrim and of Lothlórien, and Arwen's grandmother. Galadriel is the most powerful female figure in *The Lord of the Rings* and, in fact, one of the most important characters of either gender in the story. One of the three Elven ring-bearers, Galadriel uses her power for healing, not domination. As Elrond explains to Glóin at the Council:

> The Three [rings] were not made by Sauron, nor did he ever touch them. [...] They are not idle. But they were not made as weapons of war or conquest: that is not their power. Those who made them did not desire strength or domination or hoarded wealth, but understanding, making, and healing, to preserve all things unstained. (II.7.268)

The kind of power described here is the alternative to traditional, male-oriented power. Galadriel is a stronger embodiment of this power than her husband, Celeborn. It is she who is the wiser and more powerful, though both rule together, and he clearly has both wisdom and power. When the Fellowship enters Lothlórien, Haldir, the Elf, tells Frodo and Sam, "You feel the power of the Lady [not the Lord] of the Galadrim" (II.6.351). It is Galadriel, not Celeborn, who realizes that Gandalf did, indeed, set out with the company, as planned, but did not come to Lórien with them (II.7.355), and it is she who corrects Celeborn for his harsh words to Gimli (II.7.356), exemplifying "forgiveness, hospitality, understanding" that "serve as a model for toleration of difference" (Chance, *Mythology* 54). Galadriel also is the one who mentally tests each member of the Fellowship, offering him a choice between the danger that lies ahead and something else that he greatly desires (*LotR* II.7.357). And she tells the Fellowship that she is the one who first summoned the White Council and, "if my designs had not gone amiss, it would have been governed by Gandalf the Grey, and then mayhap things would have gone otherwise" (II.7.357). Clearly, Galadriel is important, not only as a queen among Elves, but as a mover and planner of the great things in Middle-earth, affecting all its peoples.

Yet, despite her own power, or perhaps because of it, Galadriel knows the dangers of power used wrongly. She even knows the temptation toward the other kind of power, that of domination and pride. When Frodo offers her the Ring, she admits her desire for it:

> I do not deny that my heart has greatly desired to ask what you offer. For many long years I had pondered what I might do, should the Great Ring come into my hands, and behold! it was brought within my grasp [...] And now at last it comes. You will give me the Ring freely! In place of the Dark Lord you will set up a Queen. And I shall not be dark, but beautiful and terrible as the Morning and the Night! Fair as the Sea and the Sun and the Snow upon the Mountain! Dreadful as the Storm and the Lightning! Stronger than the foundations of the earth. All shall love me and despair! (II.7.366)

The characteristic Elven links with nature, in its beauty and healing, become in Galadriel's momentary fantasy and temptation part of the seductive quality of the Ring and potentially forces of domination, both powerful and destructive. Had she succumbed to this temptation, Galadriel herself would have become dominated by the pride linked to this kind of power, normally most tempting to males, but here, luring this most powerful female. However, Galadriel resists the temptation and rejects the Ring. After her temptation, successfully resisted, "she let her hand fall, and the light faded, and suddenly she laughed again, and lo! She was shrunken, a slender Elf-woman, clad in simple white, whose voice was soft and sad. 'I pass the test,' she said. 'I will diminish, and go into the West, and remain Galadriel' " (II.7.366). Like her granddaughter, Arwen, Galadriel is willing to endure personal abdication of power out of love, and it is this renunciation that reveals her spiritual and moral strength.

Prior to the scene of temptation where Frodo offers her the Ring, Galadriel explains the nature of her struggle with the Dark Lord: "[D]o not think that only by singing amid the trees, nor even by the slender arrows of Elven-bows, is this land of Lothlórien maintained and defended against its Enemy. I say to you, Frodo, that even as I speak to you, I perceive the Dark Lord and know his mind, or all of his mind that concerns the Elves. And he gropes ever to see me and my thought. But the door is closed!" (II.7.365). As if symbolic of her strength of will, Galadriel's Elven ring is of Adamant (II.7.365). Her gifts to the Fellowship reflect the nature of her strength, rooted in wisdom; each gift is perfectly suited to its recipient's character, from Aragorn's kingly scabbard, reflecting his lineage and destiny, to Sam's gardening soil and seed. As Aragorn says to Boromir, who has expressed skepticism about Galadriel's intentions: "Speak no evil of the Lady Galadriel! There is in her and in this land no evil, unless a man bring it hither himself. Then let him beware!" (II.7.358). In fact, Tolkien has suggested that his depiction of Galadriel is linked to a Catholic image of Mary, the mother of Jesus. In a letter, written in 1958, Tolkien wrote: "I am a Christian (which can be deduced from my stories), and in fact a Roman Catholic. The latter 'fact' perhaps cannot be deduced; though one critic (by letter) asserted that the invocations of Elbereth, and the character of Galadriel as directly described (or through the words of Gimli and Sam) were clearly related to Catholic devotion to Mary" (*Letters* 288). And, more specifically, in another letter, written in 1971, he says: "I was particularly interested in your remarks about Galadriel [...] I think it is true that I owe much of this character to Christian and Catholic teaching and imagination about Mary, but actually Galadriel was a penitent" (*Letters* 407). Tolkien is referring to Galadriel's participation in the rebellion under Fëanor of the Noldor against the Valar, as told in *The Silmarillion*, where Galadriel, "the only woman of the Noldor to stand that day tall and valiant among the contending princes, was eager to be gone" (83–84). However, in the same letter, Tolkien says that Galadriel "was pardoned because of her resistance to the final and overwhelming temptation to take the Ring for herself" (407). And, in a letter written very close to his death in 1973, to Lord Halsbury, Tolkien offers what may be a revised view of Galadriel:

> Galadriel was "unstained": she had committed no evil deeds. She was an enemy of Fëanor. She did not reach Middle-earth with the other Noldor, but independently. Her reasons for wanting to go to Middle-earth were legitimate, and she would have been permitted to depart, but for the misfortune that before she set out the revolt of Fëanor broke out, and she became involved in the desperate measures of Manwë, and the ban on all emigration. (*Letters* 431)

This view of Galadriel would certainly seem to contradict her own words in *The Silmarillion*: "we were not driven forth, but came of our own will, and against that of the Valar" (*S* 127). Stratford Caldecott,[5] in an essay exploring the Catholic influence on *The Lord of the Rings*, suggests that "the pressure of the Marian archetype in Tolkien's imagination on the development of the character of Galadriel" specifically caused his later revision of her as having ever been involved in a prior rebellion (6); certainly, his view of Galadriel, as revealed by these letters, developed over time. However, even if Galadriel remains a redeemed sinner, by grace a penitent *can* reflect the beauty of Mary and even of Christ, and Galadriel does this certainly.

As mentioned earlier, Tolkien was not creating allegorically exact parallels to any religious figure, but instead conveying an overall sense of "evangelium," as he refers to the gospel in his famous essay "On Fairy-stories" (note 4). In this context, Galadriel suggests some of the power and beauty of Mary, the mother of Jesus. To Father Robert Murray, S. J., who had written that *The Lord of the Rings* had "a strong sense of the order of Grace" and noted a connection between the depiction of Galadriel and the image of Mary, Tolkien wrote:

> I think I know what you mean by the Order of Grace; and of course by your references to Our Lady, upon which all my own small perception of beauty both in majesty and simplicity is founded. *The Lord of the Rings* is of course a fundamentally religious and Catholic work; unconsciously so at first, but consciously in the revision. That is why I have not put in, or have cut out, practically all references to anything like "religion," to cults or practices, in the imaginary world. For the religious element is absorbed into the story and the symbolism. (*Letters* 172)

Stratford Caldecott expounds on the reference to Mary in this letter by pointing out that "as Tolkien's Catholic faith was profound and instinctive, it would have been as hard for him to separate the Virgin Mary's presence from Christ's as to separate Our Lord from Scripture or the Church" (6). Since as a Catholic Tolkien would see Mary as a reflection of Christ, symbolism linked to her would be an important part of the religious resonance permeating *The Lord of the Rings*. Other

---

5. Stratford Caldecott's article gives a detailed analysis of the Marian symbolism attached not only to Galadriel, but also to Elbereth.

symbolic associations connected with Mary, pointed out by Caldecott, include the phial of light given to Frodo, the overthrow of Sauron on March 25 (the Feast of the Annunciation to Mary of her conception of Jesus), and the overall theme of humility triumphing over power and evil pervading the entire story, specifically expressed in Mary's beautiful prayer, the Magnificat, in Luke 1 (Caldecott 6–8). In addition, closely analyzing the Loreto Litany, Fr. Michael W. Maher, S. J. links Galadriel and the land of Lórien with a large number of symbolic images of Mary, taken from this famous prayer, "Seat of Wisdom" and "Mother of Good Counsel" being two examples (230). All the Marian references serve to undergird the link between Tolkien's depiction of his female characters and power, since, as Caldecott observes, the humility of Mary is a central component of her character and, paradoxically, the one attribute that enables her, through her submission to God's will, to be instrumental in bringing about the most powerful overthrow of evil through the Incarnation. Mary's willingness to say "yes" to the Lord's request of her, through the Angel, her surrender of her own will to God, is the act that leads to her ultimate empowerment as a vehicle of grace (Caldecott 6).

Tolkien's reference to the "Order of Grace" in his letter to Fr. Murray is important with regard to the two kinds of power polarized in the story. While the conflict is, indeed, between good and evil on the largest scale, there exists even among those on the "good side" two kinds of power, with the spiritually based but physically "weaker" type of power invariably shown to be the stronger in the long run. Frodo, in his victory over Sauron, is a prime example of the power of moral and spiritual strength and courage overcoming physical strength. It is fitting that Arwen and Galadriel, being female and therefore (like the hobbit) outside the Man-dominated world of physical prowess, understand Frodo better than do many other characters. They empathize with his suffering and his sacrifice, offering help and consolation through the wisdom and power they possess.

The Christian roots of the victory of apparent weakness over physical strength are clearly outlined in Scripture. In John's gospel, Jesus graphically illustrates this concept when He takes a towel, ties it around His waist, and does the task of a slave, washing the disciples' feet (John 13.5–11). Jesus's teaching about love of one's enemies and turning the other cheek (Luke 6.27–38 and Matt. 5.38–48) inverts traditional uses of power in a way that is truly radical. And, of course, Jesus's Passion and Death present the ultimate example of the laying down of power and of life itself, leading to triumph over evil and death.

The key thing to remember with regard to Jesus's renunciation of traditional power is that it is not equivalent to weakness or passivity; rather, it is a conquering of evil through spiritual rather than physical force, ultimately through love. The resurrection proved the validity of Jesus's non-traditional use of power. In the letter to the Hebrews, the early believers are reminded: "Since then the children share in flesh and blood. He Himself likewise also partook of the same, that through death He might render powerless him who had the power of death, that is, the devil: and might deliver those who through fear of death were subject to slavery all their lives" (Heb. 2.14–15). As Tolkien says, "The Birth of Christ is the *eucastastrophe* of Man's history. The Resurrection is the *eucatastrophe* of the story of the Incarnation. This story begins and ends in joy" (*OFS* 89). Tolkien acknowledges in the same essay that his work is rooted in this ultimate *eucatastrophe* of Christ's birth, death, and resurrection: "if by grace what I say has in any respect any validity, it is, of course, only a facet of a truth incalculably rich, finite only because the capacity of man for whom this was done is finite" (88).

A key concept involved in *eucatastrophe,* in a fairy story or its gospel prototype, is the transformation of death. Linda Greenwood argues, "In Tolkien's work, love motivates faith to reach beyond the boundaries of the known, to rekindle hope in the midst of the uncertain. Love turns death into a gift and transforms defeat into victory" (171). In other words, characters who are ultimately most powerful are those, whether male or female, who willingly lay down their own power and even, in some cases, their lives for others. As mentioned with regard to Arwen, though no character in *The Lord of the Rings* perfectly represents Jesus, nor does any action perfectly convey the unequalled importance of His death and resurrection, some of the characters (including Galadriel and Arwen) do suggest aspects of His renunciation of physical power for the spiritual power of love.

This renunciation, experienced by both characters, involves giving up unending life in this world. Arwen, as we have seen, literally becomes mortal, but Galadriel also accepts the "fading" of the Elves and their quickened departure from Middle-earth. As Charles Huttar, in his discussion of Tolkien's story as an heir to the Golden Age myths of classical writers, says, Elves were "especially susceptible" to the temptation toward "the prevention or slowing of *decay*" (*Letters* 152, quoted by Huttar, emphasis in original). Both Arwen and Galadriel willingly choose to let go of the illusion of changelessness that the nearly (but not completely) immortal nature of the Elves enables them to enjoy. Huttar points out that all "Elves who remain in Middle-earth at the end of the Third Age have proved victorious over their natural 'clinging to Time' " (Huttar 102). However, Tolkien uses two female characters to emphasize the refusal of the power of endless time in this world, as it moves toward a new age dominated by mortal human beings.

The female character depicted most complexly with regard to issues of power is the human woman Éowyn, niece of King Théoden of Rohan. As a part of a culture that highly values physical prowess and strength in arms, Éowyn has grown up feeling cramped and devalued. As Gandalf explains to her brother Éomer, during Aragorn's healing of Éowyn after her heroic victory over the leader of the Nazgûl: "My friend [...] you had horses, and deeds of arms, and the free fields; but she, born in the body of a maid, had a spirit and courage at least the match of yours. Yet she was doomed to wait upon an old man, whom she loved as a father, and watch him falling into a mean dishonoured dotage; and her part seemed to her more ignoble than that of the staff that he leaned on" (*LotR* V.8.867). Through Gandalf, Tolkien is expressing a perspective on gender which, while it may not be called explicitly feminist, is certainly sensitive to the pain felt by a woman such as Éowyn living in a male-dominated world; as a woman, Éowyn has been patronizingly kept from activities that she proves herself to have been more than capable of performing. Her encounter with the Nazgûl shows the strength of her spirit and her skill in battle. She will, as Jane Chance points out, "serve Rohan in battle better than any other Rider from the Mark" (*Mythology* 72). The perfect irony of her reply, "No living man am I!" to the Nazgûl's boast, "No living man may hinder me!" turns gender expectations on their head, as she drives her spear into the invisible skull (*LotR* V.6.841).

However, Éowyn's victory is not complete with this triumph over the Nazgûl, for her understanding of power remains the male-dominated, physically oriented kind. Though her action is truly heroic and self-sacrificial, as pointed out by Lynnette Porter (99), her experience of power must deepen through renunciation of it. One of the most touching chapters in the *The Lord of the Rings*, entitled "The Steward and the King," tells of the beginning of the love relationship between Éowyn and Faramir. Both wounded in the battle with the Nazgûl, they have also been wounded by a culture that has devalued them, Éowyn (as we have seen) because she is a woman and Faramir because he is not the "typical" warrior his brother Boromir was. Both need to understand that skill in battle, though they have it to a high degree, is not enough for peace and wholeness. Together, they must find healing, which at first seems particularly far from Éowyn. Éowyn tells Faramir early in their friendship: "Look not to me for healing! I am a shieldmaiden and my hand is ungentle" (*LotR* VI.5.961). As Faramir discerns, part of Éowyn's hurt involves a mistaken "love" for Aragorn: "You desired to have the love of the Lord Aragorn. Because he was high and puissant, and you wished to have renown and glory and to be lifted far above the mean things that crawl on the earth. And as a great captain may to a young soldier he seemed to you admirable" (VI.6.964). However, Aragorn, who is in love with Arwen, has not returned Éowyn's love, a rejection that is most painful to her and part of what has led her into battle, as well as part of what still needs to be healed after the battle is over. When Faramir declares his love for her, "the heart of Éowyn changed, or else at least she understood it. And suddenly her winter passed, and the sun shone on her" (VI.6.964).

What exactly has happened to Éowyn? A superficial reading might render her transformation no more than a return to a traditional female role; she is marrying the man she loves and giving up her attempts to be a fighter; as she says, "I will be a shieldmaiden no longer, nor vie with the great Riders, nor take joy only in the songs of slaying" (VI.6.965). Fredrick and McBride sum up her transformation as a triumph of patriarchy: "an unruly impulse to transcend prescribed gender roles has been successfully thwarted" (113). However, her healing is not so easily defined. Her love relationship with Faramir is intimately linked with the healing of Middle-earth because of the destruction of the Ring. Though news of the overthrow of Sauron has not yet reached Minas Tirith, Faramir and others in the city somehow sense it. In a passage that evokes a sense of the joy of *"eucatastrophe,"* Tolkien describes the commingling of these two lives with the great event of their time:

> And so they stood on the walls of the City of Gondor, and a great wind rose and blew, and their hair, raven and golden, streamed out mingling in the air. And the Shadow departed, and the Sun was unveiled, and the light leaped forth; and the waters of Anduin shone like silver, and in all the houses of the City men sang for the joy that welled up in their hearts from what source they could not tell. (*LotR* VI.6.963)

Her personal healing involves not only being open to love, but a movement from a desire for power and domination (i.e. as a queen) to the desire to heal and to help things grow. She says, "I will be a healer and will love all things that grow and are not barren [...] No longer do I desire to be a queen" (VI.6.965). Now like Faramir, who always valued the other, gentler sort of power to the dismay of his father, Éowyn seeks only the power of healing and of peace, the power enjoyed for many years by the Elves, and now being brought into the Age of Men, through the conquering of Sauron and through Aragorn's and Arwen's incipient reign. As she and Faramir come down from the high walls, people see "the light that shone about them" (VI.6.965). Éowyn has begun to enjoy the kind of high beauty linked to the spiritual powers of love and forgiveness.

Éowyn and the other female characters in *The Lord of the Rings* are crucial to the meaning of the tale. *The Lord of the Rings* is far more than a story of battle and adventure in the external sense, where those with the greatest physical prowess prove to be the victors. It is also more than a tale of the spiritual battle between Good and Evil, though, of course, it is *at least that*. *The Lord of the Rings* is an illustration of various choices regarding the use of power, but with only one of them shown to be the best, the ultimately good choice. Arwen, Galadriel, and Éowyn (by the end of the tale) all make this good choice by opting for the Christ-like power of love, healing, and gentleness. The fact that they are female (and thus among the less valued members of the society Tolkien is depicting) emphasizes a larger theme, as clarified by Jane Chance: "Humility in Tolkien is always ultimately successful," as we see in case after case of the triumph of a "marginalized protagonist," whether Hobbit, or female, or other member of a less dominant group (*Mythology* 79). Is this kind of power *only* for females (and others perceived as weaker), somehow *relegated* to them? Definitely not. In fact, if *The Lord of the Rings* shows anything about power, it makes clear the fact that true power for *anyone* comes from renouncing earthly dominance and from giving of oneself for the healing and love of others. Aragorn, Gandalf, Faramir—to name just a few key male characters—all exhibit this renunciation and enjoy a greater power because of it (as contrasted with Denethor, Saruman, and Boromir, for instance). However, the fact that Tolkien shows female characters exhibiting this kind of power better and more significantly than many of the males undercuts much of the supposed male dominance perceived by some readers of the novel, a perception largely based on the low number of female characters (which is less significant than the roles they play) and the supposed stereotypes these female characters fulfill (stereotypes undercut by an accurate analysis of gender in connection with the definition of power in the text). In *The Lord of the Rings,* the kind of power associated with masculine strength and physical prowess is subverted through female characters who lay down their own power in Christ-like renunciation, part of the *eucatastrophe* that overturns the strongest evils in the world.

This article was published originally in Renascence: Essays on Values in Literature *59.2 (2007): 93–108 as well as in* J. R. R. Tolkien's The Lord of the Rings, *edited by Harold Bloom, New Edition (NY: Chelsea Press, 2007), 171-86. It is reprinted here with permission from both sources.*

Works Cited

Battis, Jes. "Gazing upon Sauron: Hobbits, Elves, and the Queering of Post-Colonial Optic." *MFS: Modern Fiction Studies* 50.4 (2004): 908–26. Print.

Chance, Jane. The Lord of the Rings*: The Mythology of Power*. Lexington, KY: UP of Kentucky, 2001. Print.

---, ed. *Tolkien the Medievalist*. New York: Routledge, 2003. Print.

Donovan, Leslie A. "The Valkyrie Reflex in J. R. R. Tolkien's *The Lord of the Rings*: Galadriel, Shelob, Éowyn, and Arwen." Chance, *Medievalist* 106–32. *Reprinted in this volume.*

Fredrick, Candice, and Sam McBride. *Women Among the Inklings: Gender, C. S. Lewis, J. R. R. Tolkien, and Charles Williams*. Contributions in Women's Studies, vol. 191. Westport, CT: Greenwood Press, 2001. Print.

Green, William H. " 'Where's Mama?' The Construction of the Feminine in *The Hobbit*." *The Lion and the Unicorn* 22.2 (1998): 188–95. Print.

Greenwood, Linda. "Love: The Gift of Death." *Tolkien Studies* 2.1 (2005): 171–95. Print.

Huttar, Charles A. "Tolkien: Epic Traditions and Golden Age Myths." *Twentieth Century Fantasists: Essays on Culture, Society and Belief in Twentieth-Century Mythopoeic Literature*. Ed. Kath Filmer. New York: St. Martin's Press, 1992. 92–107. Print.

Maher, Michael W., S. J. " 'A Land without Stain': Medieval Images of Mary and Their Use in the Characterization of Galadriel." Chance, *Medievalist* 225–36.

New American Standard Bible. Lockman Foundation.

Petty, Anne C. *Tolkien in the Land of Heroes*. Cold Spring Harbor, NY: Cold Spring Harbor Press, 2003. Print.

Porter, Lynnette R. *Unsung Heroes of* The Lord of the Rings*: From the Page to the Screen*. Westport, CT: Praeger, 2005. Print.

Stimpson, Catherine R. *J. R. R. Tolkien*. Columbia Essays on Modern Writers 41. New York: Columbia UP, 1969. Print.

Windling, Terri. "On Tolkien and Fairy-Stories." *Meditations on Middle-earth*. Ed. Karen Haber. New York: St. Martin's Press, 2001. 215–29. Print.

Yates, Jessica. "J. R. R. Tolkien: Overview." *Twentieth-Century Children's Writers*. 4th ed. Ed. Laura Standley Berger, 1995. *Literature Resource Center*. Online Database. Web. 7 July 2014.

Power in Arda:
Sources, Uses and Misuses

Edith L. Crowe

A fine American cartoonist, Nicole Hollander, titled one of her collections *Ma, Can I Be a Feminist and Still Like Men?* Her punch line wasn't too encouraging: "Sure, just like you can be a vegetarian and like fried chicken." (We must remember humor often exaggerates for its effects.) The question I'm here to answer is a similar one: "Ma, can I be a feminist and still like Tolkien?" Obviously my answer is going to be a more positive one, since I am, and do. To be very practical about it, fantasy readers of my generation would have had precious little to read years ago if we had limited ourselves to works fully in tune with our feminist principles.

Females of later generations are often less forgiving. The reaction of a friend's daughter, age five, upon hearing *The Hobbit* for the first time, was: "Mommy, aren't there any *girls* in this story?" Her mother was forced to admit that, by and large, there weren't. The most problematic aspect of Tolkien is indeed the disappointingly low percentage of females that appear in his best-known and best-loved works, *The Hobbit* and *The Lord of the Rings*. I don't intend to castigate Tolkien for this, though I certainly regret it. He was reflecting his sources and his times. Neither am I going to claim he was a hidden feminist—not the man who, in 1943, viewed with such alarm the possibility of a post-war world over-run with such horrors as "American sanitation, morale-pep, feminism, and mass production" (*Letters* 65).

I would dearly love to know what he had against American sanitation, and how he defined it. I would also like to know how he defined feminism, since my experience has been that no two people mean the same thing by that rather charged word. However, to say that Tolkien's work is completely incompatible with feminism is to accept not only too limited a view of Tolkien's writings, but too narrow a definition of feminism. Tolkien's work is much richer than that, particularly if we include *The Silmarillion, Unfinished Tales*, and his other posthumous works. There are many interpretations of feminism, and some aspects are more compatible with Tolkien than others.

For instance, there has been a difference of opinion in feminism between "social constructionists" and "essentialists" (although the former seem to have pretty much won the field). The former claim that an individual's identity as "male" or "female" is almost purely a result of learning—of nurture, if you will, both within the family and in the larger context of the world outside it. Essentialists feel that there is indeed a basic difference between men and women beyond the biologically obvious, and that the problem is that the natures of each sex are not equally valued. I suspect the truth, as it does in most things, lies somewhere in between.

At first, the main concern of feminists was to increase the participation and influence of women in society as it was, in politics, in professions historically closed to women, in education, etc. In a later stage, one begins to ask larger questions about the basic values of the society itself. A good example is the thorny question of women in the military—should one be working to increase the numbers of women in the military, or to change one's society in a more fundamental way and abolish or shrink the military?

We now come close to the place where Tolkien and feminism, while coming from very different places, grapple with some of the same issues. Many of those issues center on power—where it comes from, who has it, the different ways in which it is utilized, and what constitutes legitimate or illegitimate use. It is my contention that in Middle-earth, Tolkien exhibits *attitudes toward power* that are quite compatible with, if not identical to, the attitudes of many who define themselves as feminists.

The first thing to look at is the ultimate source of power in Middle-earth. That source is divine, because it resides in Eru Ilúvatar. Of all the beings that we meet in Tolkien's subcreated universe, only Eru is omnipotent. Only he possesses the Flame Imperishable, and is therefore capable of creation of the Ainur *ex nihilo*. And as he tells Melkor, "no theme may be played that hath not its uttermost source in me, nor can any alter the music in my despite" (*S* 17). Although many other beings have the ability to alter Arda in major and minor ways, for good or ill, only Eru has the power to completely transcend it as he does when Númenor is destroyed and Valinor removed from the circles of the world. In addition, only Eru is omniscient: "to none but himself has Ilúvatar revealed all that he has in store" (*S* 18), not even to the Ainur. Eru is also portrayed as male, in a manner very reminiscent of Yahweh, of "God the Father" in the Judeo-Christian tradition. In that tradition, although the Hebrew word Elohim has both feminine and masculine roots (incidentally explaining how in the first creation story in Genesis both woman and man could be created in Elohim's image), all the other appellations of the deity, such as King, Lord, Father, and Shepherd, are specifically male (Eisler 94).

So Eru—or Ilúvatar, "Father of All" in Quenya—is firmly within a familiar patriarchal religious tradition. However, Eru seems to be much better at delegating authority than Yahweh, because, with the exception mentioned above, he does not interfere directly in the further creation and operation of Arda. Here we begin to part company with the Judeo-Christian model in ways that Tolkien found acceptable within his religious tradition but also give some satisfaction to the many within and without that tradition who hunger for a female conception of deity. In his subcreation of the Valar, Tolkien has managed to incorporate female power at the penultimate level at least. At this point, he seems to reveal himself as an essentialist where male and female natures are concerned:

> But when they desire to clothe themselves the Valar take upon them forms some as of male and some as of female; for that difference of temper they had even from their beginning, and it is but bodied forth in the choice of each, not made by the choice. (*S* 21)

Although he may give pride of place to the male, Tolkien has also given us a number of powerful female characters among the Valar. Varda, for example, although technically second to Manwë, actually has a greater presence in Middle-earth (especially in *The Lord of the Rings*) due to the reverence in which the Elves hold her and their tendency to call upon her frequently. She is the closest thing Arda has to a Goddess. Although Tolkien's religious beliefs would not allow him to conceptualize her as such, her creation of the stars suggests the Queen of Heaven, an appellation not only of Mary, the mother of Jesus, but of Isis, the great goddess of the ancient world to whom Mary owes many of her attributes. A suggestion of her power and significance is the intriguing fact that Melkor "feared her more than all others whom Eru made" (*S* 26).

If Varda suggests the Great Goddess—the goddess as Creatrix—the other female Valar (the *Valier*) encompass other aspects of the

Goddess. Yavanna is very much the Earth Mother: her Eldarin surname, Kementari, means Queen of the Earth; her role as the source of growing things is suggestive of Ceres or Demeter. The maiden aspect of the Goddess (although neither are actually maidens) is found in Nessa, the sister of Oromë the hunter, who is fleet of foot and loves deer (like Artemis), and in Vaná, younger sister of Yavanna, who causes flowers to open if she looks at them and birds to sing at her coming. She is like a Persephone who need never fear that a Hades will carry her off.

The Valier associated with giving rest and healing to the hurt and weary (Estë) or with the Halls of Mandos where the dead wait (Nienna and Vairë) suggest the aspect of Goddess as Crone: that aspect associated with the end of life rather than its beginning. Therefore, although Eru is definitely portrayed as male, that is the only level of being at which a strong female presence is absent. Although one only familiar with *The Hobbit* and *The Lord of the Rings* might be forgiven for concluding that Tolkien was lacking in recognition of the importance of the feminine, the Valier alone should go far to contradict that conclusion. Although the ultimate deity is male, spiritual power, as embodied in the Valar, is almost equally the province of male and female.

Already this is an improvement over the Primary World, since its major religions are not oversupplied with images of female spiritual power. As we move to the level of the Children of Ilúvatar, Elves and Men, another significant difference appears. In Judeo-Christian (and to some extent Islamic) traditions, woman (in the person of Eve) has been "blamed for nothing less than our fall from paradise" (Eisler 190). Considering how often that belief has been used to justify the subordination and persecution of women, it is extremely refreshing to encounter a secondary world in which the Fall of both Elves and Men is a male's fault. Interestingly enough, in both cases the action which brings about the Fall is preceded by an insufficiency of the "feminine principle," as in Fëanor's case, or in active damage to it, as in Ar-Pharazôn's.

In her excellent *Mythlore* article on "The Feminine Principle in Tolkien," Melanie Rawls points out that "Through *The Silmarillion* runs this theme: in Arda and in the Heavens, the Feminine and the Masculine are present; when they are in equilibrium and in harmony, there is Good, but Evil is the result of an insufficiency or a disharmony of the attributes of one or the other of the genders" (5).

Another important point she makes is that this equilibrium and harmony can be achieved either by the balance of masculine and feminine qualities within an individual, or by a less integrated being who has "access to the nature of the other gender, usually in the form of a spouse, a sibling, or a mentor" (Rawls 5). Fëanor can hardly be blamed for the absence of his mother, but he is culpable for ignoring the advice of his wiser and more patient wife. Tolkien tells us that Nerdanel "restrained [Fëanor] when the fire of his heart grew too hot" (*S* 64). This female restraint of male misuse of power has a precedent among the Maiar: Uinen, Lady of the Seas, not only "can lay calm upon the waves, restraining the wildness of Ossë" her spouse, but she even kept Ossë from succumbing to the temptation of Melkor (*S* 30). Fëanor, alas, was not so wise.

This theme permeates Tolkien's work: the absolute necessity of both male and female elements, however defined, for the proper functioning of both individuals and societies. More importantly, he recognizes the interdependence of male and female, and suggests repeatedly that to ignore one at the expense of the other is a grave mistake which at the very least diminishes the individual and at the worst can lead to disaster for both the individual and the society. Not only are Manwë and Varda the supreme powers among the Valar, but they enhance each other's power: "When Manwë [...] ascends his throne and looks forth, if Varda is beside him, he sees further than all other eyes [...] And if Manwë is with her, Varda hears more clearly than all other ears" (*S* 26).

Although the presence of the Valier and the absence of an Eve figure provide a strong sense of female spiritual power, Middle-earth still exhibits an almost invariably patriarchal and patrilineal political and social organization. Manwë clearly possesses the highest authority among the Valar, and among the peoples of Middle-earth, the norm in both government and the family is that the highest authority is male. This follows from the position of Eru, since in the primary world, "Religions in which the most powerful or only deity is male tend to reflect a social order in which descent is patrilinear [...] and domicile is patrilocal [...] religions in which the most powerful or sole deity is female tend to reflect a social order in which descent is matrilinear [...] and domicile is likewise matrilocal" (Eisler 24).

We now move to the level of temporal power, although among the Eldar and Edain, at least, spiritual and temporal powers are to some extent interwoven. There are many varieties of temporal power, from many sources. Two of the more outer-directed are physical strength/skill; or power based in formal authority and/or the possession of tangible resources—that is, political/economic power. Power can also arise from "personal magnetism, attractiveness, or charisma" or from "access to information, particularly information that others do not have or cannot understand" (Lips 5–6). Although the latter two types are more evenly distributed between men and women, physical or political power seems to be associated rarely with women. It does, however, exist, especially among the Eldar. Aredhel Ar-Feiniel (the White Lady of the Noldor) "was tall and strong, and loved much to ride and hunt in the forests" (*S* 60).

The Galadriel that we see in *The Lord of the Rings* is clearly a great power—greatest among the Elves of Middle-earth—but in that work we see only the tip of the iceberg. Galadriel seemed to hold a particular fascination for Tolkien, since he continued to work on her character and history until the end of his life. In a letter written only a month before his death she is clearly much on his mind (*Letters* 431). After first meeting her in *The Lord of the Rings*, it is fascinating to read descriptions of Galadriel in the First Age which indicate a previously unstressed physical ability. We learn that her mother's name for her was Nerwen, or "man-maiden": that "she grew to be tall beyond the measure even of the women of the Noldor; she was strong of body, mind, and will." Her depth of knowledge comes as no surprise, but we also learn that she was "a match for both the loremasters and the *athletes* of the Eldar" (*UT* 229, emphasis added).

Her physical strength and courage are not limited to athletics. In one version of the Noldorian rebellion, Galadriel was at Alqualondë considering departure from Middle-earth for her own reasons, and "fought fiercely against Fëanor in defense of her mother's kin" during the Kinslaying (*UT* 230). In such a context, one can only assume a fight of the physical sort. In another version of the revolt, Fëanor leaves Fingolfin's people stranded in the Northern Waste, and Galadriel is among the small band that leads their people overland to Middle-earth.

"Few of the deeds of the Noldor thereafter surpassed that desperate crossing in hardihood or woe" (*S* 90).

There are enough women in Middle-earth who possess both physical courage and political leadership ability to suggest that Tolkien did not believe that lack of these qualities was an essential aspect of femaleness. Why then are examples not more frequent? Part of the reason is, as noted above, a patriarchal social structure derived from a spiritual hierarchy with Eru on top. Another part of the reason may be the fact that for so many of the peoples of Middle-earth, having to fight almost constant battles against Melkor, Sauron, or their minions, the political leader of the group was also the military leader. Although the women of the Eldar and Edain are certainly capable of fighting in many instances, it tends to be in last-ditch defense of their homes and children, rather than organized warfare taken outside their territory.

In an extensive cross-cultural study of Primary World societies, Peggy Sanday discovered that women seldom engage in warfare, not necessarily because their culture views them as incapable of it, but because this is seen as inappropriate or too risky. Even in cultures where women have power and authority, they may believe "it is more efficient for women to delegate than to monopolize power. Since women are the potential bearers of new additions to the population, it would scarcely be expedient to place them on the front line at the hunt and in warfare" (Sanday 115).

This common belief may explain the rarity of female political leaders in Middle-earth. On the other hand, it may be a result of the Primary World attitude, especially prevalent since the Industrial Revolution, that the woman's domain is the domestic and private sphere, and the public world of commerce and politics the man's—an attitude particularly pervasive in nineteenth-century Britain and America, and still influential in Tolkien's formative years.

There are actually a number of interesting examples of women warriors in Middle-earth who fit this model of defenders of the home. One of the most interesting women of the Edain is Haleth, "a woman of great heart and strength." When her father and brother were killed by Orcs, "Haleth held the people together, though they were without hope" for seven days, until rescued by a force led by the Elf Caranthir. She was not only valiant in arms, but must have been an exceptional political leader. The people "took Haleth for their chief" and they "were ever after known to Elves and Men as the People of Haleth." She kept her people moving west through difficult circumstances, "constraining them to go forward by the strength of her will" (*S* 146–47). In another description of the people of Haleth, Tolkien states: "One of the strange practices spoken of was that many of their warriors were women, though few of these went abroad to fight in the great battles. This custom was evidently ancient; for their chieftainess Haleth was a renowned Amazon with a picked bodyguard of women" (*UT* 377).

Another rather Amazonian figure is Emeldir the Manhearted, wife of Barahir and mother of Beren. Although she would have preferred "to fight beside her son and her husband than to flee," she "gathered together all the women and children that were left, and gave arms to those that would bear them; and she led them into the mountains" (*S* 155). Clearly, Beren inherited his heroism from both sides.

In the late 1800s of the Third Age, the Wainriders warred against Rohan and Gondor. Left behind to defend the home front were youths, old men . . . and young women "who in that people were also trained in arms and fought fiercely in defense of their homes and their children" (*UT* 290). Éowyn is also presumably trained in arms, although it is never explained in detail what being a shieldmaiden of the Rohirrim entails. She is a skilled enough rider to be part of the difficult ride to Gondor, and a sufficiently skilled fighter to acquit herself well in the Battle of the Pelennor Fields even before she dispatches the greatest of the Ringwraiths—with a little help from prophecy and a halfling. She is also not without a measure of political power: the suggestion that Éowyn serve as "Lord" of the Eorlingas in the absence of Théoden and Éomer comes from her own people, and is another example of the woman warrior's role as defender of the homestead. It is also an example of something we see in other peoples: that lineage and family are often more important than gender in legitimizing female political power. In Éowyn's case, being a member of the House of Eorl is apparently more important than her sex. That also may be the explanation that the eldest child of the Númenórean monarch should wear the crown, not the eldest son (although Tolkien was inconsistent on this point) (*LotR* Appendix A.I.iv.1049; *UT* 208–09, 225–26).

Women of the Eldar can be formidable in battle as well, but the nature of their power is harder to categorize. Lúthien certainly shows physical courage in her travels with Beren to confront Sauron and later Morgoth (not to mention considerable intelligence and initiative in getting away from her father, in a tale which reads like a feminist retelling of Rapunzel). But her greatest power is that of Elven "magic," for lack of a better term, which is essentially a spiritual power: "Then Lúthien stood upon the bridge, and declared her power: and the spell was loosed that bound stone to stone, and the gates were thrown down, and the walls opened, and the pits laid bare" (*S* 175).

The recovery of the Silmaril utilizes this same "magic," with a bit of that charismatic power of attractiveness thrown in. Morgoth makes the mistake of leaving Lúthien free at first so he can ogle her, giving her the opportunity to sing him and his entire court to sleep so Beren can take a Silmaril. Leveling fortresses is a talent possessed by Galadriel also; the appendix to *The Lord of the Rings* tells us that after the fall of Sauron, Celeborn leads the people of Lórien on an assault against Dol Guldur. When they were successful, "Galadriel threw down its walls and laid bare its pits" (*LotR* App.B.1094).

We have considered the source of power, and seen that it is primarily "religious" or spiritual. The creatures of Arda may be able to use that power directly, such as the Valar and Maiar; they may be capable of a "magic" that derives from it; or they may inherit political power that derives from it. The rulers of Númenor are priest-kings (and occasionally queens) and their later descendants divine-right monarchs. All these types of power are available to both males and females, though not equally.

The power of males in Middle-earth is manifested more frequently in those areas which are more obvious and which the culture of our primary world considers more important: warfare, commerce, the holding of political office. However, although Arda is hardly a feminist utopia (whatever that might be), it has its share of powerful and renowned females, and a spiritual tradition which includes a strong female dimension.

There is one more aspect of power we need to consider, however: its use and misuse. Tolkien's attitudes toward the proper and improper use of power permeate all his writings. More than anything else, his beliefs on this point toward a society that, in its ideal form, shares many traits with a society envisioned by some feminists.

Riane Eisler, in *The Chalice and the Blade* (1988), reviews a vast amount of archaeological and other evidence which suggests that Neolithic societies that worshipped a female deity or deities were not matriarchies, as turn-of-the-century scholars mistakenly concluded, but egalitarian societies which were supplanted by Indo-European invaders who associated power with the ability to destroy rather than nurture.[1] From her study of these various cultures, Eisler derives two basic models of society:

> The first, which I call the *dominator model,* is what is popularly termed either patriarchy or matriarchy—the *ranking* of one half of humanity over the other. The second, in which social relations are primarily based on the principle of *linking* rather than ranking, may best be described as the *partnership* model. In this model—beginning with the most fundamental difference [...] between male and female—diversity is not equated with either inferiority or superiority. (xvii)

In many ways, this could serve as a good description for Arda.

Although from Eru's realm down to the humblest Hobbit-hole this universe is hierarchically structured, Eisler does not view hierarchy as automatically negative. She distinguishes "domination hierarchies," based on force or the express or implied threat of force, from "actualization hierarchies" which are found in progressions from lower to higher orders of functioning (like those in biological systems, for example) (106). Many of the hierarchies in Middle-earth arise not because Tolkien thinks one group is inherently better than another, but because peoples develop differently due to choices that were made.

Throughout *Splintered Light,* Verlyn Flieger seems to suggest a spiritual hierarchy in Arda based on a group's distance from the light of Valinor, that is, from the spiritual. Thus the preeminent position of the

---

1. At the time this paper was published in 1996, the work of archaeologist Marij Gimbutas—upon which Eisler relies heavily—was controversial. It still is, although of less significance to current archaeology. Many scholars considered her interpretation of European prehistory more a feminist wish-fulfillment fantasy than rigorous analysis of the evidence. Others welcomed it as a long-needed corrective to many years of exclusively male (and possibly wish-fulfilling) interpretations of archaeological evidence. I lack the qualifications to judge, and besides, it is irrelevant to my work. How much *The Chalice and the Blade* is based on real prehistoric societies matters less than the fact that the concepts/models Eisler introduces now exist. A model that is no longer considered useful in its original field can still yield valuable insights when applied by another. A good example of this is Freud's *eros/thanatos* dichotomy. Consider this some grains of salt which you can sprinkle on this paper if you wish.

Eldar among the Elves and the Númeónreans among Men is based on the choices they made to move closer to the light, the spiritual, and their long dwelling within its influence. Tolkien's treatment of such groups as the Easterlings and the Southrons has unfortunate overtones of racism to the modern ear. I doubt Tolkien intended it that way; his ringing denunciation of German racial attitudes prior to World War II suggests otherwise (*Letters* 37–38), as does a letter sent to Christopher while he was serving in South Africa (73–74). The evil of the Easterlings, Southrons, Wainriders, etc., lies not in any inherent quality, but in the fact that they succumbed to the temptations of the Shadow. Other Men not of the Edain (Woses, Dunlendings) are good but lesser beings who never went to Númenor, but did resist Melkor and Sauron.

Tolkien certainly seems to feel that men and women have different, and sometimes contradictory, talents, interests, and attitudes. By and large, women are associated with the domestic and family sphere rather than the outer world; with insight and wisdom rather than physical prowess; with nature, especially in its domesticated form, rather than crafts of the more technological sort. However, Tolkien is not consistent in this, and the more we learn of his work the less essentialist he appears.

For example, in such couples as Tom Bombadil and Goldberry, or the Ents and the Entwives, the females seem to be associated with domesticated nature and the males with nature "in the raw." But is this really true? Tom and Fangorn are not hunters, but husbandmen. Their relationship to nature is not as different from their female counterparts as it first appears, indeed, being more a difference in degree than in kind. And in the tale of "Aldarion and Erendis" from *Unfinished Tales*, it is Erendis who values the trees for themselves, in their natural state, and Aldarion who is more concerned with their "domestication" for human use. Whatever Tolkien's personal feelings might have been—and in deference to his well-known dislike for criticism via biography I do not intend to address that—his work exhibits a more complicated attitude toward appropriate male and female roles than is immediately apparent.

The more important point is not the fixity of the boundaries between male and female spheres, but the fact that their relationship is one of linking, not ranking. To quote Melanie Rawls again: "There is no war between the sexes in Tolkien's subcreation. Complementary and mutually augmenting positive feminine and masculine qualities are set against enantiodromic, negative feminine and masculine qualities. Feminine and Masculine are diverse—not subordinate nor antagonistic to one another" (13). Not only is that a fair assessment of Tolkien's work, it's a good description of what Eisler would call a partnership society.

Another important characteristic of Tolkien's universe is the refreshing absence of violence against women *as women*. In a dominator society, this is a basic characteristic. Middle-earth certainly contains violence against women, but the perpetrators are those who are equally violent against everybody (Orcs, for example). Mutual violence and antagonism in Middle-earth depend on what people one belongs to, not which sex, and usually have their roots in some past event (such as the long-standing feud between Elves and Dwarves) or some action of Morgoth or Sauron (special hatred of Orcs for Elves explained by the possibility that the former were bred from the latter).

The most flagrant examples of violence against women are the two forced marriages of Númenórean kings in their spiritual decline—that of Ar-Gimilzôr to the Lady Inzilbêth, and later Ar-Pharazôn's treatment of Tar-Míriel. Not only did he usurp her throne but forced her into an incestuous marriage which, under the circumstances, can be viewed as nothing less than rape. This terrible and uncharacteristic (for Númenóreans in general) treatment of a woman is symbolic of the magnitude of Ar-Pharazôn's evil. Generally, men (or Elves) who treat women poorly come to a bad end. Eöl's marriage to Aredhel results as much from deceit as from force, but he comes to a bad end as well.

Another example of oppressive behavior toward women is the tendency of Elven fathers to restrict their daughters' freedom to marry. Thingol is the most blatant example, since he actually resorts at one point to imprisoning Lúthien, but Elrond also forbids the marriage of Arwen and Aragorn, at least until certain demanding conditions are met. But is this type of behavior only directed against women? Would an Elven father act the same way if his son wanted to make what he considered an inappropriate marriage? I don't think there's enough evidence to reach a judgment. Thingol aside, it's possible such prohibitions owe their power more to the reverence and love

Elven daughters (and sons) seem to have for their fathers than to any belief such prohibitions would be otherwise enforced.

Eisler describes the power she symbolizes by the blade as "[t]he power to dominate and destroy" as opposed to that of the chalice, "the view of power as the capacity to support and nurture life" (53), and points out that "many women and men are frontally challenging destructive myths, such as the 'hero as killer' " (188–89). I think Tolkien can be counted among them. One of the most pervasive themes in his work is the association of the dominating power of the blade with evil and the nurturing power of the chalice with good. The whole point of *The Lord of the Rings* is, after all, the renunciation of the power of domination, whereas "The Enemy in successive forms is always 'naturally' concerned with sheer Domination" (*Letters* 146).

Tolkien's heroes may kill, but they are by no means the hero *as* killer. When they kill without need, such as Fëanor did at the Kinslaying, this is portrayed as a great wrong, and its negative consequences reverberate throughout the ages in Middle-earth. There is a great deal of killing, particularly in *The Silmarillion*, but it is either in self-defense or evil if it is not. It is attributed to the baleful influence of Melkor or Sauron, a symptom of Arda Marred. The heroes of Middle-earth go to war reluctantly, and only when their only other choice is to succumb to the greater evil of domination by the Shadow.

In fact, some of the greatest heroes of Middle-earth are those whose decision *not* to kill proves to have important consequences: if Faramir had not stayed his hand against Frodo and Sam; if Aragorn and the Wood-elves and Frodo had not spared Gollum, Sauron would have been triumphant. One of the things that sets apart *The Lord of the Rings* from most other works of contemporary fantasy (besides its sheer quality and richness) is this theme of the renunciation of power. Those on the side of good in Middle-earth are certainly capable of wielding the Ring, but recognize in their wisdom that to use that power—the power of the blade—would lead to the destruction of their essential selves.

Creative, life-affirming, and nurturing powers are those associated with good in Middle-earth, and are found in both male and female. For example, Lúthien and Aragorn are healers. In fact, it is the ability to heal, rather than any military prowess, which marks Aragorn as the True King. Faramir, Gandalf, Galadriel, Bilbo and Frodo show reverence for the art and learning of the past; Bombadil, Goldberry, Ents and Entwives, Elves, Men and Hobbits reverence and care for the natural world in their different ways. Tolkien's ecological consciousness was ahead of its time, and in many ways worthy of a contemporary ecofeminist. The nurturing values of home and hearth may be more frequently ascribed to females, but they are given great importance and respect, not denigrated as they are so often in the Primary World.

This, then, is why I conclude that a person of feminist persuasion, while not necessarily agreeing with Tolkien's attitudes *in toto*, can find much to appreciate in his work. Arda is a world in which females share power in spiritual and temporal realms, although not always to the degree a feminist might wish. More importantly, it is a world in which attitudes and values associated in the Primary World with the feminine are highly valued. Indeed, these "feminine" values triumph at the end of the Third Age, though not always incarnate in female bodies. Though Tolkien's road was his interpretation of Christianity, and Eisler's (and mine) our interpretation of feminism, the destination seems to have a great deal in common. Our mutual task in the Fourth Age is to resist the temptation to divide and dominate, whether we characterize this misuse of power as that of the Blade or the Ring. May Varda look with favor upon our efforts.

This article was published originally in the Proceedings of the J. R. R. Tolkien Centenary Conference, 1992, *edited by Patricia Reynolds and Glen H. GoodKnight (Altadena, CA: Mythopoeic Press, 1995): 272–77. It is reprinted here with permission.*

Works Cited

Eisler, Riane. *The Chalice and the Blade.* 25th anniversary ed. San Francisco: HarperSanFrancisco, 1995. Print.

Flieger, Verlyn. *Splintered Light: Logos and Language in Tolkien's World.* Grand Rapids, MI: Wm. B. Eerdmans, 1983. Print.

Hollander, Nicole. *"Ma, can I be a feminist and still like men?": Lyrics from Life.* New York: Saint Martin's Press, 1980. Print.

Lips, Hilary M. *Women, Men, and the Psychology of Power.* Englewood Cliffs, NJ: Prentice-Hall, 1981. Print.

Rawls, Melanie. "The Feminine Principle in Tolkien." *Mythlore* 10.4 (#38) (Spring 1984): 5–13. Print. *Reprinted in this volume.*

Sanday, Peggy Reeves. *Female Power and Male Dominance.* Cambridge, UK: Cambridge UP, 1981. Print.

Specific Characters

The Fall and Repentance of Galadriel

Romuald I. Lakowski

Although Galadriel is one of the best known and best loved characters in *The Lord of the Rings*, surprisingly little has been written about her. It is true that she only really plays an important role in the Lothlórien episode in Book II.6–8, and at the very end of Book VI. Part of the problem is that the story of her past life in Middle-earth was never really told in *The Lord of the Rings*, but only hinted at in the "Lament of Galadriel" (*LotR* II.8.373–74). Tolkien himself obviously felt dissatisfied by his treatment of Galadriel after *The Lord of the Rings* was published, and he elaborated on her history in several late writings, including post-*Lord of the Rings* versions of *The Silmarillion*, some of his late letters, the section on "The History of Galadriel and Celeborn" in the *Unfinished Tales*, and some notes that Tolkien himself supplied to Donald Swann's Song Cycle *The Road Goes Ever On*, first published in 1967. In addition, Volumes 6–9 and 12 of *The History of Middle-earth* also contain early drafts of *The Lord of the Rings*, which allow us to see more clearly the emergence of Galadriel into the narrative. In several of these late writings Tolkien elaborated a story of Galadriel's Fall and Repentance, only to repudiate it in the final year of his life.[1]

Perhaps the most succinct statement of the later story of Galadriel's Fall and Repentance can be found in a letter to Mrs. Ruth Austin on 25th Jan. 1971, written only two years before Tolkien's death:

> I was particularly interested in your comments about Galadriel [...] I think it is true that I owe much of this character to Christian and Catholic teaching and imagination about Mary, but actually Galadriel was a penitent: in her youth a leader in the rebellion against the Valar (the angelic guardians). At the end of the First Age she proudly refused forgiveness or permission to return. She was pardoned because of her resistance to the final and overwhelming temptation to take the Ring for herself. (*Letters* 407)

1. For two earlier studies of Galadriel in the First Age, see Johnson 11–14 (who anticipates some of my own conclusions); Bridoux 19–23.

In the draft of an earlier letter to Mr. Rang dated Aug. 1967, Tolkien states that "The Exiles [who fled from Valimar] were allowed to return—save for a few chief actors in the rebellion of whom at the time of the *L.R.* only *Galadriel* remained" (*Letters* 386, emphasis in original). In a note attached to this passage, Tolkien further explains that

> At the time of her lament in Lórien she believed this to be perennial, as long as Earth endured. Hence she concludes her lament with a wish or prayer that Frodo may as a special grace be granted a purgatorial (but not penal) sojourn in *Eressea,* the Solitary Isle in sight of *Aman,* though for her the way is closed. [...] Her prayer was granted—but also her personal ban was lifted, in reward for her services against Sauron, and above all for her rejection of the temptation to take the Ring when offered to her. So at the end we see her taking ship. (386)

About the same time as this letter was written Tolkien added some notes to *Ai! laurië lantar lassi súrinen* "Galadriel's Lament in Lórien," no.5 in Donald Swann's 1967 Song Cycle *The Road Goes Ever On,* which was originally published in the "Farewell to Lórien" chapter in *The Lord of the Rings.* In commenting on the line *Sí man i yulma nin enquantuva?* ("Who now shall refill the cup for me?") (*LotR* II.8.377), and on the question *What ship would bear me ever back across so wide a Sea?* at the end of her earlier song ("I sang of leaves, of leaves of gold, and leaves of gold there grew") (II.8.372), Tolkien explains that

> [Galadriel] was the last survivor of the princes and queens who had led the revolting *Noldor* to exile in Middle-earth. After the overthrow of *Morgoth* at the end of the First Age a ban was set upon her return, and she had replied proudly that she had no wish to do so. She passed over the Mountains of *Eredluin* with her husband *Celeborn* (one of the *Sindar*) and went to *Eregion.* But it was impossible for one of the High-Elves to overcome the yearning for the Sea, and the longing to pass over it again to the land of their former bliss. She was now burdened with this desire. In the event, after the fall of *Sauron,* in reward for all that she had done to oppose him, but above all for her rejection of the Ring when it came within her power, the ban was lifted, and she returned over the Sea, as is told at the end of *The Lord of the Rings.* (Swann and Tolkien 68)

In another late work "Of Dwarves and Men," dating from after June 1969 (*Peoples* 293) and also referring to the notes to the "Lament of Galadriel" in *A Road Goes Ever On,* Tolkien comments that

> the Farewell was addressed direct to Frodo, and was an extempore outpouring in free rhythmic style, reflecting the overwhelming increase in her regret and longing, and her personal despair after she had survived the terrible temptation. [...] In the event it proved that it was Galadriel's abnegation of pride and trust in her own powers, and her absolute refusal of any unlawful enhancement of them, that provided the ship to bear her back to her home. (*Peoples* 320–21)

Tolkien also refers again to the "Lament of Galadriel" in yet another late work, "The Shibboleth of Fëanor," dating from after Feb. 1968: "Her Lament—spoken before she knew of the pardon (and indeed honour) that the Valar gave her—harks back to the days of her youth in Valinor and to the darkness of the years of Exile while the Blessed Realm was closed to all the Noldor in Middle-earth" (*Peoples* 338–39).

The agreement of these five late witnesses, all dating from the period between 1967 and 1971, is impressive, but unfortunately nothing about Tolkien's late writings is simple. There are other late accounts that contradict this clear narrative of Fall and Redemption. Nor is the exact nature of Galadriel's Fall ever clearly spelled out.

Galadriel in The Silmarillion

The Silmarillion, published in 1977 after Tolkien's death, has remarkably little to say about Galadriel's part in the rebellion of the Noldor. All we are told is that "Galadriel, the only woman of the Noldor to stand that day tall and valiant among the contending princes, was eager to be gone. No oaths she swore, but the words of Fëanor [her uncle] concerning Middle-earth had kindled in her heart, for she yearned to see the wide unguarded lands and to rule there a realm at her own will" (*S* 83–84).

There is no mention of a specific ban on the return of Galadriel, only of the general Doom or Curse of Mandos on the rebels, especially the House of Fëanor, for the kinslaying of the Teleri at Alqualondë (*S* 85–90). In *The Silmarillion*, Galadriel herself was not involved in the kinslaying. However, she was tainted by association, because she was the niece of Fëanor and especially because she had Telerian blood in her through her mother Eärwen, the daughter of Olwë Lord of the Teleri. Thus, in *The Silmarillion*, Galadriel's "sin" is primarily one of omission. On arriving in Middle-earth after the tortuous crossing of the Helcaraxë (the Grinding Ice) necessitated by Fëanor's burning of the ships at Losgar (*S* 97), Galadriel dwelt for a time in Doriath, where she met her future husband Celeborn, kinsman of Thingol, King of Doriath and brother of Olwë. (Thus, Thingol was also Galadriel's maternal uncle.)[2] There, Galadriel also befriended Melian the Maia, wife of Thingol and mother of Lúthien Tinúviel. From Melian, Galadriel "learned great lore and wisdom concerning Middle-earth" (*S* 115),[3] and she stayed with her when her brother Finrod Felagund went off to found Nargothrond.

When Melian asked Galadriel about the flight of the Noldor, she replied: " 'we were not driven forth, but came of our own will, and against that of the Valar. And through great peril and in despite of the Valar for this purpose we came: to take vengeance upon Morgoth, and regain what he stole.' [...] but still she said no word of the Oath [of Fëanor], nor of the Kinslaying, nor of the burning of the ships at Losgar" (*S* 127). Melian, nonetheless, guessed that Galadriel was hiding some dark secret and warned Thingol, and he eventually learned the truth from Círdan the Shipwright, who had heard dark rumors about the kinslaying. When Galadriel's brothers, the "sons of Finarfin," came to visit her in Doriath, Thingol angrily confronted them with these rumors. One of them, Angrod, confessed the truth, but tried to exonerate the house of Finarfin from blame: "Then Angrod spoke bitterly against the sons of Fëanor, telling of the blood at Alqualondë, and the Doom of Mandos, and the burning of the ships at Losgar. And he cried: 'Wherefore should we that endured the Grinding Ice [*Helcaraxë*] bear the name of kinslayers and traitors?' " (*S* 129).[4] However, Melian replied with prophetic foresight: "Yet the

---

2. See entry for Year 1280 of "The Annals of Aman" in *Morgoth* 93, 104.

3. In the draft text for this passage, we are told that there Galadriel "received the love of Melian" (*Jewels* 178); cf. *Jewels* 35, "there was much love between them" (in *The Silmarillion* this phrase is applied instead to Galadriel's relationship with Celeborn; *S* 115). See also the rumor reported in the drafts of "Of the Rings of Power and the Third Age": "For it is said by some that she was a handmaid of Melian the Immortal in the realm of Doriath" (*Peoples* 185); cf. *Treason* 265–66, n. 31 (qtd. in note 6).

4. In a draft text for this passage in "The Grey Annals," note to Year 66, §95, Galadriel herself denies any complicity on the part of her family: "and being perplexed and recalling suddenly with anger the words of Caranthir [one of the Sons of Fëanor] she said ere she could set a guard on her tongue: 'For already the children of Finrod [later Finarfin] are charged with talebearing and treason to their kindred. Yet we at least were guiltless, and suffered evil ourselves.' And Melian spoke no more of these things with Galaðriel" (*Jewels* 119).

shadow of Mandos lies on you also" (129), and like Fëanor and his sons, the sons of Finarfin also all perished in Middle-earth.

By implication, the shadow of Mandos also falls on Galadriel as well. However, at the end of the published "Quenta Silmarillion," Galadriel is clearly included in the general pardon of the Valar at the end of the First Age. We are told that the Elves of Beleriand were admitted again to the love of Manwë and the pardon of the Valar; and the Teleri forgave their ancient grief, and the curse was laid to rest. Yet not all the Eldalië were willing to forsake the Hither Lands where they had long suffered and long dwelt; and some lingered many an age in Middle-earth. Among these were Círdan the Shipwright, and Celeborn of Doriath, with Galadriel his wife, who alone remained of those who led the Noldor to exile in Beleriand (*S* 254).

In *The Lord of the Rings* itself, though there is sadness in the speech of Galadriel in the chapter "The Mirror of Galadriel," there is nothing to indicate that her stay in Middle-earth is unwilling: "For the Lord of the Galadhrim [Celeborn] is accounted the wisest of the Elves of Middle-earth, and a giver of gifts beyond the power of kings. He has dwelt in the West since the days of dawn, and I have dwelt with him years uncounted; for ere the fall of Nargothrond or Gondolin I passed over the mountains, and together through the ages of the world we have fought the long defeat" (*LotR* II.7.357).

The early drafts of this passage, written in 1942, are more explicit, and strongly suggest that Tolkien already (before Galadriel had entered the *Silmarillion* tradition in 1951) conceived of Galadriel as a (voluntary) exile from Valinor: "The lord and lady of Lothlórien are accounted wise beyond the measure of the Elves of Middle-earth, and of all who have not passed beyond the Seas. For we have dwelt here since the Mountains were reared and the Sun was young" (*Treason* 248).[5] In "Of the Rings of Power and the Third Age" in *The Silmarillion,* we find the similar statement (but with more emphasis on the power of Galadriel): "A queen she was of the woodland Elves, the wife of

5. See *Treason* 263, n.12. A further addition to the manuscript of one of the drafts makes the connection more explicit: "And I have dwelt here with him since the days of dawn, when I passed over the seas with Melian of Valinor; and ever together we have fought the long defeat" (*Treason* 265, n.31). For Galadriel's relationship with Melian, see also n.4 above.

Celeborn of Doriath, yet she herself was of the Noldor and remembered the Day before days in Valinor, and she was the mightiest and fairest of all the Elves that remained in Middle-earth" (*S* 298).[6]

Although *The Silmarillion* was published after Tolkien's death in 1973, an examination of Volumes 10 and 11 of the *History of Middle-earth* indicates that the latest material incorporated by Christopher Tolkien into the text of the 1977 *Silmarillion* dates from about 1958. At this point the emphasis is still on the Kinslaying at Alqualondë, Cain's sin of fratricide in Genesis 4, but in the later writings on Galadriel there is a radical shift in emphasis: Galadriel's besetting sin becomes that of pride, the sin of Adam and Eve in the Garden in Genesis 2–3. It is certainly an easier sin to pin on a woman than the sin of fratricide, in which Galadriel was only indirectly implicated at most as an accomplice.

The History of Galadriel and Celeborn

Before turning to consider the most striking illustration of this transformation of Galadriel's "sin" in the late work "The Shibboleth of Fëanor" which dates from after Feb. 1968 (*Peoples* 331), it is necessary at least briefly to consider the accounts of "The History of Galadriel and Celeborn," which Christopher Tolkien included in *Unfinished Tales*, published in 1982. Since these accounts deal with the history of Galadriel, Celeborn, and Amroth in the Second Age of Middle-earth, they are only indirectly relevant to the topic of this paper. Christopher Tolkien comments: "There is no part of the history of Middle-earth more full of problems than the story of Galadriel and Celeborn, and it must be admitted that there are severe inconsistencies 'embedded in the traditions'; or, to look at the matter from another point of view, that the role and importance of Galadriel only emerged slowly, and that her story underwent continual refashionings" (*UT* 294). These comments are

6. For other references to Galadriel's fairness and valor in the *Silmarillion* tradition, see *S* 90; "Galadriel, the only woman of the Noldor to stand that day *tall and valiant* among the contending princes" (*Morgoth* 112, emphasis added); and these drafts of *S* 97 and 61 (quoted below): "Therefore led by Fingolfin and his sons, and by Inglor [later >Finrod] and Galadriel *the valiant and fair*" (*Morgoth* 120, emphasis added; cf. 196) and "A sister they had, Galadriel, the fairest lady of the house of Finwë, and *the most valiant*" (*Morgoth* 177, emphasis added). Compare this with *LotR*, Appendix F, "Of the Elves": "Noblest of all was the Lady Galadriel of the royal house of Finarfin and sister of Finrod Felagund, King of Nargothrond" (*LotR* Appendix F.I.1128; *Morgoth* 181).

equally applicable to the First Age accounts of Galadriel, some of which were included by Christopher Tolkien in the introduction to "The History of Galadriel and Celeborn" (*UT* 294–301). Although Christopher Tolkien does not date this material, there is a reference in a letter by his father to Dick Plotz of the Tolkien Society of America dated 12 Sept. 1965 to the existence of "a large amount of matter that is not strictly part of *The Silmarillion*" including "the history of Celeborn and Galadriel" (*Letters* 360). In his introduction to "The History of Galadriel and Celeborn," Christopher Tolkien expressed doubts that "the conception of a ban on Galadriel's return into the West was present when the chapter 'Farewell to Lórien' was composed, many years before" (*UT* 295). Part of his reason for believing so was that: "It is very notable that not only is there no mention in this text of a ban on Galadriel's return into the West, but it even seems from a passage at the beginning of the account that no such idea was present" (302).

Undoubtedly, Christopher Tolkien is right. The earliest of the references to a specific Ban on Galadriel's return dates from 1967, a full 25 years after the drafts of Book II of *The Lord of the Rings* were first written in 1942 (*Treason* 1). This late interpretation of the "Lament of Galadriel" in "Farewell to Lorien" is clearly contradicted by a statement that Galadriel herself makes in the earlier chapter "The Mirror of Galadriel" in *The Lord of the Rings*, after Frodo has just offered the Ring to her. She refuses it, saying: "I pass the test [...] I will diminish, and go into the West, and remain Galadriel" (*LotR* II.7.366). And she makes an even stronger statement slightly earlier in the same chapter in talking to Frodo about the general fate of the Elves (in which she obviously includes herself): "Yet if you succeed, then our power is diminished, and Lothlórien will fade, and the tides of Time will sweep it away. We must depart into the West, or dwindle to a rustic folk of dell and cave, slowly to forget and to be forgotten" (II.7.365). The only reasonable or natural interpretation of these passages is that Galadriel thought at this point she was free to return to Valinor. The view that Galadriel had prophetic foreknowledge of the Pardon of the Valar is at best very strained, and seems contradicted even by the late statement in "The Shibboleth of Fëanor" (after the ban had entered the story) quoted above that her Lament was spoken before she knew of the pardon of the Valar. Tolkien obviously "overlooked" or forgot about these inconsistencies when he developed his late story of the Ban of the Valar.

The Shibboleth of Fëanor

In the late account of Galadriel in "The Shibboleth of Fëanor" (*Peoples* 336–39, 347), part of which was also included by Christopher Tolkien in the introductory matter to "The History of Galadriel and Celeborn" (*UT* 295–98), great emphasis is placed on Galadriel's pride:

> Galadriel was born in the bliss of Valinor, but it was not long, in the reckoning of the Blessed Realm, before that was dimmed; and thereafter she had no peace within. For in that testing time amid the strife of the Ñoldor she was drawn this way and that. She was proud, strong, and self-willed [...] she had dreams of far lands and dominions that might be her own to order as she would without tutelage.
>
> So it came to pass that when the light of Valinor failed, for ever as the Ñoldor thought, she joined the rebellion against the Valar who commanded them to stay; and once she had set foot upon that road of exile, she would not relent, but rejected the last message of the Valar, and came under the Doom of Mandos. Even after the merciless assault on the Teleri and the rape of their ships, though she fought fiercely against Fëanor in defence of her mother's kin, she did not turn back. Her pride was unwilling to return, a defeated suppliant for pardon; but now she burned with desire to follow Fëanor with her anger to whatever lands he might come, and to thwart him in all ways that she could. Pride still moved her when, at the end of the Elder Days after the final overthrow of Morgoth, she refused the pardon of the Valar for all who had fought against him, and remained in Middle-earth. It was not until two long ages more had passed, when at last all that she had desired in her youth came to her hand, the Ring of Power and the dominion of Middle-earth of which she had dreamed, that her wisdom was full grown and she rejected it, and passing the last test departed from Middle-earth for ever. (*Peoples* 337–38)

There are several remarkable features of this text, especially the emphasis on Galadriel's pride and self-will. In this version of the story Galadriel freely refuses the general pardon of the Valar at the end of the First Age. Unlike the account in *The Silmarillion*, she is now shown as fighting on the opposing side during the kinslaying at Alqualondë against Fëanor. There are several other features of the account in "The Shibboleth of Fëanor" that are quite remarkable. She is portrayed as being something of an Amazon: "Her mother-name was Nerwen 'man-maiden', and she grew to be tall beyond the measure even of the women of the Ñoldor; she was strong of body, mind, and will, a match for both the loremasters and the athletes of the Eldar in the days of their youth" (*Peoples* 337).

Considerable attention is also focused on her golden hair. In "The Mirror of Galadriel," it is only briefly mentioned: "the hair of the Lady was of deep gold, and the hair of the Lord Celeborn was of silver long and bright" (*LotR* II.7.354).[7] Already in *The Silmarillion* we are told: "A sister they [the sons of Finarfin] had, Galadriel, most beautiful of all the house of Finwë; her hair was lit with gold as though it had caught in a mesh the radiance of Laurelin" (*S* 61).[8] In the account of "The Shibboleth of Fëanor" this description is greatly elaborated on:

> Even among the Eldar she was accounted beautiful, and her hair was held a marvel unmatched. It was golden like the hair of her father and her foremother Indis, but richer and more radiant, for its gold was touched by some memory of the starlike silver of her mother; and the Eldar said that the light of the Two Trees, Laurelin and Telperion, had been snared in her tresses. Many thought that this saying first gave to Fëanor the thought of imprisoning and blending the light of the Trees that later took shape in his hands as the Silmarils. For Fëanor beheld the hair of Galadriel with wonder and delight. He begged three times for a tress, but Galadriel would not give him even one hair. These two kinsfolk, the greatest of the Eldar of Valinor, were unfriends for ever. (*Peoples* 337)[9]

This conception is also found in a late letter dating from 6 March 1973, the last year of Tolkien's life: "Galadriel [...] means 'Maiden crowned with gleaming hair'. It is a secondary name given to her in her youth in the far past because she had long hair which glistened like gold but was also shot with silver. She was then of Amazon disposition and bound up her hair as a crown when taking part in athletic feats" (*Letters* 428). This explanation of Galadriel's *epessë* or secondary name is also found in "The Shibboleth of Fëanor":

---

7. In the early drafts of this passage both Galadriel and Celeborn have white hair; see *Treason* 233, 242, 246, 256, 262. The golden hair of Galadriel has been overlooked in both Ralph Bakshi's and Peter Jackson's films.

8. The conception of the "golden house of Finrod [Finarfin]," later extended to the whole kindred of the Vanyar (cf. *Jewels* 382–83) and also mentioned in draft texts of Appendix F of *The Lord of the Rings*, was already present in the *Silmarillion* tradition, before Galadriel was inserted back into the history of the First Age; see *Lost Tales I* 43–44 and *Peoples* 77.

9. Galadriel's behavior here is in very sharp contrast with her gracious gift to Gimli in *The Lord of the Rings* of "three golden hairs" (*LotR* II.8.376)—though clearly Fëanor is a very different kind of character from Gimli.

> *Galadriel* was chosen by Artanis ("noble woman") to be her Sindarin name; for it was the most beautiful of her names, and, though as an *epessë*, had been given to her by her lover, Teleporno [Celeborn] of the Teleri, whom she wedded later in Beleriand. As he gave it in Telerin form it was *Alatâriel(lë)*. The Quenyarized form appears as *Altariel*, though its true form would have been *Ñaltariel*. It was euphoniously and correctly rendered in Sindarin *Galadriel* [...] The whole [name], 'maiden crowned with a garland of bright radiance', was given in reference to Galadriel's hair. (*Peoples* 347)[10]

The Repentance of Galadriel

All this emphasis on Galadriel's various names and on her golden hair in Tolkien's late writings (with their perilous associations with female pride and vanity) is very far removed from the spirit if not letter of *The Lord of the Rings*, where the emphasis on Galadriel's spiritual beauty and wisdom is coupled paradoxically to a deep sense of her humility and her own deep awareness of the limitations of her power emphasized in the double use of the verb "diminish" in the passages quoted above (*LotR* II.7.366).

We can see this clearly in examining the accounts of Galadriel's "temptation" by Frodo in *The Lord of the Rings* to take the Ring. In the initial draft outline for this passage, Galadriel dismisses Frodo's offer with a laugh: "Frodo offers Galadriel the Ring. She *laughs*. Says he is revenged for her temptation. Confesses that the thought had occurred to her. But she will only retain the unsullied Ring. Too much evil lay in the Ruling Ring. It is not permitted to use anything that Sauron has made" (*Treason* 254, emphasis added). The laughter is important (in later drafts it is stated even more strongly that she laughs "with a sudden clear laugh of [pure] merriment") (*Treason* 260, 261) as a clear sign of Galadriel's awareness of her own creaturely limitations and is retained in the printed text:

> Galadriel laughed with a sudden clear laugh. "Wise the Lady Galadriel may be," she said, "yet here she has met her match in courtesy. Gently are you revenged for my testing of your heart at our first meeting. You begin to see with a keen eye. I do not deny that my heart has greatly desired to ask what you offer. For many

---

10. For further references to Galadriel's other names (Nerwen, Artanis, and Al(a)tariel), see *Peoples* 337, 346; *UT* 298, 346 (which is based on "The Shibboleth of Fëanor"); *Morgoth* 182; *S* 360, entry *kal-*.

> long years I had pondered what I might do, should the Great Ring come into my hands, and behold! it was brought within my grasp. The evil that was devised long ago works on in many ways, whether Sauron himself stands or falls. Would not that have been a noble deed to set to the credit of his Ring, if I had taken it by force or fear from my guest?
>
> "And now at last it comes. You will give me the Ring freely! In place of the Dark Lord you will set up a Queen. And I shall not be dark, but beautiful and terrible as the Morning and the Night! Fair as the Sea and the Sun and the Snow upon the Mountain! Dreadful as the Storm and the Lightning! Stronger than the foundations of the earth. All shall love me and despair!"
>
> She lifted up her hand and from the ring that she wore there issued a great light that illumined her alone and left all else dark. She stood before Frodo seeming now tall beyond measurement, and beautiful beyond enduring, terrible and worshipful. Then she let her hand fall, and the light faded, and suddenly she laughed again, and lo! she was shrunken: a slender elf-woman, clad in simple white, whose gentle voice was soft and sad.
>
> "I pass the test," she said. "I will diminish, and go into the West, and remain Galadriel." (*LotR* II.7.365–66)

All this is in very sharp contrast to the image of Galadriel that emerges in Tolkien's late writings. In this crucial scene, first comes the manifestation of her power. But then she knows very well she is being "tested." Her laughter both before and after is a clear sign to Frodo that he has nothing to fear—she is in on the "joke." She has enough self-knowledge and humility to admit that she feels the attraction of the Ring. But she knows that she can never possess the Ring, that it would end up possessing her. She willingly and freely renounces all claim to the Ring and accepts her "diminishment." After the manifestation of her power fades, she appears "shrunken: a slender elf-woman, clad in simple white," and then follows her beautiful and moving and poignant words of renunciation. The crucial words "I will diminish" clearly echo John the Baptist's "I must diminish" in John 3:30.[11] But equally clearly the whole scene also has echoes of the Virgin Mary's *Magnificat*. Galadriel is paradoxically exulted because she is willing to be humbled.

11. Tolkien was no doubt familiar with the Vulgate text for John 3:30: "*illum oportet crescere me autem minui* [He must grow greater, but I must diminish]. *Minui* (as well as the original Greek NT verb ελαττουσθαι) is most frequently translated as "decrease," or in some modern versions as "become less important," but can be translated more literally as "diminish."

If there is any truth to Tolkien's own later claim that figure of Galadriel was modeled on the Virgin Mary (though she is clearly, as Tolkien does not say, also modeled on the traditional figure of the "Fairy Queen"), the parallel is to be precisely found in this paradoxical mixture of power with humility and renunciation.[12]

The same image of "diminishment" can also be found in the description of Galadriel in the "Farewell to Lórien" chapter, when she meets Frodo and the other members of the Fellowship for the last time: "She seemed no longer perilous or terrible, nor full of hidden power; *but elven-fair she seemed beyond desire of heart.* Already she appeared to him *(since her refusal in the garden)* as by men of later days elves at times are seen: present, and yet remote, a living vision of that which has already passed far down the streams of time" [phrases in italics not in *The Lord of the Rings*] (*Treason* 281; cf. *LotR* II.8.373). The same idea is also expressed more subtly in the final description of Galadriel as the Fellowship departs from Lothlórien:

> On the green bank near to the very point of the Tongue the Lady Galadriel stood alone and silent. As they passed her they turned and their eyes watched her slowly floating away from them. [...] Soon the white form of the Lady was small and distant. She shone like a window of glass upon a far hill in the westering sun, or as a remote lake seen from a mountain: a crystal fallen in the lap of the land. Then it seemed to Frodo that she lifted her arms in a final farewell, and far but piercing-clear on the following wind came the sound of her voice singing [her "Lament"]. (II.8.377)

This is very far removed in spirit from the late story of Galadriel's Fall and Redemption that emerged in about 1967. While Frodo's offer of the Ring to Galadriel in *The Lord of the Rings* is a real "test," it is not the

---

12. See the response, written in 1953, to a letter from his friend Fr. Robert Murray, S. J., who had read parts of *The Lord of the Rings* in manuscript, and who compared the image of Galadriel to that of the Virgin Mary. In it, Tolkien wrote: "I think I know exactly what you mean by the order of Grace; and of course by your references to Our Lady, *upon which all my own small perception of beauty both in majesty and simplicity is founded*" (*Letters* 172, emphasis added); cf. also *Letters* 49: "The woman is another fallen human-being with a soul in peril. But combined and harmonized with religion (as long ago it [the romantic chivalric tradition] was, producing much of that beautiful devotion to Our Lady that has been God's way of refining so much of our gross manly natures and emotions, and also of warming and colouring our hard, bitter, religion) it can be very noble." See also *Letters* 288 and 407, quoted above; and Purtill 84–86.

"final and overwhelming temptation" of Letter #320 quoted at the beginning of this paper. Even as late as September 1963, Tolkien was insisting that Galadriel's rejection of the Ring was reasoned and premeditated: "In the 'Mirror of Galadriel' [...] it appears that Galadriel conceived of herself as capable of wielding the Ring and supplanting the Dark Lord. [...] It was part of the essential deceit of the Ring to fill minds with imaginations of supreme power. But this the Great had well considered and had rejected [...]. Galadriel's rejection of the temptation was founded upon previous thought and resolve" (*Letters* 332).

The Final Story

A careful examination of the textual evidence suggests many and striking differences between the pictures of Galadriel that emerge in *The Lord of the Rings* and in Tolkien's late writings, especially "The Shibboleth of Fëanor." Tolkien himself seems to have realized the problems with these late accounts of Galadriel, and at the very end of his life, he made one final and extraordinary change in the story that completely exonerated Galadriel from any part in the Rebellion of the Noldor. In a letter written on 4th August 1973, almost exactly a month before he died, Tolkien wrote: "Galadriel was 'unstained': she had committed no evil deeds. She was an enemy of Fëanor. She did not reach Middle-earth with the other Noldor, but independently. Her reasons for desiring to go to Middle-earth were legitimate, and she would have been permitted to depart, but for the misfortune that before she set out the revolt of Fëanor broke out, and she became involved in the desperate measures of Manwë, and the ban on all emigration" (*Letters* 431). This account was also found in "a very late and partly illegible note" set down in the last month of Tolkien's life (*UT* 299), which Christopher Tolkien reported (in summarized or retold form) in the section on "The History of Galadriel and Celeborn" in *Unfinished Tales* (299–300). According to this very late account:

> In Fëanor's revolt that followed the Darkening of Valinor Galadriel had no part: indeed she with Celeborn [now not a Sindarin Elf but one of the Teleri] fought heroically in defence of Alqualondë against the assault of the Noldor, and Celeborn's ship was saved from them. Galadriel, despairing now of Valinor and horrified by the violence and cruelty of Fëanor, set sail into the darkness without waiting for Manwë's leave, which would undoubtedly have been withheld in that hour, however legitimate her desire in itself.

> It was thus that she came under the ban set upon all departure, and Valinor was shut against her return. (*UT* 299)

Galadriel's opposition to Fëanor at Alqualondë and Celeborn's Telerian origins are already present in "The Shibboleth of Fëanor," but in other respects this story is a radical departure from that earlier account. Gone is Galadriel's rebellious pride: she is exonerated from all blame and only falls under the Ban of the Valar on a technicality, because she had unwittingly violated their emigration policies.

Given the serious inconsistencies and even contradictions between all these late accounts, it is hardly surprising that they were never incorporated into *The Silmarillion*. In *Unfinished Tales,* Christopher Tolkien offered a defense of his decision:

> This story [...] is profoundly at variance with all that is said elsewhere. It arose from "philosophical" (rather than "historical") considerations, concerning the precise nature of Galadriel's disobedience in Valinor on the one hand, and her status and power in Middle-earth on the other. That it would have entailed a good deal of alteration in the narrative of *The Silmarillion* is evident; but that my father doubtless intended to do. [...] The book as published was however formed from completed narratives, and I could not take into account merely projected revisions. (*UT* 300)

Such a defense is hardly necessary. Second thoughts aren't always better. Tom Shippey, for one, criticizes Tolkien for exculpating Galadriel completely in this final account and sees this as another example of Tolkien's "soft-heartedness" that he criticizes in *The Road to Middle-earth* (319, n. 10; cf. 205-06).

All these late changes to the story of Galadriel's Fall and Repentance are rather bewildering. It is easier to point out the inconsistencies than to come up with a possible explanation. It would be too easy to say (though at least partly true) that Tolkien was a perfectionist and was never completely satisfied with his own artistic creations. Certainly Tolkien in his later years spent a lot of effort, not all of it productive, in trying to elaborate the mythology of the First Age that underlay *The Lord of the Rings*, part of which was later published posthumously as *The Silmarillion*. Perhaps it would be more true to say that, like many authors, Tolkien became fascinated by his own artistic creation and felt the need to "fill in the gaps." Certainly, some of the late changes in the characterization of Galadriel, especially the portrayal of her as being something of an Amazon in her youth, are quite striking. However, the problem is that these changes are ultimately inconsistent with the characterization of Galadriel in *The Lord of the Rings*, and I think Tolkien realized this. But rather than discarding the story completely, Tolkien at the very end of his life decided to rehabilitate and exonerate Galadriel in a way that can perhaps best be described with Tom Shippey as being a bit "softhearted."

Tolkien has often been criticized for failing to pay enough attention to women. Such a criticism is certainly unjustified if we consider all the important female figures in *The Silmarillion* tradition, including Idril Celebrindal, Nienor Níniel, Finduilas, Lúthien Tinúviel, Melian, and all the female Valar of whom the most important is Varda or Elbereth Gilthoniel. But even when we turn to *The Lord of the Rings*, Galadriel surely stands out in the minds and hearts of many readers as one of the more important and certainly most beloved characters in Tolkien's great epic-romance. The fact that Tolkien continued to think about Galadriel and her place in his own private mythology of the First Age right until the very end of his life indicates also how important Tolkien himself considered her.

This article was published originally in Mythlore *25.3/4* (#97/98) *(2007): 91–116. It is reprinted here with permission.*

Works Cited

Bridoux, Denis. "The Tale of Galadriel and Celeborn: An Attempt at an Integrated Reconstruction." *Amon Hen* 104 (July 1990): 19–23. Print.

Johnson, Janice. "The Celeblain [Silver Thread] of Celeborn and Galadriel." *Mythlore* 9.2 (#32) (1982): 11–19. Print.

Lakowski, Romuald I. " 'Perilously Fair': Titania, Galadriel and the Fairy Queen of Medieval Romance." *Tolkien and Shakespeare: Essays on Shared Themes and Language*. Ed. Janet Brennan Croft. Jefferson, NC: McFarland Press, 2007. 60–78. Print.

---. "Tolkien's 'Love Triangle': Aragorn's Relationship with Éowyn and Arwen" *The Ring Goes Ever On: Proceedings of the Tolkien 2005 Conference. Celebrating 50 Years of The Lord of the Rings.* 2 vols. Ed. Sarah Wells. Cheltenham, UK: The Tolkien Society, 2008. 1: 305–15. Print.

Purtill, Richard L. *J. R. R. Tolkien: Myth, Morality, and Religion*. San Francisco: Harper and Row, 1984. Print.

Shippey, Tom. *The Road to Middle-earth: How J. R. R. Tolkien Created a New Mythology*. 2nd ed. London: HarperCollins, 1992. Print.

Swann, Donald, comp., and J. R. R. Tolkien. *The Road Goes Ever On: A Song Cycle*. 2nd ed. London: HarperCollins, 2002. CD and Print.

Lúthien Tinúviel and Bodily Desire in the Lay of Leithian

Cami D. Agan

> Then Lúthien dared the most dreadful and most valiant deed that any of the women of the Elves have ever dared; no less than the challenge of Fingolfin is it accounted, and may be greater, save that she was half-divine.
>
> —The Quenta (*Shaping* 112)

> [...] Lúthien was the noblest, and the most fair and beautiful, of all the Children of Eru remembered in ancient story [...]
>
> —The Shibboleth of Fëanor (*Peoples* 364, note 53)

In the primary versions of the tale of Beren and Lúthien, also referred to as the Lay of Leithian,[1] Lúthien Tinúviel stands at the center of the narrative and moves the Quest for the Silmaril forward when male figures—Thingol, Celegorm, Curufin, Beren, Felagund—fail or thwart the personal and larger objectives.[2] By taking direct action and employing her significant powers over the natural world, over her own body, and over the bodies of others, Lúthien also affects her own future and enacts or makes possible choices she in fact desires. As the child of Melian the Maia, Lúthien's significant powers allow her to pursue a heroic purpose that even Galadriel's narrative does not match, but equally powerful are the episodes wherein Lúthien acts as a physical and (potentially) sexual

---

1. While I ground much of the discussion in the best-known version of the Tale found published in *The Silmarillion*, I will also note important passages in the larger *History of Middle-earth* that establish Lúthien's power and centrality to the Story, or that may otherwise offer insight into Lúthien's position.

2. In this claim, I align my reading with treatments of Lúthien as a powerful force, such as Chance, "Women"; Whitaker; Brückner; and Slack, and in contrast to readings such as Fredrick and McBride, which claims that Lúthien is idealized but largely immobile, a symbol who "does very little but sing and frolic through the forest" (120). In contrast, Benvenuto notes that "Lúthien is evidently superior to Beren" (41) and calls Lúthien "probably the single most important character in the fabric of Tolkien's mythology" (42). There are several excellent surveys of critical viewpoints concerning Tolkien's construction of females; in particular, see Enright; Donovan, both presented in this volume.

agent not only to alter her personal narrative, but also to act against annihilating forces and thus reframe the larger Story of Middle-earth. While the narrative threatens to objectify Lúthien by assigning her typical gendered feminine attributes of ethereal, unattainable beauty, with an affinity to nature, and placing her in the position of desired but chaste maiden,[3] the text also allows space for Lúthien to move against the will of the father, her lover, the enemy Sauron, and of course, even Morgoth. These personal rebellions and direct challenges, in tandem with her potent implementation of power, ground themselves in the body, in this case the body of a young (Elf) woman. Her power, represented as singing, weaving, transforming, healing, and shape-shifting, has its foundation in the body, works through the body, and allows her to gain a status—the Elf who becomes Human—that is defined by processes of the body.

In exploring the moments where the text foregrounds Lúthien's physical body as a site of power and agency, it becomes clear that the body is not beside the point but *is* the point. As body, acting and reacting to powerful forces, Lúthien appears as a rare textual example in Tolkien's legendarium of one who acts on sexual desire and is neither demonized as monstrous nor directly punished by the narrative for her desires. Interestingly, the locus of Beren's and Lúthien's love is the forest, a space beyond the traditional fixtures of cultural codes and systems. Because the text repeatedly places the lovers in this highly charged locale of freedom and natural power, it asks us to consider their "forest time" as Other, as atypical, and perhaps as somehow sanctioned by larger forces. Allowing ourselves to ask, "Are they sexually intimate?"[4] offers fruitful inroads both into Lúthien's episodes in the forest with Beren and into the resulting powerful reversals of domination she enacts. We might come to view the moments where the two engage in sexual union as a process that moves from equal choice to be-

3. Whitaker notes that Tolkien does fall back on the notions of Lúthien's beauty as her source of power: "his positing of female beauty as the catalyst for violent seduction or unrestrained lust remains problematic other than as understood in the mythic mode" (51).

4. Here, I follow Saxey's lead, who interrogates *The Lord of the Rings* as potentially homoerotic, suggesting that "it is helpful to ask 'What would it *mean* or *achieve* to assert that they [Sam and Frodo] are lovers?' " (130); or in this exploration, what would it *mean* or *achieve* to claim that Lúthien and Beren have a sexual relationship?

trothal to consummation, a kind of private marriage sustained by only themselves and that can exist only in "forest-time."[5] That powerful bond, constructed first by themselves alone, grounds itself in the joining of two bodies in a place beyond others—and contrasts sharply with other diseased, tortured or disfigured bodies of the tale.

Paralleling the first contact between Elwë and Melian, Beren's first interaction with Lúthien moves from sight, through enchantment and a kind of place beyond time, to naming her and finally to physical touch. Already Beren's body has transgressed magical time and space, as he has crossed through the impenetrable borders of the Girdle of Melian after the unspeakable terrors of the Ered Gorgoroth.[6] Beren awakens from his initial enchantment when Lúthien awakens the forest from winter: "the song of Lúthien released the bonds of winter [...] Then the spell of silence fell from Beren; and he called her, crying Tinúviel; and the woods echoed the name" (*S* 165).[7] As Brückner observes, "it is only when Lúthien sings that Beren becomes an active agent. He calls out to her and gives her a name [...] of his own creation" (5). Lúthien's physical actions—dancing and singing—inaugurate the fecundity of spring, and the text directly parallels this fruitful awakening with Beren's: the "waters spoke" and the "flowers sprang" (*S* 165), even as Beren names Tinúviel. Slack holds that "Beren's vision of Lúthien is acclaimed by the

5. Consider, for example, the Forest of Arden in Shakespeare's *As You Like It* (IV.i), where Rosalind "marries" Orlando first in a ceremony presided over only by herself, without sanction from family, law, or church. Shakespeare takes advantage of the forest's special conditions to allow for transgressions that, for a time, set institutions aside. Brückner explores the notion of the forest fully, and using Foucault's conception of "heterotopia," suggests that the lovers' "relationship, at this stage, is absolutely self-reflexive and asocial. It is the site where it occurs that renders it possible and safe" (7).

6. I find this process of movement through magical spaces quite significant in many ways. For the sake of this paper, it establishes a textual parallel between the horrific feminine space recalling "the fell race of Ungoliant," the female un-light that devours all into nothingness, and the powers inherent in the "mazes that Melian wove" (*S* 164). I will return to the ways in which Lúthien's power "undoes" Ungoliant's feminine devouring, below.

7. While Benvenuto suggests that "her magical powers are strongly connected to nature and growth" (49), in exploring the processes of song and spell, Eilmann observes that "If the Eldar intends a song to work as a spell, the singing causes a visible change in the physical environment or serves the intention of the singer in another way" (107). Such a power seems evident through Lúthien not only here but in all her performances in the tale.

woods that join him in echoing her name" (66).[8] Thus, the tale stages the moment of contact between the lovers as part of the natural world's verdant blossoming. In response to her physical calling forth of its reproductive renewal, the forest rebounds Tinúviel, as if to make intimate and personal her performance of seasonal transformation.

Indeed, the moments of initial connection between the lovers interlock in a series of exchanges wherein each has a violent bodily reaction to the sight, sound and touch of the other. Beren's physical binding/enchantment is released by the sight and sound of Lúthien literally calling forth spring/growth/regeneration; he gains voice to call after her—Tinúviel—and "the whole of nature calls her by the name Beren has given her" (Slack 71). The powerful choric naming from forest and Man arrests Lúthien: "Then she halted in wonder, and fled no more, and Beren came to her. But as she looked on him, doom fell upon her, and she loved him; yet she slipped from his arms and vanished from his sight even as the day was breaking" (*S* 165). While the text suggests "love at first sight" for both Beren and Lúthien, it simultaneously alludes to a more physical connection—Lúthien must "slip" from his arms, from a potentially passionate embrace that evokes her erotic response as well as their fate/doom. Although elided by Lúthien's flight response, the embrace nevertheless stresses erotic contact that overwhelms Lúthien, presumably with an emotion she does not anticipate: desire.[9]

The *Lay of Leithian* is even clearer as to the erotic charge of the moment: "His voice such love and longing filled/one moment stood she, fear was stilled;/one moment only; like a flame/he leaped towards her as she stayed/and caught and kissed that elfin maid. [...] /She left his arms and slipped away/just at the breaking of the day" (*Lays* 180). Beren's passion and his physical response arouse curiosity, and in the

8. West calls Beren's use of Tinúviel as cognomen "apt because [...] on one level it functions as a term of endearment between lovers [...] he has thereby both praised [Lúthien] and piqued her curiosity, but on another because he has *named her*—and no one knew better than Tolkien the power of names or the significance of being able to assign names" (263, emphasis in original).

9. Brückner agrees and suggests that "It might be worthwhile to interpret [their initial contact] as indicative of a sexual encounter [...]" (6n4). However, Brückner suggests that the tale may thereby suggest that emotion develops from the physical rather than vice versa.

poem Lúthien responds to his physical touch by staying with Beren through the night. Given the poem's imagery, it seems viable to assume a sexual relationship, one freely exchanged amidst the newly green forest. The erotic terminology of the poetic passage—love, longing, flame, leaped, kissed—points to a natural physical connection between the lovers, and while the narrative version appears to underline more clearly the doom and fate connected to their union, it does not completely erase the body that both magically awakes and sexually arouses in the lovers. Upon Lúthien's return to a bereft Beren—the first instance of the motif of enchantment and return—the tale establishes their secret pastoral marriage and nightly rendezvous. Once "she laid her hand in his," an evocation of betrothal and promise that consummation would seal, "they went in secret through the woods together from spring to summer" (*S* 166).[10] To assume that the lovers have consummated their desires and live in a "honeymoon" period seems appropriate to the season—spring to summer—and establishes the significance of the momentary joys they experience throughout the tale. This trope of mutability in fact becomes a structuring component of the narrative: fleeting joy in the forest prior to further testing and trials, a process that evokes their "brief" life together after the Quest is achieved.[11]

How then might it affect the text to assume that Lúthien and Beren consummate their love in the forest? In particular, it suggests their special doom, a "oneness" developed in the "other space" outside the normal rules of marriage, beyond the power even of Elven kingdoms—a transgression or break not for selfish or lustful motives but one sanctioned by natural desires echoed in the springtime of

---

10. The *Lay of Leithian* gives further agency to Lúthien in their love affair: "Each day before the end of eve/she sought her love, nor would him leave, / until the stars were dimmed, and day / came glimmering eastward silver-grey" (*Lays* 184). The Lay also employs the metaphor of the dance for their sexual union: "In Doriath Beren long ago / new art and lore he learned to know; / his limbs were freed; his eyes alight, / kindled with a new enchanted sight; / and to her dancing feet his feet / attuned went dancing free and fleet" (185). This "love dance," too, comes at Lúthien's suggestion and insistence.

11. In Slack's exploration of oaths and songs in the tale of Beren and Lúthien, she observes both the "dyscatastrophic" or "Beowulfian" (62) thematics and its resultant impact on the narrative: "The narrator is always at great lengths to communicate to the reader the brevity of their joy [...]" (71).

Doriath and one ultimately fated, as Melian foresees. As Lúthien leads Beren, her husband by her choice, to the seat of her father Thingol, it is not their bodily desire that ensnares Doriath; rather, it is Thingol's "cunning counsel" (*S* 168) to enact Beren's death-by-quest that seals the kingdom's future.[12] Their union has in some sense "already happened," because already fated. Further, to consider their union an erotic one creates strong contrast to the numerous violent and transformative physical confrontations with bodies that the tale subsequently develops. While the initial forest interlude between the lovers establishes a space where Lúthien may give her body as part of the fecund processes of nature, this bond is increasingly threatened by the distorted, tortured and perverted bodies (including Beren's) that the tale recounts. Assuming a sexual union between Lúthien and Beren also points to Tolkien's interest in subcreation, not merely in the procreative future they will have, but also in the ways that their "oneness" combats the Fallen world of Middle-earth and works to reconstruct its future. Lúthien and Beren's feats as the tale unfolds might be viewed as achievable *through* their sexual union: their union/choice beyond race, beyond politics or systems of control achieves what Beren and Felagund, two powerful and wise males bonded as brothers, could not. By acting on their "pure" desire, Lúthien and Beren construct one body in consummation that can then proceed to act on and respond to the bodies of others.

Lúthien's encounters with the sons of Fëanor, Celegorm and Curufin, underline the contrast between their desires and the physical and psychological connection Lúthien and Beren have established in Doriath. The brothers' treatment aligns clearly with Thingol's earlier imprisonment of his daughter in Hírilorn: like Thingol, "Celegorm and Curufin are exponents of the father-husband economic discourse" (Brückner 12).[13] Significantly, her father's containment leads to her crafting of the bodily sign of her power—the cloak of her own hair

---

12. Flieger, citing Stith Thompson, reminds us that such a challenge is rooted in "A traditional motif [...] in which a supernatural parent-figure tries to prevent the marriage of a daughter by assigning tasks designed [...] to ensure the death of the quester" (137).

13. Flieger's description of Thingol's attempt to exchange or hold Lúthien's light also echoes the brothers' treatment of her: "[his] possessiveness of Lúthien is wrongful, [...] [and] his motives are darkened and twisted" (138).

that renders her disguised and others unconscious. The fact that Lúthien is able to craft this object of power from her own bodily processes seems vital; what she possesses can grow, can obscure, can overcome both her father's will and eventually, others' as well.

Unlike Beren, whose sight of Lúthien prompts their union,[14] subsequent repeated references to seeing and desiring are associated with various men seeking to contain Lúthien, possess her, and use her for political, dynastic purposes. Beren's enchantment and renaming of Lúthien as Tinúviel is contrasted with Celegorm's feigning: "So great was her sudden beauty [...] that Celegorm became enamoured of her; but he spoke her fair" (*S* 173).[15] Lúthien reveals herself; she speaks the truth and withdraws the cloak from her body, while the sons of Fëanor, overwhelmed at her beauty, nonetheless feign and disguise both their personal erotic fixation and their political machinations: "they purposed to let the King [Felagund] perish, and to keep Lúthien, and force Thingol to give her hand to Celegorm" (173). Due to Lúthien's trust, her belief that they are Elves who would help their own, she loses any advantage over them: "and Lúthien was betrayed; for they held her fast, and took away her cloak, and she was not permitted to pass the gates or to speak with any save the brothers" (173). Once under their power, her body no longer commands; it is unstable and contained, locked away and ineffectual. While the bodies of Beren and Felagund simultaneously undergo torment in Tol Sirion, Lúthien is "held fast"; she is unable to move, to use her powerful weapon (the cloak), and presumably, her voice to combat their violence. Whitaker states that "The stripping of the cloak literally divests Lúthien of some power and makes her all the more visible and vulnerable for the brothers to enjoy" (63). As Celegorm and Curufin torment her body through the silencing and containing of her power, they become a kind of evil "cloak" to render Lúthien's existence invisible beyond their own desires.

---

14. Whitaker claims that, in Lúthien and Beren's initial experiences, the tale underscores "The sense of sight—and its association with (divine) enchantment" (61).

15. *The Lay of Leithian*, although it assigns the violent feelings to Curufin, is even clearer as to the motive, as Huan wonders "why Curufin looked with hot desire/on Lúthien, he pondered deep,/and felt some evil shadow creep/of ancient curse o'er Elfinesse" (*Lays* 241).

After the lovers' escape and the defeat of Sauron at Tol Sirion, Celegorm and Curufin again seek to do bodily harm, to mar Lúthien's power and to destroy her freely chosen partner. Driven from Nargothrond, the brothers "espied them and knew them from afar," and Celegorm "turned his horse, and spurred it upon Beren, proposing to ride him down," while in an another attempt to abduct her physically, "Curufin [...] lifted Lúthien to his saddle" (*S* 177). Although the lovers again overcome the violent threat, the sons of Fëanor are humiliated by their defeat; they are unhorsed, shifted bodily from a position of power to that of subjugation, the very position they had hoped to enact upon Lúthien: "In an almost comic inversion of Curufin's attempted abduction of Lúthien, Curufin must now ride as (unwilling) passenger behind his brother Celegorm" (Whitaker 65). The fact that Beren, a Man and an ally of Felagund, and Lúthien, whom they had hoped to possess, have unseated them, arouses only more violence: "Curufin, being filled with shame and malice, took the bow of Celegorm and shot back as they went; and the arrow was aimed at Lúthien" (*S* 177). The emasculated brothers, themselves bodily "brought down," seek to inflict harm and to destroy the "oneness" that Lúthien and Beren have (re)-achieved. Only Huan—the hound who had hunted with Celegorm since the days in Valinor and now "forsook [his] service" (177)—can defeat the annihilating threat that the sons embody. Lúthien must turn to a disfigured Beren, wounded by Celegorm's spear and the final arrow that "smote him in the breast" (177), and "by her arts and by her love" (178) heal his tormented and defeated body. While the episodes of Tol Sirion and the sons' violence are followed by episodes of healing, the threat of rape and annihilation that Celegorm and Curufin inject into the tale never ceases to overshadow Lúthien; instead, it is merely transferred to more powerful forces.

In subsequent episodes of escape into forests—after Lúthien's rescue of Beren from Tol Sirion and following the loss of Beren's hand and the Silmaril to Carcharoth—it is Lúthien's power over and through the body that heals, renews, and ultimately overcomes violent physical threat. She is able to heal and restore Beren fully twice, even prior to the tale's eucatastrophic conclusion. These moments of rest are possible as a result of the manipulation of the body Lúthien has enacted: she escapes Thingol's attempt to contain her by weaving a cloak from her own hair that serves as the marker of her power through the remainder of the quest. To reach Beren, Lúthien moves through a series of restraints: Thingol "caused a house to be built from which she should not escape" (*S* 172); Celegorm and Curufin "held her fast" (173); and Sauron "thought to make her captive and hand her over to the power of Morgoth" (174). From these impediments which powerful males place before her, Lúthien establishes a position of power with the wearing of the cloak, the use of her voice and song, and the aid of the hound Huan. Each episode emphasizes the power of Lúthien's physical presence in the wake of the bodily suffering of others. At Tol Sirion, her song breaks the boundaries of Sauron's walls and constructs a link to Beren, who responds with "a song of challenge that he had made in praise of the Seven Stars, the Sickle of the Valar" (174). As Huan wavers before the monstrous "Wolf-Sauron," Lúthien begins to wrest the power of Tol Sirion from Sauron by "cast[ing] a fold of her dark cloak before his eyes" (175). The being who had heard her voice and imagined her constraint now falls into "fleeting drowsiness" (175) at the touch of her hair-cloak. Lúthien forestalls the touch of Sauron with her own body, reversing the power Sauron hoped to hold over that same body.

In rescuing her lover Beren from the isle, Lúthien begins a process of opening, freeing, and healing that counters the distressed and horror-filled bodies littering the episode. Significantly, the description of Sauron's loss of control over Tol Sirion grounds itself in his own tormented, shifting and exposed body:

> Then Sauron shifted shape, from wolf to serpent, and from monster to his own accustomed form; but he could not elude the grip of Huan without forsaking his body utterly. Ere his foul spirit left its dark house, Lúthien came to him, and said that he should be stripped of his raiment of flesh, and his ghost be sent quaking back to Morgoth; and she said: "There everlastingly thy naked self shall endure the torment of his scorn, pierced by his eyes, unless thou yield to me the mastery of thy tower." (*S* 175)

As Sauron's body desperately transforms to increasingly monstrous incarnations, we understand that he, too, possesses a body under threat. The passage in fact repeatedly references "Sauron-as-body"—beast-strength, shape, wolf, serpent, monster, form, body—and underscores his fixation on his "dark house" (body). His "devil's art" (174) cannot undo Huan's physical, bodily bite "by the throat" (175). Constrained, with no escape, Sauron must consider fleeing without a body, must face the potential annihilation of his physical form. His particular bodily desire links to his power, his ability to alter his form to ever more monstrous forms; the actions of Huan and Lúthien threaten this desire and exploit it to render him powerless. In Lúthien's direct address to Sauron, the text again grounds the exchange of the isle in Sauron's body: the "raiment of his flesh" will be stripped; his "naked self" will suffer "pierced by [Morgoth's] eyes."[16] In effect, she threatens him with physical/bodily dissolution if he will not submit to her. The passage is structured clearly as a reversal of the abduction and violence Sauron would enact upon Lúthien. Under such a threat, Sauron yields the tower and transforms finally into a kind of open wound: "he took the form of a vampire, [...] and he fled, dripping blood from his throat upon the trees" (175).

Again after a process of healing and forest interlude, where we can imagine that the lovers renew their sexual bond, Lúthien and Beren turn toward the gates of Angband.[17] Lúthien's ability to transform her body and Beren's into fell creatures—Thuringwethil the vampire and the wolf Draugluin—suggests an ironic inversion of Morgoth and Sauron's power to corrupt through bodily perversion.[18] These horrific "raiments of flesh" gain them access to Morgoth's kingdom, and as disguises Thuringwethil and Draugluin function to conceal bodies and allow access to the very regions that their own could not "pierce." In her powerful if temporary "mastery" of Angband, Lúthien employs her voice and her exposed self/ body, first to cross the guarded threshold and then to allow Beren sufficient time to retrieve the Silmaril, itself concealed in the dungeons of Morgoth. In their confrontation with the wolf-guardian Carcharoth, "some power, descended from of old from divine race, possessed Lúthien, and cast-

16. The use of the phrase "raiment of flesh" for Sauron's physical form in fact evokes Lúthien's cloak, actual raiment that both conceals and acts upon others, just as Sauron's physical form can conceal his "ghost" and overpower others.

17. Whitaker writes, "But though Beren and Lúthien enjoy a brief respite after this event, there are further elements of rape narrative in Lúthien's tale as she undertakes with Beren to face Morgoth" (65).

18. It may also be significant that she and Huan, in these same forms, travel to Beren through Taur-nu-Fuin, the very region where Sauron, defeated and in vampire form, retreated, "filling it with horror" (*S* 175). Thus, Lúthien crosses geographic boundaries in the form evoking her defeated enemy, and thus she effects another humiliation of the bleeding vampire-Sauron.

ing back her foul raiment she stood forth, small before the might of Carcharoth, but radiant and terrible" (*S* 180). The tale's concern with concealing and revealing continues here, as Lúthien removes not her own cloak but the vampire-cloak she has employed to breach this space. Without her cloak's power to render her enemies unconscious, she now needs only her voice to overcome the wolf: "fall now into dark oblivion, and forget for a while the dreadful doom of life" (180).

Interestingly, Lúthien's triumph over the gatekeeper is rhetorically constructed, and we can assume magically ordered, as a release, an escape from the very consciousness of who and where Carcharoth is. As if giving a gift, Lúthien brings down the being Morgoth created to "lie unsleeping before the doors of Angband" (180). She has effected reversal once again; the very purpose of the Red Maw, to guard the gate, to resist sleep, and to destroy light, fails. Has Lúthien somehow tapped into the animal's one desire? To escape his "doom" and lie, even if for a moment, unconscious, outside of the body in which Morgoth has imprisoned him?[19] Carcharoth's "raiment of flesh" is a burden to him, and perhaps through her own wearing of the "cloak" of Thuringwethil, Lúthien intuits this desire for a (temporary) "release from bondage."

As the two lovers race to complete "the greatest deed that has been dared by Elves or Men" (*S* 180), Lúthien finds herself once again revealed, exposed and alone under the gaze of one who would constrain her. Although still in wolf-form, Beren cannot move or act; his body breaks even in its disguise. Yet, while Morgoth exposes her and "bent his gaze upon her," Lúthien "was not daunted by his eyes; and she named her own name, and offered her service to sing before him, after the manner of a minstrel" (180). Chillingly, this moment appears to enact her description of Sauron's impending humiliation: "There everlastingly thy naked self shall endure the torment of his scorn, pierced by his eyes" (175); physically and metaphorically naked before the gaze of

19. *The Lay of Leithian* has Lúthien employ her hair-cloak and emphasizes her power through weaving as well as the notion of escape from the wolf: "Her cloak / by white hands woven, like a smoke, / like all-bewildering, all-enthralling, / all-enfolding evening [...] as forth she stepped, / across those awful eyes she swept / a shadow and a mist of dreams / wherein entangled starlight gleams. [...] 'For one brief hour escape the net / the dreadful doom of life forget!' " (*Lays* 291–92).

Morgoth,[20] Lúthien is threatened with objectification, rape, and perpetual torment. However, Lúthien retains her identity, names herself, and thus solidifies her power. In naming herself,[21] Lúthien claims equal standing with Morgoth himself; she is unafraid, "not daunted by his eyes" (180), the very eyes that Sauron fears to endure in defeat. As Lúthien has subdued Carcharoth through a command that appears to enact his own desire for annihilation, here too she powerfully meets Morgoth's eye and offers him what he has desired: the possession of her body, identity, and song. We might also read the self-declaration and proposal of performance as a kind of concealed exchange or even as spell; Lúthien appears to offer "service" out of a position of weakness—and this is what Morgoth "sees"—when in reality she has worked through his bodily desire to create a space and time wherein she might take mastery of Angband.

In the performance that follows, the text appears to suspend time through the words-song-movements of Lúthien. We are privy not only to the power of her performance, "a song of such surpassing loveliness, and of such blinding power, that [Morgoth] listened perforce," but we are also privy to the bodily desire through which Morgoth is ensnared: "looking upon her beauty conceived in his thought an evil lust, and a design more dark than any that had yet come in to his heart since he fled from Valinor. Thus he was beguiled by his own malice, for he watched her, leaving her free for a while, and taking secret pleasure in his own thought" (*S* 180). Like Celegorm and Sauron before him, Morgoth clearly desires to possess Lúthien sexually, to dominate her, and by extension all the Eldar, through physical violence and constraint. As Slack notes, Morgoth's lust rests in "a desire [...] to thoroughly trammel what is in effect the last thing in Middle-[e]arth which still bears the grace of Eru's creation" (74). Worked through the body of

---

20. Whitaker in fact reads the passage as a literal "stripping," so that Lúthien stands before Morgoth's throne as body, exposed and under his violent gaze: "This same device, wherein truth, beauty, and nakedness are aligned, forms part of Lúthien's approach to Morgoth, in a scene that dares to imply female sexual power as a positive force" (65). Beren's abject position, still in wolf form and immobilized, offers her no help.

21. We might ask, in light of our reading, does she name herself Lúthien, or Tinúviel? We do not know, but in employing the "new" name she has gained through union with Beren, she would connect herself to the heroic tradition of epithets, as well as link herself to her mate.

Lúthien, his near masturbatory reverie, his pornographic ocular desire—that "secret pleasure in his own thought"—represents his "evil lust" for destruction and domination of Middle-earth itself.[22] Indeed, Whitaker reminds us that the text "equates the heinous depravity of [Morgoth's desire] with the destruction of the sacred trees of Valinor or of the marring of the music of the Ainur or of the wrongful possession of the Silmarils—it is a challenge, corruption or violation of the divine" (66). Rapt at his own imagined power over Lúthien, Morgoth loses himself, shrinks synecdotally into an eye that desires. At the locus of his power, he can do nothing; "perforce," he must attend, must acknowledge the power of this minstrel, and therein Lúthien's spell takes hold. Because Morgoth can only conceive violent control and perversion, he agrees to allow her performance, thereby "beguiling" himself through his own desire to see, to contain, to possess.[23]

As Lúthien stands exposed before the throne of Morgoth, she weaves a song that renders him blind and the court in suspension. A kind of pulsation develops in the passage as she sings: Lúthien eludes, Morgoth's eyes roam, Angband is "cast down in slumber," his fires "faded and were quenched," while the Silmarils "blazed forth" (*S* 181). Indeed, the *Lay of Leithian* emphasizes the reversal of power through images of Lúthien slipping, fluttering, constructing a "mazy-winged dance," speeding, ranging, and reeling (*Lays* 300–01), while Morgoth and the court fall into stupor. As Lúthien moves, as she sings, her power increases and her body gains increasing freedom; in contrast, her enemies grow slack, physically and, in the case of Morgoth, sexually impotent. In this state of suspension, Morgoth cannot deflect the power of Lúthien's cloak: "She cast her cloak before his eyes, and set upon him a dream, dark as the Outer Void where he

---

22. The *Lay of Leithian* allows Morgoth to speak his desires: "And who would not taste the honey-sweet / lying to lips, or crush with feet / the soft cool tissue of pale flowers, / easing like gods the dragging hours? [...] / O blinding thirst's unending fire! / One moment shall ye cease, and slake / your sting with morsel I here take!" (300). The images of crushing, devouring, and consuming suggest Morgoth's desire not only to possess Lúthien, but also to escape, to forget, to be released from the prison he has constructed.

23. The text's use of the terms "evil lust" and "beguiled" also evokes demonic overtones, as the familiar medieval motif "beguiler beguiled" begins to work itself through this episode. Like Satan, Morgoth falls by the very devices he employs to dominate others.

once walked alone. Suddenly he fell" (*S* 181). Through the use of her own body in performance, and through the power of the cloak constructed from her body, Lúthien brings Morgoth's monolithic body, literally, down to the earth. As with Sauron at Tol Sirion, Lúthien reverses power relations to render the powerful "dead," in a state of suspended consciousness, a kind of escape from the "weight of care, of fear, and of desire" they themselves have created (181). As with the sons of Fëanor, the degradation for those who would possess Lúthien is marked: "what song can sing [...] of [...] the wrath and humiliation of Morgoth, for even the Orcs laugh in secret when they remember it" (*Shaping* 113). Their own desires for domination through physical violence have rebounded through her song-cloak back onto themselves. The results are not destruction or literal death but loss of self, temporary escape from the "doom" of evil in which they live and, of course, a brief time when Lúthien and Beren may act.

When Lúthien exerts her magical power, it is grounded in the body and overcomes the distorted bodies of those around her. Through its repeated use as magical object, the cloak serves as covering for Lúthien, who is impervious to its somnolent power, and in her use and casting off the hair-cloak she overwhelms the power of those bodies that would possess hers. As Morgoth lies in suspension, "Lúthien touching [Beren] with her hand aroused him, and [...] from the iron claws that held it he cut a Silmaril" (*S* 181). Physical contact between the lovers, echoing their first encounters in Doriath, awakens Beren again, this time from abject fear and immobility rather than enchantment and desire. Lúthien thus can awaken and revive her lover, just as she can invoke slumber and unconsciousness in those who threaten her. In fact, in each instance where she is threatened by the gaze and desires of males to contain, use, and sexually assault her, those violent desires result in their own bodily disintegration—loss of object, loss of power and control, and loss of consciousness itself. When she touches Beren, however, her powers of healing and renewal emerge once again; thus, within the space of utter absence, Lúthien maintains all manifestations of her power.

However, upon emerging from the pits of Angband, Lúthien arrives at the limits of that power: "Lúthien was spent, and she had not time nor strength to quell the wolf" who "stood now in wrath upon the threshold of Angband" (*S* 181). After so long in silence or immobility, it is Beren who stands forth to challenge the wolf. Offering the sight of the

Silmaril as weapon against Carcharoth's threat, Beren only awakens "the devouring spirit within [Carcharoth] [...] and gaping he suddenly took the hand within his jaws, and he bit it off at the wrist" (181). Both lovers emerge from their quest, from the pits of Angband, with bodies maimed: Lúthien has "spent" her power in gaining entrance to Angband and then in quelling the desire of Morgoth; Beren's hand, holding the Silmaril, cannot withstand the devouring menace of the wolf. Ultimately, the text suggests that their "oneness," the force of Lúthien's physical power, and even the Light of the Silmaril, are no match for the consuming force of evil. Continuing the technique of reversal, however, the devourer and his desire to consume is itself devoured by the jewel: "swiftly all his inwards were filled with a flame of anguish, and the Silmaril seared his accursed flesh. Howling he fled before them, and the walls of the valley of the Gate echoed with the clamour of his torment" (181–82). Where the bodies and force of the two lovers cannot stand against the power of those who would devour and annihilate, the Silmaril itself consumes, flames, sears and physically torments: the devourer is devoured, the tormenter tormented.

While Carcharoth "burst from the North with ruin upon the world," Lúthien must again heal Beren's broken body: "Lúthien with her lips drew out the venom, and she put forth her failing power to staunch the hideous wound" (*S* 182). The cosmic nature of their quest—to defeat Morgoth and regain the Silmaril—now recedes to reemphasize the intimate connection between the lovers; the passage thus offers a sense of opposition between the violent forces who seek destruction and the healing power of Lúthien. In another form of physical union, Lúthien mingles her fluids with Beren's, as she employs her "failing power" to draw out the "fell and poisonous" (183) venom of the wolf. She places her mouth over the wound, the gaping absence at the wrist where Beren held the Silmaril and where Carcharoth consumed them both. Her body thus "devours" the poisons of Carcharoth and transforms the site of Beren's achievement (Silmaril) and agony (wound). As Beren traverses the borders between life and death, his body-spirit on the threshold between them, Lúthien offers the last of her powers to heal and renew; Beren "was drawn back to life by the love of Lúthien" (183), and the lovers once again enjoy a transitory time in the forest: "together they walked in the woods once more" (183).[24] Even before her final performance before Mandos, then, Lúthien here resurrects Beren, heals his body, and is "willing to wander in the wild without returning" (183). At this point, the achievement of the quest for the Silmaril appears less the focus of the narrative than Lúthien's power to call back, to transform, and to reconstruct "oneness" out of altered, broken, and "suffering" forms.

Significantly, the tale not only develops a contrast between the forces of evil Lúthien actually confronts on the quest, but on a larger scale—at the level of Middle-earth's cosmic story—it also suggests that Lúthien's narrative of love, healing, power, and song serves as counterpoint to Ungoliant's ancient tale of hatred, devastation, and devouring of all light and good. Where Ungoliant desires beauty and light as a kind of food to nourish the womb of her own evil void (a familiar anxiety about the feminine within the Ungoliant narrative), Lúthien employs her bodily power to release beauty and light from the caverns of void, Angband. In many ways, in her representation as the monstrous feminine, a being who "was able to undo the fabric of Tolkien's universe with her darkness" (Lionarons 6), Ungoliant haunts or treads the borders of the tale of Tinúviel.[25] Initially, Beren negotiates the horror between two dangerous spaces, both constructed by female power: Dungortheb, where "spiders of the fell race of Ungoliant abode, spinning their unseen webs in which all living things were snared" (*S* 164), and the girdle of Melian, where the Maia's power is woven around Doriath as a protection against penetration. Side by side, two "feminine" powers weave and constrain; both "weave fabric, flesh, and fates" (Miesel 151). More specifically, Lúthien's own embodied power, her cloak, woven from her own hair, stands as a reversal of Ungoliant's own foul web, "an Unlight, in which things seemed to be no more, and which eyes could not pierce, for it was void" (*S* 74). Both use their cloaks to escape and to mask

---

24. Brückner, too, describes Beren as "languish[ing] at the threshold of death" (16) and claims that "It is the conflict between the political and the private sphere that forces Beren to return to Menegroth, even though Lúthien suggests a joint exile in the forests" (17).

25. Miesel describes all the spider-beings of Tolkien's world: "With ravening maws that can never be filled [...] [they] are monstrous, death-dealing mothers who mate with their sons and devour them" (148).

their quests, but Lúthien's cloak casts the evil she confronts into forgetful sleep, into a place beyond their evil constructions, whereas Ungoliant's web-cloak obscures the descent of Morgoth into Aman.[26] Once confronted with the Light—the two trees of Valinor—"she sucked up all light that she could find and spun it forth again in nets of strangling gloom" (73).[27] In the fulfillment of her quest, Lúthien releases the last remaining portion of light from the "strangling gloom" of Angband. Through the work of her body—manifested in the cloak here in particular—Lúthien succeeds in a recuperative act, an act that reclaims the power of the Light from the Void that had held it captive.

In the closing instance of the intimate's influence on the cosmic, Lúthien's final song in the Halls of Mandos "weaves" the entire narrative of the Silmarillion through her bodily experience of love for Beren. The description of her song reads as a microcosm of the history that we have thus far encountered in the text: "For Lúthien wove two themes of words, of the sorrow of the Eldar and the grief of Men, of the Two Kindreds that were made by Ilúvatar to dwell in Arda, The Kingdom of Earth amid the innumerable stars" (*S* 187). As a bard equal in power to Daeron and Maglor, Lúthien adds the thread of her own story into the larger tapestry of the Story of Arda, and her reward is not only reunion with Beren and a second life, but also physical transformation, a miracle of bodily "shape-shifting." For what

---

26. Lionarons observes Tolkien's alignment of Elves and spiders: "Most importantly, both elves and spiders spin thread and weave webs [...] Both spinning and weaving are, of course, traditional occupations of women, and [...] both are associated with magic, fate, and death" (8). While Lionarons's discussion focuses primarily on the associations between Galadriel and Shelob in *The Lord of the Rings,* and while she does not reference Lúthien, she acknowledges the aligning of spider and elf in Ungoliant's primary devouring.

27. Flieger calls Ungoliant "swollen, monstrous [...] a ghastly perversion of nourishment and a perversion also of the light" (112). Donovan, in her exploration of the valkyrie complex in *The Lord of the Rings,* notes that Shelob, the descendent of Ungoliant, "reverses the weaving [...] motif related to the benevolent valkyrie" and calls Shelob "monstrous," noting the webs she spins to snare her prey (120). Lionarons aligns Shelob with "deathly sexuality," in opposition to Galadriel's "regenerative effect" on Sam (12). Chance, too, describes Shelob in terms applicable to her ancestor Ungoliant: "cruel [. . .] predatory greed" (*Mythology* 70); "mindless and immoral [...] moved solely by appetite in her actions" (79). Griessel and Kotzé, developing Garreth Hill's notion of the "Static Feminine," associate the negative aspect of the archetype [the Terrible Mother] with phrases evoking Ungoliant's horror: "smothering entanglement, inertia, [...] ensnaring and devouring" (187).

does it mean that Lúthien "would become mortal" (187)? As one of the Eldar, she is once inexorably bound to Middle-earth, to live as long as Middle-earth lasts. Once she accepts Manwë's option to become human, we might speculate that she is physiologically altered as well. In this process of "transfiguration" (Flieger 139), her own mortal body then re-enters history with Beren, outwardly the same yet inwardly changed from eternal elven to human mortal. Lúthien's final achievement in her tale, then, is one which echoes her previous deeds: song and performance, weaving, rebelling (this time against the Fate of both Kindreds), casting enchantment, attainment of the impossible quest (resurrection and transformation of bodies) and finally, a return once again to the forest idyll with Beren. Through the construction of such a character who manifests power through physical union and through acts of singing, weaving, cloaking, revealing, and reversal, it is possible to glimpse the text working to construct a female sexuality and a female-centered narrative at the core of the legendarium.

Interspersed through the tale's recounting of Lúthien's and Beren's confrontations with evil, their forest interludes remind us of their marriage/union, of Lúthien's powers of healing, and of a space beyond or outside the normal passage of time. That these moments are transitory, of course, presciently describe her chosen doom: mortality. Considering the ways in which the text grounds its narrative structure and its heroine's power in control over and through the body allows us to revise our understanding of the feminine and feminine sexuality beyond the convenient binary: divine chaste spirit beyond the world or horror-filled absence that devours.[28] Lúthien's forest encounters with Beren introduce the possibility of a healthy sexual desire that results in heroic action centered on and fulfilled largely through the female's power. In fact, Lúthien and Beren's bodily "oneness" becomes necessary and moral as read against the bodily domination of forces such as Sauron and Morgoth (and even Celegorm and Curufin). Further, Lúthien's particular choice to fulfill her curiosity, to seek out Beren, and to name herself "rebellious daughter" (*Lays* 298), and thus to identify herself as

28. Jung identified the conceptions of the feminine as just such a binary: "all that is benign, all that cherishes and sustains, furthers growth and fertility," and that which "connotes what devours, seduces, and poisons" (82).

sexually aware, constructs a woman in Tolkien's text who successfully re-writes the power of the feminine body.

That Lúthien returns in a mortal body only to die—swiftly, due in part to the glory of the Silmaril she wears after Thingol's death—beautifully evokes the ways in which her story reflects the entire "drama" that is Arda Marred. Lúthien, "whom they have lost" (*S* 187), no longer exists in body, and the physical union she and Beren construct cannot last, but their union and their quest serve as the reminder of Eru's words at the Music of the Ainur: all that Melkor has marred "shall prove but mine instrument in the devising of things more wonderful, which he himself hath not imagined" (*S* 17). Not only do Lúthien and Beren's progeny (Dior, Elwing) thwart the grand design of the Great Marrer Morgoth and, through Eärendil, elevate the Silmaril the lovers both gained, but Lúthien's body itself disappears to leave only her tale, the great narrative that will last even beyond the fading of the Firstborn.[29] She now shares the Gift of Men and will not wait in Mandos to return to her kindred; where she is, the Elves and even the Valar do not know.[30] While Morgoth has also marred this Gift so that some consider it a Curse, Lúthien appears to comprehend that mortality, and the loss of the body, while melancholy for those left behind, takes her (with Beren) beyond Arda Marred to a position envisioned by Eru himself. If Finrod's vision is correct, humans will play a central role in the fulfillment of Arda Healed, a role that Lúthien, now a human mortal, may both further in Time and participate in at its end: "This, then, I propound, was the errand of Men, not the followers, but the heirs and fulfillers of all: to heal the Marring of Arda, already foreshad-

29. As Tolkien notes in several places in his legendarium, Beren and Lúthien's position is unique and transformative for the Story and the future of Arda: "Thus from the union of Lúthien and Beren which was made possible by their return [from death, in bodies], the infusion of a 'divine' and an Elvish strain into Mankind was to be brought about, providing a link between Mankind and the Elder World" (*Morgoth* 340).

30. In "Of the Beginning of Days," Eru is recorded as claiming: "But to the Atani I will give a new gift" (*S* 41). This gift is unique, "the gift of freedom" (42) in that "[Men] should have a virtue to shape their life [...] beyond the Music of the Ainur, which is as fate to all things else" (41). In his discussion with Andreth, Finrod, too, sees the distinction between Elves and Men: "the *fëar* of Men, though close akin indeed to the fëar of the Quendi, are yet not the same. For strange as we deem it, we see clearly that the fëar of Men are not, as are ours, confined to Arda, nor is Arda their home" (*Morgoth* 315).

owed before their devising; and to do more, as agents of the magnificence of Eru: to enlarge the Music and surpass the Vision of the World!" (*Morgoth* 318).

Works Cited

Benvenuto, Maria Raffaella. "Against Stereotype: Éowyn and Lúthien as 20th Century Women." *Tolkien and Modernity 1*. Eds. Frank Weinreich and Thomas Honegger. Zollikofen, Switzerland: Walking Tree, 2006. 31–54. Print.

Brückner, Patrick. "Tolkien on Love: Concepts of 'Love' in *The Silmarillion* and *The Lord of the Rings*." *Tolkien and Modernity 2*. Eds. Thomas Honegger and Frank Weinreich. Zollikofen, Switzerland: Walking Tree, 2006. 1–52. Print.

Chance, Jane. The Lord of the Rings: *The Mythology of Power*. New York: Twayne Publishers, 1992. Print.

---, ed. *Tolkien the Medievalist*. New York: Routledge, 2003. Print.

---. "Tolkien's Women (and Men): The Films and the Book." *Tolkien on Film: Essays on Peter Jackson's* The Lord of the Rings. Ed. Janet Brennan Croft. Altadena, CA: Mythopoeic Press, 2004. 175–93. Print.

Donovan, Leslie A. "The Valkyrie Reflex in J. R. R. Tolkien's *The Lord of the Rings*: Galadriel, Shelob, Éowyn, and Arwen." Chance, *Medievalist* 106–32. *Reprinted in this volume.*

Eilmann, Julian Tim Morton. "I am the Song: Music, Poetry, and the Transcendent in J. R. R. Tolkien's Middle-earth." Kerry and Miesel 99–118.

Enright, Nancy. "Tolkien's Females and the Defining of Power." *Renascence: Essays on Values in Literature* 59.2 (2007): 93–108. Web. 15 August 2013. *Reprinted in this volume.*

Flieger, Verlyn. *Splintered Light: Logos and Language in Tolkien's World*. 2nd ed. Kent, OH: Kent State UP, 2002. Print.

Fredrick, Candice, and Sam McBride. *Women Among the Inklings: Gender, C. S. Lewis, J. R. R. Tolkien, and Charles Williams*. Contributions in Women's Studies, vol. 191. Westport, CT: Greenwood Press, 2001. Print.

Griessel, Loura, and Martine Kotzé. "The Feminine and the Masculine in the Development of the Self in Women: A Post-Jungian Perspective." *Women's Studies* 38.2 (2009): 183–212. Web. 8 September 2013.

Jung, C. G. *The Archetypes of the Collective Unconscious*. 2nd ed. Trans. R. F. C. Hull. Princeton, NJ: Princeton UP, 1968. Print.

Kerry, Paul E., and Sandra Miesel, eds. *Light Beyond All Shadow: Religious Experience in Tolkien's Works*. Madison, NJ: Farleigh Dickinson UP, 2001. Print.

Lionarons, Joyce Tally. "Of Elves and Spiders." *Mythlore* 31.3/4 (#121/122) (Spring/Summer 2013): 5–13. Web. 10 August 2013.

Miesel, Sandra. "Life-giving Ladies: Women in the Writings of J. R. R. Tolkien." Kerry and Miesel 139–52.

Saxey, Esther. "Homoeroticism." *Reading* The Lord of the Rings: *New Writings of Tolkien's Classic*. Ed. Robert Eaglestone. London: Continuum, 2005. 124–37. Print.

Shakespeare. William. *As You Like It*. *The Complete Works of Shakespeare*. 6th ed. Ed. David Bevington. New York: Pearson, 2009. 298–332. Print.

Slack, Anna. "Moving Mandos: The Dynamics of Subcreation in 'Of Beren and Lúthien.' " *The Silmarillion: Thirty Years On*. Ed. Allan Turner. Zollikofen, Switzerland: Walking Tree, 2007. 59–79. Print.

West, Richard C. "Real-world Myth in a Secondary World: Mythological Aspects in the Story of Beren and Lúthien." Chance, *Medievalist* 257–67.

Whitaker, Lynn. "Corrupting Beauty: Rape Narrative in *The Silmarillion*." *Mythlore* 29.1/2 (#111/112) (Fall/Winter 2010): 51–68. Web. 10 August 2013.

The Power of Pity and Tears:
The Evolution of Nienna in the Legendarium

Kristine Larsen

Of all the works penned by J. R. R. Tolkien, the one dearest to his heart was the one that failed to see publication until after his death: *The Silmarillion*. As he had explained a letter to Milton Waldman (circa 1951), "once upon a time [...] I had in mind to make a body of more or less connected legend, ranging from the large and cosmogonic, to the level of romantic fairy-story" (*Letters* 144). Tolkien's first characters are not elves, dwarves, or even hobbits, but rather the pantheon of Ilúvatar (the "God" figure of Tolkien's cosmology) and the demigods and demigoddesses, known collectively as the Ainur. A subset of these angelic beings takes on a greater role in the great song of creation and eagerly accepts the responsibility to be bound to the newborn world of Arda until its eventual end in the distant future. These beings become known as the Valar and with them are associated beings of the same type but lesser power, the Maiar. While the fundamental concepts of the music of creation and the Ainur enter the legendarium in its earliest forms (in *The Book of Lost Tales*), many of the basic powers, personalities, and familial relationships of the Valar shift (sometimes quite dramatically) during the six decades in which Tolkien rewrote and re-imagined his subcreation. Indeed, Verlyn Flieger warns that the "published *Silmarillion* gives a misleading impression of coherence and finality, as if it were a definitive, canonical text, whereas the mass of material from which that volume was taken is a jumble of overlapping and often competing stories, annals, and lexicons" (63).

In J. R. R. Tolkien's published *Silmarillion*, many of the Valar have clearly defined roles (such as Varda, Queen of the Stars, Mandos, Pronouncer of Dooms, and Yavanna, Guardian of Living Things) and there is no doubt of their powers and their central role in the narrative. However, others among the Valar leave the reader uncertain what their main role might be. Among these is Nienna,[1] listed third among the seven Valier (Queens of the Valar) numerated in the "Valequenta" section of the work, behind Varda and Yavanna (*S* 25). Within the main text of the "Quenta Silmarillion," Nienna is only mentioned (and quite briefly) in four specific incidents: when her tears water the Two Trees at their birth, wash away the stain of Ungoliant at their death, and attempt to resurrect them; and during the pardoning of Melkor in Valmar, when she prays on his behalf.

More than one reader of *The Silmarillion* has wondered (if they remember her at all) if she does anything more important than cry. Is Nienna nothing more than a stereotypical weepy woman? Fortunately for feminist readers of Tolkien, Nienna is one of the most powerful of the Valar and plays a central, albeit subtle, role in the legendarium. As the "Valaquenta" declares, Nienna is "acquainted with grief, and mourns for every wound that Arda has suffered in the marring of Melkor. So great was her sorrow, as the Music unfolded, that her song turned to lamentation long before its end, and the sound of mourning was woven into the themes of the World before it began" (*S* 28). She weeps for all living beings and for all hurts in the world, and from her is learned "pity, and endurance in hope" (28). Rather than reside in Valmar where all is joyous, she instead dwells close to the Halls of Mandos and comforts those of the Firstborn (Elves) who wait within its walls for rebirth. It is not to Varda that these elves cry, but rather to Nienna, who "brings strength to the spirit and turns sorrow to wisdom" (28). Nienna's propensity for tears is certainly a feminine attribute, but as Lisa Hopkins argues, in the case of some of Tolkien's female characters, "their very femininity" is the "very source of their strength" (365). The evolution of Nienna from the earliest versions of the legendarium through the post *Lord of the Rings* period indicates that, by the late 1950s, she indeed has become one of the most powerful figures behind the curtain of Middle-earth, a far cry from her initial iteration in *The Book of Lost Tales* as the pronouncer of dooms for individual humans.

---

1. Tolkien is inconsistent in his spelling of this name, vacillating between Nienna and Niënna. The former will be used consistently throughout this essay as it is the form published in *The Silmarillion*.

Nienna Mark I: The Mistress of Death

While all the Valar evolve to some extent throughout the decades, some change quite dramatically, growing and/or diminishing in prominence and powers as Tolkien revises the philosophy and cosmogony of Middle-earth. A strong example is Varda, Queen of the Stars, wife of Manwë (King of the Valar), and arguably the most important of the Valier. In a previous work (Larsen), the author detailed the evolution of Varda's personality and powers in the legendarium, roughly chronologically through four periods of Tolkien's writing: the first iteration of *The Book of Lost Tales* (1916–26), a second iteration prior to beginning *The Lord of the Rings* (1927–37), a third iteration during the writing of *The Lord of the Rings* (1938–54), and a final fourth iteration. In this work, the relative passivity of Varda in *The Book of Lost Tales* is justified as simply reflecting the traditional gender roles found in Tolkien's early work. For example, in the darkness that follows Melko[r]'s destruction of the Trees, "then were Vána and Nessa and Urwen and many maids and ladies of the Valar in tears, but Palúrien [Yavanna] girds her lord as he stands impatiently, and Varda has ridden forth from Taniquetil by her lord's side bearing a blazing star before him as a torch" (154). In this case, while most of the female Valar are paralyzed with grief, only two—Yavanna and Varda—appear to play any active role. In *Perilous Realms*, Marjorie Burns contends that in their relative passivity Tolkien's Valier resemble Norse goddesses, who are "far more static, far more focused on service and providing what others need" (153). Among her specific examples, Burns names Nienna, whom she calls "the communal mourner" (153). But mourning in Tolkien's legendarium is not necessarily passive and often serves some active purpose. More importantly, Nienna was not initially passive by any definition; indeed, initially, she was more powerful than Varda in some respects.

"The Coming of the Valar" chronicles the order and natures of the beings who enter Tolkien's world. Among these[2] are the two Tári, "la-

---

2. Melko (as Melkor was first known) enters first into the world, then Manwë and Varda and their retinue (the Mánir and Súrilu). The second wave consists of Ulmo, Aulë, and Palúrien (Yavanna), along with a variety of related lesser spirits. After these "greatest chieftains" follows a variety of sea-related spirits (including Ossë and his consort Ónen), and then Tulkas, accompanied by the brothers Vefántur Mandos, the Fantur of Death, and Lórien Olofántur, the Fantur of Dreams, as well

dies of great worship, queens of the Valar" (*Lost Tales I* 66). The first is named Fui Nienna, wife of Mandos, "fain of mourning and tears" (66). Her other names include "Núri who sighs and Heskil who breedeth winter, and all must bow before her as Qalmë-Tári, the mistress of death" (66). According to the appendix on names, *fui* is Gnomish for "night" and her Gnomish name is Fuil, "Queen of the Dark" (253). Nienna derives from the Qenya *nië* "tear" (262). The other Tári is Vána Tuivána, wife of Oromë (here, the son of Aulë and Yavanna) and the bringer of spring, also known as Tári-Laisi, "mistress of life" (67). It is interesting to contrast the differences between this original and the final listings of the Valar in the published *Silmarillion*.[3] Two important changes are the reduction in power of Vána—here seen in juxtaposition with Nienna as both goddesses of the seasons and (in a parallel symbolism) the bringers of life and death—and the eventual shift of Nienna from wife of Mandos to a solitary maiden, opening up a spot in the pantheon for Vairë the Weaver as the mistress of the Halls of Mandos.

As in the published *Silmarillion*, Mandos and Nienna dwell apart from the rest of the Valar (in the *Book of Lost Tales*, due to the brightness of the Two Trees), choosing instead dark halls delved for them by Aulë beneath the roots of northern mountains, Vê for Mandos and Fui for Nienna. Nienna prefers to dwell in her own hall, the "wider and more dark" of the two, lit by a brazier with a single coal, sitting upon a black chair beneath the roof made of bats' wings and supported by pillars of black, volcanic basalt (*Lost Tales I* 77). Much of her time is spent distilling "salt humours" from which she creates the tears of the world and which she sends forth in "lightless webs" of black clouds that bring "despairs and hopeless mourning, sorrows and blind grief" (76–77). As in the later legendarium, Mandos passes judgment on the Firstborn, and they remain in his care until they are reborn. (However, in this early permutation of the eschatology, they are specifically reborn into their

---

(note continued)

as the two Tári. Finally, come rushing into the world Makar and his sister Meásse and lesser "quarrelsome" spirits aligned with Melko, and the youngest of the Valar, Amillo the singer (*Lost Tales I* 66–67).

3. These differences include the last three characters (who were soon dropped in revisions of the legendarium), the later demotion of Ossë (with his wife, renamed Uinen) to the Maiar, the promotion of Nessa, wife of Tulkas, to the greater Valar, and the later invention of Estë, wife of Lórien.

children.) Nienna's role is a clear and significant departure from the published *Silmarillion,* as she is the judge for the human dead who come to her halls "to hear their doom" after dying from any of "the multitude of ills that Melko's evil music set within the world" (77). Christopher Tolkien explains that this initial role for Nienna is in "deep contradiction to the central thought of the later mythology," in which death is deemed the gift of Ilúvatar for humans, who go to some unknown fate beyond the world upon dying, in opposition to the Elves and Valar, who are bound to the world until its end (*Lost Tales I* 90).

While the initial version of humanity's afterlife in Middle-earth stands in stark opposition to its later description, it is transparently familiar to the reader as explicitly Christian in its symbolism. For upon treading the path to Nienna's halls (a path separate from that taken by elves to Mandos's domain), a human's heart is read by Nienna, and his or her doom pronounced. Some go to the company of Mandos, some (presumably those of evil heart) she drives out to be captured by Melko and taken to the Hells of Iron (Angamandi), and the majority set sail on the black ship Mornië to be taken to the plains of Arvalin to "wander in the dusk" under the light of the stars "and wait in patience till the Great End" (*Lost Tales I* 77). Christopher Tolkien interprets this tale and the associated poem "Habbanan Beneath the Stars" (91–92) as representing Heaven, Hell, and Purgatory (92). Interestingly, in the original Túrin tale ("Turambar and the Foalókë"), Túrin and his sister/wife Nienóri are refused entrance into the afterlife by both Nienna and Mandos. It is Manwë who shows mercy and allows the pair to enter the Fôs'Almir (bath of flame) to purify their sins and reside among the Valar (*Lost Tales II* 115). Elizabeth Whittingham draws parallels between this three-fold fate of humans and Greek and Latin mythologies as well as the Eddas (132), and, in "Norse and Christian Gods," Marjorie Burns connects Fui Nienna with the Norse Hel, daughter of Loki (173–74). Regardless of one's interpretation of this early Middle-earth afterlife, it is clear that the merciless Nienna of *The Book of Lost Tales* bears little resemblance to the kinder, gentler underworld goddess of the *Lord of the Rings*-era texts of *The Silmarillion.*

Nienna Mark II: Solitary Lady of Sorrows

In the published *Silmarillion,* Nienna is numbered among the eight Aratar (nine if one counts Melkor), those Valar of "chief power and reverence" (*S* 29). She is the "Lady of pity and mourning," sister to the Fëanturi, and dwells alone (343). In this last respect, she stands in opposition to the other Valier, who all have spouses. Among the Valar, only Ulmo (and Melkor) also live alone. This solitary existence sets her apart not only in a physical sense, but also in strength, as she needs no male consort to complement or bolster her base of power. It can be argued that this is simply because her strength lies in a traditionally feminine role. Yet, while pity and mourning may be traditionally more feminine roles, such an explanation tends to denigrate the power of pity and mourning, for to relegate something to the feminine sphere is to lower its stature in Western culture (e.g., the perceptions of such professions as nursing, teaching, and caretaking). Instead, a detailed analysis of the post-Fui metamorphosis of Nienna will reveal the shift in Nienna's powers.

After *The Book of Lost Tales,* the next legendarium texts are the brief sketch (the first "Silmarillion") and the "Quenta," followed in rapid succession by the "Annals of Valinor" and the "Later Annals of Valinor" (texts AV1 and AV2, respectively). In "Quenta," Nienna is said to be mightier than Vána (now simply called the Queen of Flowers) and remains the companion of Mandos (here called Nefantur Mandos) (*Shaping* 79). No longer does she judge the fate of humankind, but instead "Pity is in her heart, and mourning and weeping come to her," a description remarkably modern in terms of the legendarium (79). As Burns observes, this Nienna is "a more kindly, more genteel version of the weeping goddess figure" and more akin to the Norse goddesses Frigg and Freyja ("Norse" 169). The solitary nature of Nienna also quickly enters the legendarium; in AV1, Estë and Vairë appear for the first time as the wives of the brothers Lórien and Mandos, respectively (*Shaping* 270). Nienna now takes on a dual position of authority, being a single maiden of power and also the sister of Manwë and Melko (263). Estë becomes the healer and giver of rest, a natural companion to her husband, the giver of dreams.

But some hurts cannot be healed, at least not in the realm of the living, and some hopes and dreams must be left unfulfilled, especially in Middle-earth; thus, Nienna remains an important player in the pantheon. In the next expansion of the mythology, "Quenta Silmarillion" (the last major revision before the writing of *The Lord of the Rings*), Nienna once again prefers the dark halls of the dead to the light of the

Two Trees, now visiting the Halls of Mandos which lie nearer her own hidden halls. Importantly, she is "a healer of hurts, and turns pains to medicine and sorrow to wisdom;" for this reason "all those who go to Mandos cry to her" (*Lost Road* 206). This description is notable for two reasons; first, it remains relatively consistent through the legendarium's subsequent development, shifting only slightly to read "for she brings strength to the spirit and turns sorrow to wisdom" (*S* 28) in the published "Valaquenta" (a document Christopher Tolkien dates to the late 1950s [*Morgoth* 199]); second, the Elves are said to cry to her, a power not given to Varda until the later revisions of the legendarium during the writing of *The Lord of the Rings*. Therefore, while Varda's powers certainly increased during the writing of the evolution of the legendarium in the 1930s and 1940s (Larsen), those of Nienna grew earlier and remained consistent. Also, while Vairë has been created to take the place of companion to Mandos, she is no replacement for Nienna, for she has lesser importance in the eschatology. Indeed, Vairë is merely the neutral recorder of history, through her weaving of "storied webs" that hang in her husband's halls (*Lost Road* 205).

The shift in Nienna's character creates a domino effect in the Valar beyond the creation of the characters Estë and Vairë. In the first iteration of the creation of the sun and moon in *The Book of Lost Tales*, for instance, Mandos and Fui Nienna complain that there will no longer be "quiet or peaceful shadow" (*Lost Tales I* 189). Further, in "Quenta," it is Lórien and Nienna who complain that the new lights will banish "all sleep and night and peace from the earth" (*Shaping* 97), a refrain that remains in "Quenta Silmarillion" and finally changes to Lórien and Estë in the texts of the 1950s (*Morgoth* 198), many years after Estë enters the pantheon. Vána also continues to recede into the background; without a goddess of winter, there is a reduced role for a goddess of spring, and by the final version of "Valaquenta," Vána is merely known only as the Ever-young wife of Oromë and sister of Yavanna, a favorite of birds and flowers (*S* 29). A final change in Nienna that impacts the other Valar is her late shift (in the post *Lord of the Rings* manuscript LQ2) from sister of Manwë and Melkor to sister of Lórien and Mandos, a move which might be seen as diminishing her relative importance, but is quite logical given her roles and brings her full circle from *The Book of Lost Tales* as a natural visitor to the halls of the dead (*Morgoth* 149).

The Power of Pity in a Fallen World I: Examples from the Legendarium

In a letter to Milton Waldman circa late 1951, Tolkien writes that there "cannot be any 'story' without a fall—all stories are ultimately about the fall" (*Letters* 147). The fall in question is a loss of grace, the loss of Eden in a Biblical sense, and the primary reason for sorrow in the world. But as Tolkien explains in an unsent letter from 1958, the fall of Middle-earth differs from that of the Christian world because the evil caused by Melkor is woven into the very fabric of the world from its beginning, rather than being introduced after the world was born (*Letters* 286). The world of Middle-earth, therefore, is flawed from its very birth—Arda Marred, as it is termed—making pain and sorrow inevitable. This concept of the evils of the world being woven into the song of creation by Melkor dates back to the earliest version of the tale, "The Music of the Ainur" in *The Book of Lost Tales*. Here, Tolkien notes that through Melkor's actions "has pain and misery [...] cruelty, and ravening, and darkness [...] violent flame, cold without mercy, been born, and death without hope" (*Lost Tales I* 55). The 1930s version of the "Ainulindalë" records that Ilúvatar's third theme is "blended with unquenchable sorrow, from which its beauty chiefly came" (*Lost Road* 158), while in the "Ainulindalë version C" of the late 1940s the sorrow is changed to "immeasurable," a term that remains in the published form (*Morgoth* 10).

Nevertheless, it is not mere sadness that is woven into creation, but an acknowledgement of what has been lost, mourning for Arda Unmarred, set there by Nienna herself. In "Valaquenta," we read that "so great was her sorrow, as the Music unfolded, that her song turned to lamentation long before its end, and the sound of mourning was woven into the themes of the World before it began" (*S* 28). Her deep understanding of the inherent sorrows of the World That Is causes Nienna not only to weep, but provides her tears with their power. In the initial tale of the Two Trees, the powers of Yavanna and Vána (as the then goddess of spring and life) bring forth the Two Trees, and the tears (specifically tears of love) from Vána produce the last buds of the dying Trees after Melko's attack (*Lost Tales I* 71; 183–84). After the first revision of the legendarium and the above-mentioned changes to Vána and Nienna, it is the latter who helps Yavanna to sprout the trees by watering them with her tears, a change that persists in the legendarium to its publication. In this revision, Yavanna's powers of "growth and healing" solely produce the final fruit and flower (*Lost Road* 240). In the late 1950s "Annals of Aman," it is Yavanna and Nienna who are charged by Manwë with saving the Trees. While Nienna's tears do not heal the wounds, they are apparently an important part of the tale, as they remain through subsequent revisions (*Morgoth* 129–30).

Tears cannot heal all wounds, but mourning is an important part of dealing with death. This is not the first time Nienna weeps in relation to the Two Trees in this version of the tale. When Fëanor refuses to allow the Silmarils to be used to revive the trees, Nienna weeps and mourns "the bitterness of the world" (107). This passage is extended in LQII, where she "cast back her gray hood, and her eyes shone like stars in the rain, for her tears were poured out, and she washed away the defilements of Ungoliantë. And when she had wept she sang slowly, mourning for the bitterness of the world and all hurts of the Marring of Arda," a reflection of her part in the Music as described in "Valaquenta" (293). A revision of the "Annals of Aman," referred to as "AAm*" by Christopher Tolkien, blends together the two ideas, explaining that

> it is said that even in the Music Nienna took little part, but listened intent to all that she heard. Therefore she was rich in memory, and farsighted, perceiving how the themes should unfold in the Tale of Arda. But she had little mirth, and all her love was mixed with pity, grieving for the harms of the world and for the things that failed of fulfillment. So great was her ruth,[4] it is said, that she could not endure to the end of the Music. Therefore she has not the hope of Manwë. He is more farseeing; but Pity is the heart of Nienna. (*Morgoth* 68)

Tolkien later considered attributing to Varda this passage in a truncated form that importantly did not mention pity. The abridged descriptor would appear to diminish the power of Varda, who previously was a character of concrete deeds (such as the creation of the stars). However, in its complete form (centered around pity), it has the opposite effect on Nienna. Thus, this post-*Lord of the Rings* text most clearly articulates Nienna's cosmic role as the personification of not only sorrow *for* the evils of the fallen world, but also of pity and its central role *in* Arda Marred.

---

4. Bratman explains that Tolkien used *ruth* as a synonym for "pity or compassion" (419).

In a fallen world where misery abounds, pity and mercy cannot cure sorrow, but they do not add to it further. They are the proper response to living in an imperfect world filled with fallen beings. Tolkien himself calls mercy "the supreme value and efficacy of pity and forgiveness of injury" (*Letters* 252). Peter Kreeft notes that Tolkien uses pity and mercy as synonyms and to describe an action, especially in *The Lord of the Rings* (217). Mercy and pity play central roles in a number of famous tales in the legendarium, such as the tale of Beren and Lúthien, where the song of Lúthien moves Mandos to pity and tears at Beren's death. Another example is Ilúvatar's mercy towards Aulë's ill-thought attempt at being a creator; he adopts the Dwarves as his children rather than allowing Aulë to destroy them. Otherwise flawed characters reveal their potential for goodness when they show mercy in the legendarium, such as Maglor, son of Fëanor, when he adopts Elrond and Elros after the kinslaying at Sirion, and Túrin when he spares Mîm and shares in grieving the dwarf's slain son. Eärendil sails West seeking pardon "for the Noldor and pity for their great sorrows, and mercy upon Men and Elves" (*S* 249), a wish granted by the Valar. Finally, the Valar and their armies catch Melkor unawares because he could not fathom that the Valar would come to the aid of Middle-earth. In Tolkien's words, "to him that is pitiless the deeds of pity are ever strange and beyond reckoning" (251).

In light of this passage, it is all the more telling that one of the persistent actions of Nienna in the legendarium is to aid Melkor's prayers for pardon before the Valar in Valinor (before the death of the Two Trees), a reason why she was (until late in the legendarium) called his sister (*Shaping* 277). In the "Debate of the Valar over the Statute of Finwë and Míriel" (in "Laws and Customs among the Eldar" in "The Later Quenta Silmarillion"), Nienna asks not only that Míriel's wish to abandon her body be granted out of pity, but that, in their considerations of the request, the Valar put themselves in her place, a difficult task as none of them had "known the weariness of Míriel, or felt the bereavement of Finwë" (*Morgoth* 242). One outcome of this debate is a realization of the extent of Melkor's damage to "the substance of Arda, so that all those who were incarnate and drew the sustenance of their bodies from Arda Marred, must ever be liable to grief, to do or to suffer things unnatural in Arda Marred" (258–59). In such a world, there is much need for a lady of mourning, mercy, and pity.

The Power of Pity in a Fallen World II: Mercy in The Lord of the Rings

According to several letters written after its publication, Tolkien saw the central theme of *The Lord of the Rings* to be the sorrows of death (in the case of humans) and deathlessness (from the Elvish perspective) (*Letters* 146; 246; 262; 284). Mercy and pity play central roles in the novel, so much so that Tolkien was forced to revise a vital scene in *The Hobbit* in order to more closely conform to this theme. According to John Rateliff, the "key passage in the second revised edition" of *The Hobbit* is an expansion of Bilbo's thoughts as he hides from Gollum while wearing the ring (and invisible to Gollum's sight): "A sudden understanding, a pity mixed with horror, welled up in Bilbo's heart," leading Bilbo to refrain from harming Gollum and instead merely escaping (Rateliff 744; *H* 81). As the Prologue to *The Fellowship of the Ring* explains, "pity stayed him," and Bilbo decides not to harm an unarmed foe (21). The famous dialogue between Frodo and Gandalf regarding pity staying Bilbo's hand, and that "the pity of Bilbo may rule the fate of many" (*LotR* I.2.59), is so central to the novel that it reoccurs as a flashback in *The Two Towers* (IV.1.615). Ralph Wood asserts that the choice of "pity" rather than "mercy" is important here, because, despite the fact that modern connotations of pity often include a sense of patronizing the person granted the pity, to Tolkien the Latin "*pietas* entails responsibility, duty, devotion, kindness, tenderness, even loyalty" (151–52). According to the author's Kindle, the words "mercy," "merciful," "pity," and "pitiable" show up a total of 75 times within the novel, as opposed to only five uses of the words "merciless" and "pitiless" (in descriptions of the Nazgûl, Uruk-hai, and Orcs). Incidents of pity and mercy being shown to other characters are too numerous to mention, but include Théoden toward Wormtongue and the hobbits towards Saruman. The more noble the character, the more likely he or she is to demonstrate these virtues toward others; examples include Aragorn and Faramir. As noted, Frodo's mercy and pity to Gollum are central to the story, and Tolkien himself explains in a number of letters that the Ring is destroyed (and Frodo is ultimately saved from it) only through mercy and pity (*Letters* 191; 234; 251–52; 253).

But Gandalf, rather than Frodo, most clearly illustrates the handiwork of Nienna in the novel. Not only does the wizard understand the importance of pity and mercy in the thread of events that connects the Ring to Gollum, Bilbo, and Frodo, but he practices the virtue regularly. He treats Saruman with pity numerous times, explicitly calling Saruman "pitiable" when he breaks the fallen wizard's staff at Isengard (*LotR* III.10.583). Gandalf explains to Denethor that he even has pity for the slaves of Sauron (V.4.813) and refuses the Ring when offered it by Frodo, knowing it would trap him by twisting his desire to offer pity to the weak and gain "strength to do good" (I.2.61). It is not explained where Gandalf has gained this knowledge; many readers may chalk it up merely to life experience, or the fact that he is one of the "Wise." Yet the legendarium provides a definitive answer. In "Valaquenta," it is said of Nienna that "those who hearken to her learn pity and endurance in hope" (*S* 28). One of those is Olórin, a Maia, who "dwelt in Lórien, but his ways took him often to the house of Nienna, and of her he learned pity and patience" (30–31). He became "the friend of all the Children of Ilúvatar, and took pity on their sorrows; and those who listened to him awoke from despair" (31). Primary among these is Frodo, as Olórin was none other than Gandalf (*UT* 249). Thus, in the actions of Gandalf, we see the hand—or perhaps tears—of Nienna, affecting Middle-earth in ways that rival those of Varda or any other of the Valar.

Conclusion: Two Virgin Maidens of Mercy—Nienna and Mary

Ralph Wood emphasizes that "Nowhere is *The Lord of the Rings* made more manifestly Christian than in its privileging of pity—mercy and forgiveness—as its central virtue" (149). He explains the centrality of mercy to Christian theology as an understanding that the gift of life itself demonstrates God's mercy, and for this reason "God's mercy precedes his justice and serves as its very basis" (96–97). It is well known that Tolkien himself acknowledged the Christian overtones of his work in a 1953 letter to Robert Murray. In this and other letters, Tolkien acknowledges that readers saw a reflection of the Virgin Mary in several characters of the novel, including Galadriel and Elbereth/Varda (*Letters* 172; 288; 407). Numerous Tolkien scholars have picked up this thread and expanded upon it; for example, Wood explains that Varda is "an angelic, mercy-bearing figure with distinctive kinship to the Virgin Mary" (122). Stratford Caldecott argues that Mary's presence is felt in *The Lord of the Rings* in four ways: in the virtue of humility, in the characters of Galadriel and Elbereth, as a symbol of light (most especially the phial of Galadriel), and in the Ring's destruction date falling upon the date of the Annunciation. In a meta-analysis that draws upon earlier works, Farid Mohammadi cites specific plot points and themes that relate characters and events in *The Lord of the Rings* to Marian attributes, including these instances as well as connections between the Flame Imperishable and the Holy Spirit. Mohammadi concludes that Tolkien's well-known, "profound devotion for the Blessed Virgin Mary" led to the theme of pity and mercy that is so central to novel, as Mary is "the universal symbol of Mercy and Compassion" (207).

Certainly, Tolkien would have considered Mary to be such a symbol, as a pillar central to his Catholic faith. For example, St. Augustine penned a famous prayer to "Our Lady of Mercy," which not only thanks Mary for "having rescued a fallen world" but implores upon her to "help the miserable, strengthen the discouraged, comfort the sorrowful" (Beyer 59). The *Raccolta*, a 1910 Catholic book of prayers and indulgences, includes a "Prayer to Our Lady of the Pity," in which the petitioner comes "to thee in my sorrow and distress" (St. John 117). "Our Lady of Sorrows," a prayer to Mary attributed to St. Bonaventure, acknowledges Mary's "overwhelming grief" at the death of her son and begs Mary to "look upon me with eyes of compassion and awaken in my heart a tender commiseration for those sufferings" (O'Brien 14). September is also traditionally the month of devotional practices to Mary as "Our Lady of Sorrows" (14). Is it a mere coincidence that Bilbo (whose pity sets into motion the destruction of the Ring) and Frodo (who both gives mercy to many and experiences extreme suffering in his quest to fulfill the task appointed to him) are both born in this month?

That question cannot be answered with certainty. It is clear, however, that Nienna owes many of her later attributions to virtues Tolkien felt were central to living successfully in our fallen world, namely mercy and pity, and the faith to reach out in our suffering toward a virginal divinity who (in Tolkien's mind) could both understand and ease our suffering. As Wood notes, Nienna is the Valar's "very soul of suffering" (48–49); I would take an additional step and suggest that Tolkien meant for us to consider Nienna's later role in his subcreation as parallel to the role of Mary in the Catholic world.

Like any real-world mythology, Tolkien's legendarium evolved in its repeated telling, leading to sometimes significant changes in the relative importance and powers of certain characters. Nienna begins as a merciless death goddess whose clouds send tears and "despairs and hopeless mourning, sorrows and blind grief" (*Lost Tales I* 77). As Tolkien revised the legendarium through the next few decades, and especially during the writing of *The Lord of the Rings*, Nienna's character both softened and strengthened, for as Peter Kreeft notes "it is mercy, not justice or courage or even heroism that alone can defeat evil" (217). Nienna takes on a role separate and distinct from the other two Valar related to the dead, Mandos and Vairë, being neither a merciless judge nor a detached chronicler. Nienna certainly illustrates Lisa Hopkins's insightful crystallization of the power of Tolkien's women, as women who are "not portrayed solely in the light of their relationships to men." Hopkins notes that "traditional roles for women in epic narratives are seriously limited: they can normally appear either to be wooed, to be rescued, or occasionally to be killed" (365). None of these apply to Nienna.

It is true that the living among the Firstborn cry to Varda in their need; however, the dead cry to Nienna (*S* 28). As the ages pass, Nienna's followers increase in number, as the Halls of Mandos accept more of the Firstborn due to grievous injuries and unbearable grief at the marring of the world and the continued fading of the beauty it contains. Anne Petty reminds us that "The dilemmas of impermanence, mortality, loss, and longing are what gives Tolkien's world its heart and soul" (179). Nienna *is* the very personification of that soul. At the end of days, when the Firstborn and Secondborn meet again in whatever reunion Ilúvatar has planned (but has not revealed), the Queen of the Stars will not lead the playing of the theme aright, but rather, the Queen of Pity, Mercy, and Mourning. In the end, Nienna will reveal her true power, and her centrality to both the World That Is, and the hope of attaining a better World That Can Be.

Works Cited

Beyer, Richard J. *Blessed Art Thou*. Notre Dame, IN: Ave Maria Press, 1996. Print.

Bratman, David. "Mercy." *J. R. R. Tolkien Encyclopedia*. Ed. Michael D. C. Drout. New York: Routledge, 2007. 418–19. Print.

Burns, Marjorie. "Norse and Christian Gods: The Integrative Theology of J. R. R. Tolkien." *Tolkien and the Invention of Myth*. Ed. Jane Chance. Lexington, KY: UP of Kentucky, 2004. 163–78. Print.

---. *Perilous Realms: Celtic and Norse in Tolkien's Middle-earth*. Toronto: U of Toronto P, 2005. Print.

Caldecott, Stratford. "The Lord & The Lady of the Rings: The Hidden Presence of Tolkien's Catholicism in *The Lord of the Rings*." *Touchstone Magazine* 15.1 (Jan/Feb 2002). Web. 1 Sept. 2013.

Flieger, Verlyn. *Interrupted Music: The Making of Tolkien's Mythology*. Kent, OH: Kent State UP, 2005. Print.

Hopkins, Lisa. "Female Authority Figures in the Works of Tolkien, C. S. Lewis and Charles Williams." *Proceedings of the J. R. R. Tolkien Centenary Conference*. Eds. Patricia Reynolds and Glen H. GoodKnight. Milton Keynes, UK: The Tolkien Society, 1995. 364–66. Print.

Kreeft, Peter, J. *The Philosophy of Tolkien*. San Francisco: Ignatius Press, 2005. Print.

Larsen, Kristine. "(V)Arda Marred: The Evolution of the Queen of the Stars in Tolkien's *Legendarium*." *Mallorn: Journal of the Tolkien Society* 45 (2008): 31–36. Print.

Mohammadi, Farid. "In Search of the Holy Presence of the Blessed Mary in Tolkien's Middle-earth." *International Journal of Applied Linguistics and English Literature* 2.4 (2013): 200–11. Web. 8 Sept. 2013.

O'Brien, Joseph. "Prayer of the Month: To Our Lady of Sorrows." *The Catholic Times* 89.18 (2013): 14. Web. 8 Sept. 2013.

Petty, Anne C. *Tolkien in the Land of Heroes*. Cold Spring Harbor, NY: Cold Spring Harbor Press, 2003. Print.

Rateliff, John D. *Return to Bag-End*. Boston: Houghton Mifflin, 2007. Print.

St. John, Ambrose. *The Raccolta or Collection of Indulgenced Prayers & Good Works of the Oratory of St Philip Neri, Birmingham*. London: Burns & Oates, 1910. Web. 22 June 2014.

Whittingham, Elizabeth A. *The Evolution of Tolkien's Mythology*. Jefferson, NC: McFarland and Co., 2008. Print.

Wood, Ralph C. *The Gospel According to Tolkien*. Louisville, KY: Westminster John Know Press, 2003. Print.

At Home and Abroad:
Éowyn's Two-fold Figuring as War Bride in *The Lord of the Rings*

Melissa A. Smith

Raised in the company of great warriors, in a society that has taught her to glorify the battle-arts, Éowyn, Lady of Rohan, seems an unlikely choice as a participant in *The Lord of the Rings*' single romantic storyline. Noble, cold, and stern, she desires to find death, not to renew life; she searches for glory, not healing. Yet, amid the carnage and hopelessness of combat in *The Return of the King*, J. R. R. Tolkien develops a courtship centered on Éowyn, one that is ultimately imbued with the same wartime ethos that surrounded the young women of World Wars I and II.[1] Éowyn, shieldmaiden of the Rohirrim, and Faramir, a former captain newly succeeded to the title of Steward of Gondor, figure principally in what is popularly termed a "wartime romance"—a relationship characterized by an accelerated intimacy attributed to the pressures and fears of war, including the uncertainty of prolonged separation and death. As Tolkien constructs it, however, Éowyn's attachments are not so simplistically binary: Aragorn, son of Arathorn, has also attracted her affections, creating a system that actually allows for a comprehensive representation of the several incarnations of the World Wars' "war brides." Éowyn's respective relationships with Aragorn and Faramir thus cast her in the dual roles of war bride-left-behind and foreign war bride, and while comparison of her experiences with the courtship, marriage, and assimilation experiences of women in the war-torn twentieth century reveal her to be a negative example of the former, she is clearly, for Tolkien, a positive exemplar of the latter.

---

1. The influence of the events and atmosphere of the two World Wars upon the works of J. R. R. Tolkien has been extensively investigated. He has even been classed, by Brian Rosebury, Croft tells us, with the "killed war poets," a group that included Wilfred Owen and Edmund Blunden, because of thematic similarities amongst their works (qtd. in Croft 13). Of the many analyses of the war's influence on Tolkien available, perhaps the best source is Janet Brennan Croft's *War and the Works of J. R. R. Tolkien*—though war brides do not enter her discussion.

Though not usually pinpointed as a social issue in past periods of international warfare, the principles that lie behind the concept of the "war bride" make it a timeless and world-encompassing phenomenon—perhaps every bit as old as the span of human history.[2] Yet the term "war bride" is itself a relatively new one, seeming to rise into prominence in the social and cultural upheavals of the First World War that Tolkien experienced so intimately. Indeed, the first citation of the term's use in the *Oxford English Dictionary*—a project that famously provided Tolkien with his first post-war job[3] (researching for the W's, no less) (Gilliver et al. 7)—is dated 1918, the year the Great War ended ("War"). *OED* aside, the term appears often in the literature and even in the pop culture of the time. Writing during the First World War, for example, a woman named Ruth Wolfe Fuller, whose husband was drafted into the United States army two months after their marriage, subtitled her brief reminiscences, *The Experiences of a War Bride*. Even earlier, in September of 1914, a short play entitled "War Brides" was written by Marion Craig Wentworth and was staged for the first time in January of 1915 (Wentworth 6). Detailing the choices of women in a war-torn country, Wentworth's drama enjoyed some notable success in the climate of the times.

Little different is the climate of the Second World War; the term "war bride" surfaced repeatedly in the media, in movies like *I Was a Male War Bride* (1949), starring Cary Grant, and in popular radio shows, like "Fibber McGee and Molly." In one episode of "Fibber McGee," aired on 3 March 1941, Fibber receives a letter informing him that he is to report for induction into the Army, as he has been drafted into the armed services ("Could it be"). Although the letter turns out to be a copy of his original World War One draft notice, Fibber is convinced throughout the episode of the letter's contemporary authenticity. Upon hearing of her husband's seeming re-call into the army, his wife Molly cries, "Imagine me! A war bride! Again!" Molly's dismay at the prospect of a repetition of her experiences confirms that the previous war had

2. As but one example, in an article examining Roman-Barbarian marriages in the late Empire (about 250–550 CE), Blockley notes that, of the thirty-three connubial unions he lists, "Most involve military men, who, by the nature of their careers, are mobile" (71).

3. Tolkien worked for the *OED* from 1919 to 1921 (Crabbe 16).

produced a social figure that was being recognizably reproduced in 1941. War brides from Molly's generation even saw enough common experience between themselves and the new brides to introduce themselves on those terms—one newlywed from London who had made Canada her new home wrote, "I recall that the day after I arrived a friend of my husband's family came to call. She told me that she had been a war bride from the first World War" (Hibbert 147).

Of the two waves of newlyweds, the focus of research generally tends to the war brides of WWII because of the greater scope of the phenomenon during this time—war brides were documented as entering America from over fifty different countries, including nearly 30,000 from Great Britain (Shukert and Scibetta 2), both during and after the war. By accepting the definitions of a war bride as provided by Ruth Fuller and the *OED*, it can be judged that these war brides generally belonged to one of two categories: the newlywed wife left in the homeland by the soldier, as Ruth Fuller defines herself (6), or a bride of foreign origin married after a necessarily hasty engagement to a serviceman of the occupying, usually friendly, country (Shukert and Scibetta 2). The slightly derisive connotation saddled upon the term "war bride"[4] emerged from the widespread popularity of these latter "lightning marriages" (Shukert and Scibetta 19) during the war—hasty alliances made attractive to native young women by the war-created shortage of marriageable men and to soldiers by the loneliness of being abroad (Glenn 60). While the motive for such marriages may have appeared questionable to an older generation with more traditional courtship ideals[5] (and who, with the character of Hedwig in Wentworth's "War Brides," would probably have said, "You make a mock of marriage!"—lines 270–71), "[t]ime was precious for lovers who made the most of every minute [...] before one or both had to return to ships or planes or stations to fight the war again" (Shukert and Scibetta 18). Tol-

4. Some women have expressed a preference for the term "international bride," finding "war bride" to be derogatory (Houston 1). "War bride" is used throughout this paper precisely because of the baggage, both derogatory and romanticized, that the term carries with it. It is also useful because it defines at once both of Éowyn's roles.

5. According to Hibbert, the majority of war brides were in their twenties. One woman, though a little older than the majority, still tells of a conservative English village's shocked reaction: "[M]y fast-moving courtship caused quite a stir [...]. The villagers thought I'd taken leave of my senses!" (Hibbert 22).

kien was aware of and understood this trend, explaining in response to a criticism of Faramir and Éowyn's too-speedy courtship: "In my experience feelings and decisions ripen very quickly (as measured by mere 'clock-time', which is actually not justly applicable) in periods of great stress, and especially under the expectation of imminent death" (*Letters* 324). This summary directly defines the psychology of wartime marriages that produced the war brides of WWI and II.

Éowyn's first figuring as a war bride is as the beloved wife left alone in the soldier's land of origin. Although not Aragorn's wife,[6] the representation of this initial relationship is portrayed through the interactions of the two while Aragorn sojourns at Dunharrow before passing through the Paths of the Dead.[7] The White Lady's reactions at times mirror those of Ruth Fuller, whose husband is called away to training camp, and then France, during WWI. Further comparisons can be drawn with the experiences of Edith Tolkien, whom Tolkien married "shortly before he was posted to France" (Croft 14) on 22 March 1916.[8] Éowyn receives the news of Aragorn's perilous proposed journey in much the same manner that Fuller accepts the news of her husband's recruitment: shock, followed by a frightening internal struggle. Lady Éowyn stares at Aragorn "as one that is stricken" and goes white upon hearing of his plans. Though she confides her fears

---

6. Apropos to this argument is the fact that "[f]or some time while writing this part of *The Lord of the Rings* Tolkien intended that Aragorn and Éowyn should marry" (Hammond and Scull 406).

7. Critics have put several faces on Éowyn's love. Part of Aragorn's attractiveness is obviously his heroic stature. In explanation, Siegfried Sassoon's "Glory of Women" criticizes, "You love us when we're heroes, home on leave / Or wounded in a mentionable place. / You worship decorations; you believe / That chivalry redeems the war's disgrace" (lines 1–4). A slight twist to this idea is Croft's argument that Éowyn's feelings are also typical of the kinds of homoerotic, non-physical "crushes" experienced by soldiers in the First World War. "Handsome young soldiers were attractive in part because they were doomed," she reports, and "sometimes the lower ranks had hero-worshipping crushes on their officers as well" (Croft 52). Faramir suspects this as well, and he theorizes to Éowyn, "[A]s a great captain may to a young soldier he seemed to you admirable" (*LotR* VI.5.964).

8. Several commentators attribute the timing of Tolkien's marriage to the permeating wartime mood. Croft goes inside Tolkien's head, claiming he must have been motivated by an awareness of the possibility of his death in battle (14), while Garth notes the outward signs: "He had grasped the urgency of the moment, as his official graduation, his attempt at publication, and his marriage all demonstrate" (131).

to no one, she is later observed to be in a "great torment of mind" (*LotR* V.2.783). Similarly, Fuller recalls an overall feeling of "helplessness" concerning the difficult decision she is forced to make—should she and her husband claim exemption?[9]—in the face of the "mass of conflicting emotions" which beset her (4–5). Éowyn's torment is attributed to her fear, not only that Aragorn will never return from his endeavor, but also that the course he is choosing will not bring him honor; she begs him instead to ride boldly to battle (*LotR* V.2.783). Fuller is also interested in the glory of her husband: she and her husband ultimately choose not to claim exemption because to do so would be a "compromise with honor" (5).

The women are also united in their desire to accompany their loved one, and again joined in their grief at being parted from him. Éowyn pleads, "Lord [...] if you must go, then let me ride in your following. For I am weary of skulking in the hills, and wish to face peril in battle." Aragorn refuses her wish, replying, "Your duty is with your people" (*LotR* V.2.784).[10] Indeed, the role of the war bride at home is to set aside grief and "carry on" single-handedly, as Éowyn does in her watch over her people, preserving as closely as possible the status quo. When her king inquires how she fares, Éowyn replies, "All is well. [...] All is now ordered, as you see. And your lodging is prepared for you" (V.3.795). Fuller, too, cannot bear to be parted from her husband, and taking a job in Boston to be near his training camp, she must still bid him a permanent farewell as he crosses the ocean for France. She is determined, however, to "do her bit" (31), allowing herself only a minute or two for tears and immediately embarking upon a sort of private mission in her involvement with the Red Cross (42) and enduring in her day-to-day existence (35). Still, however busy they might be, the lonely women hunger for news of the action and their loved ones. Éowyn terms her isolation an exile (*LotR* V.2.783) and listens eagerly to the descriptions of the battles and of her relatives' deeds as related to her by

9. Fuller is probably referring to the Conscription Act of 1917, under which "men with dependents were specifically exempted by law" from the draft (Jacobs and Gallagher 10).

10. Aragorn is not being merely dismissive. He implies that he, too, is denying his own desires in order to perform what he knows to be his duty: "I do not choose paths of peril, Éowyn. Were I to go where my heart dwells, far in the North I would now be wandering in the fair valley of Rivendell" (*LotR* V.2.784).

Aragorn's men (V.2.782–83). Likewise, Fuller plans with her husband for the sending of cablegrams before he even departs (25) and comes to rely upon them to make France seem "not so far away" (41). Motivated by a similar sentiment, Tolkien "adopted a code of dots" which allowed him to communicate his location to Edith while she, in her turn, "traced his movements on a large map pinned to the wall" (Garth 144). Éowyn's vigil upon the walls of Minas Tirith, waiting for Aragorn's return, is also a reflection of this war bride characteristic. "Does not the Black Gate lie yonder?" she asks Faramir, demonstrating her faithful watchfulness. "And must he not now be come thither? It is seven days since he rode away" (*LotR* VI.5.962). This anxiety, as all three women demonstrate, is the fate of the war bride.

Although Éowyn, as we have seen, represents what we might call the Anglo-Saxon equivalent of a modern homebound war bride, she fails to be an exemplary one. Ruth Fuller meant her book as a prescription to women dealing with wartime separation from their spouses: "[T]he *women* of the Country [have] a very definite and necessary part to play; they [are] to maintain optimism and courage, keeping the Lamp of Inspiration trimmed" (14–15, emphasis in original), she opines, declaring also the "great need for cheery courage and patriotic loyalty among the women" to buoy up the confidence of the as yet amateur soldiers (18). "Morale is a woman's business," concurs a smiling face on a WWII advertisement in New Zealand (Montgomerie 24). Thus, while their men waged physical battles, women battled the intangible, spiritual foes of uncertainty: falling spirits and the strain of helpless anticipation. Éowyn's experiences,[11] tempera-

11. It is easier to be sympathetic to Éowyn's plight when one considers her situation. She is an orphan, raised by men in a warrior society where being male is the norm, and she is trained in battle arts but forbidden to fight (Rogers and Rogers 109). While playing the "ignoble" part of waiting upon an uncle who is decaying into a "mean dishonoured dotage," she is also continually subjected to the "poison" of Wormtongue, who is cunningly twisting the words of his master: *"Dotard! What is the house of Eorl but a thatched barn where brigands drink in the reek, and their brats roll on the floor among their dogs?"* (*LotR* V.8.867, emphasis in original). Wormtongue is guilty on two counts, this "son of lechery" having lusted after Éowyn as she grew in beauty (Rogers and Rogers 108–09). "Such a reaction from such a person can make a young woman feel downright dirty," suggest Rogers and Rogers (109).

ment,[12] and desires[13] are in direct opposition to compliance with this mode of thinking, and with negative results. She bitterly complains of her lot: "Shall I always be left behind when the Riders depart, to mind the house while they win renown, and find food and beds when they return?" (*LotR* V.2.784). Here, she and Edith find in common their reluctance to put up a plucky façade. Edith, shunted from village to village[14] and finally fed up with her circumstances, which now included a new baby, called hers a "miserable wandering homeless sort of life" (Garth 246). Éowyn's own powerful expressions of discontent are not beneficial to Aragorn's spirits. Instead, he is greatly troubled—"[H]e kissed her hand and [...] rode away, and did not look back; and only those who knew him well and were near to him saw the pain that he bore" (*LotR* V.2.785). She also attempts to divert him from his duty,[15] calling his quest to seek the Paths of the Dead "madness" (V.2.783). Edith too, seems to find more to be thankful for in Tolkien's convalescence than in his military service—"Every day in bed means another day in England,"[16] she reminded him (qtd. in Garth 232). Éowyn later abandons her place with her people, seeking honor of her own on the battlefield,[17] whereas Fuller finds her little duties as an army Hostess

---

12. Gandalf observes to Éomer, "[S]he, born in the body of a maid, had a spirit and courage at least the match of yours" (*LotR* V.8.867). She is also "fearless and high-hearted" (III.6.523) and describes herself as one who "cannot lie in sloth, idle, caged" (VI.5.959). Agreeing, Porter calls her "a woman of action; being patient and passive is difficult for her in the best of times and certainly not wartime," citing Éowyn's desire to help in the Houses of Healing (95).

13. Probably because of the former two, Éowyn desires a glorious death in battle, which has been attributed on Tolkien's part to the Anglo-Saxon basis for Rohirric culture (see Dickerson 37). She also desires the unattainable love of Aragorn, which is synonymous with her first desire, since, as Aragorn says, "[I]n me she loves only a shadow and a thought: a hope of glory and great deeds, and lands far from the fields of Rohan" (*LotR* V.8.867).

14. In two years, Edith and her cousin, Jennie Grove, had lived in 22 different sets of lodgings while following Tolkien from camp to camp (Garth 246).

15. For a discussion of Éowyn as a female temptress, see Petty 59.

16. Sassoon again casts aspersions upon such sentiments in a poem bitingly called "Their Frailty": "He's got a Blighty wound. He's safe; and then / War's fine and bold and bright. / She can forget the doomed and prisoned men / Who agonize and fight" (lines 1–4).

17. Even on the battlefield, Éowyn contends with purely spiritual foes. "The Nazgûl whom she destroys is not a mortal being," comments Dickerson. "[I]t is not a physical enemy—but a spiritual foe: a wraith" (30). Like Sauron, the power of the Nazgûl seems to be in the despair it creates in the hearts of those in its proximity

exhilarating (Fuller 20) and regards it as her obligation to send her husband away with a smile (9). Perhaps delving into his own wife's discontented experiences for inspiration, Tolkien, who would probably claim along with C. S. Lewis that he had no insider knowledge of "the mysteries of the Bona Dea" or her doings during wartime (Carpenter 153), seems to reflect on the hardships and ill effects of female passivity in his stern Lady of Rohan. Éowyn, in her petulance and reluctance to accept her role, is clearly not the model war bride typified by Ruth Fuller.[18]

Though Éowyn is unsuccessful as the war bride-left-behind, Tolkien offers her a second chance to distinguish herself, this time as an "international" war bride, through her relationship with Faramir. Unlike the war brides that waved goodbye as their husbands were posted overseas, foreign war brides were not forced to experience to the same degree the demoralizing passivity that caused so much difficulty for Éowyn in her relationship with Aragorn. Her new role caters instead to her strengths, requiring the intrepid spirit and desire for activity so prominent in her character. A study of Japanese war brides noted that "many of the women had shown a taste for independence before [their] marriage[s]" to Anglo soldiers in Japan (Glenn 61). This is certainly true of Éowyn, whose war deeds and disobedience demonstrate a hunger, rather than a mere taste, for independence. The position of the Japanese girls is, of course, reversed in *The Return of the King*; Éowyn has entered Faramir's country in the name of war, rather than he hers, but the courtship between the two nevertheless has many similarities to descriptions of courtship as experienced by young soldiers and their lovers in foreign lands. The noble pair's relationship develops quickly, beginning with an almost immediate decla-

---

(note continued)
(143), and despair was probably a feeling many war brides contended with, metaphorically, at home.

18. This is not to condemn Éowyn, however. Few of the women left at home found it easy to follow Fuller's model and remain chipper or even faithful. In the play "War Brides," a pregnant character named Hedwig dramatically refuses to do "her bit" for the fatherland and shoots herself after writing to the emperor, "I refuse to bear my child until you promise there shall be no more war." (Wentworth, lines 668–70). And, unfortunately, "wartime separation sometimes gave rise to wartime adultery," although the number of illegitimate births during WWII did show a decrease from peace-time numbers (Montgomerie 157).

ration from Faramir. In but their first interview together, Faramir half-confesses, half-requests, "[I]t would ease my care, if you would speak to me, or walk at whiles with me. [...] Neither flower nor lady have I seen till now in Gondor so lovely, and so sorrowful" (*LotR* VI.5.960 939). This direct type of approach to a relationship was common among the young soldiers on tour. A war bride from Sussex describes her surprising experience with a fast-moving Canadian: "I met my [future] husband at a local hotel where I'd been invited to a party. He introduced himself and, after an hour or so, informed me that I would like living in Canada after we were married" (Hibbert 32). Such forward acknowledgement of interest is uniquely acceptable in wartime romances, when relocation and even death loom large in the future, and relationships must grow quickly if they are to endure separation. "There was a sense of urgency about the whole thing," one bride explains, "You never knew whether you'd be there tomorrow" (Hibbert 19). The love of Faramir and Éowyn transpires rapidly indeed, and mere days[19] after meeting, the two have confessed their love. Her dual roles clash, however, and the idealistic faithfulness of the war-bride-left-behind does battle with the readiness of the foreign war bride, making her remarkably resistant to becoming attached too quickly. She is not immediately overwhelmed by "a man in uniform"—or rather, she has already been impressed by a man in uniform, in the form of the Heir of Isildur. It is Faramir who pursues while Éowyn muses quietly on her love for Aragorn. True to war bride form, however, the uncertainty of both Aragorn's return and reciprocal affection influences her to surrender her heart to Faramir, who so willingly offers the latter. As one girl from Scotland observed, the reason GIs were so attractive to Scottish girls was the fact that "they were *there*—all young Scottish men were gone into service" (Shukert and Scibetta 7). To most civilian girls, absence—and the pressures of wartime—made the heart willing to accept the more available romantic offerings.

---

19. Éowyn and Faramir stand on the walls together for the first time five days after meeting on 25 March. The second time, when they confess their love, occurs before 30 April, when the pavilions appear (according to Tolkien's schema). A closer estimate of the date would be sometime around 8 April, as Éowyn has been invited to the celebrations on the Field of Cormallen, but declines to go. See *LotR*, Appendix B.

To a participant in the war marriage fervor, the betrothal of Éowyn and Faramir would also have looked familiar. Enlisted men were obliged to complete a very long and sometimes exhaustive application process to their superiors in order to marry while on duty. In other words, it required the approval of fellow men-at-arms in order to make a marriage possible (Shukert and Scibetta 23). Those present to offer them congratulations upon the exchange of wedding vows were also usually limited to fellow servicemen and -women; soldiers were stationed far from family and were not frequently allowed leaves of absence. Catherine Roberts-Swauger relates, "My bridesmaids were buddies stationed with me at Old Sarum. [...] We were married in the little church of St. Mary's on the grounds of Tidworth House. The uniforms of the United States on one side and the Air Force Blue of the Royal Air Force on the other. A young GI sang *Oh, Promise Me* and *I Love You Truly*" (Shukert and Scibetta 27). In similar fashion, Faramir and Éowyn receive approval for their union from their battle-mates and celebrate their happiness at a feast meant to commemorate the deeds of valor performed on the battlefield, especially those of the deceased Théoden. Éomer announces, "[T]hey shall be trothplighted before you all," and the health of the pair is drunk by all of the company of valiant hearth-companions (*LotR* VI.6.977). Éowyn continues to figure as a war bride as she is betrothed and toasted in a gathering of soldiers.

A major concern for the war brides of the two World Wars was the process of assimilation. Acceptance by the husband's family and culture was a difficult barrier to overcome,[20] and the prospect was especially intimidating for wives who spoke a foreign tongue (Glenn 64) or had been on the side of the enemy during the war. Parents were sometimes very adamant against their daughter's association with soldiers because they feared the girl would accompany the soldier to his homeland upon the war's termination and never be seen again (Shukert and Scibetta 24).

---

20. Sidenotes that would only add further complexity to the argument are Edith's "international bride" symptoms. She not only had to be accepted by Father Morgan and the Roman Catholic Church, but by the TCBS. The fraternity had always been threatened with a break-up whenever a woman entered the picture, and the friends' "congratulations were tinged with the anxiety that they might lose a friend" (Garth 33). Such an apprehensive acceptance must have been bothersome for Edith and a point of anxiety to her husband.

Some of these young girls were even ostracized by their countrymen: "the local papers in Edinburgh did not write articles in favour of the local girls marrying GIs. On the contrary, we were made to feel like traitors!" remembers Beverly Schoonmaker (25). Colored turncoats in their homelands, many women faced ill receptions in their husbands' countries as well. "Even middle-aged women seemed resentful that I had 'caught' one of their boys. 'Pity they didn't wait to marry a nice, clean, American girl,' I was told by a professor's wife," Brenda Hasty recalls (Shukert and Scibetta 80). The welcome was even more unkind if the new relatives considered the bride to be of inferior stock. Reports one woman: "Mother-in-law was a fine woman. [...] But a shadow had fallen over her life. Her son, in the eyes of the villagers, had degraded himself by an alliance with *l'ennemi*. He had betrayed them by wedding une Anglaise. She was kind to me, but I was not on a level with une bonne Canadienne" (Hibbert 110). Others were treated with respect, though as oddities: "We had the dubious distinction of being placed on the train[21] ahead of the natives," recounts Gwen Chushcoff, "and [we were] led through a huge crowd [by a woman] calling officiously 'Make way for the War Brides.' [...] Needless to say we felt like freaks" (Shukert and Scibetta 80–81). Whether welcomed with joy, animosity, or indifference into their new families and countries, nearly all felt apprehensive of the drastic change in locale:

> My friends and I [...] had many discussions as to just what we had done by marrying men we hardly knew and preparing to leave all that was dear and familiar for a life in a land completely unknown. We went to a brides club each week, where we were shown films and given lectures about our new country, and these were a help. But the fears still crept in. What had we done? (Hibbert 36–37)

Éowyn, though a foreigner, is able to overcome the problem of language through her learnedness in the Common Speech, but she voices her anxieties about acceptance in her new home and removal from Rohan by saying wistfully to Faramir, "Then must I leave my own people, man of Gondor? And would you have your proud folk say of you:

---

21. European war brides and other dependents were transported en masse over the Atlantic Ocean on luxury liners like the *Aquitania*. After landing, they were put on trains and carried to various stations around the United States and Canada, where, hopefully, someone would claim them.

'There goes a lord who tamed a wild shieldmaiden of the North! Was there no woman of the race of Númenor to choose?' " (*LotR* VI.5.965). Here, Éowyn's fears exactly prefigure the experiences of her modern counterparts, in which the dread of resentment, the discomfort of being considered inferior or abnormal, and the anxiety of separation from home are all addressed. Some of these fears are well founded—both Aragorn and Faramir at some point express the sentiment that the Rohirrim are a lesser race (Straubhaar 102). For his part, Faramir describes them as loving war and valor for its own sake—a diminished state, according to him—and while Gondorians are from a High race, the Rohirrim are Middle Peoples, Men of the Twilight (*LotR* IV.5.679).[22] Interestingly, Éowyn is ultimately successful as a foreign war bride because of her ability to adapt;[23] she renounces the "lower" ways of the Rohirrim, declaring, "I will be a shieldmaiden no longer, [...] nor take joy only in the songs of slaying. I will be a healer, and love all things that grow and are not barren" (VI.6.965). Thus changed, she can perform with ease her role as the hand of revitalization to a darkness-inflicted land and as Princess within her new culture, having been well-schooled by her upbringing in a royal house.[24] Figuring so prominently in their society,[25] Faramir and Éowyn's marriage, like many wartime marriages, is viewed as the positive unification of two cultures. "Thus

22. Shippey reinforces the idea of the Rohirrim as a "savage," less sophisticated people, comparing them to the Sioux or Cheyenne (127).

23. Taft provides a comprehensive list of requirements whereby an immigrant may be judged "fully assimilated" The list includes cultural knowledge and skills (including proper language use), social interaction (especially interpersonal contact), membership identity and social integration (includes filling an accepted social position), social and emotional identification with the new country, and conformity to group norms (233–35). By marrying Faramir, conforming to Gondorian ways, filling an accepted and highly visible social and political role, and even receiving the blessing of the king himself, Éowyn can be said to be well on her way to complete assimilation.

24. Though niece to Théoden, Éowyn was raised in the court of her uncle after her mother, Théodwyn, died, and Tolkien provides evidence, to the keen eye, of Éowyn's royal eligibility. Taking leave of Faramir in the Houses of Healing, for instance, she "[does] him a courtesy" (*LotR* VI.5.961). She also bears a filled cup to Éomer (VI.6.977) during the burial feast (a move prefigured by Wealhtheow in *Beowulf*). Both indicate her gentility and training in the ways of the court.

25. The Prince of Ithilien would be the greatest noble after Dol Amroth in the new Gondorian state, and would bear many responsibilities. Faramir also remains the Steward, who acts as chief counselor in the Council of Gondor during the king's absence. See *Letters* 323.

[...] is the friendship of the Mark and of Gondor bound with a new bond, and the more do I rejoice" (VI.6.977), exclaims Éomer upon the couple's betrothal. Similar sentiments were later expressed by those commending the value of the intercultural marriages inspired by wartime activities: "Thomas O. W. Brevner, New Zealand Consul in New York, told a *New York Times* reporter, 'It's a jolly good thing. It brings us all closer together. There's nothing like a baby or two to break down international barriers' " (Shukert and Scibetta 20).

The analogy or comparison of Éowyn to the war brides of Tolkien's time adds further proof to the influence of the World Wars on Tolkien's works. However, the promotion of the idea that the women whom men leave behind can only cope by defeminizing themselves and abandoning their traditional roles (and necessitating the introduction of foreigners in order to restabilize society), as supported by Éowyn's failure to fulfill the role of war bride-left-behind, is unsettling—unless one reads it as a subtle condemnation, on Tolkien's part, of war as a disturber of a valuable social equilibrium. It certainly reveals, however, his sympathies with the difficulty of the role that war imposes upon women, striking down the theory that Tolkien is simply a narrow-minded misogynist who dooms the women in his work to weakness and failure. Knowing from experience that the war would defeat the women's attempts to maintain the status quo despite their best efforts, he diminishes Éowyn's original role, focusing instead on her potential to rebuild and renew. His heavy focus on Éowyn's success as a foreign war bride thereby magnifies Éowyn's courage in taking up a new life in a new culture, perhaps symbolizing the way in which the women of his time aided the reforging of society after the war, and the bravery with which they and their husbands faced a new post-war culture, determined to look forward and heal the ravages that war had wreaked upon their way of life. It is this same spirit that would make the White Tree flower again.

This article was published originally in Mythlore *26.1/2 (#99/100) (2007): 161–72. It is reprinted here with permission.*

Works Cited

Blockley, R.C. "Roman-Barbarian Marriages in the Late Roman Empire." *Florilegium* 4 (1982): 63–79. Print.

Carpenter, Humphrey. *J. R. R. Tolkien: A Biography. Boston: Houghton Mifflin, 2000. Print.*

"Could it be...Fibber drafted?" *Fibber McGee and Molly*. NBC. 18 March 1941. Television.

Crabbe, Katharyn W. *J. R. R. Tolkien*. New York: F. Ungar, 1981. Print.

Croft, Janet Brennan. *War and the Works of J. R. R. Tolkien*. Westport, CT: Praeger, 2004. Print.

Dickerson, Matthew. *Following Gandalf: Epic Battles and Moral Victory in* Lord of the Rings. Grand Rapids, MI: Brazos Press, 2003. Print.

Fuller, Ruth Wolfe. *Silver Lining: The Experiences of a War Bride*. Boston: Houghton Mifflin, 1918. Print.

Garth, John. *Tolkien and the Great War*. New York: Houghton Mifflin, 2003. Print.

Gilliver, Peter, Jeremy Marshall, and Edmund Weiner. *The Ring of Words: Tolkien and the* Oxford English Dictionary. New York: Oxford UP, 2006. Print.

Glenn, Evelyn. *Issei, Nisei, War Bride*. Philadelphia: Temple UP, 1986. Print.

Hammond, Wayne G., and Christina Scull. The Lord of the Rings*: A Reader's Companion*. Boston: Houghton Mifflin Harcourt, 2005. Print.

Hart-Davis, Rupert, ed. *The War Poems of Siegfried Sassoon*. London: Faber and Faber, 1983. Print.

Hibbert, Joyce, ed. *The War Brides*. Toronto: PMA Books, 1978. Print.

Houston, Velina Hasu. *Tea: Teacher's Study Guide*. Los Angeles: L. A. Theater Works, 1994. Print.

Jacobs, Clyde E., and John F. Gallagher. *The Selective Service Act: A Case Study of the Governmental Process*. New York: Dodd, Mead, 1967. Print.

Montgomerie, Deborah. *The Women's War*. Auckland: Auckland UP, 2001. Print.

Petty, Anne C. *One Ring To Bind Them All: Tolkien's Mythology*. University, AL: U of Alabama P, 1979. Print.

Porter, Lynnette R. *Unsung Heroes of* The Lord of the Rings*: From the Page to the Screen*. Westport, CT: Praeger, 2005. Print.

Rogers, Deborah Webster, and Ivor A. Rogers. *J. R. R. Tolkien*. Boston: Twayne, 1980. Print.

Sassoon, Siegfried. "Glory of Women." Hart-Davis 100.

---. "Their Frailty." Hart-Davis 101.

Shippey, Tom. *The Road to Middle-earth*. 2nd ed. Boston: Houghton Mifflin, 2003. Print.

Shukert, Elfrieda Berthiaume, and Barbara Smith Scibetta. *War Brides of World War II*. Novato, CA: Presidio Press, 1988. Print.

Straubhaar, Sandra Ballif. "Myth, Late Roman History, and Multiculturalism in Tolkien's Middle-earth." *Tolkien and the Invention of Myth: A Reader*. Ed. Jane Chance. Lexington, KY: UP of Kentucky, 2004. 101–18. Print.

Taft, Ronald. "Problems of Adjustment and Assimilation in Immigrants." *Psychology and Race*. Ed. Peter Watson. Baltimore, MD: Penguin Books, 1973. 224–39. Print.

"War." *The Oxford English Dictionary*. 2nd ed. 1989. Print.

Wentworth, Marion Craig. "War Brides." New York: Dramatists Play Agency, 1928. Print.

Earlier Literary Contexts

The Valkyrie Reflex
in J. R. R. Tolkien's *The Lord of the Rings*: Galadriel, Shelob, Éowyn, and Arwen

Leslie A. Donovan

Since the first publication of *The Lord of the Rings* in 1954–55, many readers have considered the paucity of female characters in J. R. R. Tolkien's novel not only a disappointment but also a serious flaw in his work. Edith L. Crowe sums up this response when she writes, "The most problematic aspect of Tolkien is indeed the disappointingly low percentage of females that appear in his best-known and best-loved works, *The Hobbit* and *The Lord of the Rings*" (272). Other critics interpret the lack of women in *The Lord of the Rings* as indicative of weak technical craft or a latent misogyny[1] in Tolkien's character. An early writer, Catherine Stimpson, states such a position with her criticism that Tolkien's women are built on "the most hackneyed of stereotypes" (18). More recently, Patrick Curry notes *The Lord of the Rings* would be "seriously impoverished" without its women characters, but he concedes that Tolkien's presentation of women represents a "paternalism if not patriarchy [that is] unmissable" (127). In contrast, attempting to justify Tolkien's portrayals of women, scholars like Crowe insist "he was only reflecting his sources and his times" (272). Those with similar perspectives argue that, as women played central roles in few medieval texts, it would have been inappropriate for Tolkien's modern reweaving of traditional materials to emphasize or substantially expand female roles. Such scholars reason that, since most of Tolkien's life predated advances in contemporary women studies and gender theory, his works cannot be expected to reflect feminist approaches in women characters.

Focusing on the significance of Tolkien's existing women characters rather than their infrequency, Helen Armstrong, however, asserts

---

1. Fredrick and McBride examine biographical evidence in an attempt to discern rationale and patterns for what they see as the idealized, stereotypical, even to a degree antifeminist, presentations of women in Tolkien's works as well as the works of Lewis, Williams, and other members of the Inklings.

that "Despite the conventionally, even doctrinally, male-centred aspects of Tolkien's world, he also bucked that same system [...] by creating active heroines" (250). In accord with such views, Lisa Hopkins writes that "Power in the works of Tolkien is often to be found in the hands of a woman" and that "women in Tolkien are not portrayed solely in the light of their relationships to men" (365). Although Crowe admits readings of Tolkien as a "hidden feminist" are untenable, she contends "Tolkien exhibits attitudes toward power that are quite compatible with, if not identical to, the attitudes of many who define themselves as feminists" (272). Studies from similar feminist perspectives perceive that Tolkien's

> small number of women have a range of parts to play whose importance is remarkably disproportionate to their numbers. Their very scarcity seems to invest them with an air of uniqueness and of almost talismanic status, and in some cases their very femininity [...] is in Tolkien the very source of their strength. (Hopkins 365)

Seeking to support readings of Tolkien's women as strong, authoritative characters with pivotal narrative importance, some writers situate Tolkien's works within the contexts of classical epics, Christian typology, psychological archetypes, or contemporary gender constructs. For example, Mac Fenwick has found echoes of Homer's Circe and Calypso in Tolkien's Galadriel and parallels between Shelob and Homer's Sirens, Scylla, and Charybdis. As evocative as such classical connections are, by limiting his only study to these two diametrically opposite female characters, Fenwick cannot account for the motif throughout Tolkien's work of women as empowered forces. In addition, although convincing analogies may be made between Galadriel and the Virgin Mary,[2] such applications of Christian typology hold little promise for explaining the authority of other women in Tolkien's text. Peter Goselin uses Jung's mythic archetypes to describe the polar relationship between Tolkien's women characters as a manifestation of the female anima, but again uses only Galadriel and Shelob to exemplify this dimension of women's power. Other studies analyze the ways in which Tolkien's women operate within a larger gender construct of masculine and feminine principles. From this viewpoint, Melanie Rawls explains that

---

2. For readings of Galadriel's resemblance to the Virgin Mary, see Maher; Sly.

> his Feminine Principle is *not* the negative of the Masculine Principle, but is another kind of being, equal yet other in stature and power. This diversity adds dimension and complexity to his characters, as they dance the dance of complementarity. (13)

Yet, valuable as these examinations are for comprehending the variety of resources, allusions, and narrative functions of women in Tolkien's works, their discussions are peripheral to Tolkien's primary interests and goals, and none explore fully the multiply rendered features of women's power within Tolkien's most famous work, *The Lord of the Rings*. The extraordinary strength of women characters in the novel can be explained, however, within a context of specific relevance to Tolkien's background—that of the medieval Germanic heroic literatures that played such a crucial role in Tolkien's personal and professional consciousness.[3] Despite Tolkien's own frequently recorded distaste for scholarship seeking to identify the original sources for later works,[4] not only Tolkien's women characters but all his Middle-earth fiction have their heritage in the literature and culture of the Middle Ages. Many studies have acknowledged with C. W. Sullivan that Tolkien's "traditionally patterned narrative" may be better understood "not through the lenses of modern critical methods but through lenses developed for the study of earlier works" (11). Confirming such views, Jonathan Evans writes that Tolkien's Middle-earth fiction reflects "a dependence upon medieval developments of the motif and narrative type that preserves and highlights aspects of the tradition and at the same time extends them" (22), and Marjorie Burns summarizes the medieval origins that enrich the texture of Tolkien's narratives by stating that "Behind every setting and every character in J. R. R. Tolkien's writings on Middle-earth, lies a history of literary, mythological, and linguistic complexity" (219).

Beyond such general acknowledgments of the medieval backgrounds for Tolkien's work is a recognition of his particular debt to

---

3. Although his works contain many female figures indebted to medieval Germanic literatures, *The Lord of the Rings* provides a particularly rich context for such an examination and is representative of this tendency in all Tolkien's creative works. Because of this and the constraints of this article, this study restricts its discussion only to these female characters in Tolkien's work.

4. See, for example, Tolkien's discussion of origins in his essay "On Fairy-stories" (45–57).

medieval Germanic texts. While it would misrepresent Tolkien's accomplishments to speak of texts from the Old Norse, Old Icelandic, and Anglo-Saxon cultures as direct sources for *The Lord of the Rings*, few scholars deny that literary resonances from such cultures infuse Tolkien's work. Well-attested by his professional scholarship as well as by his personal letters, Tolkien possessed an abiding appreciation for medieval literature from northern Europe. Early in the history of Tolkien scholarship, Charles Moorman even went so far as to assert that "The greatest single influence upon Tolkien's work is the eddas and the sagas of the North" (212), a statement echoed by Lynn Bryce's later remark that "Throughout his life works of Old Norse continued to have a profound appeal to Tolkien's imagination" (113). Even when arguing Tolkien's debt to classical literature, Fenwick acknowledges the validity of an earlier statement by Auden when he admits "There can be no denying that for Tolkien North was indeed a sacred direction and that the bulk of his imaginative enterprise is based upon a lifetime's intimate acquaintance with the literature of the ancient North" (17). Attesting specifically to the relevance of Old Norse material to Tolkien's literary aesthetic, Tom Shippey identifies a Germanic "combination of pride, ferocity and sadness" as a "note that Tolkien often aimed at" in his works on Middle-earth ("Sources" 155). More recently, Gloriana St. Clair comments,

> The concept of fate in Northern works, the need for courage, a conception of evil, the tragedy of mortality, the doom of immortals, and the paradox of defeat are themes common to Northern literature and *The Lord of the Rings*. ("Overview" 66)

The cumulative voice of such scholarship confidently asserts Tolkien's legacy to medieval Germanic traditions, especially those of Old Norse and Old English literature. None of these studies, however, offers detailed scrutiny of the female analogues in medieval Germanic literatures that serve as likely patterns for Tolkien's strong women characters.[5] In particular, as independent individuals, personally responsible and socially empowered to affect change on a global scope,

---

5. Although none discuss in detail the specific relationships of Tolkien's women characters to medieval Germanic sources, some studies mention briefly the debt of characters such as Galadriel, Shelob, and Éowyn to Old English and Old Norse texts. See, for example, Bryce; Shippey, *Road* 177–222.

Tolkien's primary women characters in *The Lord of the Rings*—Galadriel, Shelob, Éowyn, and Arwen[6]—are narrative agents charged with the authority of distinct heroic women figures from Old Norse mythology and literature called the valkyries.[7]

In their varying emphasis on the themes of light, prophecy, physical prowess, self-sacrifice, cultural leadership, unwavering will, public ceremony as a binding commitment, and the support of a chosen hero, the heroically rendered characterizations of Galadriel, Éowyn, and Arwen partake of the conventions common to medieval valkyrie figures.[8] Through valkyrie-associated imagery, these women function as emblems for the often conflicting Germanic motifs of grievous loss and glorious fulfillment, individual will and community responsibility, determined constancy and unlooked-for revitalization so central to Tolkien's fictional vision. Providing a contrast to these positive figures, Shelob's dark inversion of such themes punctuates their epic significance. As relief images carved from heroic tableaux featuring Germanic valkyries, Galadriel, Shelob, Éowyn, and Arwen stand out from the narrative's background as more than secondary, incidental literary figures. In them, Tolkien seeks his own contemporary response to medieval traditions by establishing his valkyrie-indebted women as elemental forces whose presence in the text allows the pos-

6. While *The Lord of the Rings* contains other notable women characters, space limitations make it necessary to restrict discussion to those women characters most central to the narrative's development and most distinctly evocative of Germanic valkyrie traditions—Galadriel, Shelob, Éowyn, and Arwen.

7. For general discussions of valkyrie figures in Old Norse literature and culture, see Jochens; Davidson.

8. The body of Germanic mythological and heroic literature dealing most explicitly with valkyrie figures and cited in this study include the following medieval Old Norse texts: *Hervör's saga* (in C. Tolkien); *The Poetic Edda* (Neckel); *The Prose Edda* (Sturluson) abbreviated here as *PrE*; and *Völsunga saga* (Jónsson) abbreviated here as *VS*. Texts commonly collected as part of *The Poetic Edda* are cited by strophe number and abbreviated as follows: the *Helgi Lays—Helgakviða Hjörvarðssonar (HHv), Helgakviða Hundingsbana I (HH I), Helgakviða Hundingsbana II (HH II); Fáfnismál (Fáf); Sigrdrífomál (Sigdr); Sigurðarkviða en skamma (Sigsk); Völundarkviða (Völ)*; and *Völuspá* (*Vsp*). In addition, due to close affinities between the Old Norse and Anglo-Saxon cultures, Old English texts such as *Beowulf* (Klaeber), *Judith* (Timmer), and *Juliana* (R. Woolf) include women frequently characterized in terms of valkyrie attributes. References to these Old English poems are made by line number. All Modern English translations of Old Norse and Old English material are my own.

sibility of human and heroic completion. For example, unlike medieval valkyrie counterparts such as Sigrún and Sváva, Arwen's choice of mortality results not in Aragorn's tragic death but in a life lived with her beloved. Similarly, Éowyn realizes a full human potential that joins both her masculine and feminine selves, which was impossible for other valkyrie antecedents such as Brynhild and Hervör.

Yet, the valkyrie-associated figures of Wealhtheow, Sváva, Sigrdrífa, Brynhild, and Hervör that so peopled Tolkien's imagination are not simply plucked from the pages of medieval manuscripts and inserted whole into *The Lord of the Rings*. Rather, as with all the medieval sources from which he drew material for his secondary world fiction, Tolkien reshapes the valkyrie tradition to suit his own purposes and the needs of his culture. Specifically, the heroically situated Galadriel, Éowyn, and Arwen are built from those valkyrie characteristics that held the most potency for Tolkien's Christian, post-World War II, prefeminist vision of modern epic. By eliminating from his primary women figures the concept common in valkyrie typology of the female inciter and her accompanying vengeance for kin or personal insult,[9] Tolkien constructs them as reflective of moral good, heroic ideals, noble behavior, and responsible leadership by means of a female identity concordant with contemporary perceptions of women as significant forces within society and the world. Although admittedly idealized, his construction of strong women characters results most likely from Tolkien's personal admiration of women such as his mother and his wife, Edith, as well as the historical climate of his times. After World War II, the professional, religious, and societal cultures to which Tolkien belonged both continued to emphasize traditional roles for women while simultaneously recognizing the possibilities of new familial models, employment opportunities, and social as well as political importance for women. Like medieval valkyrie figures, it was more socially possible for post-World War II women to maintain independent identities without sacrificing their expected cultural validi-

---

9. See, for example, Hervör in *Heidrek's saga* and Brynhild in *VS*. While Lobelia Sackville-Baggins eventually takes action for the insults to herself and her hobbit community by striking a physical blow against the Shire's enemies, I have restricted this study to those women characters who play a major or primary role in the text's narrative development.

ty, a concept the morally conservative but broad thinking Tolkien may have found attractive.

Other women in *The Lord of the Rings* occasionally behave in ways suggestive of the medieval valkyrie tradition, but their valkyrie associations are less developed than those of Galadriel, Shelob, Éowyn, and Arwen. For example, Goldberry is a shining, radiant, otherworldly figure who serves food and drink, but she exhibits no ceremonial function, no loss of a central element of her life, and no martial abilities. Ioreth speaks words that indicate foresight or a prophetic knowledge of events, but her words, inherited from oral tradition and gossip, never suggest the character herself has prescient abilities. In her independent personality and her willingness to strike a physical blow for her people near the end, Lobelia Sackville-Baggins may be valkyrie-like, but her greediness and covetousness early in the texts are not common valkyrie traits. Although Rosie Cotton's teasing of Sam may be vaguely reminiscent of the inciter functions of medieval valkyrie figures,[10] her wholesome ordinariness has no relationship to Odin's battle goddesses. Appropriately, it is not in the rural setting of the hobbits, in the urban city-dwellers of Minas Tirith, or in the spirits of nature's woodlands that the valkyrie figure finds her place in Tolkien's work. Instead, Tolkien situates his version of the valkyrie in Middle-earth's heroic sphere, where battles and legends, prophecies and heritage, nobility and courage lead to difficult, even painful, choices with large scale consequences for the future.

Belied by their apparent marginality in Tolkien's text, the significance of Galadriel, Shelob, Éowyn, and Arwen resides primarily in the heroic choices each makes based on the necessities that drive their valkyrie-associated wills. The individual wills of valkyries are conceptually equivalent to the mode of desire frequently discussed in contemporary feminist and gender theory,[11] in that the choices

---

10. Inciting the hero to action is one of the most frequently discussed characteristics of Old Norse women characters, especially those portrayed in the valkyrie tradition. However, since Tolkien basically eliminates this characteristic from his valkyrie-associated women, the inciter role is not discussed in this study. For discussion of medieval inciter figures, see Jochens.

11. Thorough explorations of Tolkien's women in *The Lord of the Rings* using feminist or gender theory approaches (such as those of Hélène Cixous, Julia Kristeva, Judith Butler, or Luce Irigaray) would be valuable additions to contemporary

they make determine the fate of both the women characters themselves and their world's history. Evocative of a similar process by which the wills of Tolkien's women influence events in *The Lord of the Rings,* but in the context of women's actions in Old English literature, Gillian Overing writes,

> we see how marginal desire, whether this is monstrous, feminine, or even heroic, continually intrudes upon and deflects the progress of dominant desire [... by presenting] us with a polyphony of voices, an interplay of desires, which contribute to its [the text's] restless complexity and dynamic irresolution. (220)

Tolkien's Galadriel, Shelob, Éowyn, and Arwen are characters whose words and actions in *The Lord of the Rings* provide a similar polyphony of motives that shift the plot's course of events as well as the reader's expectations of an appropriate outcome.

Galadriel, Shelob, Éowyn, and Arwen partake of the same Germanic or northern themes found throughout the larger text by means of character traits patterned on standardized, stereotypical attributes of benevolent valkyrie figures such as Wealhtheow, Sváva, Brynhild, Sigrún and Hervör. These characteristics commonly include: 1) divine or semidivine origins or ancestry; 2) noble social status; 3) superior wisdom, intellect, or acumen; and 4) exceeding beauty. As many women in early literature and mythology possess these same qualities, it is no surprise that in *The Lord of the Rings* Tolkien incorporates these conventions into his portrayals of Galadriel, Éowyn, and Arwen. However, other attributes specifically connoting valkyrie traditions offer greater significance for Tolkien's women characters. The dominant valkyrie-specific traits of women in heroic settings relevant to *The Lord of the Rings* are that such figures 1) exhibit an otherworldly radiance, sometimes associated with the glittering shine of armor or with the fractured illumination linked to battle fires; 2) possess physical prowess equaling or exceeding that of male heroes; 3) serve ceremonial functions within the hall such as ritual cup-bearing at official occasions, gift-giving to heroes, and sewing or preserving special heroic garments, which challenge heroes to fulfill their destinies; 4) per-

---

(note continued)
studies of Tolkien's work. However, as such studies are outside the scope of this article's primary focus, discussion of these concepts is featured here only briefly.

form prophetic acts or engage in other speech acts that determine some future fate; 5) choose actions based on the operation of their own strong wills; and 6) undergo the loss of something central and precious to their lives. Illustrated by Shelob in *The Lord of the Rings*, the obverse valkyrie aspect, which incorporates many of these same characteristics in a negative chroma, is typified by baleful, vengeful, destructive female figures such as Grendel's mother in the Old English *Beowulf* and Hrímgerth in the Old Norse *Helgi Lays*.

The word "valkyrie" comes from the Old Norse *valkyrja*, meaning "battle-determiner" or "chooser of the slain." It refers to a semidivine female figure whose pagan religious associations derive from her position as a battle maiden under Odin's command. Like the *dísir*, other closely allied Old Norse female figures, the valkyries are characterized as "armed, powerful, priestly. They function as arrangers of destinies and intermediaries between men and the deity" (Damico, "Valkyrie" 176). Jenny Jochens describes the traditional mythological function of the valkyries when she writes:

> At Óðinn's bidding they select the men who are destined to fall in battle and they reward victory to the survivors. As such they form an important link between the divine and the human world. Having withdrawn the heroes from human life, the valkyries continue to look after them in the divine world, where they serve them drink. (39)

In heroic Germanic poetry, some valkyrie women also form compelling relationships with male heroes that alter the course of events in the human world. Helen Damico explains the authority to establish such relationships resides in the valkyrie's

> acts of choosing the hero in battle, of laying upon him the task that will shape his heroic identity, of investing him with an unwearying, heroic energy that will secure victory in battle, and then, if necessary, of accompanying him to the afterlife. (*Wealhtheow* 67)

Further, through her archetypal interaction with warriors slain in battle, "The valkyrie offers death, embodies contact with death; her semi-religious, priestess function gives her tremendous power as the repository of men's fears and ambivalence" (Overing 229).

In Old Norse literature, valkyrie figures are commonly presented in two distinct aspects, either as "fierce, elemental beings," who sometimes "require sacrificial appeasement," or as "benevolent guardians," who serve the hero in "the court as well as the battlefield" (Damico, "Valkyrie" 176–77). The grim, malevolent aspect of the valkyrie is generally considered a remnant of an earlier mythic conception, while the benevolent figure is considered a development of later Germanic mythology and literature. Although the Old English term *wælcyrge*, linguistically equivalent to Old Norse *valkyrja*, appears consistently only in references to "creatures who are malevolent, destructive, corrupt, and associated with slaughter" (177), Anglo-Saxon writers tended to depict women in heroic texts using conventions associated with both benevolent and malevolent Old Norse valkyrie figures. In his seminal article "Beowulf: The Monsters and the Critics," Tolkien expresses his acute awareness of such parallels between Old Norse and Old English literary practices when he remarks on the "fundamentally similar heroic temper of ancient England and Scandinavia" (25). A product of this common Germanic legacy shared by Anglo-Saxon and medieval Scandinavian peoples, this valkyrie reflex[12] allows benevolent Old English women characters, such as *Beowulf*'s Wealhtheow, Judith, and Juliana, to be considered valkyrie-indebted figures. Just so, through their inherited associations with valkyrie traditions, Tolkien's women take their models from these same heroic Germanic women. Whether his presentations of Galadriel, Shelob, Éowyn, and Arwen are based on his direct response to valkyrie figures in Old Norse literature, to the valkyrie reflex he recognizes in portrayals of women in Old English literature, or to a combination of these is irrelevant. What is relevant for the purposes of this study is that Tolkien's women inherit valkyrie-like characteristics carrying medieval cultural connotations, which Tolkien adapts to the modern heroic, cultural, and moral attitudes promoted in his texts.

Like the valkyrie-associated Wealhtheow in *Beowulf*, Tolkien's Galadriel is "the ideal queen, [who] reigns over a hall resplendent with light" (Damico, *Wealhtheow* 9). Galadriel rules her Elven environment with similar composure and resplendence, enhanced by allusions to light and radiance common in valkyrie imagery. Constantly referenced by terms connoting radiant or shining qualities, Galadriel's name itself means "lady of light" in Tolkien's invented Sindarin lan-

12. For further discussion of the Old English valkyrie reflex, see Damico, "Valkyrie" and *Wealhtheow*.

guage.[13] Although her radiance is not derived from the metallic brightness of armor, arm-rings or necklaces typical in the portrayals of Old English and Old Norse valkyrie figures, Galadriel's external brilliance is described in terms related to a general heightened intensity of color, especially the whiteness of her dress, her shining eyes, her fair physical features, and her blonde hair. The first time we see Galadriel, she is "clad wholly in white" (*LotR* II.7.354), echoed later by "clad in simple white" (II.7.366). At the close of the story, Galadriel appears "robed all in glimmering white, like clouds about the Moon" (II.7.366). Throughout his descriptions of Galadriel, Tolkien uses the term "white" to suggest the illuminative qualities of starlight, moonlight, and sunlight so strongly associated with her character. Further associating the Elven queen with visual intensity, Tolkien consistently identifies Galadriel as "tall and white and fair" (II.7.361) and later as simply "tall and white" (II.8.372). Whether these references refer to the whiteness of the Lady's raiment or to the white flawlessness of her skin, also described by "her white arms" (II.7.365), they establish her overall brightness and indicate an intensity of hue that is an inseparable part of her physical nature.

In Eddic literature, several valkyrie figures are described, like Galadriel, as "hvít" (white) (*HHv* 28), "fögr" (fair) (*Völ* 2), and "liósa" (shining) (*Sigsk* 53). In addition, Galadriel's white clothing echoes the "álptarhamir" (swanskin cloaks) of the valkyries in *Völundarkviða* (*Völ* prose before 1). Similarly, Galadriel's appearance in her Elven swan barge (*LotR* II.8.373) echoes the Eddic descriptions of the *Völundarkviða* women, who are identified as both valkyries and swan-maidens. Another Old Norse valkyrie, Brynhild, is presented through swan imagery as "álft af báru" (a swan upon a wave) (*VS* 177). Galadriel's white features and her swan barge link her to these valkyries in images formed from the brightest naturally occurring color. Through such references, Tolkien establishes his visual treatment of the Elven queen to reflect the uppermost extreme on the spectrum of light. Thus the whiteness of Galadriel's own physical form, combined with the exter-

13. Since the "Galadhriel" variant form of her name, meaning "tree-lady," is used only in *The Silmarillion,* it is clear Tolkien made a conscious choice in *The Lord of the Rings* to emphasize qualities of light associated with this Elven queen.

nal trappings of her dress and her ship, equates the Lady with lightness and, by extension, moral goodness in its most saturated form.

In addition to using the color white and a fair appearance to establish the visual intensity of Galadriel's physical presence as indicative of a heightened moral state, Tolkien highlights the Lady's supremacy of form and nature by including references to shining eyes and gold in his portrayal of the Elven queen. When first introducing Galadriel and her husband, Celeborn, Tolkien writes, their eyes "were keen as lances in the starlight" (*LotR* II.7.354). Such an identification of the Lady's eyes as one of her shining features suggests a similar brightness in the eyes of many valkyries. For example, the skaldic poem *Hrafnsmál* describes a valkyrie with "gloegghvarmr" (gleaming eyes).[14] Galadriel's "deep gold" hair (II.7.354) further accentuates her identification with heightened expressions of light as well as links her portrayal to descriptions of the valkyries' physical features. Recalling Old Norse valkyries whose hair is described generally as pale or golden, Gimli eloquently addresses the shining, golden qualities of Galadriel's hair, when he claims a strand of it "surpasses the gold of the earth as the stars surpass the gems of the mine" (II.7.376). Illustrating this same principal of brightness associated with light-colored hair, the same *Hrafnsmál* valkyrie with gleaming eyes also features "hvíta hadbjarta" (brightly light hair). These additional visual motifs of radiant eyes and golden hair serve to emphasize the brilliance inherent to Galadriel's character as reflective of her enhanced physical and moral state.

Further concordant with Eddic descriptions of valkyries, Galadriel's radiance is an innate part of her very being. When the Company leaves Lothlórien, the "white form" of Galadriel "shone like a window of glass upon a far hill in the westering sun, or as a remote lake seen from a mountain: a crystal fallen in the lap of the land" (*LotR* II.8.377). At the end of *The Lord of the Rings*, the Lady's innate radiance is summarized in the statement that "she herself seemed to shine with a soft light" (I.9.1028). Like the valkyrie in the *Helgi Lays*, who is "biartlituð" (bright of form) (*HHv* 17), such a description presents Galadriel as the very image of the Old English term "ælfscūnu" (Elf-shining) (*Judith* 14),

14. References to *Hrafnsmál* are taken from Kershaw 76–87.

a term that appears in connection with the heroine Judith.[15] The immanent brilliance of this Elf-shining light so central to the Elf queen's nature is later emphasized in the tunnels of Cirith Ungol, when Frodo sees "a light in his mind, almost unbearably bright at first, as a sun-ray to the eyes of one long hidden in a windowless pit [...] he saw the Lady Galadriel" (*LotR* IV.9.720). In this image of Galadriel, sun imagery offers an additional connection to valkyrie-associated figures whose brightness is also often likened to the sun. To cite two examples, the Old English Juliana is described as "sunscīene" (sun-shining one) (*Juliana* 229), and the Old Norse Sigrún as "sólbiört" (sun-bright) (*HH II* 45).

Enlarging upon the gold motif as well as incorporating the illuminative qualities typical of valkyrie figures, Galadriel's concealed Elven ring of power, Nenya, provides another piece of evidence that links her to the medieval valkyries. When Frodo first sees Galadriel's ring, "it glittered like polished gold overlaid with silver light, and a white stone in it twinkled as if the Even-star had come down to rest" (*LotR* II.7.365). While Nenya's magical power makes the ring different in nature from the gold rings of adornment and currency that frequently bedeck Germanic valkyies, its effect as part of Galadriel's external brilliance associates her with other ring-wearing valkyrie figures, such as Judith, who is "bēahhrōdene" (ring-adorned) (*Judith* 138), and Sigrún, who is "baugvarið" (ring-wearing) (*HH II* 35) and "gullvarið" (gold-wearing) (*HH II* 45). Much as the medieval valkyrie's actions are typically motivated by the woman's strong will, Nenya responds to Galadriel's will by intensifying the Lady's own inherent light at moments of import. Illustrating this property, at Galadriel's consideration of Frodo's offer to her of the One Ring, Nenya "issued a great light that illumined her alone and left all else dark" (*LotR* II.7.366).

Accentuating the valkyrie-like emphasis on light in Tolkien's characterization of Galadriel is the phial of light she gives Frodo as a parting gift. Like Galadriel, so, too, medieval valkyries are sometimes recorded as bestowing on their heroes special gifts of power with properties of brightness or glittering. For example, the valkyrie Sváva grants Helgi an especially illustrious sword described as "varið gulli./Hringr er í hialti" [adorned with gold, ringed on the hilt] (*HHv* 8–9). In *Beowulf*, Wealh-

15. Damico discusses the biblical figure Judith in Old English as characterized through the valkyrie reflex ("Valkyrie" 185).

theow, another valkyrie-associated figure, gives the hero "wunden gold/stum geēawed, earm[h]rēade twā, / hrægl ond hringas, healsbēaga mǣst" [wrought gold, granted in good will, two arm-bands, mail and rings, and the greatest neck ring] (1193–95). Like these brightly gleaming gifts from valkyrie-associated women, Galadriel's phial

> glittered as she moved it, and rays of white light sprang from her hand. "In this phial," she said, "is caught the light of Eärendil's star [...] It will shine still brighter when night is about you. May it be a light to you in dark places, when all other lights go out." (*LotR* II.8.376)

Serving just such a purpose, the phial provides Frodo and Sam not only illumination but the strength of Galadriel's spirit necessary for them to battle the darkness and malice of Shelob and Cirith Ungol. Although Galadriel's gift of magically captured starlight has no direct parallels in medieval Germanic texts, Tolkien's inclusion of it in his text echoes gifts to medieval heroes in its qualities of illumination.

While the main narrative of *The Lord of the Rings* never shows Galadriel wielding valkyrie-like martial skills or physical prowess,[16] she is portrayed through the valkyrie-associated act of ceremonial cup-bearing at occasions of narrative import. Such occasions typically involve either the welcoming of heroes, as in the case of the valkyries who welcome fallen warriors to Valhalla, or the departure of heroes, as in the case of Sigrún's farewell to Helgi (*HH II* 46–47). As Jane Chance describes this activity of valkyrie-associated women in human halls, "The mead-sharing ritual and the cup-passer herself come to symbolize peace-weaving and peace because they strengthen the societal and familial bonds between lord and retainers" ("Grendel's" 254). Like the Old English Wealhtheow and other Eddic women[17] who participate in official court ceremonies involving the sharing of ritual drink as a means of establishing loyalties and commitments from heroes, Galadriel enacts this valkyrie function at the Company's departure from Lothlórien. As Tolkien describes,

---

16. That Galadriel possesses physical prowess equal to or superior to that of a male is suggested by the comment that "Galadriel threw down its [Dol Goldur's] walls and laid bare its pits" (*LotR* Appendix B.1094).

17. See, for example, Sigrdrífa (*Sigrd* 2–4) in *The Poetic Edda,* and Brynhild in *VS,* chap. 21.

> Now Galadriel rose from the grass, and taking a cup from one of her maidens she filled it with white mead and gave it to Celeborn.
>
> "Now it is time to drink the cup of farewell," she said. "Drink Lord of the Galadrim! [...]"
>
> Then she brought the cup to each of the Company, and bade them drink and farewell. (*LotR* II.8.374)

The sequence here in which Galadriel offers the ceremonial "cup of parting" (II.8.374) filled with a special drink, first to the king and then to the heroes, parallels the process by which other valkyrie figures in medieval literature serve their ceremonial function of official cup-bearing. To cite one example from *Beowulf,* Wealhtheow, seeking to establish public bonds of loyalty between her sons and Beowulf, first takes the ceremonial cup to her lord Hrothgar, then to Beowulf, and then to the rest of the warriors (1162–233). Like the specially noted "white mead" in Tolkien's text, the "wīn" (wine) Wealhtheow serves also has specific ritual implications. In *Beowulf,* the term "wīn" is used rather than the more common drink of mead or beer primarily to denote the ceremonial drink served by Hrothgar's queen.[18] In similar fashion, the "vín" (wine) in *Eiríksmál*[19] Odin calls the valkyries to bring is a special drink for it must be such "sem vísir come" (as if a prince were coming) (1).

Immediately following her cup-bearing scene, Galadriel's ritual aspect further resembles the court functions of valkyrie figures when she grants gifts to each member of the Company. Much as the gifts awarded by medieval valkyries strengthen the commitment of the hero to both the woman and his heroic destiny, Galadriel's gifts are chosen to aid each individual hero's quest as well as to confirm their commitments to the Lady and her world of honor, beauty, and peace. Gimli's three golden hairs from the Lady's tresses, Sam's box of gardening soil from Lothlórien, and Aragorn's Elfstone brooch of ancient heritage from his beloved—all speak to those desires deepest within these heroes' hearts in an effort to inspire them to future action, while

---

18. Of the three times this word appears in *Beowulf,* twice it is associated with Wealhtheow's cup-bearing ritual, and its only remaining occurrence is used to describe Unferth as "wīne druncen" (line 1467). Even the latter reference may reflect the wine's ritual connotation, for it recalls a scene in which Unferth in his officially sanctioned role of thyle bestows on Beowulf a special sword of ancient heritage.

19. References to *Eiríksmál* are taken from Kershaw 93–99.

reminding them of the bonds forged to Galadriel and Lothlórien, bonds associated with the mythological past that the Elven queen, like the valkyries, embodies. By assuming such ceremonial functions at this point in the narrative, Galadriel acts as a force that unifies conflicting motives and desires among the Company. Although the members of the Company will be later separated from each other, their intensely powerful personal experiences of Galadriel and Lothlórien, coalescing in the combined cup-bearing and gift-giving ceremony, establish a commonality that continues to join the individuals to each other and to their larger purpose throughout the work.

An important adjunct to Galadriel's gift-giving function is her preparation of special garments for Tolkien's heroes. The grey Elven cloaks, given at the Company's parting from Lothlórien, show that the heroes are "indeed high in the favour of the Lady! For she herself and her maidens wove this stuff; and never before have we clad strangers in the garb of our own people" (*LotR* II.8.370), as one Elf explains. Galadriel's construction of these cloaks with properties that conceal the heroes from detection underscores her relationship to medieval Germanic valkyrie figures not only in her giving of such magical gifts, but also in the weaving motif. In medieval literature, valkyrie figures frequently prepare special garments or weavings intended to assist, inspire, or incite the hero's quest. The valkyrie's association with sewing, embroidering, or weaving may be a literary remnant of an earlier attribute that linked such figures with other Old Norse mythological women called the *dísir* or *norns* who wove the tapestried fates of humans. Examples of the weaving or sewing skills associated with valkyrie-like women include the *Völundarkviða* valkyries who "línn spunno" (spin flax) (*Völ* 1), Signy who gruesomely tests her sons' courage by stitching their shirts to their skin (*VS* 122), and Brynhild who "kunni meira hagleik en aðrar konur. Hún lagði sinn borða með gulli ok saumaði á þau stórmerki, er Sigurðr hafði gert" [was more skilled in handwork than other women. She adorned her tapestry with gold and embroidered on it the great deeds, which Sigurd had accomplished] (*VS* 166).

Galadriel's ability to assess and test the Company's motives is another powerful attribute connecting her to the traditions of the Old Norse seers, *norns*, or *dísir*. While normally these prophetess figures are not rendered as valkyries, the valkyrie Brynhild foretells future events (*Sigsk* 52–63), and Skuld is identified as both a valkyrie and a norn (*PrE* 44 and 61). Galadriel's prophetic perceptions of the heroes' inner thoughts is summarized in Gimli's comment that she reads "many hearts and desires" (*LotR* V.2.766), and in Sam's description of her searching look at their first meeting as "looking inside me" (II.7.358). In addition, Galadriel has prescient abilities that allow her to "perceive the Dark Lord and know his mind" (II.7.364), while hiding her own power. Like the valkyrie-norn Skuld, Galadriel's prophetic abilities also involve a special relationship to a sacred body of water. Her prescience is partly a result of her involvement with the magical water of a well, her Mirror, in which Frodo and Sam are allowed to look for information about the future. While her command of it is somewhat limited,[20] Tolkien's description of Galadriel's actions and words regarding her Mirror show it functions only through her interaction. The ritual process by which Galadriel invokes the prophetic powers of her Mirror is described thus:

> With water from the stream Galadriel filled the basin to the brim, and breathed on it, and when the water was still again she spoke. "Here is the Mirror of Galadriel," she said. "I have brought you here so that you may look in it, if you will." (II.7.361)

When the hobbit heroes look into the water, they see visions of an apocalyptic future evocative of the Old Norse Ragnarök, which the valkyrie-norn Skuld prophesies by looking into her own magical well. Although these foretellings from Galadriel's Mirror both trouble their souls and warn them of potential dangers, the visions also allow Frodo and Sam to understand and accept more fully the hazards of their quest.

Like the valkyries who intercede with Odin on behalf of exceptional heroes for the world's sake, Galadriel wields her personal and prophetic power in a battle of universal impact. In Galadriel's case, her refusal of the One Ring (*LotR* II.7.366) is valkyrie-like in that it is an action undertaken as the result of a supreme exertion of the character's

---

20. Expressing her limited control of the Mirror, Galadriel explains: "Many things I can command the Mirror to reveal [...] and to some I can show what they desire to see. But the Mirror will also show things unbidden, and those are often stranger and more profitable than things which we wish to behold. What you will see, if you leave the Mirror free to work, I cannot tell. For it shows things that were, and things that are, and things that yet may be. But which it is that he sees, even the wisest cannot always tell" (*LotR* II.7.362).

will. Both her Elven nature and prophetic abilities make Galadriel acutely aware of her responsibility to her culture. By refusing Frodo's offer of the One Ring, Galadriel exhibits her concerned awareness not only of herself and her people but also of a universe in which good and evil struggle for supremacy. Galadriel's prophetic powers enable her to recognize that her acceptance of the One Ring would be the destruction of herself, her Elven people, and the larger world of Middle-earth, for by doing so she would become a tool of evil, "beautiful beyond enduring, terrible and worshipful" (II.7.366). Like Sigrún, Brynhild, and other valkyrie figures who choose to aid a hero rather than battle against him, Galadriel exerts the force of her will to turn away from a choice that would make her a vehicle for violence and destruction.

Further linking her to Odin's battle maids, Galadriel's choice to sacrifice the paradisial haven of Lothlórien in order to save her world alludes to the theme of the valkyrie's sorrow precipitated by extreme personal loss. As Damico describes the Old Norse analogues' treatment of this theme, the medieval valkyrie figure "is touched with sorrow [that] follows convention, for the quality appears as a consistent attribute of the female figures in Eddic and Anglo-Saxon heroic poetry" (*Wealhtheow* 20). For Germanic valkyries such as Brynhild and Sigrún, grief results from a choice made by the valkyrie herself which leads to giving up her immortality, to the betrayal of a lover, or to the death of a beloved hero. Similarly, Galadriel's choice to reject the One Ring seals the already apparent fate of Lothlórien's disappearance from the world. After the destruction of the One Ring, she acknowledges her "power is diminished, and Lothlórien will fade, and the tides of Time will sweep it away. We must depart into the West, or dwindle to a rustic folk of dell and cave, slowly to forget and to be forgotten" (*LotR* II.7.365). It is this loss eternal, which can be neither denied nor succumbed to, that Tolkien himself has identified as the "real theme" of *The Lord of the Rings*.[21] In his study of the loss eternal theme, Len Sanford identifies the impact of this theme on Germanic literature and mythology when he writes, "Northern mythology takes a darker view—that the struggle between man and monster must end in man's defeat, yet he continues to struggle; his weapons are [...] na-

---

21. See Tolkien's letter to Joanna de Bortadano (*Letters* 246–47).

ked will and courage" (17). Galadriel's most profound expression of this loss-eternal theme[22] finds voice in her song about Lothlórien's fading. Resonant with the *ubi sunt* motifs commonly found in Old English elegiac poetry,[23] Galadriel laments:

> Ah! like gold fall the leaves in the wind, long years numberless as the wings of trees! The years have passed like swift draughts of the sweet mead in lofty halls beyond the West, beneath the blue vaults of Varda wherein the stars tremble in the song of her voice, holy and queenly. Who now shall refill the cup for me? For now the Kindler, Varda, the Queen of the Stars, from Mount Everwhite has uplifted her hands like clouds, and all paths are drowned deep in shadow; and out of a grey country darkness lies on the foaming waves between us, and mist covers the jewels of Calacirya for ever. Now lost, lost to those from the East, is Valimar! (*LotR* II.8.378)

While the *ubi sunt* motif in Old English poetry is not associated specifically with valkyrie figures, its definitive connection to heroic themes and its presentation by Galadriel, a female speaker, provide a matrix of personal loss, the heroic world, and women's power highly evocative of valkyrie literature.

Providing a thematic antithesis to Galadriel, Shelob typifies the inverse image of the benevolent valkyrie reflex in *The Lord of the Rings*. As Tolkien's only example of the baleful, malevolent valkyrie figure found in Germanic mythology and literature, Shelob represents an opposition that serves to intensify Tolkien's emphasis on the benevolent valkyrie motifs reflected in his other women characters. While Joe Abbott closely examines Shelob's affinity to monstrous female figures in Old Norse and Old English literature, his study omits exploration of Tolkien's spider creature as indicative of the medieval valkyrie figure in her negative, perverted aspect. His recognition, however, of Shelob as reminiscent of Old Norse and Old English giantess figures—who live in geographically liminal spaces, are associated firmly with darkness, and are begotten from ancient races of beings—parallels the themes and conventions commonly attached to the malevolent forms of the valkyrie.

---

22. Another detailed discussion of Tolkien's loss eternal theme may be found in Senior.

23. Among the Old English elegiac poems containing the *ubi sunt* or loss eternal theme are "The Wanderer" and "The Seafarer" (Pope).

An emblem of unconquerable evil will, Shelob's gigantic, dark, bloated presence establishes an extreme contrast to Galadriel's humanly proportioned qualities of light, beauty, and heightened moral goodness. As Shelob offers a parodic inversion of the benevolent valkyrie aspects of Tolkien's Elven queen whose maternal virtues guide and protect her people, so too has the valkyrie-associated Grendel's mother been described as "a parodic inversion, both of the Anglo-Saxon queen and mother, the ideal of which was embodied in the Virgin Mary" (Chance, "Grendel's" 252–53). Like Galadriel, Shelob too is a force with mythological associations beyond Middle-earth, a creature with the ability to affect conflicts in the scope of the larger world (*LotR* IV.9.723). But, while Galadriel, like the benevolent valkyries, interacts extensively with her community of Lothlórien and serves as a responsible leader of her people, Shelob operates in isolation, devoid of community, "unabated in malice" (IV.9.724). Unlike Galadriel who cares for other beings and races outside her scope of direct influence, Shelob broods only on herself. As Tolkien explains,

> Little she knew of or cared for towers, or rings, or anything devised by mind or hand, who only desired death for all others, mind and body, and for herself a glut of life, alone, swollen till the mountains could no longer hold her up and the darkness could not contain her. (IV.9.724)

Her insatiable desire to continue her monstrous existence is, as Jane Chance remarks, "the embodiment of the primordial desire for survival" (*Mythology* 114). Further, Shelob's will is enacted not as Galadriel employs the power of her will to preserve other peoples of Middle-earth, but to satisfy her ultimately selfish greed for the meat she acquires by destroying those same peoples. For Rawls, "Shelob is what happens when the feminine concern with the individual and the inner life is taken to its extreme" (10). Similarly, Fenwick explains Shelob is "a force that denies all ends except her own gloom and hunger" (23). Her kinship with baleful, valkyrie-associated figures is based on such destructive purposes. Unlike Tolkien's other primary female characters, but very like the malevolent valkyrie figures who are almost always bent on the hero's destruction, Shelob always seeks to destroy rather than to preserve or create.

Complementing the destructive aspects of her nature, the malevolent valkyrie figure is most often presented as an unnatural version of heroic appearance and behavior. Because the excessive strength of such valkyries is portrayed generally as monstrous in its inversion of medieval ideals of femininity, the malevolent valkyrie is often portrayed as the hero's most physically specific and powerful opponent. Just so, Shelob is Tolkien's most vivid, terrifying force of evil and the most substantial of the physical threats Frodo encounters. In Tolkien's vision, the Orcs are foul and powerful but conquerable, while battles with the Ringwraiths and the Ring itself are more properly conflicts of the spirit than they are of the body. Not even Sauron, that preeminent force of evil whose most explicit description is rendered as a large baleful eye, can match the overwhelmingly visceral vision of evil found in the spiderlike Shelob. Her evil nature, like the monstrous valkyrie-associated Hrímgerth of the *Helgi Lays* and Grendel's mother of *Beowulf,* is evidenced in her inhuman form. As Hrímgerth and Grendel's mother are unnaturally formed humans in their immense size and sea-monster connotations, Shelob is not a naturally evolved spider as indicated by her hugeness as well as by Tolkien's statement that she is not precisely a spider, but rather "an evil thing in spider-form" (*LotR* V.9.723). Shelob's unnaturalness is emphasized by her claws as well as by her size. In addition, while neither creature takes Shelob's spiderlike form, both Grendel's mother and Hrímgerth have claws,[24] just as on Shelob "at each leg's end there was a claw" (V.9.725). Odd additions for a spider-like creature, Shelob's claws may be derived from Tolkien's knowledge of Hrímgerth and Grendel's mother. If so, this detail of Shelob's anatomy, which has no direct purpose in Tolkien's plot development, offers additional acknowledgment of this character's valkyrie roots. Other evidence linking Tolkien's spider creature to the inhuman qualities of such grim battle demons is that her hide resembles Grendel's mother's skin or body covering in that it is tough enough to deflect weapons (1518–29), much like the armor commonly worn by valkyries. Describing this nearly impenetrable quality of Shelob's "age-old hide," Tolkien writes that it was "ever thickened from within with layer on layer of evil growth. The blade scored it with a dreadful gash, but those hideous folds could not be pierced" (*LotR* V.9.728).

---

24. See Grendel's mother's "atolan clommum" (terrible claws) (1502), and Hrímgerth's "klymmor" (claws) (*HHv* 22).

Further, in Old English and Old Norse literature, the fierce battle-demon type of valkyrie character reverses the weaving or sewing motif related to the benevolent valkyrie in that the monstrous woman is often presented as destroying warriors by fettering or binding them.[25] Functioning in much the same way, Shelob "bound in cords" (*LotR* V.9.728) her victims as a precursor to eating them. Similarly, Modthrytho in *Beowulf* weaves bonds especially designed to destroy warriors, described as "wælbende weotode tealde / handgewriþene" [slaughter-bonds woven by hand, reckoned and ordained] (1936–37). Shelob's binding cords resemble not only Modthrytho's bonds but also the fetters used by warrior women in the *First Merseberg Charm* whom Damico has identified as associated with the valkyrie tradition (*Wealhtheow* 43). In addition, the cords with which Shelob binds Frodo and her other victims are closely related to the webs with which she seals the opening to her den. Her web of "countless cords" (*LotR* V.9.722) further recalls the weaving or sewing traditions of the Germanic valkyrie figures. As Tolkien describes his spider creature's web, "Across the width and height of the tunnel a vast web was spun, orderly as the web of some huge spider, but denser-woven and far greater, and each thread was as thick as rope" (V.9.722). While the weaving motif in Old Norse texts is not generally suggestive of violence, in one skaldic poem, *Darraðarljóð* in *Brennu-Njáls saga*, women specifically identified as valkyries use their own weapons and the body parts of dead warriors to weave a garment that determines the deaths of warriors.

Shelob also exhibits the typical valkyrie trait of unusually intensified eyes. Unlike the shining eyes of the benevolent valkyries, malevolent valkyrie figures commonly display terrifying and baleful eyes, as in the "ötul augo" (fearsome eyes) (*HH II* 4) of one Eddic valkyrie. Just as terrible, Shelob possesses "two great clusters of many-windowed eyes" that are "Monstrous and abominable" (*LotR* V.9.720). Her eyes also shine, but with "fell light" (V.9.725) and "pale deadly fire" (V.9.720). The terror of Shelob's eyes reflects her unnatural origins and responses for they are "bestial and yet filled with purpose and with hideous delight" (V.9.720). Like Shelob, *The Wonders of the East*, an Old English

25. See *The Poetic Edda*'s valkyrie Herföðr (warrior-fetter) (*Vsp* 30) and the *First Merseburg Charm*'s warlike women who "hapt heptidun" (fastened fetters) (Barber 65).

travelogue preserved in the *Beowulf* Codex, describes one of its female monsters as having "wælcyrian eagan" (valkyrie eyes) and "eahta fet" (eight feet) (Orchard 186). While we cannot be certain Tolkien had this specific monster in mind when he created Shelob, the cluster of imagery referring to a terrible-eyed, eight-footed, valkyrie-associated creature, in a text Tolkien must have known, suggests more than a casual connection between Shelob and *The Wonders of the East* monster.

Yet as closely as the monstrous and malevolent Shelob parallels baleful valkyrie figures, the most direct and compelling evidence for the valkyrie tradition in Tolkien's texts resides in the character of Éowyn. Like Tolkien's Éowyn, the figures in Germanic literature and mythology most clearly identified as valkyries are martial maidens, helmeted women, armored for battle[26] who are sometimes garbed as men. Such medieval women participate in ambiguous definitions of their gender roles, which reject traditional binary definitions of gender.[27] While the attributes elaborated earlier are significant elements in representations of Germanic valkyrie figures, it is the warrior aspect that most securely identifies a woman character's debt to Odin's battle maids. Tolkien's Éowyn is modeled explicitly on such benevolent warrior women as Brynhild, who "fór með hjálm ok brynju ok gekk at vígum" [took up helmet and mail and went to battle] (*VS* 165), and the two Hervörs in *Heidrek's saga* who wage war alongside men. Like these medieval valkyrie antecedents, Éowyn not only has been trained for battle but also has martial abilities equal to those of the most heroic men, as is typical of such cross-gendered valkyrie figures. As Gandalf tells Éomer, she possesses "a spirit and courage at least the match of yours" (*LotR* V.8.867). By showing Éowyn armed for battle several times in his text, Tolkien insists on her martial abilities as a major facet of her character's identity. Her martial depiction is founded on the fact that she is "a shieldmaiden" (V.2.784; VI.5.961; VI.5.965), a term cognate with the Old Norse *skjaldmeyjar*, used frequently to describe valkyrie figures. As a shieldmaiden, Éowyn is part of an order of nobly born women warriors

26. Examples include the valkyries in *Hákonarmál*, who are described as "hjalmaðar sátu / ok höfðusk hlífar fyrir" [helmeted they sat and they carried shields before them] (Kershaw 106); the "mey und hiálmi" [woman under the helm] (*Fáf* 44); and the "hiálmvitr" [helmeted-spirits] (*HH II* 54).

27. For more extensive discussions of gender roles in relation to Old English women, see Overing; Dockray-Miller.

who appear "clad like a Rider and girt with a sword" (V.2.785), who "ride and wield blade" (V.2.784), and who do "not fear either pain or death" (V.2.784). Paralleling such descriptions in both word choice and conceptual content, the Old Norse valkyrie Brynhild identifies herself by saying, "Ek em skjaldmær, ok á ek með herkonungum hjálm, ok þeim mun ek at liði verða, ok ekki er mér leitt at berjast" [I am a shieldmaiden. I wear a helmet and ride with the warrior kings. I must support them, and I am not averse to fighting] (*VS* 168).

Like other valkyrie-identified women, Éowyn's female identity does not preclude her from wielding power, regardless of whether Tolkien presents her character gendered as a courtly princess or as an armored warrior. Gifts suitable for a warrior rather than a courtly woman, Éowyn's arms are awarded to her by her king. As Tolkien writes, "Éowyn knelt before him [Théoden] and received from him a sword and a fair corslet" (*LotR* III.6.523). By accepting these gifts, Éowyn accepts not only arms but an obligation as defender of her people. This valkyrie-like obligation is evident as the warband sets off to Helm's Deep in the image of Éowyn standing outside the doors with a sword "set upright before her, and her hands [...] laid upon the hilt" (III.6.523). Continuing this martial imagery, Éowyn later wears "a helm and was clad to the waist like a warrior and girded with a sword" (V.3.795). Such a description closely echoes that of the valkyrie Brynhild who "hefir sverð í hendi ok hjálm á höfði ok var í brynju" [had a sword in her hand and a helmet on her head and was in mail] (*VS* 177). Part of her martial aspect requires Brynhild to assume the role of military leadership at times of need, as indicated in her statement "Ek mun kanna lið hermanna" [I must review the troops of warriors] (*VS* 168). Just so, Éowyn's training for battle grants her the authority to lead her people, govern them, and provide for their welfare in the absence of Théoden. Háma validates her right to such authority when he asserts, "She is fearless and high-hearted. All love her. Let her be as Lord of the Éorlingas, while we are gone" (*LotR* III.6.523). Although her desire to physically engage in battle is rejected by Théoden, Éowyn has the valkyrie's personal power and social obligation to take up arms herself as a means of protecting her people. Where some critics view Éowyn's character as either reflective of the powerlessness inherent in traditional female roles that trap women in their femininity or as indicative of her rejection of femininity through her warrior trappings, Háma's words indicate instead her authority to be simultaneously a woman and a warrior. Her personal courage, martial skill, innate virtue, and noble genealogy make her a suitable leader of the Rohirrim, illustrating that in Tolkien's world other factors "are often more important than gender in legitimizing female political power" (Crowe 275).

Not only is Éowyn related to Old Norse and Old English battle maidens in training and leadership within her culture; she also resembles valkyries in her psychological configuration. Recognizing the formidable nature of this woman's spirit at their first meeting, Aragorn notes "strong she seemed and stern as steel" (*LotR* III.6.515). Like the medieval valkyrie figures Brynhild and Sigrún, Éowyn is a character whose nature houses a will that must be satisfied by physical action. She articulates this aspect of her psychology when she tells Aragorn, "I am weary of skulking in the hills, and wish to face peril and battle" (V.2.784). What Éowyn fears most is that, by fulfilling her duty to remain at home to protect her people, her shieldmaiden spirit will remain caged until "all chance of doing great deeds is gone beyond recall or desire" (V.2.784). To gain her freedom and to achieve her desire of serving her people honorably in battle, Éowyn, like the Old Norse Hervör and Thorbjörg,[28] disguises her female identity with male clothes and an assumed male name. Éowyn's desire to ride into battle as a male warrior named Dernhelm is an effort to fulfill her shieldmaiden training and heritage, while maintaining her personal honor. Her disguise is not an attempt to hide the fact that she is a woman, for her training verifies that in the Rohirrim culture it is acceptable for women to engage in battle, but rather her disguise is necessary to conceal the fact that she is Éowyn, the niece Théoden has forbidden to ride to this particular battle with him.

Yet, in Tolkien's medieval analogues, the valkyrie's will often results in tragedy, death, and destruction. In *Beowulf*, the valkyrie's desire for violent action, accomplished through the female form, is represented by Modthrytho's actions that reveal a "death-centred masculine desire versus female as life-giver" (Overing 254). In the *Helgi Lays*, Sigrún's love for the hero leads to his death. Echoing the tragic results common to such valkyrie counterparts, Éowyn's choice

---

28. Thorbjörg appears in *Hrólfs saga Gautrekssonar* (Jónsson).

to don male garb in order to fulfill her role as shieldmaiden arises from her expectations of heroic failure as well as her own death. These expectations are foregrounded in Merry's recognition that, disguised as Dernhelm, hers "was the face of one without hope who goes in search of death" (*LotR* V.3.803). Éowyn's act of volition, however, results not in tragedy but in unforeseen victory. Although Théoden and Aragorn attempt to thwart her desire to engage in physical battle, Éowyn fulfills this desire by clothing herself as Dernhelm, an act of her own volition and determination. As she whispers in Merry's ear, "*Where will wants not, a way opens*" (V.3.804, emphasis in original). Like her brother Éomer, when Éowyn rides to battle as Dernhelm, she embodies what is best and most heroic in the Rohirrim. Where he recalls the image of the great warrior of Rohan's past, the shieldmaiden Éowyn is the very form of her people's continuing history, a symbol of Rohan's living heritage, its recent struggle against disintegration and hopelessness, as well as the potential transformation of its future. As such, her shieldmaiden's skill and courage, intensified by the extremity of her need, join with the force of her valkyrie will to accomplish one of the text's most heroic deeds, the prophesied battle impossible for anyone else to win, the killing of the Ringwraiths' Black Captain. Yet, it is not simply her strength of will that enables Éowyn to vanquish the Black Captain; her victory also owes much to the tension between the masculine and feminine gender roles inherent in the valkyrie reflex that Tolkien has appropriated for her characterization. Like Eddic valkyries who wield their physical power to aid beloved heroes, Éowyn's blows against the Black Captain are struck to aid Théoden, for "on the battlefield, it is love, a feminine attribute which motivates her and gives her the power to act—again, an interplay of feminine and masculine attributes" (Rawls 10).

Éowyn's connection to the valkyrie reflex, however, is founded on more than her role as a warrior maiden and the exertion of her strong will. As with Galadriel, Éowyn is portrayed in terms of the intensification of light common to the benevolent Germanic valkyrie figures. Éowyn resembles the Elven queen in that she too is clad "in white" (*LotR* III.6.512; VI.5.961) or "a white robe girt with silver" (III.6.515). Also similar to Galadriel's, Éowyn's "long hair was like a river of gold" (III.6.515), and "her bright hair, released from its bonds, gleamed with pale gold" (V.6.841). The goldness of her hair in such passages is associated with treasure, but its shining qualities contribute to her valkyrie-like radiance in descriptions of her "long braided hair gleaming in the twilight" (V.3.795) and the "light fell about her, and her hair shone in the sunrise" (V.6.842). Like other valkyrie figures in Tolkien's texts and in Germanic literature, Éowyn's illumination is featured in her eyes as well as with her hair. Two particular passages highlighting this element of her radiance comment that "her eyes were shining" (III.6.522) and "her eyes were on fire" (V.2.784). But, as in Galadriel's characterization, Éowyn's valkyrie radiance is also a generalized facet of her physical nature, for she appears as "a glimmer in the night" (V.2.784) and "golden as the sun and white as snow" (III.7.977). Unlike Tolkien's other primary women characters, however, Éowyn's brilliance is sometimes associated with battle gear, as his statement "clad now in mail [... she] shone like silver in the sun" (III.6.523) makes clear. The glittering qualities imparted by her armor are identical to the medieval valkyries' most often identified source of radiance.

Further, Éowyn functions in the valkyrie's court aspect by bearing both female witness and a ceremonial cup at moments of social significance. In her role of court princess, the Germanic valkyrie commonly attends a king and, like Éowyn in her first appearance in the text (III.6.512), is often presented standing beside or behind the king's chair during occasions of sociocultural import. In Tolkien's text, Éowyn is present not only at the Company's entrance to Meduseld's hall, but also at Gandalf's initial rejuvenation of Théoden. While she is not shown at Théoden's address to his people, Éowyn presides at the king's board and attends his subsequent arming of the heroes. In this scene, Éowyn performs the traditional court valkyrie act of ritual cup-bearing. Like Wealhtheow in *Beowulf*, as well as the other valkyrie figures discussed in connection with Galadriel's cup-bearing aspect, Éowyn, in what can only be described as a ritualistic ceremony, brings a cup of wine to her king as a means of confirming the verbal commitments made previously by the heroes. Blessing Théoden's reaffirmed heroic leadership through this ceremonial act, she using the ancient language of her people,[29] "*Ferthu Théoden hál*. [...] Receive now this

29. "*Ferthu Théoden hál*" is Old English meaning "Go you Théoden whole / healed." In *The Lord of the Rings*, Tolkien uses Old English as the native language of the Rohirrim. It is the only language in the text he did not create, suggesting the

cup and drink in happy hour" (III.6.522, emphasis in original). Éowyn then offers the cup to each guest in much the same ritual common to medieval valkyrie court figures such as *Beowulf*'s Wealhtheow.

At her first appearance in Tolkien's text, Éowyn, like Rohan, is a diminished power, helpless to do more than stand behind the king. Nonetheless, after fulfilling the valkyrie role of ceremonial cup-bearer at the king's board, Éowyn has become an image of Rohan in the process toward rejuvenation and represents its urgent need to reestablish appropriately healthy social bonds. Later, Éowyn again serves the cup in a formal fashion; but this time she serves it to Aragorn before he sets off on the Paths of the Dead. As Tolkien writes,

> In her hand she bore a cup, and she set it to her lips and drank a little, wishing them good speed; and then she gave the cup to Aragorn, and he drank, and he said: "Farewell, Lady of Rohan! I drink to the fortunes of your House, and of you, and of all your people. Say to your brother: beyond the shadows we may meet again!" (V.2.785)

In this instance, the cup ceremony establishes Éowyn's authority to publicly sanction the venture as well as provides Aragorn an official opportunity to show her appropriate honor and to offer her heroic hope. Since Éowyn is dressed as a warrior in this scene, her blessing also carries martial connotations in keeping with the Company's needs at this moment. Her final ritual offering of the shieldmaiden's cup occurs near the end of the story as a fulfillment of her people's past and an affirmation of their future. As part of the Mark's custom to honor the memory of Théoden by including him in their list of former kings, Éowyn "bore a filled cup to Éomer" (VI.6.977), which then initiates the ceremony by which Éomer formally assumes his rightful place as Rohan's new king. Like Wealhtheow and other valkyrie-associated queens who preside over ceremonies by bearing ritual cups, Éowyn's formal actions and female presence acknowledge her culture's debt to an honorable past and its equal responsibility to an heroic future.

While Éowyn is not associated with the usual valkyrie motif of sewing or weaving heroic garments, like other benevolent valkyrie figures, she is responsible for arming Merry with heroic battle gear

---

(note continued)

close relationship between the Riders and the Anglo-Saxon culture so important to Tolkien's professional life.

and for bestowing special heroic gifts. Although it is at Aragorn's request that she arms Merry, the choice of gifts is clearly Éowyn's responsibility, as indicated in her words to him, "I will show you the gear that I have prepared for you" (V.3.802), and then, "I have granted it [selecting arms for Merry] as I could" (V.3.802). In gratitude for Merry's achievement in helping to destroy the Black Captain and as a "memorial of Dernhelm" (VI.6.978), Éowyn later performs the traditional valkyrie role as the giver of heroic gifts when she awards Merry "an ancient horn, small but cunningly wrought" (VI.6.978).

Éowyn's final relationship to medieval valkyrie figures is that, like them, she struggles with a loss which is not only deeply personal, but has societal implications. For Éowyn, her loss involves the common valkyrie theme of conflicting loyalties to herself and her society. In Éowyn's case, the division she combats is a battle between her individual needs and her cultural responsibilities. Dogged and "haunted" (III.6.520) for years by Wormtongue whose desire for her was ignoble and unwholesome, Éowyn sacrificed her own self esteem and dreams of a fulfilling future in order to tend the ailing Théoden. As an individual woman and a representative of the governing class of her people, Éowyn is desperate for the healing and hope a noble liberator can offer both her and her Rohirrim culture. Even though the Company's efforts free Rohan from the progress of Wormtongue's evil, Éowyn and her Rohirrim culture have been only partially rejuvenated. Mirrored by Éowyn's considered and thoughtful reaction after Théoden's response to Gandalf (III.6.515), the despair and hopelessness of her people have been stayed by the dismissal of Wormtongue but have not yet been obliterated. In Aragorn, Éowyn recognizes the heroic potential to revive the health of her failing self and people. Yet, Aragorn's different destiny cannot allow him to function as the complete answer to Rohan's needs. For Éowyn and her people, the definitive rejection of their despair comes only after the incomplete image of freedom and hope Aragorn represents is replaced by a corrected vision which stimulates social growth and healing, while preserving the independent spirit of Rohan represented by Éowyn.

Like Old Norse women who disarm themselves after falling in love with a hero,[30] Éowyn's corrected vision effects her transformation from an ambiguously gendered valkyrie whose sole desire is to perform the functions of a warrior into a valkyrie who gains human fulfillment as a wife. Until she meets Faramir, Éowyn's individual and cultural needs are confused; she wants to engage in physical combat, but she also desires Aragorn because of the hope he has inspired in her and her people. Although both needs are aspects of the same desire made manifest in different forms of her awareness, her dual nature wars against itself. For Rohan, the heroic measure of its culture and history, represented by Théoden, is only partially revived by Wormtongue's removal. Full restoration of cultural health rests on Théoden leading his warriors to battle and on the promotion of Éomer, both emblems of a past glory's unstained heroism. For Éowyn, however, the public standard of heroism in Aragorn that she interprets as the ideal salvation for her culture offers no possibility for the restoration and reintegration of her personal needs. Aragorn becomes an imperfect image of rejuvenative heroism for her people and for herself. Although Aragorn as the returned king can motivate the recovery of Éowyn's body from the wound inflicted on her by the Black Captain, her true "recuperation transcends merely physical healing" (Chance, *Mythology* 99). Requiring a "psychological bridging of her despair" (Chance, *Mythology* 97) as much as her body's health, Éowyn's complete restoration relies on the new possibility of love as the foundation for her future. Despite his appreciation of her personal strengths and public efforts, Aragorn cannot love Éowyn as an individual woman.

In contrast, Faramir loves the public and private aspects of Éowyn's identity, thereby enabling a resolution between her individual and cultural needs. Although in a different context, Chance suggests the significance of emotion as the basis for such resolution, when she writes that for Éowyn "hope as the remedy for despair arises from love" (*Mythology* 97–98). Yet despite the answers love provides, Éowyn, like her valkyrie counterparts, retains her shieldmaiden spirit, "tamed" (*LotR* VI.5.965) to be sure, but not diminished. Rather, with her marriage to Faramir, she commits her public and private selves to

---

30. Brynhild in *Völsunga saga* as well as Sigrdrífa and Sigrún in *The Poetic Edda* are examples of such valkyrie figures.

a union that satisfies both aspects of her nature. Although she says, "I will be a shieldmaiden no longer, nor vie with the Great Riders, nor take joy only in the songs of slaying. I will be a healer and love all things that grow" (VI.5.965), the use here of the word "only" insists that in the future she will not simply reject but transcend the limitations of her shieldmaiden role. Her new awareness acknowledges the effects of healing as well as of battle, of growth as well as of death. In this, Éowyn integrates her dual nature by joining her valkyrie-identified public goal of restoring her people to their previous cultural glory to her newly perceived individual needs of pursuing love as well as battle. By not permitting the former to dominate, however, her transformation allows both to coexist and draw strength from each other. To live with Faramir in Ithilien is not a rejection but an extension of Rohan, for her cultural identity as a valkyrie is still authoritative, though it is now completed by her personal, emotional fulfillment as well. In this unified state, her character becomes more than a lord's second in command. Instead, Éowyn's future offers her ruling side by side with Faramir through her personal volition and with cultural purpose, each individual completing the other.

Although Arwen's character is less developed than Tolkien's other primary heroic women characters, she too is consistently described in terms of valkyrie typology, including physical radiance. Unlike Galadriel, whose valkyrie-like radiance is metaphorized in a variety of astronomical images, Arwen's radiance is consistently identified with starlight, as her Elven epithets Undómiel and Evenstar emphasize (II.1.227). The association of Arwen's physical presence as a light in the dark is illustrated when Frodo sees her "glimmering in the evening, with stars on her brow" (VI.5.927). Further connecting her to the valkyrie topos, the motif of shining light residing in the eyes is also attached to Arwen. At Frodo's first sight of her in Rivendell, he sees "the light of stars was in her bright eyes" (II.1.227). Later, the motif of the valkyries' intensified eyes is compounded by light imagery as an element of her personal power, when Tolkien writes of Arwen that "the light of her eyes fell on him [Frodo] from afar and pierced his heart" (II.1.238).

Arwen is not only radiant in her person, but she also partakes of the courtly attributes of Germanic valkyrie figures by bestowing gifts of inspiration and reward with illuminative properties to heroes. Reminiscent of Brynhild's tapestry in the *Völsunga saga*, Arwen's gift to

Aragorn of the banner standard she prepared herself reminds him of his rightful heritage and offers a talisman of hope that inspires the despairing warriors at its unfurling. Once revealed in all its glorious implications, upon the standard

> flowered a White Tree, and that was for Gondor; but Seven Stars were about it, and a high crown above it. [...] the stars flamed in the sunlight, for they were wrought of gems by Arwen daughter of Elrond; and the crown was bright in the morning, for it was wrought of mithril and gold. (V.6.847)

When Halbarad presents this standard to Aragorn, he highlights Arwen's role in its making by telling Aragorn, "It is a gift that I bring you from the Lady of Rivendell. [...] She wrought it in secret and long was the making" (V.2.775). By emphasizing Arwen's role as the maker of this potent, radiantly shining, heroic standard, the half-Elven woman becomes further linked to the valkyrie women who sew, weave, or otherwise prepare garments and other textile objects for heroes. But, it is not only Aragorn on whom Arwen bestows a shining gift of heroic implications; Frodo also receives from her the gift of her own necklace. In a formal setting, evocative of the gift-giving scenes of Galadriel and other valkyrie figures that use imagery associated with weaving, Arwen tells Frodo,

> "wear this now in memory of Elfstone and Evenstar with whom your life has been woven!" [...] And she took a white gem like a star that lay upon her breast hanging upon a silver chain, and she set the chain about Frodo's neck. "When the memory of the fear and the darkness troubles you," she said, "this will bring you aid." (VI.6.975)

By virtue of its close association with Aragorn's queen, Arwen's gift grants Frodo heroic reward, while her words concerning how it may serve him in the future hint at the possibility of Arwen as a prophetic figure as well.

In addition, Arwen's characterization evokes the Germanic valkyrie reflex in more than the superficial actions of gift-giving and banner embroidery. She also gives up the shining otherworld, that rightful part of her cultural heritage. In awarding her Elven birthright to Frodo, Arwen says,

> "A gift I will give you. For I am the daughter of Elrond. I shall not go with him now when he departs to the Havens; for mine is the

> choice of Lúthien, and as she so have I chosen, both the sweet and the bitter. But in my stead you shall go, Ring-bearer." (VI.6.974)

In contrast to Éowyn's characterization as a woman whose love for Faramir allows her to reconcile her personal and political obligations, Tolkien presents Arwen as the type of valkyrie who must forsake obligations to her race and family in order to realize the power of love as part of her identity. St. Clair remarks that Tolkien's late addition to the text of Arwen as Aragorn's spouse may reflect Tolkien's desire to highlight the theme of an immortal's love for a mortal, which so interested him in the *Silmarillion* ("Reviser" 148). However, this theme of divided loyalties, which prompts the valkyrie-like loss of Arwen's immortality in order to gain her fulfillment in romantic, human love, also places her alongside the tradition of Germanic literary figures such as Brynhild, Sigrún, Sváva, and Sigrdrífa. Like Sigrún and Brynhild, Arwen can achieve personal fulfillment as Aragorn's wife only by rejecting the immortality that comes with her Elven heritage. Hers, like her Germanic predecessors, is a bittersweet choice in which joy and tragedy intertwine. The profound consequences of Arwen's renunciation of her birthright result in the bitterness of her final interaction with her father, Elrond. At their farewell, Tolkien writes that "they went up into the hills and there spoke long together, and bitter was their parting that should endure beyond the ends of the world" (*LotR* VI.6.978). The common motif of the valkyrie's loss of something precious and central to her life is obvious. Unlike Éowyn's marriage to Faramir, Arwen's marriage to Aragorn establishes no newly forged alliance between the woman's individual and cultural selves. As appropriate and fulfilling as their marriage is described in Tolkien's text,[31] it represents the beginning of a different Arwen standing at the head of a changed society, whose new self and new culture are gained only at the cost of her own individual heritage. What she gives up of her own volition in order to help initiate the coming of the New Age remains as important in the reader's mind as what she has gained. Necessary though her break with her cultural heritage might be for the purposes of Tolkien's final resolu-

31. Tolkien describes the joyousness of their marriage when he writes, "together they went up into the High City, and all the stars flowered in the sky. And Aragorn the King Elessar wedded Arwen Undómiel [...] and the tale of their long waiting and labours was come to fulfillment" (*LotR* VI.5.972).

tion, it reverberates with a pathos that cannot be ignored, a pathos that resonates at the same frequency as the Germanic valkyrie-brides' rejection of their divine heritage for the love of a human hero.

Representatives of heroic modes and motivations, women characters in *The Lord of the Rings* are most appropriately understood as agents of power and influence who develop their empowered literary contexts from that pivotal perspective through which Tolkien asks us to look fully into the future only by gazing intently into the medieval past. Shaped by Tolkien's admiration for and desire to transcend the conventions of medieval heroic literature, valkyrie-associated themes transform the characters of Galadriel, Shelob, Éowyn, and Arwen from mere literary accessories to figures whose words and actions carry intrinsic importance. In his treatment of women characters by means of traditional valkyrie typology, Tolkien appropriates, as he does throughout his epic fantasy, "an established element from the Old Germanic past, accepts what is useful in it and constructs something greater in its place" (Boenig 12). Without these heroically rendered women, Tolkien's texts would lack the epic completion only truly possible through the union of heroic oppositions: male and female, good and evil, life and death, joy and grief, individual and community, hope and despair.

By recasting medieval valkyrie analogues as his own contemporary models of heroism and sacrifice in *The Lord of the Rings*, Tolkien establishes what he considers the most appropriate narrative purpose for a fairy tale; that happy fulfillment he defines elsewhere as the accumulated power of Recovery, Consolation, and Eucatastrophe.[32] The "good catastrophe" or "joyous 'turn' " (*OFS* 86), which Tolkien sees as the most potent ending for a fairy story, comes not without grief and sorrow. So the actions of Galadriel to save Middle-earth cause the fading of Lothlórien, and the choice Arwen makes to construct a New Age results in her eternal separation from her Elven kindred. Although Éowyn, like Arwen, gains the joy of love, she must leave behind the singular independence of her shieldmaiden identity in order to express the full potential of romantic union. The valkyrie resonances from which Tolkien builds these heroic women enhance the

32. For discussion of Tolkien's views on the appropriate structural elements of fairy tale literature, see *OFS*.

eucatastrophic fulfillment at the work's close. Enabling that end to be "Far more powerful and poignant," the characters of Galadriel, Éowyn, Arwen, and even Shelob, like the Eddic valkyries on whom they are patterned, serve to establish "a piercing glimpse of joy, and heart's desire, that for a moment passes outside the frame, rends indeed the very web of the story, and lets a gleam come through" (*OFS* 87). Reinforced by the antithesis represented in Shelob, Tolkien's modern benevolent valkyries—Galadriel, Éowyn, and Arwen—are preservers of tradition, defenders of their culture, bearers of the future, and forces for moral good. But, most of all, shining with the radiance of their valkyrie forebears, their images and names flame like candles in the dark for his heroes. The memory of Arwen inspires Aragorn to reclaim his kingship, the sight of Dernhelm revealed as Éowyn battling the Black Captain kindles Merry's hobbit courage, and the name of Galadriel calls forth Sam's extraordinary effort outside Shelob's lair. Finally, this is the true heritage of the valkyrie reflex in *The Lord of the Rings*. Like their medieval counterparts whose heroic qualities form a bridge between the divine and human worlds, so Tolkien's valkyrie women weave together both the humble and the sublime in the same pattern of Middle-earth's heroic history.

> *This article was published originally in* Tolkien the Medievalist, *edited by Jane Chance (New York: Routledge, 2002): 106–32. It is reprinted here with the permission of Taylor & Francis Books, current representative for Routledge.*

Works Cited

Abbott, Joe. "Tolkien's Monsters: Concept and Function in *The Lord of the Rings*." [Part II: Shelob the Great]. *Mythlore* 16.2 (#60) (1989): 40–47. Print.

Armstrong, Helen. "Good Guys, Bad Guys, Fantasy and Reality." Reynolds and GoodKnight 247–52.

Barber, Charles C. *An Old High German Reader*. Oxford: Basil Blackwell, 1964. Print.

Boenig, Robert. "Tolkien and Old Germanic Ethics." *Mythlore* 13.2 (#48) (Winter 1986): 9–12, 40. Print.

Brennu-Njáls saga. Íslenzk Fornrit. Vol 12. Ed. Einar Ól Sveinsson. 1954. Reykjavík: Hið íslenzka fornritafélag, 1971. Print.

Bryce, Lynn. "The Influence of Scandinavian Mythology on the Works of J. R. R. Tolkien." *Edda: Nordisk Tidsskrift for Literaturforskning* 2 (1983): 113–19. Print.

Burns, Marjorie. "Gandalf and Odin." *Tolkien's Legendarium: Essays on The History of Middle-earth*. Eds. Verlyn Flieger and Carl F. Hostetter. Contributions to the Study of Science Fiction and Fantasy, vol. 86. Westport, CT: Greenwood Press, 2000. 219–32. Print.

Chance, Jane. "Grendel's Mother as Epic Anti-Type of the Virgin and the Queen." Fulk 251–63.

---. The Lord of the Rings: *The Mythology of Power*. New York: Twayne Publishers, 1992. Print.

Clark, George, and Daniel Timmons, eds. *J. R. R. Tolkien and His Literary Resonances: Views of Middle-earth*. Contributions to the Study of Science Fiction and Fantasy, vol. 89. Westport, CT: Greenwood Press, 2000. Print.

Crowe, Edith L. "Power in Arda: Sources, Uses and Misuses." Reynolds and GoodKnight 272–77. *Reprinted in this volume.*

Curry, Patrick. " 'Less Noise and More Green': Tolkien's Ideology for England." Reynolds and GoodKnight 126–38.

Damico, Helen. Beowulf's *Wealhtheow and the Valkyrie Tradition*. Madison, WI: U of Wisconsin P, 1984. Print.

---. "The Valkyrie Reflex in Old English Literature." *New Readings on Women in Old English Literature*. Eds. Helen Damico and Alexandra Hennessey Olsen. Bloomington, IN: Indiana UP, 1990. 176–90. Print.

Davidson, Hilda Ellis. *Roles of the Northern Goddess*. London: Routledge, 1998. Print.

Dockray-Miller, Mary. "The Masculine Queen of 'Beowulf'." *Women and Language* 21.2 (Fall 1998): 31–38. Print.

Evans, Jonathan. "The Dragon-Lore of Middle-earth: Tolkien and Old English and Old Norse Tradition." Clark and Timmons 21–38.

Fenwick, Mac. "Breastplates of Silk: Homeric Women in *The Lord of the Rings*." *Mythlore* 21.3 (#81) (Summer 1996): 17–23. Print.

Fredrick, Candice, and Sam McBride. *Women Among the Inklings: Gender, C. S. Lewis, J. R. R. Tolkien, and Charles Williams*. Contributions in Women's Studies, vol. 191. Westport, CT: Greenwood Press, 2001. Print.

Fulk, R. D., ed. *Interpretations of* Beowulf*: A Critical Anthology*. Bloomington, IN: Indiana UP, 1991. Print.

Goselin, Peter Damien. "Two Faces of Eve: Galadriel and Shelob as Anima Figures." *Mythlore* 6.3 (#21) (Summer 1979): 3–4. Print.

Hopkins, Lisa. "Female Authority Figures in the Works of Tolkien, C. S. Lewis and Charles Williams." Reynolds and GoodKnight 364–66.

Jochens, Jenny. *Old Norse Images of Women*. Philadelphia: U of Pennsylvania P, 1996. Print.

Jónsson, Guðni, ed. *Hrólfs saga Gautrekssonar. Fornaldar sögur Norðurlanda*. Vol. 4. 1954. Reykjavík: Íslendinga-sagnaútgáfan, 1981. Print.

---. *Völsunga saga. Fornaldar sögur Norðurlanda*. Vol. 1. 1954. Reykjavík: Íslendinga-sagnaútgáfan, 1981. Print.

Kershaw, Nora, ed. *Anglo-Saxon and Norse Poems*. Cambridge, UK: The University Press, 1922. Print.

Klaeber, Fr., ed. Beowulf *and The Fight at Finnsburg*. 3rd ed. with 1st and 2nd supplements. Lexington, MA: D. C. Heath and Company, 1950. Print.

Moorman, Charles. "The Shire, Mordor, and Minas Tirith." *Tolkien and the Critics: Essays on J. R. R. Tolkien's* The Lord of the Rings. Eds. Neil D. Isaacs and Rose A. Zimbardo. Notre Dame: U of Notre Dame P, 1968. 201–17. Print.

Neckel, Gustav, ed. *Edda: Die Lieder des Codex Regius nebst verwandten Denkmälern*. 4th ed., rev. Hans Kuhn. Heidelberg: Carl Winter, 1962. Print.

Orchard, Andy. *Pride and Prodigies: Studies in the Monsters of the Beowulf-Manuscript*. Cambridge, UK: D. S. Brewer, 1995. Print.

Overing, Gillian. "The Women of *Beowulf*: A Context for Interpretation." Beowulf*: Basic Readings*. Ed. Peter S. Baker. New York: Garland, 1995. 219–60. Print.

Pope, John C., ed. *Seven Old English Poems*. New York: W. W. Norton and Co., 1981. Print.

Rawls, Melanie. "The Feminine Principle in Tolkien." *Mythlore* 10.4 (#38) (Spring 1984): 5–13. Print. *Reprinted in this volume.*

Reynolds, Patricia, and Glen H. GoodKnight, eds. *Proceedings of the J. R. R. Tolkien Centenary Conference, 1992*. Altadena, CA: Mythopoeic Press, 1995. Print.

Sanford, Len. "The Fall from Grace—Decline and Fall in Middle-earth: Metaphors for Nordic and Christian Theology in *The Lord of the Rings* and *The Silmarillion*." *Mallorn* 32 (September 1995): 15–20. Print.

Senior, W. A. "Loss Eternal in J. R. R. Tolkien's Middle-earth." Clark and Timmons 173–82.

Shippey, Tom. *The Road to Middle-earth*. London: George Allen and Unwin, 1982. Print.

---. "Tolkien's Sources: The True Tradition." *Readings on J. R. R. Tolkien*. Ed. Katie de Korster. The Greenhaven Press Literary Companion to British Authors series. San Diego: Greenhaven Press, 2000. 153–61. Print.

Sly, Debbie. "Weaving Nets of Gloom: 'Darkness Profound' in Tolkien and Milton." Clark and Timmons 109–19.

St. Clair, Gloriana. "An Overview of the Northern Influence in Tolkien's Works." Reynolds and GoodKnight 63–67.

---. "Tolkien as Reviser: A Case Study." Reynolds and GoodKnight 145–50.

Stimpson, Catherine R. *J. R. R. Tolkien*. Columbia Essays on Modern Writers, vol. 41. New York: Columbia UP, 1969. Print.

Sturluson, Snorri. *Edda: Prologue and Gylfaginning*. Ed. Anthony Faulkes. Oxford: Clarendon Press, 1982. Print.

Sullivan, C. W., III. "Tolkien the Bard: His Tale Grew in the Telling." Clark and Timmons 11–20.

Timmer, B. J., ed. *Judith*. Exeter: U of Exeter P, 1966. Print.

Tolkien, Christopher, ed. and trans. *The Saga of King Heidrek the Wise*. London: Thomas Nelson and Sons, 1960. Print.

Tolkien, J. R. R. "Beowulf: The Monsters and the Critics." Fulk 14–44.

---. "Tree and Leaf: On Fairy-stories." *The Tolkien Reader*. New York: Ballantine Books, 1966. 33–99. Print.

Woolf, Rosemary, ed. *Juliana*. Exeter: U of Exeter P, 1966. Print.

Speech and Silence in *The Lord of the Rings*: Medieval Romance and the Transitions of Éowyn

Phoebe C. Linton

In *The Lord of the Rings*, Éowyn represents a literary articulation of the resistance to silence which medieval female romance figures negotiate in their attempts to achieve speech and autonomy. The privilege of voice initially is denied to Éowyn, provoking tensions between invisibility/visibility and passivity/action. Structurally, Éowyn can be better understood by considering the text's narrative interlacing, where the plot's focus alternates between characters or groups of characters, relying upon hiatuses and shifts to propel the story forward. These hiatuses may be partially responsible for the comparative neglect of Éowyn in criticism, as well as paradoxically may reveal one of the very techniques that help to develop her character. As a modern romance inspired by medieval models, *The Lord of the Rings* may be analyzed similarly to such texts, where the "primary function of the medievalist is to locate missing stories," and where works of medieval literature "always bear witness to an *other* text [...] Sometimes the work remains other to itself and must be (re)assembled" (Scala 1, emphasis added). Tolkien's Éowyn provides one such missing story. Her character reassembles after spaces between receiving narrative attention, generating a momentum that structurally prepares the apex of her journey and trial against the Witch-king of Angmar.

Key to Éowyn's oscillation between speech and silence is depth: both the implicit suggestion of depth by the author and her complexity as one of the main protagonists. No character's choice to speak or to be silent would be at all significant without complexity in the appearance, personality, and actions of that character. Derek Brewer's observation that the "whole immense story is strung out on Frodo's journey" is true as regards characters' community-oriented motivations for their actions, but this idea also encapsulates the common misconception that those who are not Ringbearers are peripheral in *The Lord of the Rings* (256). For a romance that was, according to Tolkien, "large and much-embracing," it is necessary to discard this notion (*Letters* 161). Michael Camille argues that the center of a work of art is "dependent upon the margins for its continued existence," which is also true of the effort wrought by the ostensibly secondary quest figures in Tolkien's work (10). Leslie A. Donovan sees Éowyn, among others, as a key contributor in the quest: "Galadriel, Shelob, Éowyn, and Arwen stand out from the narrative's background as more than secondary, incidental literary figures" (109).

One comment Tolkien makes of his life's work in response to criticism is helpful:

> I think the simple "rustic" love of Sam and his Rosie (nowhere elaborated) is *absolutely essential* to the study of his (the chief hero's) character, and to the theme of the relation of ordinary life (breathing, eating, working, begetting) and quests, sacrifice, causes, and the "longing for Elves", and sheer beauty. But I will say no more, nor defend the theme of mistaken love seen in Eowyn and her first love for Aragorn. I do not feel much can now be done to heal the faults. (*Letters* 161)

Tolkien mentions several themes in this statement, themes that he clearly would have liked the chance to justify further. What can be gleaned from such a defense is his deep belief that seemingly inconsequential details have complete relevance to the story, and indeed rely on their interdependence with larger, overarching themes. Humphrey Carpenter corroborates this idea, providing the insight into Tolkien's intentions that when he wrote *The Silmarillion*, "Tolkien believed that in one sense he was writing the truth," even in the case of his supernatural beings (91). For instance, Tolkien's description of the eyes of Treebeard, a tree-being, or "Ent," underlines in fiction the idea expressed in the letter cited above: "One felt as if there was an enormous well behind them, filled up with ages of memory and long, slow, steady thinking; but their surface was sparkling with the present; like sun shimmering on the outer leaves of a vast tree, or on the ripples of a very deep lake" (*LotR* III.4.463). If Tolkien intended so clearly to imbue even non-human plants and animals with depth, then depth must also be sought in other areas and levels of the text. Just as Tolkien believed the relationship between Sam and Rosie had significance to the greater quest, descriptions of any character can be used to understand aspects of characters hitherto undervalued. To demonstrate, when first introduced to the text, Éowyn is seen as a woman whose life is constricted by the court of Rohan and by tending to her uncle Théoden the King, immobile and impotent due to the machinations of Saruman and Wormtongue. Yet, one could say there is an "enormous well" of feeling beneath Éowyn's social facade. She possesses like Treebeard—and many other characters on the quest—this "deep lake" of latent power implied in the first description of her appearance: "Grave and thoughtful was her glance [...] fair and cold, like a morning of pale spring that is not yet come to womanhood" (III.6.515).

Regarding her trajectory within the story, Tolkien models Éowyn on the medieval female knight, using romance quest conventions as points of inspiration from which he transcends traditional patterns. Éowyn is "stern as steel," a woman ready to "face peril and battle," a vocal character who challenges the value-system represented by figures such as her uncle Théoden and Aragorn (*LotR* III.6.515; V.2.784). Tolkien portrays Éowyn as an integral quest agent, a conflation of the medieval female knight and courtly woman. As Brewer confirms, "to understand *The Lord of the Rings* we have to understand the true nature of romance" (249); likewise, Donovan subscribes to the view that "all his Middle-earth fiction has its heritage in the literature and culture of the Middle Ages" (107). Tolkien's women are often, but not entirely, "narrative agents charged with the authority of distinct heroic women figures from Old Norse mythology and literature called the Valkyries," which demonstrates his intent to create strong female characters (Donovan 108). The interlacing narrative structure allows the strength of characters to grow or diminish due to the neutral space afforded by turning from one quest to another within the larger structure. The medieval English analogue most easily comparable to Tolkien's *Lord of the Rings* in style is Sir Thomas Malory's *Le Morte Darthur*, written in the 1460s. Where female characterization is concerned, the two differ significantly. Nevertheless, that Tolkien would have drawn heavily on Malory for his inspiration is borne out by the fact that he wrote his own Arthurian work, an epic poem entitled *The Fall of Arthur*, published posthumously in May 2013.[1] Malory's work

1. Tolkien clearly held up Malory as a paradigm of medieval romance, as he found comparisons of it with his *Lord of the Rings* "too much for my vanity!" (*Letters* 181).

typifies the narrative pattern of interlacing that Tolkien emulates, where the story linguistically transitions from one incident to the next with conceits such as, "Now leve we sir Trystram de Lyones and speke we of Sir Launcelot du laake" (477). Similarly, Éowyn moves from periods of silence to periods of speech; the narrative focus pans in and out from her character as in medieval texts.

For my present purposes, I will limit the definitions of "romance" or "quest" and their models of (female) knights, since these evoke so many themes and components that they can entirely evade definition. Essential to romance quests from the Middle Ages to the present day are adventures of a fantastical and marvelous nature that traverse the boundary from everyday existence to the strange and unprecedented. Social rules and conventions are therefore often exceeded, giving the sense that heroes or heroines are *more* than they were at the beginning of their quests. Achieving wholeness and completion is one of the prime aims, though as Helen Cooper writes, in the "longer romances, and especially in interlaced romances that follow the adventures of more than one protagonist, the deferral of ending becomes part of the point" (46). This idea is sympathetic to Tolkien's grand work. Readers are familiar with the timeless supernatural elements of quest romances, such as enchanted objects and animals that aid or thwart protagonists on their journey to final aims of winning treasure, wooing a deserving partner, or destroying a supernatural foe. Importantly, however, Éowyn is a mortal agent as well as one who possesses no extraordinary help; instead she typifies the romance trope of the significant noble in disguise, and the less common figure of the female knight.

The idea of "womanhood," and women's involvement on the quest, is engaged differently by many medieval romances. Crucially, medieval female knights should be virginal, since this underlines the nobility of their cause and excuses their temporary exceeding of ordinary social limitations or boundaries. To the best of my knowledge, the only female knights in European medieval romance are Silence, Joan of Arc, and Avenable. The eponymous protagonist of the thirteenth-century poem, *Le Roman de Silence* (Roche-Mahdi), lives in disguise since birth and embarks upon a series of adventures as a man, first travelling as a minstrel harpist and then as a male knight, proceeding to win prowess in jousts and battle. At the end of the narrative, Silence's identity is discovered, and she is married to an eligible king. The well-known historical figure Joan of Arc also won prowess in battle, but at the end of her career was burned at the stake. She has been represented in texts such as Christine de Pizan's poem of 1429, *Le Ditie de Jehanne d'Arc*. Avenable appears in the mid fifteenth-century *Prose Merlin* (Conlee) as knight and steward, and, like Silence, is also married to an emperor at the end of her tale. Despite their chivalric acts these three female figures are subjugated at the end of their stories in an attempt to conform them to a conventional model of femininity. If this is impossible, as in the case of Joan of Arc, the female knight is consigned to death in order to diminish her political power and erase her transgressions of acting as a man. The shocking nature of the way in which she subverted her own gender is conveyed in notes from a translation of Joan of Arc's trial, where it is written that "she wore with an astonishing and monstrous brazenness, immodest garments belonging to the male sex" (Barrett).

Another woman who typifies these concerns is Enide from Chrétien de Troyes's tale "Erec and Enide." Maureen Fries, in her essay on "Female Heroes, Heroines, and Counter-Heroes," suggests that Enide is a female hero, though not "consistently" because Erec's kiss at the end of the tale "turns her again, as in the archetypal fairy tale, into a heroine" (65–66). Whether Enide is an active party in the quest of this tale is debatable, as her husband's success depends upon her speaking out, whereas Enide's success in marriage depends upon her silence. Two more women who adopt a knightly stance or engage in battle on a minimal scale are found in Malory's *Morte*: a lesser lady of the lake and one Lady Alys, respectively (40; 388). King Arthur admonishes the former lady for the transgression of wearing weaponry, asking, "Damesel, for what cause ar ye gurte with that swerde? Hit besemyth [befits] you nought" (40). The second woman is praised because Alys acts for the benefit of her paramour, Alisaunder.

In *Gender and the Chivalric Community*, Dorsey Armstrong asserts that many medieval romances focus "on the masculine activity of chivalry—fighting, questing, ruling—while simultaneously revealing the chivalric enterprise as impossible without the presence of the feminine in a subjugated position" (1). The issue of whether women are subjugated in quest romances or not is both complex and disputed. The criticism Tolkien received that his work contained "no Women" demonstrates that *The Lord of the Rings*, similar to Malory's *Morte*, has accrued a critical readership where interpretations "are by tradition tacitly inclined to concede to the feminine only a supporting place" (*Letters* 220; Heng 835). Fries writes on the subject, "there were very few heroic role models for females in medieval life: they were only infrequently rulers and forbidden to wear arms or enter the priesthood" (59). However, Tolkien explains Éowyn's character in one of his letters: "Though not a 'dry nurse' in temper, she was also not really a soldier or 'amazon', but like many brave women was capable of great military gallantry at a crisis" (*Letters* 323). The medieval period did see precedents, and some women

> proved themselves the social equals of men. Eleanor of Aquitaine, married serially to the kings of France and England, ruled more land than either of her husbands. Joan of Arc led armies, shocking the Middle Ages not so much by her mysticism as by cutting off her hair and wearing men's clothes. Margaret Paston defended one of her husband's estates, alone with only nineteen servants for support, against a thousand men for over a day (Fries 60).

Tolkien develops the feminine chivalric models further with Éowyn the shieldmaiden, whose narrative arc can be seen as transitioning between four main phases in *The Lord of the Rings*: (1) Court lady, (2) Acting lord, (3) Female knight, or Shieldmaiden of Rohan, and (4) Wife and healer.

Court Lady

Éowyn should be understood both as an individual and as a member of her community. As in Malory, where knights win honor and renown, for their own pride as well as to increase the worth of the fellowship of the Round Table, characters in Tolkien act according to both motives. Éowyn is a dormant character when she is introduced, since her kingdom has been paralyzed by the forces of Sauron and Saruman. Tolkien's diction prefigures the inflicted court that Gandalf, Aragorn, Legolas and Gimli will discover, as the land is seen in shades of "grey," "red fire," and the "hue of blood," while the atmosphere is influenced by the time of sunset, one where "smoke seemed to rise up and darken the sun's disc [...] as if it had kindled the grass" (*LotR* III.5.501–05). On their way to Edoras, the remaining Fellowship see around them that all "was silent, and there was no sign or sound of living thing" (III.5.506). Tolkien creates environments sympathetic to his characters; just as Éowyn lives in an oppressive environment under the surveillance of Wormtongue, she possesses the burning frustration that complements the landscape just described. She is also like the symbolic flower of Rohan, "Evermind," called " '*simbelmynë* in this land of Men, for they blossom in all seasons of the year, and grow where dead men rest' " (III.6.507). Théoden is as a dead man at this point in the narrative, and Éowyn blossoms in "all seasons," even—or especially—during this turbulent period in Middle-earth.

The strength of Éowyn, which is the solitary aid to the king and last remaining symbol of the power of Rohan, is belied by her silence: "Behind his chair stood a woman clad in white" (III.6.512). Brent D. Johnson asserts that this "woman clad in white" is, at this point in the tale, "a flat character who fills a space in the hall, a woman who has no name" (120). It is true that her presence is simultaneously passive as well as regal, since she is unnamed at first and silent. However, Éowyn is associated visually with the powerful queen Galadriel who is described always in terms of light and the color white. Galadriel's associations through appearance are commented upon by Donovan:

> In addition to using the colour white and a fair appearance to establish the visual intensity of Galadriel's physical presence as indicative of a heightened moral state, Tolkien highlights the Lady's supremacy of form and nature by including references to shining eyes and gold in his portrayal of the Elven queen (113).

Furthermore, just before Gandalf banishes Wormtongue's influence over Théoden, he explicitly invokes Galadriel: "Galadriel! Galadriel! [...] White is the star in your white hand" (*LotR* III.6.514). Éowyn can be seen to derive some of her power from these connections, which the landscape of Rohan, other Rohirrim, and an Elven queen demonstrate. In discussion of the medieval romance *La Fille du comte de Pontieu*, Evelyn Birge Vitz addresses the problem of "the subject," or "main character," as is used in terms of popular literature. Vitz states that in some cases:

> we have neither the simplicity of a single medieval Subject nor even of a pair of antagonistic Subjects, nor yet the tidiness of a Marxist view that would make of men a great single entity, mankind. Rather we have a clutch of rather independent characters, only more or less unified by the fact and the sense that they belong to something greater than themselves, by the fact that they share a common Object (103–04).

Éowyn's potential to contribute powerfully toward the "common Object" in Tolkien's text is established in her first description. When read as part of the chapter "The King of the Golden Hall," it is possible to overlook her significance, as the narrative purports to focus on Théoden. However, when read in relief Éowyn appears differently:

> The woman turned and went slowly into the house. As she passed the doors she turned and looked back. Grave and thoughtful was her glance, as she looked on the king with cool pity in her eyes. Very fair was her face, and her long hair was like a river of gold. Slender and tall she was in her white robe girt with silver; but strong she seemed and stern as steel, a daughter of kings. Thus Aragorn for the first time in the full light of day beheld Éowyn, Lady of Rohan, and thought her fair, fair and cold, like a morning of pale spring that is not yet come to womanhood. And now she was suddenly aware of him: tall heir of kings, wise with many winters, greycloaked, hiding a power that yet she felt. For a moment still as stone she stood, then turning swiftly she was gone (*LotR* III.6.515).

Much can be gleaned from this short excerpt. First, Éowyn's visual introduction to the text is characterized by an emotional detachment; she is simply "The woman" at the beginning, seen from a distance as she turns back at the doors. Éowyn's remoteness combined with waxing strength here foreshadows her martial role under the guise of Dernhelm. Susan Crane's argument that "chivalric incognito, as a motif of romance and as a historical practice, amounts to a peculiar kind of self-presentation, a self-dramatization that *invites* rather than resists public scrutiny," which is borne out in Éowyn's portrayal here (63, emphasis added).

Second, the excerpt underlines Éowyn's regal nature, which partially relies upon her juxtaposition with two major male characters for its impact. Théoden is less a king at this point than an invalid; when Gandalf wakens Théoden and he stands for the first time, the extent of his weakness is apparent: "The woman hastened to the king's side, taking his arm, and with faltering steps the old man came down from the dais" (*LotR* III.6.515). When Éowyn leaves the hall, "she looked on the king with cool pity in her eyes," as cited in the excerpt above. This action elevates Éowyn to the most prestigious position at court. Furthermore, designated "a daughter of kings," Éowyn is aligned with the male line of succession in Rohan rather than with the female line, as she would be if she were named "a daughter of queens" (III.6.515). Again, this could be seen to augur her later stewardship in Théoden's absence. "Lady of Rohan" indicates that Éowyn is the supreme woman at court and more than an archetypal, unnamed princess or quest damsel, as is found in Malory. As well as achieving a high local status, Éowyn compares favorably with the foreign king-to-be, Aragorn. While her description is based on what Aragorn sees, it is not a typical example of a woman defined by the male gaze, since Éowyn is not objectified and her beauty is outlined unsentimentally. Rather, the descriptive ordering emphasizes Éowyn for the reader. Aragorn is described cursorily, as is Théoden. Similarities are drawn between Aragorn and Éowyn, which mark them both as the leaders they will become: Éowyn is "like a morning of pale spring that is not yet come to womanhood," Aragorn is "hiding a power that she yet felt"; Éowyn is "daughter of kings," and Aragorn is almost identically an "heir of kings" (III.6.515).

Third, this outline of Éowyn establishes her potential for martial action. Besides her association with kings more than queens, her dress is described as "girt with silver," which evokes the image of armor—of chainmail or sword—on a woman already described as "stern as steel." Éowyn is the only mortal woman to be involved directly in one of the battles for Middle-earth, and though she comes from a society which valorizes "shieldmaidens," it is noticeable that she is still the only woman from her community to engage in direct warfare. This fact reflects the desperation of the situation of those who fight for Frodo's cause. Gandalf states: "Doom hangs still on a thread. Yet hope there is still, if we can but stand unconquered for a little while" (*LotR* III.6.516). The "we" is inclusive, and the image of their fate as threadbare reaffirms the idea that the burden of the ring is the responsibility of an international community, of which Éowyn is a part. At this point in the narrative, however, Éowyn is limited by her role as Lady of Rohan. While this is a prestigious role to inhabit, thus far Éowyn has been entirely silent. The only interruption of Éowyn's silence occurs at the ceremonial draught of health to the departing warriors as Théoden, Aragorn, and the rest of the company leave to prepare for battle at Helm's Deep: "Hail Aragorn son of Arathorn!" are her only words (III.6.523).

The first transition of Éowyn's role from lady to acting steward occurs at the court's emptying of all the Rohirrim. Éowyn appears not to have the choice of engaging actively in events. Conventionally, as

Jennifer Ward details, a medieval noblewoman was "expected to be obedient, submissive and virtuous, but to be able to carry out men's duties as needed within the family and on the estates. Her world centered on the family and its interests, and her life and prospects were affected by [...] fortune and accident" (9). The idea of fortune and accident is especially important, as at this point Éowyn is at the mercy of chance and she is not in a position to choose how she will negotiate it, since decisions over how the court will function is decided entirely by her male family members. Théoden states, "to some one I must now entrust my people that I leave behind, to rule them in my place," at which point, "No man spoke" (*LotR* III.6.523). When he asks, "In whom do my people trust?" Théoden misinterprets what one of his men means when he replies, "In the House of Eorl" (III.6.523). It appears that Théoden has been so unaware of the condition of his court that he has failed to notice the progress of his niece. P. J. P. Goldberg observes of the medieval model of femininity, "The exercise of power and authority was [...] a particularly masculine attribute, though wives and widows were in fact variably seen as competent to substitute for absent husbands in the running of the household or family estate" (9). Being fixated on the idea of a patrilineal succession, Théoden sees only Éomer as his remaining heir. But his man Háma corrects him: "I said not Éomer," answered Háma. "And he is not the last. There is Éowyn, daughter of Éomund, his sister. She is fearless and high-hearted. All love her. Let her be as lord to the Eorlingas, while we are gone" (*LotR* III.6.523). Leo D. Lefebure summarizes some of the aspects of traditional medieval chivalry as "a set of virtues, including courage, courtesy, generosity, loyalty, fidelity, and humility" (59). Háma's description parallels these models of chivalry exactly. That Éowyn is "fearless and high-hearted" means she has courage. She evinces an awareness of etiquette, through her deference to Théoden. Her willingness to wait evidences her loyalty and fidelity, while acceptance of Théoden's decision proves her humility. It is interesting to consider how the court knows Éowyn so well when all the reader is offered at this point is a silent portrayal. Her election to the stewardship is majestic: " 'It shall be so,' said Théoden. 'Let the heralds announce to the folk that the Lady Éowyn will lead them!' " (III.6.523). Silently, Éowyn is initiated into her new role in the way of the male knight: "Éowyn knelt before him and received from him a sword and a fair corslet" (III.6.523). As Donovan observes, this action is a "public ceremony as a binding commitment" (109). Significantly, Éowyn displays neither pride nor happiness at receiving this honor, since it is paired with the farewell of her nearest kin and she has no honorable exit from this responsibility. She laments, "A year shall I endure for every day that passes until your return" (*LotR* III.6.523).

Éowyn is frequently a marker of departure and homecoming, and her character is interwoven with the identity of Rohan itself. When the Rohirrim leave, Aragorn's last sighting of Edoras, like his first, is of Éowyn: "Alone Éowyn stood before the doors of the house at the stair's head; the sword was set upright before her, and her hands were laid upon the hilt. She was clad now in mail and shone like silver in the sun" (III.6.523). If this sequence is considered in the context of the text as a whole, the final words of the chapter "The King of the Golden Hall" are filled with pathos; considering Éowyn's detestation of inaction, her passivity and silence here contrast sharply with the noise and movement of her male companions. For, where "with a *rush* like the sudden onset of a *great wind* the last host of Rohan rode *thundering* into the West," Éowyn merely "saw the glitter of their spears, as she stood *still, alone* before the doors of the *silent* house" (III.6.525, emphasis added).[2]

Acting Lord

Éowyn's first sequence makes evident that her community role has necessitated the sublimation of personal feeling. The second sequence begins to unravel tensions that now become apparent: Éowyn now also represents two forms of responsibility, duty and choice. The former is one imposed from without, a responsibility which requires silence; the latter is a responsibility that arises from within and is expressed through speech. In this phase of her role as steward of Rohan, Éowyn experiences tensions between honoring the community and honoring herself, which gives rise to the first signs of emotion the reader is allowed to discern. This is caused by her increase in status as well as her contact with Aragorn. In a chivalric society, Heng argues, the function of love "is the displacement of a purely masculine and primarily mar-

2. Éowyn's position here in front of the hall is almost apotropaic, perhaps an omen of her later role as protector.

tial discourse with another of greater civilizing value: a sophisticated, feminine-presided discourse of emotion and relation" (839). This complements Donovan's analysis that over time in *The Lord of the Rings*, "Éowyn realizes a full human potential that joins both her masculine and feminine selves" (109).

In her new role as acting lord, Éowyn has already assumed both a more martial *and* emotional attitude: "when she heard of the battle in Helm's Deep and the great slaughter of their foes, and of the charge of Théoden and his knights, then her eyes shone" (*LotR* V.2.783). She is also more outspoken, for when Aragorn explains he will not stay long at Edoras, Éowyn replies that it is kind of him to visit her "in her *exile*" (V.2.783, emphasis added). It is notable that, as well as being more openly interested in battle, Éowyn also reveals more of her emotions. Before, she was remote, cold, and compared to stone and steel; now Éowyn "stared at him as one that is stricken," and "blanched" when Aragorn tells her he intends to traverse the Paths of the Dead (V.2.783). Being now emotionally invested in the outcome of Aragorn's exploits, Éowyn questions him—asking, "is it then your errand to seek death?"—and even challenges him: "this is madness" (V.2.783). Éowyn struggles between her role as acting lord of Rohan, one of authority, and her position as a lady of the court, a subordinate one, by alternately admonishing and pleading with Aragorn. On one hand, she attempts to direct him, arguing "here are men of renown and prowess, whom you *should* not take into the shadows, but *should* lead to war," but on the other hand she adopts a dependent tone: "I *beg* you to remain [...] all our hearts will be gladdened, and our hope be the brighter" (V.2.783, emphasis added). Where before it was impossible to read Éowyn, now it is obvious to many people "that she was in great torment of mind" (V.2.783).

Éowyn begins to develop the capacity for decision-making, as she becomes aware that a critical juncture approaches. Rather than remaining silent as she has done in the past, Éowyn continues to challenge Aragorn. Of relevance to this decision is that he represents not only an emotional attachment (whether romantic or not) but more than this, a patriarchal authority due to his close alliance with her uncle. Clearly, Éowyn would like to move beyond her function as a figure either of salutation and valediction and be an active component of those groups she has merely observed in the past, as "suddenly she laid her hand on his arm. 'You are a stern lord and resolute,' she said; 'and thus do men win renown.' She paused. 'Lord,' she said, 'if you must go, then let me ride in your following. For I am weary of skulking in the hills, and wish to face peril and battle' " (V.2.784). Notably, this is her first voiced complaint and Aragorn's reply is: "Your duty is with your people" (V.2.784). Éowyn refutes the idea that women are born to certain roles, asking, "am I not of the House of Eorl, a shieldmaiden and not a dry-nurse?" and dreading the prospect of a life where she is always "left behind when the Riders depart, to mind the house while they win renown, and find food and beds when they return" (V.2.784).

Comparison with the medieval romance "Erec and Enide" by Chrétien de Troyes is sympathetic to Éowyn's situation in this instance. Enide is caught between wishing to spend time with her new husband and acting dutifully by spurring her partner to honorable action. Likewise, Éowyn would like to follow Aragorn because she loves him in some undefinable way; however she also knows that the honorable action is to remain at Edoras. Equally, she does not believe the path Aragorn has chosen is the best decision, since it appears to be the coward's way out.

In her role as acting lord of the Riddermark, Éowyn is faced with her dislike of enforced responsibility, and she regrets, "Too often have I heard of duty," asking, "Shall I always be chosen?" (V.2.784). She possesses her own individual idea of what responsibility to her people entails: direct action in battle. Aragorn's view of the honor she might achieve is bleak. He believes she might well have the opportunity to display the acts of renown she so craves, that when the war is lost she will have the chance to act in "deeds that are done in the last defense of your homes" (V.2.784). Aragorn does not consider that on the battlefield, a warrior simply dies in battle; if war is brought to the houses of a defeated kingdom or race, then rape and pillage inevitably ensue. Aragorn fails to acknowledge this, effectively encouraging silence and regression. Rather than praising Éowyn's desire for battle in a wide community of soldiers, he argues for the solitary fight at home, saying "the deeds will not be less valiant because they are unpraised" (V.2.784). To be "unpraised" is to be unheard, which is exactly Éowyn's situation when she is introduced to the narrative. Aragorn's depiction of the glory attainable for women is polarized by what Éowyn has envisaged, particularly because she views the home not as a place of safety or comfort, but of silence and oppression; her memories have been shaped by the presence of Wormtongue. Her activities so far have been defined predominantly by the limitations of a gender that require her not to act vocally, politically, or martially – despite her training. Éowyn challenges Aragorn's conservative mindset: "All your words are but to say: you are a woman, and your part is in the house. But when all the men have died in battle and honor, you have leave to be burned in the house, for the men will need it no more" (V.2.784). Éowyn's statement clarifies that, for her, to have the home is to have nothing because it is silent, barren, and belongs to another regardless of whether this "other" is friend or foe. Éowyn's single fear is a "cage," to "stay behind bars, until use and old age accept them, and all chance of doing great deeds is gone beyond call or desire" (V.2.784). This is a moment of decision for Éowyn, even though she does not defy Aragorn openly and cannot prevent him following his own convictions.

Next, Éowyn oscillates strangely between supplication and resolve. She falls on her knees, begging Aragorn not to follow the Paths of the Dead, but equally she "stood still as a figure carven in stone," which is an image of strength despite its silence. Similarly, when Aragorn is gone, "she turned, stumbling as one that is blind," although the next time she meets Théoden at his return from Helm's Deep she appears in the image of a knight, "a woman with long braided hair gleaming in the twilight, yet she wore a helm and was clad to the waist like a warrior and girded with a sword" (V.2.795). She is professional and composed, proving to Théoden that she is worthy of the position of Lord of the Riddermark that he bestowed upon her. Although she suffers personal griefs—"it seemed to Merry that her voice belied her, and he would have thought that she had been weeping, if that could be believed of one so stern of face"—she gives her uncle an account of their situation: "All is now ordered [...] your lodging is prepared for you; for I have had full tidings of you and knew the hour of your coming" (V.2.795). Seated at dinner, Éowyn's increased status is clear from her position at table, as she sits with a select group of lords: "at a small table sat Théoden with Éomer and Éowyn, and Dúnhere, lord of Harrowdale" (V.2.796). This is a significant change from the reader's introduction to her as a nameless woman who waits behind the king's chair, subservient.

Shieldmaiden of Rohan

Considering the nature of the fairy tale queen, Sandra M. Gilbert and Susan Gubar ask:

> If the Queen's looking glass speaks with the King's voice, how do its perpetual kingly admonitions affect the Queen's own voice? Since his is the chief voice she hears, does the Queen try to sound like the King, imitating his tone, his inflections, his phrasing, his point of view? Or does she "talk back" to him in her own vocabulary, her own timbre, insisting on her own viewpoint? (2024)

Fairy tale, myth, romance and fantasy are interrelated forms of fiction, and since Éowyn's character is inflected by all of them, Gilbert and Gubar's question about female voice is highly pertinent to her. Much folklore demonstrates through the narrative process that "the behavior of women, at least at certain times or under certain circumstances, must be improper or nonconformist for the greater good of the whole" (Allen 2112). It is respectable for Éowyn to display her status as an armor-wearing shieldmaiden whilst she inhabits her function as hostess. However, conflict occurs when she attempts to assume the same level as a male Rohirrim and she is told to stay at home. She draws attention to the fact that she is of the same lineage, saying, "I am of the House of Eorl [...] I can ride and wield blade, and I do not fear either pain or death," a key issue that this section will address (*LotR* V.2.784). As well as expressing her contrary opinions to Aragorn, this section also explores the way in which Éowyn "talks back" to Théoden, in a paradoxically silent way. Éowyn assumes invisibility through temporarily adopting male garb and joins the critical battle for Gondor. Ultimately, her nonconformist attitude benefits the community of Rohan due to her individual success, which adds to the larger battle's outcome.

Éowyn's knighting ceremony at Théoden's earlier departure represented merely a coming-of-age, "simply an acknowledgement that the recipient was of an age to bear arms," a "basic form of knighting" (Barber 22). Éowyn becomes temporary lord of Rohan out of necessity rather than through Théoden's choice. Moreover, true reputation in a knight's career must involve further proof of worth. Éowyn achieves this by her self-sacrifice, going within a hair's breadth of dying for her uncle and her fellowship of Rohirrim. Her spatial and physical quest is not lengthy; rather, her quest is more one of character than of a literal journey.

Prior to Éowyn's incognito state as shieldmaiden, Merry's voice is worth considering, as it acts as substitute to the kinds of comments Éowyn might make, were she to disclose her feelings. Merry poignantly addresses issues such as the right to inclusion, opportunities to prove one's loyalty, a frustration with domesticity, and the shame of being left behind by one's community to remain in hiding while others fight. On their night before the departure of Minas Tirith, Merry is informed he cannot accompany the Rohirrim. In a nightmare, he murmurs, "I won't be left behind, to be called for on return!" echo Éowyn's words, "Shall I always be left behind when the Riders depart, to mind the house" (*LotR* V.3.800, V.2.784). Théoden remarks upon the morning, "at least there is no longer need for hiding," but this is a privilege he extends only to his riders and the juxtaposition of Merry's and Éowyn's words with Théoden's highlights the inequality of their positions (V.3.801).

Applying what is known about the development of Éowyn's personality thus far, her calmness is incompatible with her prior defiance. When Merry is indignant and distressed with his lot, Éowyn merely says, "Come now, Meriadoc! [...] I will show you the gear that I have prepared for you" (V.3.802). This time, rather than being left behind, Éowyn implies she is in possession of knowledge that elicits a different mood: "my heart tells me that you will need such gear ere the end [...] maybe we shall meet again, you and I" (V.3.802).

Not long after, Éowyn as Dernhelm is seen for the first time in a line of warriors, through the gaze of Merry. Their eyes meet in recognition, "one looked up glancing keenly at the hobbit [...] he returned the glance," which reinforces the relationship between the two characters (V.3.803). As well as acting under the guise of Dernhelm to make her identity invisible, Éowyn remains silent. Crucially, however, silence here is her own choice and therefore is polarized with her original appearance. In the Golden Hall, Éowyn is not in mortal danger, even though, as Gandalf accuses Wormtongue: "When all the men were dead, you were to pick your share of the treasure, and take the woman you desire" (III.6.520). While now Éowyn places herself in mortal risk, she does so of her own free will, and her independent judgment will be the deciding factor in her success or failure. Cooper writes: "No knight is ever certain of returning from his quest; every one is undertaken on the premiss that the knight will take the adventure that will fall to him, be it life or death" (368). And indeed, Merry sees this approach to fate in Dernhelm's visage: "He caught the glint of clear grey eyes; and then he shivered, for it came suddenly to him that it was the face of one without hope who goes in search of death" (*LotR* V.3.803). Furthermore, Éowyn is alone despite Merry's presence because, in following the Rohirrim to the besieged Minas Tirith in Gondor, she commits the social transgression of going against the orders of her lord and kin. As Cooper additionally observes, honor "remains crucially important in romance, but it can strain other value systems beyond breaking-point" (25).

Structural interlacing diverts the narrative from Rohan once more, during which time no more is written of Éowyn. Consistent with earlier developments in her personality as someone who either speaks or is silent with increased conviction and agency, the next time we see Dernhelm is in the battle she has been building up to. Interestingly, up to this point in the narrative the Nazgûl and dark riders have been portrayed as terrifying creatures of indeterminate physical appearance. However, before Éowyn's ultimate test as a female knight and shieldmaiden, the reader is provided with a detailed, visceral description of the Nazgûl. Bird-like, it is a "winged," "naked" creature bearing "neither quill nor feather," and its wings "were as webs of hide between horned fingers; and it stank" from feeding on "fell meats" (*LotR* V.6.840). The passage is emphasized the opening interjection "behold!" and accompanying exclamation. Having the description before Éowyn's struggle presents it as a significant obstacle, since describing the beast during the battle would have a dissipative effect. As it is, the reader is encouraged to be impressed with the Nazgûl's opponent because the wraith is a seemingly insurmountable foe, mounted on a "creature of an older world," and having already killed Rohan's king (V.6.840).

When Éowyn elects to fill the newly vacant role, her voice becomes her own again. Through Merry's perspective, the reader hears "Dernhelm speaking; yet now the voice seemed strange, recalling some *other* voice that he had known" (V.6.841, emphasis added). This relates back to Elizabeth Scala's comment that medieval texts, specifically romances, "always bear witness to an *other* text [...] Sometimes the work remains other to itself and must be *(re)assembled*" (Scala 1, emphases in original). This female character has been assembled and reassembled multiple times through interlacing and spaces of silence, which provide a neutral space for the reader to forget partially what they know of Éowyn so that when she reappears each development in her personality seems natural, illuminating nuances in her voice. Likewise, she is assembled or reassembled as Dernhelm and Éowyn again at this important juncture in her career as female knight. She commands: "Begone, foul dwimmerlaik, lord of carrion! Leave the dead in peace!" in response to which,

> A cold voice answered: "Come not between the Nazgûl and his prey! [...] No living man may hinder me!" [...]It seemed that Dernhelm laughed, and the clear voice was like the ring of steel. "But no living man am I! You look upon a woman. Éowyn I am, Éomund's daughter. You stand between me and my lord and kin. Begone, if you be not deathless! For living or dark undead, I will smite you, if you touch him" (*LotR* V.6.841).

These words are a rhetorician's, displaying the "art of using language effectively so as to persuade or influence others" (*Oxford*). As Tolkien writes, "the helm of her secrecy had fallen from her," which incites Merry to act: "She should not die, so fair, so desperate!" (V.6.841). This echoes the description of Éowyn as she takes the blow of the Nazgûl in the following passage. Notable also is the pattern of chiasmus by which the parts of the narrative pertaining to Éowyn are placed on either side of the Nazgûl's text in this key act. Narrative structure is again shown in synthesis with Éowyn's success. To clarify this pattern, I highlight the sections accordingly:

> *Still she did not blench: maiden of the Rohirrim, child of kings, slender but as a steel-blade, fair yet terrible. A swift stroke she dealt, skilled and deadly. The outstretched neck she clove asunder,* and the hewn head fell like a stone. Backward she sprang as the huge shape crashed to ruin, vast wings outspread, crumpled on the earth; and with its fall the shadow passed away. *A light fell about her, and her hair shone in the sunrise* (V.6.842).

This act immortalizes Éowyn in fulfillment of Elven prophecy, and in the history of Middle-earth she is remembered as "the Lady of the Shield-arm" (Appendix A.II.1070). Beauty and strength are not mutually exclusive in Tolkien's representation of this female character; naturally, therefore, *both* inspire those who look upon her, namely Aragorn in her first incarnation, Merry in the battle, and Faramir in the fourth and final stage which I will now consider.

Wife and Healer

Once the battle for Gondor is over, in the healing houses of Minas Tirith, characters have time and opportunity to converse. Éomer discusses with Gandalf his lack of awareness of Éowyn's pain at Edoras and Gandalf reminds him, "you had horses, and deeds of arms, and the free fields; but she, born in the body of a maid, had a spirit and courage at least the match of yours" (*LotR* V.8.867). Aragorn agrees, "her deeds have set her among the queens of great renown" (V.8.867). They echo praise of Avenable in the *Prose Merlin*, where she is praised for her "engyn," meaning skill or ability, and is called "the beste maiden and the trewest withynne youre reame" (Conlee 353–55).

In medieval romance characters such as Silence and Joan of Arc, female knights' strength derives from their conditions as virgins and having led pure lives. However, Tolkien modifies the traditional paradigms by demonstrating that strength comes from personal character rather than physical purity. Not only is Rohan a corrupted state when it is introduced to the narrative, but within it exists an ambiguity present in another of Gandalf's insights into Éowyn's possible experiences during the occupation of Rohan. Gandalf asks Éomer: "Think you that Wormtongue had poison only for Théoden's ears?" (*LotR* V.8.867). He relates how Saruman spoke derogatively about Rohan's people, in one comment saying, "What is the house of Eorl but a thatched barn where brigands drink in the reek, and their brats roll on the floor among their dogs?" (V.8.867). These words can be understood on a general level, though I would argue this quote was designed to have more sinister undertones. As Gandalf tells Éomer, "if your sister's love for you, and her will still bent to her duty, had not restrained her lips, you might have heard even such things as these escape them. But who knows what she spoke to the darkness, alone, in the bitter watches of the night" (V.8.867). A "watch" is something held in anticipation of danger, so Gandalf's words imply undisclosed occurrences that Éowyn may have had to guard against, such as rape, physical abuse, or psychological manipulation. Éowyn's deeply felt duty, in connection with Gandalf's implication of what she may have had to endure, allows a new understanding of her anger at Aragorn when she wishes to follow him on the Paths of the Dead. "Your duty is with your people," Aragorn says, to which Éowyn replies "Too often have I heard of duty" (V.2.784). Crucially, the structure of Tolkien's narrative delays

Gandalf's suggestion until all knightly action has been completed for Éowyn; if Gandalf had spoken these words when he first deposed Wormtongue in Théoden's hall, she would have been framed more as a victim than a shieldmaiden.

Sensing Éowyn's frustration at being confined to the Houses of Healing, the former steward of Gondor, Faramir begins an acquaintance with her on similar terms: "I also am a prisoner of the healers" (VI.5.959). He also prevents her reverting into her usual state of silence-in-pain. When she frostily declares "I do not desire the speech of living men," he simply tells her that she is beautiful and would like her company, saying "you and I have both passed under the wings of the Shadow, and the same hand drew us back" (VI.5.960). There is a cyclical nature to the image of Éowyn, as Faramir also sees her classically "clad all in white" and from a distance. When she is healed, she is not again prevented from going to a battlefield, as she would have been by Aragorn. The complexity of Éowyn's silences or moments when she chooses to speak is developed over narrative time, and no longer corresponds to binaries of active/passive, agent/recipient, and fulfilled/unfulfilled, as demonstrated in Éowyn's choice not to join her brother when he sends for her. Now she is silent by not telling Faramir her reasons for staying, but remains so by her choice.

When Éowyn and Faramir finally admit their affection for one another, Tolkien writes, "her winter passed, and the sun shone on her," and Éowyn says, "I will be a healer" (VI.5.964–65). The completion Éowyn realizes after her ordeals, not least her battle with the Nazgûl, is apparent in these words with Faramir:

> "No longer do I desire to be a queen," she said.
>
> Then Faramir laughed merrily. "That is well," he said; "for I am not a king. Yet I will wed with the White Lady of Rohan, *if it be her will*. And *if* she will, then let us [...] dwell in fair Ithilien [...] All things will grow with joy there, *if* the White Lady comes." (VI.5.965, emphasis added)

They are portrayed simply as a man and a woman, not as holders of a rank as is Éowyn's burden in her first incarnation as a court lady. Moreover, Faramir insists three times that the transition to wife would be of her own free will, unlike in the medieval romances where the decision for Silence and Avenable to become wives is made by male characters. The light so repeatedly associated with Éowyn's appearance surrounds them both, which can be seen as a metaphor for her choice here: "the light [...] shone about them as they came down from the walls and went hand in hand to the Houses of Healing" (VI.5.965). Importantly, the enclosure of court or house is no longer an imprisonment. When the warden of the healing-house says she is free to go, Éowyn says, "now that I have leave to depart, I would remain. For this House has become to me of all dwellings the most blessed" (VI.5.965).

Conclusion

Éowyn transitions between four roles in *The Lord of the Rings*: court lady, acting lord of Rohan, shieldmaiden or female knight, wife and healer. Tolkien accomplishes these transitions by employing techniques inspired by medieval romance literature, such as interlacing narrative structure, alternating states of speech and silence, the motif of the knight incognito, deadly supernatural foes, and resolution of narrative with a marriage. However, he uses these as points of inspiration rather than as fixed tropes. In his work, Tolkien develops the idea of a female knight to create a liminal character who moves between ideals, societies and forms, contributing to the larger quest narrative as well as surmounting the female knight's usual obstacle of an arranged marriage bringing the narrative to a normative resolution. Speech and silence never remain fixed in Tolkien's work, meaning he creates a free-moving female character both in the world of the story and in reader interpretation. Éowyn's relationship with Faramir is a reward rather than a sentence, as Faramir accepts her multi-dimensional nature. Nowhere does this manifest more purely than in a vignette from the Houses of Healing, where "he called to her, and she came down, and they walked on the grass or sat under a green tree together, now in silence, now in speech" (VI.5.961).

Works Cited

Allen, Paula Gunn. "Kochinnenako in Academe: Three Approaches to Interpreting a Keres Indian Tale." Leitch 2108–26.

Armstrong, Dorsey. *Gender and the Chivalric Community of Malory's Morte d'Arthur*. Gainesville, FL: UP of Florida, 2003. Print.

Barber, Richard. "Chivalry and the *Morte Darthur*." *A Companion to Malory*. Eds. A. S. G. Edwards and Elizabeth Archibald. Cambridge, UK: D. S. Brewer, 1996. 19–35. Print.

Barrett, W. P., trans. "The Trial of Jeanne d'Arc." *Medieval Sourcebook*. Ed. Paul Halsall. Fordham U, Sept. 1999. Web. 28 August 2013.

Brewer, Derek. "*The Lord of the Rings* as Romance." *J. R. R. Tolkien, Scholar and Storyteller: Essays in Memoriam*. Eds. Mary Salu and Robert T. Farrell. Ithaca, NY: Cornell UP, 1979. 249–64. Print.

Camille, Michael. *Image on the Edge: The Margins of Medieval Art*. London: Reaktion Books, 1992. Print.

Carpenter, Humphrey. *J. R. R. Tolkien: A Biography*. London: George Allen and Unwin, 1977. Print.

Conlee, John, ed. *Prose Merlin*. Kalamazoo: Medieval Institute Publications, 1998. Print.

Cooper, Helen. *The English Romance in Time: Transforming Motifs from Geoffrey of Monmouth to the Death of Shakespeare*. Oxford: Oxford UP, 2004. Print.

Crane, Susan. "Knights in Disguise: Identity and Incognito in Fourteenth-Century Chivalry." *The Stranger in Medieval Society*. Eds. F. R. P. Akehurst and Stephanie Cain Van D'Elden. Minneapolis: U of Minnesota P, 1997. 63–79. Print.

de Pizan, Christine. *Le Ditie de Jehanne d'Arc*. Ed. Angus J. Kennedy. Oxford: Society for the Study of Medieval Languages and Literature, 1977. Print.

de Troyes, Chrétien. "Erec and Enide." *Chrétien de Troyes: Arthurian Romances*. Trans. Carleton W. Carroll. Ed. William W. Kibler. London: Penguin, 1991. 37–122. Print.

Donovan, Leslie. "The Valkyrie Reflex in J. R. R. Tolkien's *The Lord of the Rings*: Galadriel, Shelob, Éowyn, and Arwen." *Tolkien the Medievalist*. Ed. Jane Chance. London: Routledge, 2003. 106–32. Print. *Reprinted in this volume.*

Fries, Maureen. "Female Heroes, Heroines, and Counter-Heroes: Images of Women in Arthurian Tradition." *Arthurian Women*. Ed. Thelma S. Fenster. London: Routledge, 1996. 59–73. Print.

Gilbert, Sandra M., and Susan Gubar. "The Madwoman in the Attic: The Woman Writer and the Nineteenth-Century Literary Imagination." Leitch 2023–35.

Goldberg, P. J. P. *Medieval England: A Social History 1250–1550*. London: Hodder Arnold, 2004. Print.

Heng, Geraldine. "Enchanted Ground: The Feminine Subtext in Malory." Malory 835–49.

Johnson, Brent D. "Éowyn's Grief." *Mythlore* 27.3/4 (#105/106) (2009): 117–28. Web. 9 Sept. 2013.

Lefebure, Leo D. "Authority, Violence, and the Sacred at the Medieval Court." *Violence in Medieval Courtly Literature*. Ed. Albrecht Classen. New York: Routledge, 2004. 37–66. Print.

Leitch, Vincent B., ed. *The Norton Anthology of Theory and Criticism*. New York: W. W. Norton and Company, 2001. Print.

Malory, Sir Thomas. *Le Morte Darthur or The Hoole Book of Kyng Arthur and of His Noble Knyghtes of the Rounde Table*. Ed. Stephen H. A. Shepherd. London: W. W. Norton and Company, 2004. Print.

Oxford English Dictionary. 2013. Web. 20 Aug. 2013.

Roche-Mahdi, Sara, trans. *Silence: A Thirteenth-Century French Romance*. East Lansing, MI: Colleagues Press, 1992. Print.

Scala, Elizabeth. *Absent Narratives, Manuscript Textuality, and Literary Structure in Late Medieval England*. New York: Palgrave Macmillan, 2002. Print.

Tolkien, J. R. R. *The Fall of Arthur*. Ed. Christopher Tolkien. London: HarperCollins, 2013. Print.

Vitz, Evelyn Birge. *Medieval Narrative and Modern Narratology: Subjects and Objects of Desire*. New York: New York UP, 1989. Print.

Ward, Jennifer. Introduction. *Women of the English Nobility and Gentry 1066–1500*. Ed. Jennifer Ward. Manchester: Manchester UP, 1995. 1–14. Print.

Hidden in Plain View:
Strategizing Unconventionality in Shakespeare's and Tolkien's Portraits of Women

Maureen Thum

Both Shakespeare and Tolkien have been charged with confining women to traditional roles that buttress the patriarchal status quo.[1] Recent studies have pointed, however, to subtle strategies used by both authors to resist the dominant patriarchal codes of their respective times.[2] I will make the case that both Shakespeare and Tolkien use similar strategies to disarm reader resistance and to provide a sympathetic view of women in assuming powerful roles. Shakespeare's *Twelfth Night* and Tolkien's *The Lord of the Rings* are cases in point. Both works use carnival strategies to contradict the view that women and power are a toxic combination, or even an abomination resulting in disorder, evil, and chaos, an abomination that must be contained or eradicated. Both *Twelfth Night* and *The Lord of the Rings* resist traditional stereotypes of women and expand gender roles beyond the limitations imposed by a society in which men were granted power and authority that was not granted to the majority of women.

Like all well-educated Englishmen of his time, Tolkien was closely acquainted with Shakespeare's plays. But there is no indication of a direct connection between his work and Shakespeare's plays, so I therefore wish to refrain from making the case for a one-on-one comparison which would suggest direct influence. Instead, I will propose that both writers drew on a similar tradition of carnivalized literature and that both writers used strategies central to carnivalized literature in order to question and subvert traditional views of women's roles.

---

1. Those who charge Shakespeare with reinforcing the status quo include Freedman (184); Greenblatt (86–93). Partridge (179–89), Fredrick and McBride (108), and Stimpson (18) have argued that Tolkien's writings are anti-feminist.

2. Dunn, Dash, and Levin have made a strong case for the power and unconventionality of many of Shakespeare's heroines. Critics arguing for a reassessment of Tolkien's female figures include Donovan, who compares Arwen and Galadriel to the Valkyrie. See also Rawls, who has interpreted Tolkien's female characters as hybrid mixtures of archetypally masculine and feminine principles.

Both Shakespeare and Tolkien create alternative fictive worlds that are characteristic of carnivalized literature. In these worlds of fantasy, dream, or vision, the norms of society can be explored and tested. Gender hierarchies can be shown and analyzed from an unusual, and defamiliarizing, perspective. Within these fictive worlds, both writers use key strategies of role reversal and masquerade to unsettle normative gender codes. Role reversal demonstrates that social roles are fluid, while masquerade, understood in its traditional sense as disguise and parody, confounds the sense of order on which official society is based. Donning a mask signals the adoption of an alternative identity and thereby blurs normative social and cultural distinctions. In order to demonstrate how Shakespeare and Tolkien use carnival strategies to disrupt and expand traditional gender boundaries, I will first provide an overview of Carnival and carnivalized literature and explore the binary constructions of gender to which the majority of both Shakespeare's and Tolkien's contemporaries subscribed. I will then focus on how both writers deploy carnival strategies such as experimental fantasticality, role reversal, and masquerade to press against restrictive codes confining women to traditionally sanctioned roles.

Carnival and Carnivalized Literature

As M. M. Bakhtin has demonstrated, carnivalized literature derives from the medieval and early modern pre-Lenten Carnival. In medieval times, during specific feast days including the Feast of Fools (Twelfth Night), the strongly enforced social and cultural hierarchies of the everyday world were suspended (*Rabelais* 15). The custom of carnival license allowed a permitted or licensed "time-out" from official orthodoxies without the danger of punishment or reprisal. In *Twelfth Night,* Olivia refers specifically to carnival license when she states that a licensed (allowed) fool is not to be reprimanded or censured for criticizing his social superiors: "There is no slander in an allowed fool, though he do nothing but rail" (1.5.90–91). Carnival license during specific feast days permitted role reversals, the wearing of masks, and the assuming of alternative identities, all of which implicitly put into question the hierarchical structures of the medieval world (Bakhtin, *Problems* 107–09). Although Carnival was often contained, and served merely as a venting mechanism,[3] it could lead, as Natalie Zemon Davis (131–50) and Susan Crane (129–30) have argued, to a permanent state of questioning and subversion outside the confines of the officially licensed carnival world. During the Renaissance, especially, the rebellious and unruly spirit of Carnival often spilled over into the everyday world (Davis 140).

Like Carnival itself, carnivalized literature is infused with the unruly spirit of Carnival and uses recognizable carnival strategies to challenge received ideas, including fixed views of gender and social class. Fundamental to this challenging of received ideas is the creation of a fictive world which lies outside, yet parallel to, the empirical realities of everyday life. Bakhtin refers to this strategy as "experimental fantasticality" (*Problems* 116). Experimental fantasticality involves the invention of an alternative dream or fantasy world which provides an unusual and defamiliarizing perspective. Both Shakespeare and Tolkien create such imaginary and hypothetical worlds. Within these worlds, the familiar carnival strategies of role reversal and masquerade allow accepted categories, received opinions, and traditional beliefs to be symbolically tested and disrupted. Examining the intersection of gender and Carnival in *Twelfth Night* and *The Lord of the Rings* allows us to discover how Shakespeare and Tolkien use previously unexplored strategies for questioning and resisting normative codes and for expanding traditional gender boundaries.

Traditional Views of Gender: Shakespeare's and Tolkien's Historical Contexts

Separated by over three centuries, both Shakespeare and Tolkien wrote in worlds where traditional views of women—while being challenged and tested—still held sway. Numerous studies, especially in the last three decades, have explored the powerful impact of inherited binary views of gender construction on our concepts of both men and women (Ortner 71–72; Rosaldo and Lamphere 1–3). According to a long-standing tradition, men's and women's roles were defined by divine providence, or by natural law, in strictly separated categories. In a tradition dating back to Aristotle, men were viewed as rational, as superior spiritually and intellectually, while women were viewed as

3. Barber and Hassel view the disruptions of carnival as a reinforcement of the status quo.

inferior. Men were seen as leaders and creators of culture, who played an active, legitimate role in public life. Women, by contrast to men, were viewed as followers, as creators of children rather than culture. Denied an officially sanctioned public role, their activities were seen as properly confined to the household and the domestic sphere where they could exercise power but only within a limited area of activity. While men were deemed by nature to be powerful, active, and independent, women were the reverse: powerless, passive, and dependent (Dunn 15–16). Women in the Renaissance could be powerful and influential, but, with few exceptions, they lacked recognized authority which would legitimize claims to power in the public arena.

During Shakespeare's time, the fixed gender roles were being challenged (Neely 5). The fact that Elizabeth I had remained on the throne successfully for decades and had, through careful negotiation, achieved authority as well as power, disrupted traditional views (Levin and Robertson iii). Inherited norms were further unsettled by the fact that, during the sixteenth and seventeenth centuries, numerous upper class women were educated far beyond contemporary expectations for their sex (Dunn 17–28).

However, although the challenging of traditional paradigms led gradually to new views of women's roles, such challenges to normative codes also elicited angry and frightened responses. During Shakespeare's time, sermons, conduct guides, and pamphlets inveighed against unruly women and reaffirmed the patriarchal status quo (Aughterson 68). Thus, in 1617, William Whatley urges that a woman must submit "herself with quietness, cheerfully, even as a well-broken horse turns at the least turning, stands at the least check of the rider's bridle, readily going and standing as he wishes that sits upon his back" (34). As the title of John Knox's 1558 *First Blast of the Trumpet against the Monstrous Regiment of Women* implies, women who step outside their divinely ordained roles are no less than monsters.

As Knox's diatribe suggests, during this period, women who resisted tradition and who assumed powerful roles were viewed as usurpers in a territory to which they held no claim. Resistance was frequently met by censure, punishment, accusations of heresy and witchcraft, and even execution. It is no accident, surely, that the virulently anti-feminist witch craze was at its height from about 1570 to 1700. During this time between 60,000 and 200,000 witches were executed, over 75% of whom were women. They stood as a powerful warning to those who stepped outside narrowly defined norms (Coudert 61–62). Even Queen Elizabeth, who successfully held a radically unconventional position in Renaissance society, was demonized and accused of being a baby-killer, a murderer, and an unnatural perversion of womanhood (Levin, "Power" 101–05).

Comparing Tolkien's views of women to Shakespeare's might at first seem somewhat astonishing, especially since extreme manifestations of anti-feminism such as the execution of witches had long ceased before Tolkien began writing *The Lord of the Rings*.[4] However, several factors allow for a fruitful comparison. Tolkien's world appears—on the surface—to represent a nostalgic revisiting of an age when patriarchal power structures were still intact, an age similar to that represented by Shakespeare in *Twelfth Night*. In addition, Tolkien wrote from a relatively traditionalist context. The members of his circle of Inklings, particularly C. S. Lewis, shared strongly conservative views about women. Finally, like Shakespeare's England, Tolkien's mid-twentieth-century Britain was characterized by rapid change and cataclysmic events which brought about a rethinking of accepted orthodoxies, including the place of women in the social order. World War II had thrust numerous women into the workforce to play unconventional roles while men were at war. But, while opportunities opened during the war, a backlash followed after the war ended. The men returned home, and women were encouraged, if not exhorted, to return to the domestic sphere (Friedan 184).

The paradoxes of this period are reflected in Tolkien's writings. During the early decades of the twentieth century, despite vocal and often high profile women's movements for suffrage, equal education, and equal recognition in the workplace, women's roles for the most part remained relatively traditional. Virginia Woolf's *A Room of One's Own* (1929) speaks of the major universities in Great Britain as bastions of male power where women were as yet granted only limited access (6–24). Simone de Beauvoir, writing in the 1950s, argues in *The Second Sex* that women's roles had remained essentially unchanged for

4. As Purkiss notes, "the popular beatings and lynching of women for witchcraft [...] continued into the late nineteenth century" and popular witch stories continued to be circulated as late as 1962 (111).

centuries. In a thought-provoking article, Patricia Sullivan and Carole Levin compare the attitudes toward women and power during the sixteenth and twentieth centuries, noting that in 1992, Hillary Rodham Clinton was portrayed on the cover of the *American Spectator* as "The Wicked Witch of the West" (278). In the same year, Pat Robertson, the self-styled spokesman for the "Moral Majority," spoke out against the passage of an equal rights amendment in Iowa. He censured the amendment as the product of a "feminist agenda" which was part of "a socialist, anti-family political movement that encourages women to leave their husbands, kill their children, practice witchcraft [...] and become lesbians" (qtd. in Levin and Sullivan, "Politics" 4). Even now, the question of women and power has remained vexed, and the anxieties concerning female power have not yet been allayed.

During the Renaissance and beyond, mainstream literature reflected, and often reinforced, traditional views of women and power. Powerful, active women in the literature of the Renaissance were frequently demonized and punished, meeting a horrible end. While disobedience was decried, submission was rewarded. In traditional fairy tales deriving from the Medieval and the Early Modern periods, passive, silent women, like Sleeping Beauty and Snow White, were allowed happy endings, while active women, such as Snow White's wicked stepmother, were portrayed as evil, and even demonic, and were often killed in the course of the narrative. Such portraits reflected the rejection of powerful, independent women in a patriarchal society. During the twentieth century, witches and witch-like figures continued to appear frequently in literature and film, including the children's books written by Tolkien's friend, C. S. Lewis. In the Walt Disney versions of fairy tales such as *Snow White* (1937), *Cinderella* (1950), *Sleeping Beauty* (1959), and *The Little Mermaid* (1989), the witch-like figures are even more strongly demonized and more spectacularly punished than in their much earlier fairy-tale counterparts.[5]

5. In Perrault's eighteenth-century "Sleeping Beauty," on which the Disney film is based, the wicked fairy plays only a brief cameo role at the beginning of the tale. In Disney's film, by contrast, the wicked fairy, named Maleficent (evil-doer) appears as a full-fledged witch complete with familiars including a crow and other frightening creatures. The epitome of the monstrous, demonic woman, she is transformed into a dragon which the prince is forced to kill with his sword of virtue and shield of truth.

Carnival Worlds: Experimental Fantasticality in Shakespeare's and Tolkien's Texts

Both Shakespeare and Tolkien explore, test, and expand the binary constructions of gender by creating alternative worlds in which traditional views can be turned on their head. In the world of Carnival, the very fact that women can dress as men, peasants as kings, laity as monks and bishops upsets the prescribed social order. Role reversal and masquerade allow Shakespeare and Tolkien to present intelligent, powerful women who are not demonized as witches and punished for their transgressive roles. Instead, their unconventional behavior is validated and even rewarded, indicating that women who step outside traditional roles are neither monstrous nor perverse.

The site for these transgressions is the fictive carnival world where the writers can stage experimental hypotheses concerning the potential for both men and women to think and act outside the boundaries of their traditional roles. In *Twelfth Night*, the mythical, vaguely medievalized country of Illyria becomes the imaginary site where Shakespeare can subvert fixed concepts of identity associated with gender and social class.[6] Here, male and female roles can be reversed without risk of censure, and a woman can don the mask of a man without fearing the angry responses and reprisals which she would be forced to face in the real world of Shakespeare's time (Levin, *Heart* 126–27; Williams 77). The notion that Shakespeare has created a carnivalized world in *Twelfth Night* is corroborated by the fact that the title specifically links the play to Carnival and the carnival tradition, referring to the Twelfth Night festival which was also known as The Feast of Fools (Hassel 151).

Like Shakespeare, Tolkien creates a fictional world complete with maps to chart its geography and multiple peoples and languages with their own history and cosmology. Although closer to reality than the half-mythic world of *The Silmarillion*, it is still a world peopled by magical creatures who interact with ordinary and extraordinary mortals.

---

6. Illyria was "the ancient name of an area of the Adriatic Coast roughly corresponding to what was for long known as Yugoslavia" (Warren and Wells 8). By Shakespeare's time, the name was applied to city states under the governance of the Venetian Republic. But while Illyria has links to an actual area of the Adriatic, it is also a mythic territory and imaginary world.

Creating this carnivalized world allows Tolkien, like Shakespeare, to challenge traditional views of power and gender in a setting where the realities of the official, everyday world can be turned upside down. Although the kings, princes, lords, and ladies in Tolkien's writings appear to uphold the ancient hierarchies of the medieval texts from which their images are drawn, a closer look reveals that beneath the veneer of nostalgically re-visioned myth and legend, Tolkien actually invents figures who revise the normative codes even of his own time (Thum 235–38). As with Shakespeare, the alternative perspective of the invented world allows gender hierarchies to be seen from an unusual, defamiliarizing, and critical point of view.

Role Reversal in Twelfth Night and The Lord of the Rings

Within the carnivalized worlds of *Twelfth Night* and *The Lord of the Rings*, expected gender roles are switched. By destabilizing essentialist views of both men's and women's roles as divinely ordained, they suggest that these roles are far more fluid than traditional paradigms would suggest. In *Twelfth Night*, both men and women exchange expected attributes. Critics and directors alike have frequently viewed the non-traditional male character, Duke Orsino, as a fool because his attributes are not those of the stereotypical male (Hassel 160–61). He is not the epitome of the manly ideal: independent of others, dispassionate, and in charge of his emotions. Instead, he is emotional, overwhelmed by love and by his passions, and dependent on the Countess Olivia, whom he loves from afar and who has consistently refused his offers of marriage. His emotional swings go beyond accepted "courtly" behavior. He even describes himself as "unstaid and skittish" (2.4.18), and claims that he is more emotional and passionate than a woman (2.4.93–103).

Orsino's assumption of a non-traditional role fairly stands for the reversal of gender roles throughout a comedy in which none of the male characters display the expected behavior patterns associated with the traditional ideal of manhood. Sir Toby Belch and Sir Andrew Aguecheek are both dependent on the graces and charity of a woman, Countess Olivia, for room and board. Both men are knights and, therefore, among the higher orders. Nevertheless, both are subject to Olivia's commands as mistress of a large household, over which she holds complete sway. Like Malvolio, the victim of their cruel practical joke, they are prone to folly and cut ridiculous figures throughout the comedy. Viola's brother, Sebastian, weeps openly in grief for his sister and is swayed by an irrational love and admiration for Olivia, whom he met only minutes before. Moreover, he decides to marry her, all the while wondering whether or not he is mad or dreaming.

The female characters, Viola, Olivia, and Maria, all share attributes commonly ascribed to men and, thus, are highly unconventional figures. They are witty, outspoken, and intelligent, and they claim areas of power generally reserved for men. Viola befriends the Duke and gains his confidence dressed as a man, while Olivia runs her estate without the guidance of a male authority figure. Maria, the mastermind of the plot to bring about Malvolio's fall through pride and self-love, has scarcely been mentioned in critical studies, even though she plays the role of "player king," a manipulator of men's destinies. This role of mastermind is generally assigned to a male character, as in *The Tempest*, where it is played by Prospero, or in *Much Ado About Nothing*, where the role is taken by Don Pedro, Prince of Aragon.

In *The Lord of the Rings,* Tolkien has also reversed gender expectations. Critics who view Tolkien as an anti-feminist writer object that he has reproduced female stereotypes. But Tolkien has actually turned traditional paradigms on their head. We see this reversal especially in the expectations attached to the male hero in *The Lord of the Rings*. Jane Chance observes that "Tolkien recast the medieval hero [...] in new, unlikely, and multiple forms. These include small Hobbits, suspiciously dark rangers like Strider, sisters and sister-daughters (nieces) like Éowyn [...] and second sons like Faramir" (175). Moreover, many of the powerful males in *The Lord of the Rings* prove to be singularly unheroic. They are often weak, subject to temptation, and unable to carry out heroic deeds or exercise their authority. King Théoden is mesmerized by Wormtongue and unable to carry out his kingly duties, while, in a reversal of expectations, Éowyn, a woman, resists Wormtongue's spells. Boromir, the great warrior, cannot resist the temptation to take the Ring from Frodo and thus fails the Fellowship. Ironically, his failure results from his attempt to fulfill the traditional heroic role: to save his people from the enemy. His father, Denethor, Steward of Gondor, fails his sons and abdicates his responsibilities as leader because he has also reached for greater power in order to protect Gondor, but in so doing, he has fallen into the thrall of the Dark Lord.

In both cases, traditional heroic qualities—the desire to accomplish great deeds, the desire to shore up and enhance the power of the realms with which they are charged, the desire to challenge the enemy head-on and win the game—all prove to be traps. In a complete reversal of traditional values, among the heroes are Frodo and Sam, "two small dark figures, forlorn, [standing] hand in hand upon a little hill, while the world shook under them" (VI.4.951).

By the same token, Tolkien reverses expectations attached to female roles in medieval romance.[7] In Tolkien's anti-epic/romance, women who at first appear to fulfill the stereotype associated with romance genres actually resist the accepted patterns of gender roles associated with the genre. Women—Éowyn, Galadriel, and Arwen—play powerful roles and, contrary to expectations, are not censured or punished for assuming both the power and the authority reserved traditionally for men. Tolkien, like Shakespeare, turns the gendered roles associated with both men and women on their heads.

Carnival Masquerade in Twelfth Night

Within these experimental worlds, both Shakespeare and Tolkien employ traditional carnival maskings and unmaskings in order to explore the intersection of gender and power in an essentially male-dominated society. By disguising themselves as men, female characters escape the confines of the woman's part. By hiding beneath the mask of conventional femininity, women can even more successfully expand gender roles, since the conventional masquerade is more subtle and difficult to detect. Citing Luce Irigaray, Susan Crane has made a strong case that "resistance to the feminine position is possible through mimicry, that is, through the deliberate acting out of prescribed femininity" (59). Conscious manipulation of gender roles allows women to meet societal expectations while simultaneously circumventing them. During the Renaissance, as Carol Levin has demonstrated, Queen Elizabeth I participated in this form of disguise by careful manipulation of the image of the Virgin Queen, who always appears ready to accept a suitor as her husband, but who puts off matrimony indefinitely by setting up obsta-

---

7. In medieval romance, "the social position occupied by those gendered male becomes conflated with that of humanity at large, exiling those gendered female to the position of difference, otherness, and objectification" (Crane 13).

cles to the seemingly wished-for union. Elizabeth I thus provided a model for Shakespeare's heroines who use a similar strategy (*Heart* 127–28). Tolkien also depicts this form of disguise when he presents female characters who only appear to fulfill expected stereotypes, but whose actual role and nature expands gender definitions in defiance of traditional restrictions.

VIOLA'S MASQUERADE

With few exceptions, critics and directors have viewed the two main female characters of *Twelfth Night,* Viola and Olivia, as polar opposites.[8] Viola has been interpreted as a positive, winsome, endearing young woman who, despite her unconventional mask, reaffirms traditional views of gender. Olivia, by contrast, has been viewed negatively, as a mutilated, narcissistic, frigid, obsessive, and haughty woman who is unable to love, incapable of connecting with other human beings, and prone to folly.[9] However, neither of these views fully explores the complexity of Shakespeare's two woman characters. I wish to argue that Viola and Olivia are far more closely connected than numerous critics have allowed.[10] Each character uses a different strategy of masquerade to lay claim to areas of action and to forms of power which would otherwise be closed to them.

To judge from the angry response to cross-dressing in writings by Renaissance moralists, a woman's adoption of male clothing and a male role was seen as undermining the public order (Williams 78). As Levin and Robertson note, "the boy actor challenges biological essentialism and acknowledges, albeit not in our terms, the cultural construction of gender. Femininity becomes simply something played" (vii). One can extrapolate that masculinity can also be played, putting into question equally fixed ideas about men's roles. Viola's donning of a male mask is hence a subversive and audacious act in itself, an act

8. Freedman views both figures negatively: Viola as self-alienated by her mask, and Olivia as self-alienated by her failure to connect with reality (216).

9. For Hassel, Viola and Sebastian are "comic types of the incarnate Christ" who represent "good will and selfless love, forgiveness and humility" (150). Olivia, by contrast, is a folly-ridden, obsessive woman engaged in "self-indulgent posturing as a grief-stricken sister" (154).

10. See Irene Dash and Catherine Dunn who make a strong case that both women are positive, independent, witty, and unconventional characters.

which is only one of many that demonstrate her intelligence, her ingenuity, and her independence of spirit. Cast upon a foreign shore, uncertain of her reception in a strange land, alone and unprotected, she is at risk in a society which is threatening even to male strangers (3.3.9–11). It is not surprising that she is unwilling to be "delivered to the world"—that is, to allow her identity to be disclosed—"Till that [she] had made [her] own occasion mellow, / What [her] estate is" (1.2.43–44). She wishes to control the outcome of this chance arrival on a foreign shore, but as a woman, she has little leeway for doing so. By taking the initiative and disguising herself, she immediately takes charge of her destiny, allowing herself to claim the freedom of movement otherwise granted only to men.

Viola's mask, while seemingly restricting her love relationship with Duke Orsino, nonetheless allows her an unusual freedom in her relationship with him, thus countering accepted views of the appropriate relationship between men and women who contemplate marriage and even stretching the boundaries of relationships considered appropriate among male friends. Unmarried women were exhorted to avoid the company of men unless escorted by a chaperon (Vives 71). Disguised as a man, Viola has the freedom to become the friend and trusted confidante of the man she comes to love. Thus, they are friends before they become lovers, a completely unconventional approach to traditional views of marriage and the relationships between men and women, especially among the privileged classes. Even among men, the relationship would be unusual, since they are not simply comrades, but have a private, intimate relationship during which Orsino bares his very soul to her.

Significantly, mediated by masquerade, Shakespeare pairs Viola in marriage not only with a partner who has become her friend, but with a man who is himself unconventional and, therefore, more likely to accept a similar unconventionality in a woman. When we first meet him, Orsino is clearly suffering from an even more advanced case of Petrarchanism than Romeo with his imagined love for Rosalind in *Romeo and Juliet*. Shakespeare demonstrates the ludicrous nature of such a stance when, in a sudden and amusing turnabout, Orsino, like Romeo, is instantly cured of his Petrarchan affliction. Reality, as opposed to the conventional projections he had imagined in his amorous fancy, has the power to dispatch the poetic illusion of a distant lover and to readjust Orsino's vision almost without delay. Unlike Romeo who only gets to know Juliet briefly, Orsino has the good fortune to have found a marriage partner to whom he has been able to "unclasp" his bosom and tell his innermost thoughts (1.4.13–14).

Furthermore, Orsino is unconventional in his acceptance of Viola's actions and, especially, her disguise. A stereotypical response would be suspicion and anger, as indicated by the numerous sermons and conduct guides inveighing against female cross-dressing (Levin, *Heart* 127). Unlike the sermons, conduct books, and even the order of James I condemning cross-dressing as an abomination, Orsino does not censure Viola for her disguise, and even though he wishes to see her, finally, in her "woman's weeds," he is not threatened by an intelligent woman who has the independence, the skill, and the sheer bravado to maintain her disguise successfully. Orsino's final words to Viola suggest that their marriage also has the possibility of altering expected male-female power relations in matrimony. His words have at least two possible conflicting meanings, allowing for two opposed readings of their future relationship:

> Your master quits you; and for your service done him,
> So much against the mettle of your sex,
> So far beneath your soft and tender breeding,
> And since you called me master for so long,
> Here is my hand. You shall from this time be
> Your master's mistress. (5.1.321–26)

His statement about the power relationship between the two remains suffused with irony, since Orsino appears to claim his patriarchal role of master, all the while declaring himself henceforth to be subject to Viola as his mistress. As we have seen in his previous relationship, Orsino is not in charge of women; they hold sway over him.

Olivia and the Mimicry of Convention

Olivia first appears to the audience wearing the mask of conventionality. What we first know of Olivia is only by hearsay. Her identity is concealed by the mask of the cold Petrarchan mistress, distant, unfeeling, rejecting the passionate lover out of cruelty and caprice. Her father and brother have both died, and everyone, including Orsino, expects her to be in want of a protector without whom she can scarcely be expected to run her estate, let alone live a fulfilled life.[11] Olivia has rejected Orsino's advances by claiming that she will not wed until she has grieved for seven years. Critics have interpreted this behavior as evidence of Olivia's morbid introspection, her "self-indulgent posturing as the grief-stricken sister" (Hassel 154), her "ego-reification" and her "refus[al] to interact with others" (Freedman 216), when it is, in reality, a strategy on Olivia's part to avoid an unwanted suitor.

When we actually meet Olivia, the above views of the men who describe her—the Captain, Orsino, and Valentine—are put into question. When Viola, posing as Cesario, a seemingly attractive youth, comes to woo Olivia in the name of Orsino, Olivia after very little prompting removes her veil of mourning. What we discover during their exchange is not the grief-obsessed, folly-ridden woman described by so many critics. Instead, she is witty, ironic, and down to earth. Viola/Cesario begins her petition in the high-flown terms we have come to expect from Orsino, but interrupts herself to state that she does not wish to waste her breath speaking poetry that she has learned by heart if she is not dealing with the "lady of the house." Viola thereby shows her ironic distance from the artificial verses she has "conned" or learned by heart (1.5.170).

Viola's down-to-earth approach strikes a chord in Olivia, who has a similar sense of irony concerning set poems of praise and the poses they represent. Olivia retorts that verses learned by heart are "the more like to be feigned" (1.5.192), revealing with these words that she is not amused by Orsino's posing. Indeed, since she says several times that she does not love Orsino, her apparently exaggerated mourning, like her seeming coldness and inability to respond to Orsino's suits, may actually be seen as her successful fending off of an unwanted suitor (1.5.278). But, since he refuses to accept "no" for an answer, she advances her mourning, at least in part, as a means of keeping Orsino's importunities at bay. The mask of the distant lady who makes somewhat exaggerated claims for mourning is conventionally acceptable, while an outright refusal in order to retain her independence is not. Despite strong pressures to normalize her situation by marrying an appropriate

11. In most European countries and Britain, "all widows and unmarried women [were required by law to choose] a male guardian who was to oversee their financial affairs and appear for them in court" (Wiesner 4).

and eligible bachelor, she deflects his advances and maintains her independence without being censured for inappropriate behavior.

Olivia demonstrates that she is ironically and humorously distanced from Orsino's poses. When Viola makes the traditional "carpe diem" argument that Olivia's beauty will go with her to the grave if she does not wed and leave a "copy," that is, a child, Olivia replies ironically by reinterpreting the word "copy" to mean a list of attributes (1.5.239). She then presents a list that parodies the fixed tropes of the conventional love sonnet much as does Shakespeare in his well-known satire, "My Mistress' Eyes are Nothing like the Sun":

> Oh, sir, I will not be so hard-hearted. I will give out divers schedules of my beauty. It shall be inventoried, and every particle and utensil labeled to my will: as item, two lips, indifferent red; item, two grey eyes, with lids to them; item, one neck, one chin, and so forth. (1.5.239–44)

Clearly, Olivia is no fool, nor is she the cold, cruel woman Orsino has described. Instead, she is witty, astute, and able to voice her ironic objection to Orsino's taking of the conventional role as the rejected courtly lover. Her itemized list demonstrates that she not only understands the conventions of courtly love, but she also recognizes and rejects the objectification of women which these conventions of male admiration conceal. Significantly, when Orsino does marry, he is able to abandon his former stance with an alacrity that demonstrates the superficiality of his former pose. Olivia clearly understands him better than he understands himself.

Olivia's mask of convention not only hides an intelligent, witty, insightful young woman. It also deflects attention from the fact that she has power and autonomy as an orphan who is subject neither to her father's nor her brother's will. She proves to be quite capable of running an entire estate efficiently and effectively. Sebastian, who arrives just in time to "save" Olivia from an impossible match with a disguised woman, questions her sanity and even his own. And yet, Sebastian recognizes that he cannot be mad, nor can Olivia, for as he observes, "[I]f t'were so, / She could not sway her house, command her followers, / Take and give back affairs and their dispatch / With such a smooth, discreet and stable bearing" (4.3.16–19). Olivia is passionate and independent in her actions. She chooses her lover and marries according to her own wishes, disregarding social class in order to do so.

Indeed, Sebastian's lower social class may be welcome to Olivia, since she may not wish to relinquish her power to an overbearing man, and above all, to a man she does not love. If we are to believe Sir Toby, she has sworn many times never to marry above her station, and thus she refuses to play the subordinate role, either as woman or as a lower ranked spouse who must be grateful for her rise in status (1.3.107–09). Olivia does not put off marriage altogether, as did Queen Elizabeth I. Instead, she makes sure that her partner is willing to play by her rules. Her wish to Sebastian and his response are significant: "Would thou'dst be ruled by me!" Acquiescing to her wish to rule him, Sebastian replies without hesitation, "I will" (4.1.63–64). This is not a partner who will play the expected role of lord and master in the household. Practical and in charge, Olivia follows up immediately by fetching the priest and making the arrangements for the exchange of vows.

Some critics have seen her love for Cesario as a humiliation, and her marriage to Sebastian alternately as a gift of grace, or as a further humiliation. But her comment upon seeing the twins revealed is an undisguised exclamation of pleasure: "Most wonderful!" (5.1.225). These are scarcely words of humiliation and shame.[12] Furthermore, if we accept the fantasy of visually identical twins, male and female, whom the other characters are unable to tell apart, we can also accept the fantasy of a Sebastian who actually is, as Viola tells the audience, similar to her played Cesario in every respect, "For him I imitate" (3.4.385). As Levin notes,

> Olivia, a powerful woman who stays in her female dress but stretches the boundaries of gender expectation, gets what she wants. Olivia is certainly not a direct and complete parallel to Elizabeth, but the queen's presence allowed Shakespeare sympathetically to present—and his audience to accept—a powerful, articulate woman who retains the accoutrements of femininity [...] Olivia, like Elizabeth, does not need to cross-dress to be powerful. (*Heart* 137)

The humorous ending which rights all wrongs and appears to return the characters from carnival topsy-turvy to the "real world" is, as so often in Shakespeare's comedies, a sprung ending. The harmonious

12. Levin notes that her exclamation "sounds like a rapturous triumph" (*Heart* 137).

return to convention, which signals closure in many Shakespearean comedies, does not necessarily provide containment for the critical, questioning spirit which has been liberated during the carnival time-out. Like the spirit of Carnival itself, it spills over the accepted boundaries, leaving questions unanswered, issues unresolved, and gender roles destabilized.

Masquerade in The Lord of the Rings

Tolkien, like Shakespeare, uses carnival masquerade in his depiction of two major woman characters, Éowyn and Galadriel. Given the romance/epic genres from which Tolkien drew in his construction of *The Lord of the Rings* (Chance 175), one would expect to find a traditionalist approach to women's roles. Indeed, several critical studies have viewed Tolkien's female characters as traditional women, mere counters who play a symbolic role as objects in male games of power and control. However, Tolkien presents subtle variations similar to the masks described in *Twelfth Night* which can deflect the attention of his more conservative audience from the unconventional implications of the powerful women in his novel.

Éowyn's Masks

Éowyn wears two masks: first, the conventional mask of the romance heroine, which is stripped away when she dons a second mask, that of the male warrior, Dernhelm. In both cases, she resists traditional roles to which women have been relegated. Her mask of unconventionality allows Tolkien to depict her independent nature in far stronger terms than if she stated her rebellion against women's traditional roles in overt and clearly discernible forms. When the reader first encounters Éowyn, she is wearing the conventional mask, appearing to fulfill stereotypical expectations of medieval romance. She is simply a "woman clad in white" (*LotR* III.6.512), an unnamed object, standing in a subordinate position behind King Théoden's chair. But her body language almost immediately resists the implications of the mask she wears. Instead of looking at Théoden as would a subordinate, with unquestioning obedience, "she looked on the king with cool pity in her eyes" (III.6.515). By the same token, she speaks no words and obeys the command to go, seeming to be silent and obedient. Tolkien's description of her also appears to show her as fulfilling the traditional expectations of the beautiful heroine: "Very fair was her face, and her long hair was like a river of gold" (III.6.515). But again, the impression is almost immediately contradicted: "Slender and tall she was [...] but strong she seemed and stern as steel, a daughter of kings" (III.6.515).

Aragorn believes her to be "fair and cold, like a morning of pale spring that is not yet come to womanhood" (III.6.515). But we discover that, contrary to the expectations raised by this male judgment, she is a woman of power, passion, and resolve. Gandalf suggests that she has been viewed as a pawn in Saruman's game—again a typical role for women—since she has been promised as the prize to Wormtongue if he succeeds in undermining Théoden's power. Gandalf's words, spoken once Wormtongue has been banished, seem to suggest that she has been rescued: "Éowyn is safe now" (III.6.520). Nevertheless, reading between the lines, we recognize that this seemingly fragile, beautiful, and typical romance figure, whom we would expect to be relegated to the position of object in a man's world, has demonstrated greater power than Théoden in resisting the spells of Wormtongue, Saruman's emissary. Wormtongue has successfully cast a spell on King Théoden, but he has been unable to overpower Éowyn's will as her pitying glance toward the king suggests. She also appears prominently in all the gatherings of men. This is their sign of respect for her rank and, as the reader discovers, for her qualities which are recognized and applauded by the men of Rohan.

Contrary to traditional expectations, Tolkien presents a society in which the men respect and admire a woman's power, skill, and merit. Thus, when Théoden plans to go to war, Háma puts Éowyn forward as the leader of the people who remain behind: "She is fearless and high-hearted. All love her. Let her be as a lord to the Eorlingas, while we are gone" (III.6.523). Unlike Viola in *Twelfth Night*, or the other disguised women in Shakespeare, Éowyn does not simply claim power unofficially, but is officially granted both power and authority. During a special ceremony, she kneels, as would a knight, and receives a sword and "fair corselet" from the king as signs of her office. As the departing Aragorn looks back at her, she appears almost as an emblem of power, standing before the doors of the house in the traditional pose of the knight: "the sword was set upright before her, and her hands were laid upon the hilt. She was clad now in mail and shone like silver in the sun" (III.6.523). The mask of the conventional heroine has been replaced by that of the leader whose power has, astonishingly given the medievalized context of the novel, been officially authorized.

Éowyn uses her authority to empower Merry, a young male Hobbit who, like herself, has been marginalized in the battle preparations. She is marginalized because of her gender and he because of his size as a "Halfling," about the size of a human child of ten. She prepares a tent, weapons, and armor, using her authority to do so. When Merry is to be left behind, she secretly takes him with her, riding on the horse before her. Tellingly, Tolkien does not reveal her identity to the reader throughout the long trek to Gondor. In *Twelfth Night*, the audience knows that Viola is disguised, so that the discrepancy between her real and her assumed identity becomes the source of irony and humor. In the case of Tolkien, to avoid the suggestion of a woman warrior, unacceptable to Théoden and his advisors, he conceals Éowyn beneath the male disguise of the warrior, Dernhelm.

Unlike Viola, who comments consistently on the burden of her disguise, Éowyn is equally at home in the roles of woman and warrior, subject and leader. Unlike Viola, whose inability at sword play is the source of much horse-play and slapstick humor, Éowyn has a skill equal to that of a man. Unlike Viola, she is fearless, and unlike Viola, she recognizes clearly that traditional women's roles are a trap. Objecting to Aragorn's arguments, she says, "All your words are but to say: you are a woman, and your part is in the house. [...] But I am of the house of Eorl and not a serving-woman. I can ride and wield blade, and I do not fear either pain or death." When Aragorn asks what she fears, she replies "A cage [...] To stay behind bars, until use and old age accept them, and all chance of doing great deeds is gone beyond recall or desire" (V.2.784). It is difficult to imagine a more overtly feminist statement than one questioning the limitations not only of women's accepted roles, but of the heroic desire for doing "great deeds."

When Éowyn, with the indispensable help of Merry, a child-like Hobbit, kills the Witch-king and his dragon-like beast, Tolkien's narrator does not express astonishment at the deed. Instead, he validates both her disguise and her role as a warrior. Tolkien makes it clear that only Éowyn was destined to fulfill this role and save the people of Gondor from the devastation of the Witch-king, whom no man could kill. Furthermore, the male characters do not condemn her for donning a disguise in order to go to war. Instead, they recognize and honor her for her qualities as a warrior.

Like Viola, Éowyn marries a man who is her friend. Éowyn abandons her vain admiration for Aragorn, a hero whom she worships from afar, to marry Faramir, a man who not only becomes her friend, but who is her empathetic support in the Houses of Healing while she is recovering from the wound she received in battle. As Leslie Donovan has stated, unlike the Valkyrie whom she resembles, Éowyn is not punished by meeting a dreadful end. Instead, like the other women in the novel, she is allowed "the possibility of human and heroic completion" (109). Tolkien thus validates Éowyn's unconventional role by rewarding her with happiness and fulfillment, not as a man, but as a woman. She is not a male in disguise; she is a powerful woman who retains her womanly characteristics, all the while demonstrating that she can gain public honor in ways normally allowed only to men. In his portrait of this unconventional woman who is both warrior and tender lover, power and femininity do not prove to be a toxic mixture, producing an unnatural being or an abomination. Even at the height of the battle, she remains human and womanly: "slender but as a steel-blade, fair yet terrible" (*LotR* V.6.842). In Éowyn, the mask does not indicate self-alienation or a sense of a usurped identity. Instead, the mask *is* the woman. Éowyn is a hero.

Galadriel: Masked Power

Critics have frequently overlooked the powerful role played by Galadriel in *The Lord of the Rings*.[13] This is probably not surprising, since, like Olivia, Galadriel wears a conventional mask which deflects the reader's attention and conceals the extent of her power and influence in the novel. At first glance, Galadriel seems to be an expected heroine of romance. She appears to be confined to a garden-like realm, Lothlórien or Blossom of Lórien, where time stands still and where evil is kept at bay. She therefore seems to live in an edenic or fairy-tale world which has little connection with the "real" world of Middle-earth. She does not leave Lothlórien. Like a medieval lady, she presides over a court with Lord Celeborn. She grants gifts to the members of the fellowship, to-

---

13. For Fredrick and McBride, "Galadriel is a female of great power and importance, yet that power has little relevance to [*The Lord of the Rings*]" (112).

kens similar to those granted in medieval traditions, and she has admirers who worship her from afar for her beauty. Even Gimli the dwarf, like the hero of romance, is prepared to fight anyone who disputes his claim that she is the most beautiful of women.

This mask of traditional attributes is not assumed by Galadriel herself. Unlike Olivia, Galadriel has no need to dissemble to assert her authority and to exercise power. On the contrary, Tolkien expresses her powers implicitly to make them more acceptable to members of his audience, many of whom still subscribe to more conservative views of women. Behind the mask, however, Galadriel is a woman of unusual power and authority. Unlike women who are confined to the domestic sphere and the garden, Galadriel is not imprisoned in the confines of her garden. On the contrary, she has created this world. As we later discover, she has been entrusted with Nenya, one of the three Elven Rings of Power, which allows her to protect Lothlórien from the spreading evil of the Dark Lord. When members of the fellowship first arrive in Lothlórien, they feel her strong presence. The Elves inform them, "You feel the power of the Lady" (II.6.351). She is no objectified image without identity or subjectivity. Her subjectivity is so powerful as to be felt throughout her realm.

Her garden is not just a limited territory. It extends over many miles and has an Elven city at its center. She runs the defenses of the realm, keeping in direct contact with the guards who meet the Fellowship and destroy the Orcs who have been following them. She protects the realm not just with her powers, but with her wise provisions for secrecy. No one who could betray its secrets may enter the realm unless they are blindfolded. Those who enter may not, under normal circumstances, leave. The realm thus is protected from the growing influence of the Dark Lord.

Her creative powers are reflected as well in the great beauty of her realm. When Frodo first sees the city of Cerin Amroth, which lies at the heart of Lothlórien, he is struck by its unearthly beauty: "It seemed to him that he had stepped through a high window that looked onto a vanished world. A light was upon it for which his language had no name" (II.6.350). Galadriel even has the ability to keep illness and other human imperfections and evils at bay.

In addition to playing the role of creator and protector of the realm—traditionally male roles—she is also shown to possess further powers. She possesses a mirror which can show possible futures; she can read the minds of the members of the fellowship and understand their thoughts without words. They feel, when she looks upon them, as if she had questioned each one of them deeply. Such powers are frequently associated with witchcraft and sorcery. Recognizing the potential prejudice of readers who might deem Galadriel to be a witch and therefore to be evil and perverse, Tolkien preempts such judgments by putting them in the mouths of those who, like Wormtongue, have an evil agenda and whose assessment is not to be trusted. Furthermore, all those in the novel who are good, sympathetic characters see her in a positive light, validating her role as a powerful woman without demonic attributes.

Galadriel's power extends far beyond the realm over which she reigns. As Leslie Donovan has indicated, her gifts are similar to those of the Valkyrie (112–18), gifts with special powers such as the bow and arrow with which Legolas shoots the Ringwraith in the dark, the phial of light which has the power to keep darkness and evil at bay, the elven rope which unties itself, the elven cloaks that conceal members of the Fellowship from their enemies, and the waybread that sustains Frodo and Sam throughout their journey to Mordor. Her presence is so powerful that Gandalf invokes her in song when he exorcises the demonic thralldom of Saruman's minion, Wormtongue, from King Théoden. Galadriel demonstrates political acumen and insight. She calls the first White Council. She advises them to take Gandalf as their leader, advice which proves to be valid in the long term. She even summons the Dúnedain to Aragorn's aid at Helm's Deep. From the time the Fellowship visits her in Lothlórien, her presence and power permeate the novel.

Galadriel's mask of conventionality thus allows Tolkien to validate a powerful and positive woman and to contradict prejudices that would cause women with such powers to be condemned as witches. Indeed, it is significant that while the writings of C. S. Lewis, Tolkien's more conservative friend, feature numerous female witches, Tolkien himself has no female witches whatsoever in his writings. The only witch in Tolkien is male: the Witch-king. In this novel, even the traditional witch figures have been reversed and re-gendered as male.

Conclusion

As Doris Earnshaw notes in her discussion of medieval romance lyric, "the female voice within the overwhelmingly male-dominated literary tradition in written form, can function as a carrier of undercurrents of social values not generally permitted or approved" (13). Shakespeare and Tolkien use similar strategies to disrupt traditional gender paradigms. The fictive carnival worlds in *Twelfth Night* and *The Lord of the Rings* are not merely used as venting mechanisms which reinforce the status quo after a brief time-out. Instead, these fictional spaces reflect back critically on the normative world of mainstream society. Within these worlds, both Shakespeare and Tolkien reverse expected roles both of men and of women. Both writers depict female characters—Viola and Éowyn—who disguise themselves as men either to escape a position of vulnerability and to enjoy the freedom of movement granted only to men (Viola), or to assume a powerful role otherwise denied to women (Éowyn). At the same time, both writers portray women—Olivia and Galadriel—who appear to be confined to women's traditional spaces, but who, in reality, are not. The fact that their transgressive behavior is concealed allows them greater power and flexibility than would overt masquerade. The woman cloaked in conventionality blends in; her mask is invisible, so that she expands gender roles even while her unconventionality remains hidden in plain view.

This article was published originally in Tolkien and Shakespeare: Essays on Shared Themes and Language, *edited by Janet Brennan Croft, Critical Explorations in Science Fiction and Fantasy 2 (Jefferson, NC: McFarland, 2007). It is reprinted here with the permission of McFarland Publishing.*

Works Cited

Aughterson, Kate, ed. *Renaissance Woman: A Sourcebook*. New York: Routledge, 1995. Print.

Bakhtin, Mikhail M. *Problems of Dostoevsky's Poetics*. Ed. and trans. Caryl Emerson. Minneapolis: U of Minnesota P, 1984. Print.

---. *Rabelais and His World*. Trans. Helene Iswolsky. Bloomington, IN: Indiana UP, 1984. Print.

Barber, C. L. *Shakespeare's Festive Comedy: A Study of Dramatic Form and its Relation to Social Custom*. Princeton: Princeton UP, 1972. Print.

de Beauvoir, Simone. *The Second Sex*. Trans. and ed. H. M. Parshley. New York: Knopf, 1953. Print.

---. "Tolkien's Women (and Men): The Films and the Book." Croft 175–93.

Brink, Jean, Allison Coudert, and Maryanne Horowitz, eds. *The Politics of Gender in Early Modern Europe*. Kirksville, MO: Sixteenth Century Journal Publishers, 1989. Print.

Coudert, Allison. "The Myth of the Improved Status of Protestant Women: The Case of the Witchcraze." Brink et al. 61–89.

Crane, Susan. *Gender and Romance in Chaucer's* Canterbury Tales. Princeton: Princeton UP, 1994. Print.

Croft, Janet Brennan, ed. *Tolkien on Film: Essays on Peter Jackson's* The Lord of the Rings. Altadena, CA: The Mythopoeic Press, 2004. Print.

Dash, Irene G. *Wooing, Wedding, and Power: Women in Shakespeare's Plays*. New York: Columbia UP, 1981. Print.

Davis, Natalie Zemon. *Society and Culture in Early Modern France: Eight Essays*. Stanford: Stanford UP, 1975. Print.

Donovan, Leslie A. "The Valkyrie Reflex in J. R. R. Tolkien's *The Lord of the Rings*: Galadriel, Shelob, Éowyn, and Arwen." *Tolkien the Medievalist*. Ed. Jane Chance. New York: Routledge, 2003. 106–32. Print. *Reprinted in this volume.*

Dunn, Catherine. "The Changing Image of Woman in Renaissance Society and Literature." *What Manner of Woman: Essays on English and American Life and Literature*. Ed. Marlene Springer. New York: New York UP, 1977. 15–38. Print.

Earnshaw, Doris. *The Female Voice in Medieval Romance Lyric*. New York: Lang, 1988. Print.

Fredrick, Candice, and Sam McBride. *Women Among the Inklings: Gender, C. S. Lewis, J. R. R. Tolkien, and Charles Williams*. Contributions in Women's Studies, vol. 191. Westport, CT: Greenwood Press, 2001. Print.

Freedman, Barbara. *Staging the Gaze: Postmodernism, Psychoanalysis, and Shakespearean Comedy*. Ithaca, NY: Cornell UP, 1991. Print.

Friedan, Betty. *The Feminine Mystique*. 1963. New York: Dell, 1983. Print.

Greenblatt, Stephen. *Shakespearean Negotiations: The Circulation of Social Energy in Renaissance England*. Oxford: Clarendon, 1988. Print.

Hassel, Chris. *Faith and Folly in Shakespeare's Romantic Comedies*. Athens, GA: U of Georgia P, 1980. Print.

Knox, John. *First Blast of the Trumpet against the Monstrous Regiment of Women*. 1558. Aughterson 138–39.

Levin, Carole. *"The Heart and Stomach of a King": Elizabeth I and the Politics of Sex and Power*. Philadelphia: U of Penn P, 1994. Print.

---. "Power, Politics, and Sexuality: Images of Elizabeth I." Brink et al. 95–110.

Levin, Carole, and Karen Robertson, eds. *Sexuality and Politics in Renaissance Drama*. Lewiston, NY: Mellen, 1991. Print.

---, and Patricia Sullivan, eds. *Political Rhetoric, Power, and Renaissance Women*. New York: SUNY P, 1995. Print.

---. "Politics, Women's Voices, and the Renaissance: Questions and Context." Levin and Sullivan, *Political* 1–14.

Neely, Carol. "Constructing Female Sexuality in the Renaissance: Stratford, London, Windsor, Vienna." Levin and Robertson, *Sexuality* 1–26.

Ortner, Sherry. "Is Female to Male as Nature is to Culture?" Rosaldo and Lamphere 67–88.

Partridge, Brenda. "No Sex Please–We're Hobbits: The Construction of Female Sexuality in *The Lord of the Rings*." *J. R. R. Tolkien: This Far Land*. Ed. Robert Giddings. London: Barnes, 1983. 179–97. Print.

Purkiss, Diane. *The Witch in History: Early Modern and Twentieth-Century Representations*. New York: Routledge, 1996. Print.

Rawls, Melanie. "The Feminine Principle in Tolkien." *Mythlore* 10.4 (#38) (Spring 1984): 5–13. Print. *Reprinted in this volume.*

Rosaldo, Michelle, and Louise Lamphere, eds. *Woman, Culture, and Society*. Stanford, CA: Stanford UP, 1974. Print.

Shakespeare, William. *The Complete Works of William Shakespeare*. Ed. David Bevington. New York: Pearson, 2004. Print.

Stimpson, Catherine R. *J. R. R. Tolkien*. Columbia Essays on Modern Writers, vol. 41. New York: Columbia UP, 1969. Print.

Sullivan, Patricia, and Carole Levin. "Women and Political Communication: From the Margins to the Center." Levin and Sullivan, *Political* 275–82.

Thum, Maureen. "The Sub-Subcreation of Galdriel, Arwen, and Éowyn: Women of Power in Tolkien's and Jackson's *The Lord of the Rings*." Croft 231–58.

Vives, Juan Luis. *The Instruction of a Christian Woman*. 1523. Aughterson 69–74.

Warren, Roger, and Stanley Wells. Introduction. *The Tempest*. William Shakespeare. Oxford: Clarendon, 1994. Print.

Whatley, William. *A Bride Bush*. 1617. Aughterson 31–35.

Wiesner, Merry. "Women's Defense of their Public Role." *Women in the Middle Ages and the Renaissance: Literary and Historical Perspectives*. Ed. Mary Beth Rose. Syracuse: Syracuse UP, 1986. 1–28. Print.

Williams, John. "A Sermon of Apparell." 1619. Aughterson 77–79.

Woolf, Virginia. *A Room of One's Own*. 1929. New York: Harcourt, 1957. Print.

Women Readers

Finding Ourselves in the (Un)Mapped Lands:
Women's Reparative Readings of *The Lord of the Rings*

Una McCormack

It came as a point of interest to me—if not exactly a surprise—to learn, at a recent conference on Tolkien, that there are more named horses than named women in *The Lord of the Rings*. As a woman reader and writer, I often find myself in the position of explaining that I love Tolkien *despite*... Despite the absence of women, despite the late Victorian/Edwardian aspects of the ones that are there, despite the uneasy racialization of Orcs and Númenóreans, despite the hierarchical social structures—despite all of this, I continue to love *The Lord of the Rings*, returning to it yearly (at least) to derive comfort and pleasure from it and from the friends I have made not only through multiple rereads, but through the reading, sharing, and discussion of fanfiction based upon Tolkien's books. And this occurs *despite* the comparative absence of women—of people like me—in those books.

Does it matter if a reader is in some way absent from a loved text? Junot Díaz, in his Pulitzer Prize-winning novel *The Brief Wondrous Life of Oscar Wao*, presents the life of a Dominican-American boy, Oscar, a geeky child who loves Tolkien and continues to love his books beyond adolescence, but who, by virtue of his ethnicity, will always be excluded in a fundamental way from this most beloved of books. As Oscar's life nears its close, he returns to Tolkien:

> He read *The Lord of the Rings* for what I'm estimating the millionth time, one of his greatest loves and greatest comforts since he'd first discovered it, back when he was nine and lost and lonely and his favorite librarian had said, Here, try this, and with one suggestion changed his life. Got through almost the whole trilogy, but then the line "and out of Far Harad black men like half-trolls" and he had to stop, his head and heart hurting too much. (307)

Here, Díaz conveys how a reader's absence from a loved text—or, more precisely, presence in ambivalent terms—makes love for that text difficult and even painful, even as the reader continues to derive comfort from reading. Such ambivalent relationships come at some cost. Deepa D., in an essay on non-Western responses to the Western hegemony of fantasy fiction, indicates how absent readers have to conduct extra labor in order to find themselves in fantastic texts and gain the cultural capital to participate in the communities that surround them. She writes, "Dragons are not universal. If I am defensive, it is because I have had to learn how to love Tolkien while trying to find myself in the unmapped lands in the East where the Green and Blue wizards disappeared to."

The complexity of such reading and writing practices and the ambivalence of the creative labor involved in making repairs upon such texts have driven some women readers to find a presence for themselves in *The Lord of the Rings* through writing fanfiction as a creative-critical response to Tolkien's text. By weaving female characters into the familiar narrative, or else focusing upon marginalized characters such as nurses, servants, and non-combatants, these authors write themselves—or those like themselves—into the events of the War of the Ring. In so doing, they perform acts of transformation, reparation, and radicalization on *The Lord of the Rings*, establishing female presences, queer presences, and urban working class presences in a text chiefly concerned with the masculine and the heroic.

While the problem of Tolkien's missing women is endemic and has inspired much more writing than I can possibly discuss here, a set of texts written by a group of women writers working more or less in proximity across a period of 10–12 years after the 2001 release of Peter Jackson's film of *The Fellowship of the Ring* provides a useful sample for examining women's responses to Tolkien's work. Most of these writers met initially via the *Henneth Annûn* mailing list and its associated fanfiction archive.[1] Writing and discussion was later supported through other social media outlets (such as LiveJournal) and online communities (such as the Silmarillion Writers' Guild[2] and its annual fiction festival). Although these mailing lists, forums, and communities archive a range of fanfiction responding to the whole of Tolkien's legend-

1. This online community is accessed at www.henneth-annun.net.
2. See www.silmarillionwritersguild.org.

arium, the stories selected for the present study focus almost entirely on Gondor, Minas Tirith, and the Houses of Healing.[3]

I take as given that fanfiction is a valid creative activity, which encompasses a wide variety of styles, employs varying techniques, and is written for numerous purposes. I specifically want to avoid popular mainstream accounts of fanfiction (as pornography for women; as "training wheels" for "immature" young female writers) and the celebratory tone of early scholarship on fanfiction, which emphasizes it as a mode of resistant reading. Fanfiction can be one or all of these things at once; it can be a legitimate creative response that involves complex critiques of a source text, while simultaneously diverting the creativity of its writers into a genre from which they are unable to earn much social capital or financial remuneration.[4] I have, in the main, chosen works I consider successful as fiction in their own right. However, it is sufficient for my purposes simply to argue nothing more than that fanfiction exists, that it is written predominantly by women, and that examining fanfiction based upon *The Lord of the Rings* allows some insight into different ways in which these women writers negotiate and repair representational gaps in Tolkien's work.[5]

Missing Women: Reinscribing "Her-story"

The simplest strategy available to a writer attempting to make up for the lack of women in *The Lord of the Rings* is to create female characters and write stories about them. Since there is no textual evidence *against* the existence of these women—and since women are so often

---

3. These fanfiction texts were chosen for this study not least because this is where my own fanfiction practice has occurred, under the pen-name "Altariel."

4. Amazon's venture Kindle Worlds provides the first licensed online space where authors can upload and sell fanfiction. The experiment may well provide an interesting avenue for licensed publication of fanfiction, depending on the franchises licensed. (Problems with Kindle Worlds should also be noted: for example, Amazon holds the rights to Original Characters created by the fanfic author and published by them, which is worrying).

5. See Abrahamson for a general defense of fanfiction as a creative-critical response to the works of Tolkien. As well as providing a theoretical grounding for fanfiction in general, Abrahamson convincingly asserts the legitimacy of fanfiction based on Tolkien's works and draws out affinities with Tolkien's own creative practice. Abrahamson also notes the general tendency to analyze fanfiction in terms of sociology and popular culture rather than as literature worth studying in its own right (64); I hope this essay to some degree achieves the latter.

erased from history or placed in the margins—the fanfiction writer is arguably reinscribing a history that has somehow been lost in translation or transmission. Firerose, in the notes to her story "Missing," addresses the absence of women in *The Lord of the Rings*, explains its thematic centrality to her story, and provides good reason for assuming their existence:

> Though no daughter of the Steward's family is ever mentioned, the sex ratio of the Númenorean and Gondor nobles mentioned in the Appendices simply *would not support species survival*. The marginalisation of women in *The Lord of the Rings* and in Gondor society is a theme of the story, and the circumstances of Lóriniel's life and death would tend to contribute to the silence about her. (Emphasis added.)

The lack of women in the original text is therefore a flaw in world-building: a gap and an implausibility that the writer can exploit to her own advantage. "Missing" posits a younger sister for Boromir and Faramir, Lóriniel, who is dead before the end of the War of the Ring, whose life is glimpsed by Faramir only from the corner of his eye, and whose tragedy he assembles piecemeal through clues and hints: pages torn from journals, memories of an angry encounter between his brother and his father, a wisp of cloth on a brooch. Denethor, driven by grief over the loss of his wife, Finduilas, and to madness by the *palantír*, has turned to Lóriniel for sexual comfort, eliding wife and daughter. This uneasy and troubling story, with hints of the Gothic in the doubling of the two women of the family and the pale ghostly figure of Lóriniel who haunts its margins, lifts the veil that can be thrown over the lives even of high-born women. As the narrator, Faramir, notes: "Indeed, beyond the bare facts of birth and death, in truth, I knew scarce more about my sister than our mother." Beneath this veil, within the domestic sphere, lie tragedy and exploitation unimagined by the men whose own troubles provide the subject matter of the source text.

My own story, "Lady of Silences," similarly suggests if not a conspiracy of silence where the absent women are concerned, then an unwillingness to speak the truth about how their lives might have been. Finduilas, wife of Denethor, mother of Boromir and Faramir, and the story's first-person narrator, is shown shortly before her death. Here, the strategy is not to create a female character from nothing, but to take the passing mentions of her from the main text of the book and the Appendices to conjecture what life she might have led. We know from the book only that she "died untimely" (*LotR* VI.5.961) and from the Appendices that "she withered in the guarded city, as a flower of the seaward vales set upon a barren rock" (A.I.iv.1056). The focus of "Lady of Silences" is, again, domestic; Finduilas is seen with her younger son while the elder spends the day with his father. Denethor, when he appears, has a silencing effect upon his wife and younger son, who stop singing in his presence. These silences are the mechanism by which this dysfunctional nuclear family is able to operate. When Boromir, upset to have hurt his mother by grasping her clumsily by the arm, confronts her with the physical violence to which her husband subjects her (and, crucially, blames Finduilas for it), the fragile balance of the family is disrupted beyond repair. Finduilas takes a sleeping draught, and a question mark remains over the nature of her death: Is it suicide, as Denethor commits suicide in time? Is the suicide intentional, or is it an accident? The story (and certainly not the Appendices) can offer no definitive account.

A more joyous expansion of a named, but little developed, character can be found in Dwimordene's "Speaking of Love." The story concerns Ioreth, the garrulous wise woman from the Houses of Healing, and is told from the point of view of an unnamed female narrator who is Ioreth's lover. This short reflective piece, set on the day of Aragorn's coronation, describes their long relationship, begun when both women were young, and how they have lived quietly among the more "respectable" residents of Minas Tirith, who have failed to understand the nature of the lives being lived in plain sight:

> [W]e have lived comfortably now for many years. Right under the noses of all the respectable citizens of the city, and indeed, should they discover what exists before them, she shall truly be the death of me. And I of her. But men are blind, happily, and they know "our" tale [...] A great pity, folk said gravely in those days, that two lovely young women should know such things, and how brave we were, to come so far and to begin again with only each other. Endearing, they called our devoted attachment to each other. They still call it endearing—touching, a fine example of womanly love. Oh aye, "touching" and "womanly" ... they know not the half of it. (Dwimordene)

Again, voice is used as the chief symbol for women's absence from the written text of *The Lord of the Rings* and here becomes the means by which their presence is inscribed. Ioreth's talk is transformed in the story from the diffuse chatter that strains Aragorn's patience in *The Return of the King* into something more radical: an account of a life lived fully alongside the events of the War of the Ring and among everyday "respectable" citizens and heroes alike. Leveraging the space offered by the source text (Ioreth provides a running commentary during the coronation scene into which this story is placed), the history of Ioreth and her lover weaves into the fiber of the grand narrative of the book:

> And of course, I admired my Ioreth—admired her, that in the midst of her joy, *she could weave our "story" seamlessly into her profusion of words*. "Oh, Cousin, and you must remember—or did I tell you? Never mind, 'tis not important. You were going to tell me how it was at home, in Imloth Melui, whether it was terrible or how was it? But the Halfling, my dear, the one who went to Mordor? Yes, he is related to the one who marched with the host, and also to the one who remained. Merry, his name is, and he does merit it and—oh, no, no, Merry is Meriadoc, in truth, and he was the King of Rohan's esquire. Not the one who went to Mordor, no. But did I tell you...?" And so on, *putting the elements of our "lives" into her speech while the day lasted*, while I clung to her arm, and squeezed her hand and stayed fast at her side, shy thing that I am known to be. And where others could not see, she squeezed back, and we knew that all was right, as it had not been since we were parted. (Dwimordene; emphasis added)

"Speaking of Love" addresses a triple absence from history that occurs through the intersection of sexuality, gender, and class. Ioreth and her lover are working class women, servants. If women appear in written history, they are likely, the story suggests, to have a quite different social status:

> I have never been one for lofty aspirations [...] 'Tis enough for me to rebuild my life, which is also Ioreth's; not for me to save my people with my very body, for I am not the White Lady of Rohan. One so golden as she should indeed give birth to many things, *epics not the least*. (Dwimordene; emphasis added)

In contrast, Alawa's story "Keepers of the Hearth" addresses, celebrates, and even sanctifies the role of homemaker. The point-of-view character, Winfrith, has served the King of Rohan, Théoden, as housekeeper since the death of his queen, Elfhild, in childbirth. The story follows Winfrith (*Mrs Dalloway* style) across a 24-hour period during which the wedding of the new king, Éomer, to Lothíriel of Dol

Amroth restores a Queen to the Golden Hall.[6] Throughout the course of the day, while involved in last minute preparations for the wedding feast, Winfrith recalls her long years of service to the royal family: first as wet-nurse to the king's heir, Théodred, then as nanny to him and his cousins, Éomer and Éowyn, and later as housekeeper during the king's widowerhood and decline. Domesticity—the lives, cares, and unceasing responsibilities of women—are placed at the heart of the polity, not as marginal, but as central:

> Near as long as the Riddermark had lived the Golden Hall had beat at the heart of it. Joy it had seen in its time—and sorrow. Births, hand-fastings, funeral feasts, one ever followed the other in endless round, and Winfrith had seen her share of them all. (Alawa)

The necessity of women's stories, and their power, is asserted. Winfrith teaches her charges that warriors, and war, are without purpose if the women and the home are destroyed, invoking a rare woman mentioned in the source text:

> On a foolish impulse she opened her door and lit the children's night-light from the torch burning in the hall. Chuckling wryly at herself she placed it where it cast a little warmth around the room. Then reaching to a shelf, set a bit apart, she took down the figure she still held most dear; Hild, Helm's sister, safely hiding in Dunharrow with her son, that the Hall could be cleansed and a new line of kings begun. *For hope remains while women endure,* so she always told the tale, for it was right young warriors remembered what they were to be shielding from harm. (Alawa)

The story culminates not in the wedding, but in a short and beautiful ceremony at the evening feast in which Winfrith hands over her keys, and her charge, to Lothíriel, and, together, the two women ask for the blessing of Varda. Kingdoms may enjoy the return of their kings, but, as this piece suggests, restoration is not complete without a fully powerful queen. Unlike Tolkien's book, where Arwen's wedding, to some extent, represents a transaction between Elrond and Aragorn,

---

6. Lothíriel is a popular choice for fanfiction writers seeking to expand upon the brief mentions of female characters in the text. She appears in Firerose's "Missing" as a breath of fresh air, with the vibrancy and wit of a heroine from a Georgette Heyer novel. She is greatly developed in Isabeau of Greenlea's novel *Captain My Captain* as part of a richly characterized expansion of the royal family of Dol Amroth.

this is a celebration of women's power focused entirely upon an exchange between women:

> Quickly [Winfrith] lit the brand from the brazier by the door and walked towards the hearth. The two women exchanged smiles as Winfrith grasped her hand and together they held the torch above the well-primed tinder; gnarled, blue veined fingers on slender ones, strong and white. Winfrith heard her take a steadying breath then both their voices were firm as together they said the words that had come down to them, the same words Winfrith had last spoken with Léofric's mother all those many years ago:
>
> *Keeper of the Hearth   kindle us*
> *Gather us up   under your mantle*
> *And restore to us   remembering.*
> *Mothers of our mother   remind us how*
> *Foremothers strong   show us the way*
> *To kindle the hearth   keep it bright*
> *Preserve the flame's   flicker in darkness.*
> *Your hands upon ours   our hands within yours*
> *Day and night   now keep light kindled.* (Alawa)

Taken together, these stories offer a corrective to the heroic grand narrative of *The Lord of the Rings*, suggesting that different forms of history happen alongside what the annals tell us, and that these histories have their own worth. They see different possibilities in narrative from those Tolkien saw in the Fourth Age. In a late letter from 1972, he writes: "I of course discovered that the King's Peace would contain no tales worth recounting; and his wars would have little interest after the overthrow of Sauron" (*Letters* 419). These fanfiction stories demonstrate how history in its traditional narrative forms will always pass over the lives and accomplishments of women as unworthy of note. The Record of Days written in his father's hand, over which Faramir pores in "Missing," cannot tell him the stories of his mother and his sister. Voices such as these are transitory, easily lost, but these stories attempt to capture something of the nature of the lives that must have been lived—the mothers, the sisters, the daughters, the lovers, the healers, the housekeepers—so that the lives of men may appear on the written page as history. They suggest, furthermore, that the story of the Fourth Age, of the King's Peace, need not be one of wars and policies, but instead one of progress, healing, and repair.

Exceptional Women: Reconfiguring the Text

If the quiet, undocumented lives of women form the subject matter of the stories discussed previously, other texts focus upon female characters distinguished by their exceptionality. Three novel-length texts featuring a female protagonist who—as soldier, healer, or adventurer—sets herself apart from the "ordinary" exemplify this fanfiction approach. In contrast to the quieter lives detailed (usually in vignette or short story form) in the previous section, these "exceptional" characters have a different and more demanding relationship to the source text. Rather than finding a space for themselves in the margins, these characters demand that the text and its story-world reconfigure around their presence.

Isabeau of Greenlea's *Captain My Captain* is told from the point of view of Hethlin, the only woman to serve with the Ithilien Rangers during the War of the Ring and after, when she is the first woman to enter the service of Imrahil, Prince of Dol Amroth, as a Swan-Knight. This long (over 300,000 words) episodic novel is arguably picaresque: Hethlin invariably finds herself embroiled in (or at least witnessing) many of the main events that take place in and around Minas Tirith during *The Lord of the Rings*. Told with great humor and a sharp eye for opportunities offered by a non-canon character editorializing on events, Isabeau of Greenlea's characterization humanizes the source text: the noble men and elves whom Hethlin encounters become more grounded in the everyday.

The novel is split into two distinct parts. The first sixteen chapters closely follow and retell events of *The Lord of the Rings* from the point of view of the Rangers during the siege of Minas Tirith up to the coronation of Aragorn and the installation of Faramir as Prince of Ithilien. Throughout this part of the novel, Hethlin is, in effect, a "grunt": a minor player in a much larger war, whose proximity to Faramir is the means by which she gains access to the main players and events of the book. Her love for Faramir goes unrequited, particularly with the arrival on the scene of Éowyn, a more suitable partner for a nobleman of Gondor.

After Faramir's elevation to princedom and throughout the rest of the novel (more than thirty chapters), Hethlin's status undergoes a steady transformation. She learns of her aristocratic connections to the northern Dúnedain, and is sent by Aragorn to serve Imrahil of Dol

Amroth as one of his elite Swan-Knights. A romance with Elrohir, son of Elrond, and the revelation of Hethlin's own noble birth complicate the relationship with Faramir. The narrative of these remaining chapters focuses on Hethlin's journey to Rohan with Théoden's honor guard, and then to Lothlórien to meet Arwen and form part of her guard on her journey south to her wedding. Imrahil emerges as another potential suitor, and multiple opportunities open up for Hethlin. These provide the narrative drive for the second part of the novel: will she travel south to Dol Amroth to be a great warrior, travel north to adventure with her long-lost family, or marry a prince?

From this point onward, Isabeau of Greenlea's novel moves away from close adherence to the source text and exploits gaps in *The Lord of the Rings* to create a lively, funny, and very human account of the early days of King Elessar's reign. Hethlin, to some extent, operates much as hobbits do in the source—offering an ordinary person's perspective on the doings of the noble and the wise. She has one foot in the Citadel of Minas Tirith and another in the lower circles of the city; the last few chapters involve two weddings, one of her former captain, Mablung, and the other of Aragorn and Arwen. A quarrel with Faramir (over Éowyn's desertion of her post in Dunharrow) moves Hethlin from lovelorn dependant to young noblewoman in the making.

The second part of *Captain My Captain* therefore explores the theme of the opportunities available to a young woman in a patriarchal (if changing) society. As the story progresses, Hethlin increasingly insists upon her right to self-determination, even as her elevation to the nobility closes off many of the freedoms she has enjoyed as a member of the ranks. Echoing what Éowyn has to say in the source text, Hethlin argues with kings, princes, and stewards that she is not there to be disposed of according to the whims of the men around her. The narrative's playful insertion of this character into the context of *The Lord of the Rings* in fact serves a serious purpose: asserting the right of a woman to decide her future, whatever the men around her may think is in her best interests.[7]

---

7. Hethlin chooses to follow her career, heading to Dol Amroth to train as an elite soldier. Another story by Isabeau of Greenlea, "Doggerel," explores Hethlin's struggle to be accepted by her all-male comrades (a story, in effect, about sexual harassment in the workplace). Other works give accounts of Hethlin's arrival among

Fallen, by Aliana, also asserts the right of its female protagonist to decide her future, and insists upon a broad conception of what constitutes history and who constitutes an historical actor. (Indeed, the novel opens with a quotation from Alan Bennett's play *The History Boys*: "What is history?" asks the single female character in the play, before answering her own question: "History is women following behind with the bucket.") The novel is told from the first-person perspective of an unnamed "Narrator," a young nurse in the Houses of Healing during the War of the Ring.[8] It documents the harrowing events of the siege of Gondor and the Battle of the Pelennor Fields, emphasising the traumatic effects of war upon a whole generation and intentionally evoking the "greatest generation" that fought the Second World War. The novel asserts that the cumulative experience of a society is what constitutes history, and that no story is too small to be significant:

> Keep stepping back, now, back beyond living memory [...] when a song of malice was spun in time with a bit of gold, and our history was born. [...] When everything seemed to coalesce here, and all the forgotten people who stood on the outside of the great deeds and tales could only shudder at the sweep of events that came to gather them up. When that story began, all of our tales became small and melted in the face of it, and *all our tales became one.* (Aliana; emphasis added)

History is great deeds, yes; it is also women, following behind with a bucket. If either of these is small, all are small; if either is exceptional, all are exceptional.

A key theme of the novel is that the trauma of war is not the sole province of young men on the battlefield. A society that has prioritized violence and warfare, even out of necessity, is a traumatized society; nobody is immune from the effects. Narrator's rape at the hands of a troubled veteran is not, as is so often the case, used narratively as a means to provide characterization for male characters (e.g., an opportunity for an incensed father or lover to pursue his woman's assailant), but is directly compared to the trauma being suffered by the

---

(note continued)

and initiation into the Ithilien Rangers and her childhood; see "Blackbow" and "Cage No Bird," respectively.

8. "Narrator" is how Aliana refers to her character in discussion, so I follow that convention here.

men who are at war. As Gondor falls, the author suggests, the burden is shared equally by men and women (and children, and across classes): the effects of war are felt not solely on the field, but send shockwaves through the whole of society.

Near the end, Narrator, along with the rest of the city, begins her own healing; able at last to "confess" the fact of her rape to her suitor, Beren, she learns that he does not perceive her as a "fallen" woman, as she had feared, and that he wishes to continue their courtship. This catharsis enables her to embark on the next necessary step toward full healing; she insists that her practical experience during the siege and beyond be given full recognition, and that she be able to study to become a surgeon—a post previously open only to boys and men.

Aliana brilliantly draws upon the source text here: the ban on women surgeons arises from the same period in which the Steward Pelendur rejects the claim of Arvedui to the throne of Gondor via his marriage to Fíriel, the only surviving child of the dead king, Ondoher. Pelendur's refusal of Arvedui's claim is a rejection of the Númenórean law of succession that allows for a ruling queen. The ban on women surgeons is a ban on armed women: that is, on the risk of a queen when a warrior-king is required. The course of the War of the Ring—or, more precisely, the War of the Ring as documented in *Fallen*—demonstrates the meaninglessness of this ban. Its removal—and Narrator's ability to train as a surgeon—is endorsed as a progressive move, part of the wider restoration Gondor will undergo in the Fourth Age, as it transitions from war-state to peaceful polity. Narrator's insistence that she be accorded the same respect and formal position as the men around her expands and transforms ideas latent in the source text to a fully thought-through stance on what a healing and healthy society should be.[9]

Amid the Powers and Chances of the World by Azalais is another long novel (183,000 words) that exploits its readers' high degree of familiar-

---

9. *Fallen* allies itself with other progressive agendas: one subplot concerns a senior surgeon who is "struck off" after mercy-killing a dying soldier. The case is pursued by an administrator who argues it is a corruption of the healing mandate of the Houses. Not coincidentally, the two men had an affair in their youth; the administrator, now respectably married, fears this might become common knowledge. At the end of the War of the Ring, the administrator acknowledges his bias in the case, withdraws the charges, and the surgeon is reinstated.

ity with *The Lord of the Rings* for many of its effects. The story concerns a young woman, Rowanna, of Dúnedain descent but brought up in Rohan, who, following an attack on her outpost, sickens with the Black Breath and is taken, near-death, to Rivendell. Her party reaches its destination in advance of the Ring-bearer, during which time Rowanna is healed and establishes a friendship with Bilbo, the only other "Sickly One" among the elves. This friendship brings her into close contact with the other hobbits once they arrive (a narrative device allowing Rowanna close access to the events of the source text). After the Fellowship departs, Rowanna, aware that the situation outside Rivendell is becoming desperate, resolves to leave in order to be with her mother when war comes to Rohan. A substantial part of the novel weaves her journey south around that of the Fellowship—there is a chance meeting on the plains of Rohan shortly before Aragorn, Gimli, and Legolas meet Éomer and his party—and, having reached Rohan only to find that her mother has returned to her childhood home in Minas Tirith, Rowanna travels there in advance of the city's siege to help in the Houses of Healing throughout the rest of the war.

I have foregrounded Rowanna's travels and adventures here, since they provide her main motivation throughout. Yet, the story is also a romance. During her time in Rivendell, Rowanna meets Legolas; they strike up a friendship and, after the Fellowship departs, realize in each other's absence a mutual attraction. The romance is complicated after Legolas's experiences at Pelargir awaken the sea-longing in him. After the War of the Ring, as the full story of Aragorn and Arwen becomes apparent to them, the couple part, seeing no chance for happiness together. An intervention by Faramir finally brings them together in the newly established princedom of Ithilien.

The story is therefore both romance and adventure. Rowanna's exceptionality is repeatedly asserted: she is tomboyish, dark-haired among fair-haired Rohirrim, and earning her own living as a horse-breeder. In addition, her earthiness, practicality, excellent appetite, and courage in heading to the war in Gondor for the sake of her mother (and not to chase a lover) make her an unusually attractive and likeable character. A major theme of the novel concerns her insistence on being treated as fully adult—not as an incapable woman among capable men or a sickly mortal among immortal Elves—and her right to journey southward and refuse well-meaning attempts by relatives to marry her off. The romance does not end conventionally in marriage and a family; her move to Ithilien gives her independence as a horse-breeder (i.e., a woman who earns professional respect on her own terms), and she embarks upon a life with a lover who will not give her children, who may be pulled away at any moment, and with whom, according to the beliefs of both, there is no chance of reunion after death.

These three novels are driven by the insertion of a newly created, exceptional female character into the main narrative of *The Lord of the Rings*. Those familiar with terminology used within fanfiction communities might, at this point, be thinking of the "Mary Sue." For those unfamiliar, "Mary Sue" refers to an "original" (i.e., non-canonical) female character who often represents an idealized version of the author. Mary Sue has historically been (and continues to be) one of the most reviled figures in fanfiction; in many circles, distaste for her seems to arise from a sense that the author's desire for ownership of the text has overstepped reasonable or respectable bounds. Gentler complaints might suggest that an author's inexperience has led her to over-ambitiously impose herself upon the original.

Nevertheless, I would praise Mary Sue rather than bury her. More complex readings of the phenomenon point to her capacity to provide a specific point of insertion for readers who do not find themselves present in many mainstream texts. Willis, in a poignant 2006 discussion of the absence of queer adolescents in the *Harry Potter* books, discusses her intentional use of the Mary Sue in her *Harry Potter* fanfiction. She creates the character Hestia Jones as an adult model of queerness for queer children looking to find possible ways in which their lives can be lived. While I leave it to the authors concerned to accept or refuse the Mary Sue designation for their creations, in the case of the protagonists in the three novels discussed, I believe that they apply a corrective to *The Lord of the Rings* similar to what Willis describes. We have Hethlin, mixing with the great and good of Middle-earth, humanizing them and asserting her agency; Narrator, insisting upon her right to become the first woman surgeon in the Houses of Healing; and Rowanna, adventuring along the same path as the Fellowship and capturing the heart of one of its members. All three novels directly address the limitations others attempt to place upon their protagonists. Responding to a book in which many exceptional men exist (and exceptional elves, dwarves and hobbits), these three novels insist that there must have been exceptional women too, and that their exceptionality is all the more extraordinary given how the source and its world are stacked against them. The authors' fluency with Tolkien's original text, and the quality of the prose, demonstrates how these novels are carefully considered reconfigurations of a familiar, well-understood text. Showing deference and worrying about one's respectability has historically not served exceptional women well. Imposing themselves audaciously upon the source text, the heroines of these novels instead assert their right to be present on equal terms with Tolkien's heroes.

These are only a few examples of how women writers attempt to redress the under-representation of women in their creative-critical responses to *The Lord of the Rings*. How these writers use major characters from the original could form a lengthy discussion in itself; Éowyn, for example, is not written in fanfiction as an unequivocally heroic figure, but instead becomes a site for debate over whether the ultimate success of her actions vindicates her decision to desert the charge she was given to lead her people in Dunharrow.[10] Tolkien's male characters also provide the means whereby heroism and masculinity are scrutinized in fanfiction; my novel *A Game of Chess*, an account of the early days of Faramir and Éowyn's marriage, begins with the wedding (an intentional subversion of romantic fiction), and then traces the effects on the couple of Faramir's emerging post-traumatic stress disorder, which leaves him unable to function as a soldier, and of Éowyn's attempts not to be imprisoned by the realities of marriage and motherhood. The use of alternating first person throughout makes the focus domestic and psychological, with the intention of politicizing the private sphere of the family.

I have only scratched the surface of how fanfiction authors working within the milieu of Gondor reimagine characters. In addition, the vast body of work by fanfiction writers working within other milieus cannot possibly be addressed here. Sturgis, for example, points out

10. See the stories under the challenge "Éowyn: Heroine or Deserter?" at the *Henneth Annûn* website, which draw out the complexities of the responses to this character on the part of women readers. If Éowyn is intended as the focal point for the representation of female desire in *The Lord of the Rings*, she is by no means universally received in a positive fashion by a female audience. Isabeau of Greenlea and I also debate this question through many of our co-written stories.

how Hobbit women too are "noteworthy for their recurring absence" (165), and that the "mothers, sisters, and future wives [...] repeatedly appear as faceless names" (166). She further outlines how Rosie Cotton is brought to life and reimagined by female writers: as healer and helpmeet of both Sam and Frodo; as willing participant in a happy polyamorous relationship[11]; even as vampire or taker of the One Ring. This single character is recast in numerous fanfiction stories variously as "the paragon of the hearth, the iconoclast of the bedroom, or the agent of the supernatural" (Sturgis 183). The writers of these stories also take advantage of the textual space that is Rosie Cotton to rework the source for their own multiple purposes.

It seems a shame that stories such as those I have discussed are not more widely read, or are dismissed unread as amateurish. Popular attention has in general focused on male-authored responses to Tolkien such as Kirill Yeskov's *The Last Ringbearer* and Steve Hillard's *Mirkwood,* which attracted some notoriety when the Tolkien Estate attempted to halt publication. The former is a lively and entertaining spy thriller that radically and imaginatively plays with the source text to suggest Mordor was a nation shifting toward Enlightenment before being destroyed by a religious alliance of elves and wizards reminiscent of the Inquisition. Nevertheless, it finds less for its female characters to do than the original; Éowyn is reduced to a trophy girlfriend, and the single new female character, Alviss, is a clichéd "tart with a heart." As a result, the overall effect is considerably less radical than intended; through female readers' eyes, it is less an enlightened retelling and more business as usual. While Hillard's novel sets out to address the absence of women in the original text, it suffers from incoherence and a poor ear for language.

Why these texts receive attention when more accomplished ones do not, I cannot say. But this attention highlights the double bind in which women—and, perhaps, other marginalized readers—find themselves when reading texts from which they are absent or ambivalently

11. Cruisedirector, in her Fourth Age story *Seasons of Wonder,* similarly puts Aragorn, Arwen, Faramir, and Éowyn in a polyamorous relationship. In this story, which inspired several spin-offs, the four characters find healing through multiple expressions of love for each other, a provocative and joyful interpretation of the Fourth Age as sexual utopia.

present. Participation in mainstream or canonical culture can come at a cost; a reader must position herself with characters that are only loose approximations of herself, and she runs the risk (as Junot Díaz writes) of suddenly and rudely finding herself reminded that she has no real place in the text and that she has been granted only temporary permission to come along on the journey. To deliberately and consciously construct a space of one's own in the original text—as these fanfiction writers do—runs numerous risks: to go unread; to go dismissed; to have one's creative work categorized as derivative or adolescent. Working to place oneself in such texts comes with some considerable creative labor—labor that rarely translates into social or economic capital.

The modernist writer May Sinclair, in her classic 1919 account of the making of a female writer and artist, *Mary Olivier*, describes the struggle of her young heroine to articulate a position of agency from which she can narrate her experience:

> The nicest way of all, though, was not to be yourself, but to be him; to live his exciting, adventurous, dangerous life. Then you could raise an army and free Ireland from the English, and Armenia from the Turks. You could go away to beautiful golden cities, melting in sunshine. [...] You could find out all sorts of things.
>
> You were he, and at the same time you were yourself, going about with him. You loved him with a passionate, self-immolating love. There wasn't room for both of you on the raft, you sat cramped up, huddled together. Not enough hard tack. While he was sleeping, you slipped off. A shark got you. (227)

This is the condition of marginalized readers in relation to canonical and mainstream culture: to be there, but not there; to be always struggling to find one's own space on the raft, without going over and drowning; to live a double life within a beloved text. Fanfiction can provide one means of repair, but not without cost to the writer.

Works Cited

Abrahamson, Megan B. "J. R. R. Tolkien, Fanfiction, and 'The Freedom of the Reader.' " *Mythlore* 32.1 (#123) (Fall/Winter 2013): 53–72. Print.

Alawa. "Keepers of the Hearth." *Tolkien Fan Fiction*. Tolkien Fan Fiction, 31 July 2004. Web. 8 Oct. 2013.

Aliana. *Fallen*. *Tolkien Fan Fiction*. Tolkien Fan Fiction, 31 Mar. 2012. Web. 8 Oct. 2013.

Altariel [Una McCormack]. *A Game of Chess*. *Archive of Our Own*. The Organization for Transformative Works, 6 July 2011. Web. 8 Oct. 2013.

---. "Lady of Silences." *Archive of Our Own*. The Organization for Transformative Works, 16 Sept. 2011. Web. 8 Oct. 2013.

Azalais. *Amid the Powers and Chances of the World. Henneth Annûn*. henneth-annun.net, 24 Aug. 2011. Web. 8 Oct. 2013.

Cruisedirector. *Seasons of Wonder. Henneth Annûn*. henneth-annun.net, 11 Nov. 2003. Web. 30 Jan. 2014.

Deepa D. "I Didn't Dream of Dragons." *Kabhi Kabhi Mere Dil Mein, Yeh Khayal Aata Hai... Deepa D's blog*. Dreamwidth Studios, 13 Jan. 2009. Web. 8 Oct. 2013.

Díaz, Junot. *The Brief Wondrous Life of Oscar Wao*. London: Faber and Faber, 2008. Print.

Dwimordene. "Speaking of Love…" *Henneth Annûn*. henneth-annun.net, 27 Feb. 2003. Web. 8 Oct. 2013.

Firerose. "Missing." *Tolkien Fan Fiction*. Tolkien Fan Fiction, 14 Jan. 2005. Web. 8 Oct. 2013.

Hillard, Steve. *Mirkwood: A Novel about J. R. R Tolkien*. Austin, TX: Cruel Rune Publications, 2010. E-book.

Isabeau of Greenlea. "Blackbow." *FanFiction*. FanFiction.Net, 7 Oct. 2009. Web. 8 Oct. 2013.

---. "Cage No Bird." *homepage.ntlworld.com*. n.p., n.d. Web. 8 Oct. 2013.

---. *Captain My Captain. Fanfiction.Net*. 28 Nov. 2003. Web. 8 Oct. 2013.

---. "Doggerel." *FanFiction*. FanFiction.Net, 18 Aug. 2012. Web. 8 Oct. 2013.

Sinclair, May. *Mary Olivier: A Life*. 1919. London: Virago, 1980. Print.

Sturgis, Amy H. "Reimagining Rose: Portrayals of Tolkien's Rosie Cotton in Twenty-First Century Fan Fiction." *Mythlore* 24.3/4 (93/94) (Winter/Spring 2006): 165–87. Print

Willis, Ika. "Keeping Promises to Queer Children: Making Space (for Mary-Sue) at Hogwarts." *Fan Fiction and Fan Communities in the Age of the Internet*. Eds. Karen Hellekson and Kristina Busse. London: MacFarlane, 2006. 153–70. Print.

Yeskov, Kyrill. *The Last Ringbearer*. Еврей без ярлыков. LiveJournal, 1999. Web. 8 Oct. 2013.

Contributors

Cami D. Agan is Professor of English and Chair of Language and Literature at Oklahoma Christian University. She teaches British and world literature and in the Honors program. She has published on Tolkien in *Mythlore,* and her recent publications include a chapter in *Approaches to Teaching Tolkien's* The Lord of the Rings *and Other Works* (forthcoming from MLA) as well a chapter on teaching eighteenth-century dramatist Frances Sheridan. She is currently working on a project exploring cultural geography and the Silmarillion, specifically the Ainulindalë.

Janet Brennan Croft is Head of Access and Delivery Services and Faculty of Research and Instructional Services at the Rutgers University libraries. She is the author of *War in the Works of J. R. R. Tolkien* (Praeger, 2004; winner, Mythopoeic Society Award for Inklings Studies) and has written on the Peter Jackson films, J. K. Rowling, Terry Pratchett, Lois McMaster Bujold, and other authors. She is the editor or co-editor of four collections of literary essays and contributes a regular column on libraries and copyright to *Oklahoma Librarian*. She also edits the refereed scholarly journal *Mythlore* and serves on the Mythopoeic Press Editorial Board.

Edith L. Crowe is Librarian Emerita at San José State University, after a thirty-five-year career. She joined the Mythopoeic Society as soon as she discovered it in 1973 and has been active in it ever since. This year marks the end of fifteen years of service for her on the Council of Stewards. She has published numerous articles and reviews in *Mythlore, Mythprint, San José Studies,* and *Tolkien Studies*. Many a Mythcon has been subjected to one of her papers, presentations, or panels. While serving as moderator of the last, Neil Gaiman kissed her. She has also presented at the Tolkien Symposium, the SW/TX Popular Culture Association and the Tolkien Centenary Conference (a peak experience). Co-author (with Janet Brennan Croft) of the *Mythlore Index*, Edith is currently working on the *Mythlore Art Index*.

Leslie A. Donovan is a Professor in the Honors College at the University of New Mexico, where she teaches interdisciplinary humanities courses for undergraduates. Among her publications are studies of valkyries in *The Lord of the Rings* (included in this collection), Tolkien's mythology, women saints' lives in Old English prose, the character of Hunferth in *Beowulf,* and various pedagogical topics. She has edited *Approaches to Teaching Tolkien's* The Lord of the Rings *and Other Works* forthcoming from the Modern Language Association. In addition, she is the Editor of the Mythopoeic Press.

Nancy Enright is an Associate Professor of English and Catholic Studies at Seton Hall University and Coordinator of Journey of Transformation, the first of three required "Signature" core classes. She also serves on the Core Advisory Board and the Catholic Studies Advisory Board. She has been actively involved in planning and teaching courses in Seton Hall's core curriculum, which includes classic core texts explored in connection with questions about the meaning of life, death, service, and community. She has published articles on Dante, Augustine, C. S. Lewis, J. R. R. Tolkien, Julian of Norwich, and William Hazlitt.

Kristine Larsen is an Astronomy Professor at Central Connecticut State University. She is the author of *Cosmology 101* and *Stephen Hawking: A Biography* and co-editor of *The Mythological Dimensions of Doctor Who* and *The Mythological Dimensions of Neil Gaiman*. Her Tolkien scholarship has been published in a variety of books, as well as *Tolkien Studies, Mallorn, Silver Leaves,* and *Amon Hen*.

Romuald I. Lakowski is a member of the English Department at Grant MacEwan University in Edmonton, Canada, where he has taught courses on Shakespeare, Medieval Drama, Early Medieval Literature, History of the English Language, and Children's Literature, as well as seminars on Spenser, Early Modern Utopias, Tolkien, and Renaissance English Poetry. He has published several articles on Tolkien in *Mythlore, Mythprint, The Ring Goes Ever On: Proceedings of the Tolkien 2005 Conference, The Mirror Crack'd: Fear and Horror in J. R. R. Tolkien's Major Works,* and *Tolkien and Shakespeare: Essays on Shared Themes and Language.*

Phoebe C. Linton is a doctoral student funded by the Arts and Humanities Research Council at the University of Edinburgh, where she completed her M.A. in English literature in 2011, followed with an M.Sc. by research in 2012. In her explorations of medieval literature, Phoebe is concerned primarily with female voice or silence, considering ambiguities between the boundaries of the public and private lives of characters. She draws on Early and Late Middle English sources, maintaining also a keen interest in Old French chivalric literature and Neomedieval romances. Outside her research, Phoebe is a reader for the literary James Tait Black Award.

Una McCormack is Lecturer in Creative Writing at Anglia Ruskin University, Cambridge, UK. The author of seven science fiction novels and numerous short stories in that genre, she specializes in TV tie-in novels based on franchises such as *Star Trek* and *Doctor Who*. She is also a *New York Times* bestselling author (for her novel *The Crimson Shadow*). A prolific fanfiction writer, she has set up and organized several online writing groups and resources for fanfiction writers. She lives in Cambridge, UK, with her partner, Matthew, and daughter, Verity.

John D. Rateliff is best known for his work on Tolkien's *Hobbit* manuscripts, particularly in his book *The History of* The Hobbit. He has contributed to collections such as *Tolkien's Legendarium,* the Blackwelder festschrift, and the Shippey festschrift *Tolkien in the New Century*. His interest in the emergence of fantasy as a modern literary genre found expression both in his dissertation on the work of Lord Dunsany, the great fantasy short story writer, and in an on-line column *Classics of Fantasy*. He lives in the Seattle area with his wife, two cats, and a great many books.

Melanie A. Rawls earned her master's degree in English from Florida State University and is a composition instructor at Florida A & M University. She is a board member of Anhinga Press and an assistant fiction editor for the *Apalachee Review*. She is a published poet, essayist, and short story author. *Mythlore* has published several of her essays, including "The Rings of Power," "The Verse of J. R. R. Tolkien" and "Witches, Wives and Dragons: The Evolution of the Women in Ursula K. Le Guin's Earthsea."

Robin Anne Reid is a Professor of Literature and Languages at Texas A&M University-Commerce. Her scholarly and teaching interests are creative writing, marginalized literatures, digital humanities, and critical theory, specifically cultural studies, intersectional studies, and queer studies. Recent publications include work on female bodies in *The Lord of the Rings* and on anti-racist work in online sff fandom. She has published collaborative scholarship on Peter Jackson's film with

Judy Ann Ford, a medieval historian, and is working with a group of linguistics and literature scholars on the Tolkien Corpus Project.

Sharin Schroeder is an Assistant Professor of English at Taipei Tech with research interests in Victorian literature and J. R. R. Tolkien's nineteenth-century influences. She has published in *Nineteenth-Century Prose* as well as in *Picturing Tolkien* and in the forthcoming MLA *Approaches to Teaching Tolkien's* The Lord of the Rings *and Other Works.* Her archival research on the effect of Andrew Lang's writings on Tolkien's imaginative writing and scholarship was generously funded by a 2012–13 grant from Taiwan's National Science Council.

Melissa A. Smith is a Ph.D. candidate in the Department of English at the University of Texas at Austin, where she also earned her M.A. She earned her B.A. in English at the University of Rochester. She has published in *Mythlore* and the *Dickens Studies Annual*. She is currently working on her dissertation on nineteenth-century stewardship and the British novel.

Maureen Thum teaches English and Honors at the University of Michigan-Flint where she is the Director of the Honors Program. She has presented numerous papers on writers such as Shakespeare, Tolkien, Barrett-Browning, the Grimm Brothers, and Wilhelm Hauff. In addition, she has published articles focusing on nineteenth- and twentieth-century German and British literature in the *Philological Quarterly*, the *Germanic Review, The Children's Literature Quarterly, Children's Literature, Short Story,* and *the Michigan Academician.*

Ulla Thynell is a freelance illustrator based in Finland. She is a faithful Tolkien fan and has created numerous Middle-earth themed artworks, including *Yavanna Kementári* featured on the front cover of *Perilous and Fair*. She wound up studying philosophy after high school and graduated from University of Helsinki in 2008. She decided to pursue a career in illustration in 2012 and her first book illustrations were published the very next year. Currently, Ulla studies graphic design at Helsinki Metropolia UAS and works as a professional illustrator, focusing on fantasy and children's books. Her online gallery is located at www.ullathynell.com.

Index

Tolkien's works are listed independently. Tolkien's characters and fanfiction characters in Middle-earth also have their own entries, as do primary world historical and mythical figures; characters belonging to other works are entered under their authors or, for anonymous works, under their work titles.

Abbott, Kasia 57
actors, boys 291
Adam 158
adaptation studies 6, 26–27
Adriatic coast 287n6
adultery 86, 211n18
The Adventures of Tom Bombadil 33, 45n8
agency 5, 37, 169, 172n10, 274, 322, 325
aggression and aggressiveness 35, 101, 107n2
Agnes, Mother M. 54
Ainsworth, W. Harrison 78n10
Ainur 34, 137–38, 180, 186, 189, 196
Aitkin, Daniel Ferguson 56
Akers-Jordan, Cathy. "Fairy Princess or Tragic Heroine? The Metamorphosis of Arwen Undómiel in Peter Jackson's *The Lord of the Rings* Film" 27
Aldarion 111n3, 146
allegory 35–36, 71, 83, 124, 128
Allen & Unwin 56, 58
Allen, Grant 82
alphabets and writing systems 44n6
Alqualondë 141, 155–56, 158, 160, 165–66
alternate worlds 33, 287
Alviss (fanfiction character) 324
Amazon (online retailer) 311n4
Amazons 116, 120, 143, 160–61, 167, 263
American Spectator 286
Amillo 192n2
Amroth 158
Amundsen, Roald 41
Ancrene Wisse 29, 58
Anderson, Douglas 14
Andreth 186n30
Anduin 133
Angamandi (Hells of Iron) 193
Angband 177–84
angels 25, 129
Anglo-Saxon literature and culture 6, 28, 33, 209, 210n13, 224, 225n8, 230, 238, 240, 248n29; *see also* Old English language and literature
Angrod 156
anima (Jungian analysis) 16, 222
antiquity 17, 85; *see also* time
Apollo 90
Aquitania (ship) 214n21
Aragorn 6, 29, 32, 90–91, 100, 101n1, 110, 116, 118, 120, 122–25, 127, 131–34, 147–48, 199, 204, 207–12, 215, 226, 235, 245–46, 248–250, 252–53, 255, 259–60, 263, 265–66, 268–72, 275–77, 298–300, 302, 315; as Elfstone 123, 252; as Strider 289; in fanfiction 314, 317–18, 321, 324n11
Arathorn 204, 266
archaeology 144–45
archetypes 19, 73, 106, 120, 184n27, 222, 229, 262, 266, 281n2
archival materials in scholarship 17
Arda Marred 148, 186, 196–98
Aredhel Ar-Feiniel 35, 108–09, 113, 141, 147
Ar-Gimilzôr 113, 147
Aristotle 283
armor 228, 231, 241, 243, 247–49, 266, 268, 272, 298–99
Armstrong, Helen. "Arwen" 29
Ar-Pharazôn 108, 113, 139, 147
Artemis 139
Arthurian legends 18, 36, 60n22, 260–61; *see also* Malory, Thomas
Arvalin 193
Arvedui 320
Arwen 6, 25, 27, 29, 37, 99, 106–07, 120–26, 129–33, 147, 225–28, 230, 235, 251–55, 259, 281n2, 290, 315; banner woven for Aragorn 123, 252; eyes 251; in fanfiction 318, 321, 324n11; other names 251
Association for the Higher Education of Women 49n14, 50; *see also* Oxford University: Women's colleges: St. Anne's
astronomy 93
Athena 27
Atwood, Margaret 81
Auden, W. H. 74n6, 224

Augustine, St. 201
Aulë 115, 191n2, 192, 198
Austen, Jane 75
authority 5, 20, 113, 120, 140–42, 194, 222, 225, 244–45, 248, 260, 267, 269, 281, 284, 289–90, 298–99, 301

Bag End (farm belonging to Jane Neave) 45
Bakhtin, Mikhail 33, 282–83; *see also* carnival and carnivalized literature
Ballantyne, R. M. 78n10
Balrog 25, 90
Barahir 143
Barrie, James 79, 82
Basso, Ann McCauley. "Fair Lady Goldberry, Daughter of the River" 33–34
Battle of the Pelennor Fields 143; in fanfiction 319
beauty 3, 17, 35, 66, 73, 84, 88–92, 121–22, 126, 128, 133, 161–63, 164n12, 169, 179, 183, 228, 235, 238, 240, 259, 275, 295, 298, 301
Beleriand 157, 162
Belladonna Took 103
Benvenuto, Maria Raffaella. "Against Stereotype: Éowyn and Lúthien as 20th-Century Women" 29, 168n2, 170n7
Beowulf 28–29, 48, 54n18, 57, 172n11, 215n24, 225n8, 229–30, 235, 241, 243, 245, 247–48; Clark-Hall translation 58. Characters: Beowulf 29, 235; Grendel's mother 229, 240–41; Hrothgar 235; Modthrytho 242, 245; Unferth 235n18; Wealhtheow 28, 215n24, 226, 228, 230, 234–35, 247–48
"Beowulf: The Monsters and the Critics" 54, 230
Beren 3, 26, 105, 114, 116, 122, 143–44, 168–86 passim, 198
Beren (fanfiction character) 320
Besant, Walter 80n15
Bible 5, 31, 83, 118, 128–30, 138, 158, 163, 196
Bilbo Baggins 70n1, 103, 148, 199, 201; in fanfiction 321
Birmingham Oratory 41, 46, 47n11
Birmingham School Board 44
Black Breath 321
Black Captain *see* Witch-king of Angmar
Black Gate 209
Blackwood's Magazine 79–80
Błaszkiewicz, Maria. "Tolkien's Queen-Women in *The Lord of the Rings*" 36–37
Bliss, A. J. 61
Bloom, Harold—theory of anxiety of influence 24
Blunden, Edmund 204n1
bodies and corporeality 5, 37–38, 168–87
The Book of Lost Tales 191–95. "Habbanan Beneath the Stars" 193; "The Music of the Ainur" 196; "Turambar and the Foalókë" 193. Textual history 189–90, 196
Boromir 32, 92, 102–03, 105, 110, 118, 127, 132, 134, 289; in fanfiction 312–13
Boston 208
botany 43–45, 93–94
Bowen, Elizabeth 81
boys' books 70–94
Bratman, David 14
Bratt, Edith, *see* Tolkien, Edith
Bree 121
Brennu-Njáls saga 242
Brontë sisters 93
Brooke, Rupert. "The Old Vicarage, Grantchester" 45; "Town & Country" 45
Brooklands Hospital, Hull 52n16
Buckhurst, Helen 54n18, 56, 58, 61; influence on troll scene in *The Hobbit* 58
Burchfield, Robert 60

Cabell, James Branch 66
Cain 158
Calacirya 239
Calypso 20, 222
Cambridge University 62–63, 88; allowing women professors 61n23
Canada 206, 212, 214
Caranthir 142, 156n4
Carcharoth 175, 177–79, 181–82
Carnegie, Andrew 66
carnival and carnivalized literature 33, 281–83, 287–88, 290, 296–97, 303
Carpenter, Humphrey. *Tolkien: A Biography* 41, 47–48, 52, 55, 59n21, 259
Carter, Susan. "Galadriel and Morgan Le Fey: Tolkien's Redemption of the Lady of the Lacuna" 30
Cather, Willa 81
Catholicism and Catholic symbolism 25, 36, 127–28, 153, 201, 213n20
caves and cave symbolism 25
Cecil, Lord David 62

Celeborn 17, 90, 114, 122, 125, 144, 153–54, 156–62, 165–66, 232, 235, 300; original name Teleporno 162
Celebrimbor 106
Celegorm 168, 173–76, 179, 181, 185
Celtic literature and mythology 34, 36
Ceres 139
Cerin Amroth 123, 301
chalice, symbolism of 148
Challans, Mary *see* Renault, Mary
Chambers, R. W. 54n18, 60, 62
chance 267
Chance, Jane. *The Lord of the Rings: The Mythology of Power* 118–19, 121, 131, 133; ed., *Tolkien the Medievalist* 25–26
charisma 141, 144
Chaucer, Geoffrey 45n8
childbirth 105
Childe, W. R. 54n18
children readers 72
chivalry 18, 262–63, 267–68
Christ imagery and symbolism 31, 118, 123–24, 128–30, 133–34, 138, 291n9; Incarnation 129–130
Christianity and Christian themes 5, 18–19, 30, 120, 149, 153, 193, 196, 200, 222
Churchill, Winston 80
Cimarron Review 1, 16
Cinderella (film) 286
Circe 20, 222
Círdan 106, 156–57
Cirith Ungol 37, 233–34
civil rights movement 1, 15n7
Clark, George, and Daniel Timmons, eds. *J. R. R. Tolkien and His Literary Resonances: Views of Middle-earth* 24
class and class theory 15n7, 24, 39, 283, 287, 310, 314
classical literature and mythology 20, 34, 43, 130–31, 222, 224
Clinton, Hillary Rodham 286
Coghill, Nevill 62–63
Cold War 83
commerce 142, 144
Common Speech 214
compassion 101, 115, 201
complementarity 18, 99–101, 116, 223
Conscription Act of 1917 208n9
consent 35
Consolation (element of fairy-stories) 19, 254
Constable, Mrs. Strickland 52n16
Cooper, Helen 63
Corlett, A. C. 56
Council of Elrond 121–22
counsel and advice 100–01, 103–07, 109–12
courage 103, 116, 129, 141–43, 202, 209, 216, 224, 227, 236, 239, 267
courtesy 267
courtship 32, 41, 204, 206–07, 211, 320
critical theories 3, 13, 24, 38–39
Croft, Janet Brennan, ed. *Tolkien and Shakespeare: Essays on Shared Themes and Language* 32; ed., *Tolkien on Film: Essays on Peter Jackson's* The Lord of the Rings 26; *War in the Works of J. R. R. Tolkien* 204n1
Crook, Ruth A. 56
Crowe, Edith. "Power in Arda: Sources, Uses and Misuses" 5, 19–20, 27, 136–49, 221–22
cultural studies 24, 38–39
cup-bearing 215n24, 228, 234–36, 247–48, 266
Curtis, Sir Henry 79
Curufin 168, 173–76, 181, 185
Cutter, Charles 66

Daeron 184
Dagnall, Susan 58
dance 100–01, 105, 172n10
Dante. *Divine Comedy* — characters: Beatrice 36
d'Ardenne, Simone 29, 42, 54n18, 59, 61; living with Tolkien family 59; thesis 59
darkness, symbolism 24, 239–40
Davis, Norman 61
death 124, 130, 181, 191–99 passim, 207, 212, 229, 240, 245–46, 251, 254, 269, 272–74; *see also* mortality
de Beauvoir, Simone. *The Second Sex* 285
Defoe, Daniel. *Robinson Crusoe* 77, 78n10
Demeter 139
Denethor 103, 134, 200, 289; in fan-fiction 312–13
de Pizan, Christine. *Le Ditie de Jehanne d'Arc* 262
Dernhelm *see* Éowyn
despair 210–11n17, 249, 252
DeTardo, Merlin 14
de Troyes, Chrétien. "Erec and Enide" 262, 270. Characters: Enide 262, 270; Erec 262, 270

Díaz, Junot. *The Brief Wondrous Life of Oscar Wao* 309, 325
Dickens, Charles 78n10, 93. Works: *The Pickwick Papers* 78n10
Dickerson, Matthew. "Finwë and Míriel" 29
digital humanities 7
Dior 186
disguises and cross-dressing 6, 110, 245–46, 261, 265, 272–74, 278, 282, 287, 290–93, 296–300; *see also* masquerade
dísir 229, 236
Disney, Walt 286
disobedience 166, 211, 286
dissertations 36
Dol Amroth 103, 215n25, 314–15
Dol Guldur 144, 234n16
domination and dominator societies 5, 31, 118, 125–26, 129, 131, 133, 145, 147–49, 179–81, 185, 290
Donne, John 67
Donovan, Leslie A. "The Valkyrie Reflex in J. R. R. Tolkien's *The Lord of the Rings*: Galadriel, Shelob, Éowyn, and Arwen" 6, 25, 27, 221–55, 259–60, 264, 268–69, 281n2, 300, 302
Doriath 114, 155–58, 172–73, 181, 183
Dostoevsky, Fyodor 93
doubling 312
Doughan, David. "Women, Oxford and Tolkien" 33–34
Downey, Sarah. "Cordial Dislike: Reinventing the Celestial Ladies of *Pearl* and *Purgatorio* in Tolkien's Galadriel" 35–36
Doyle, Arthur Conan. Sherlock Holmes stories 73n3, 93
draft *see* Conscription Act of 1917
dragons 75, 286n5, 310
Draugluin 177
Drayton, Michael 32
dreams 101n1, 282–83
dream-vision genre 33, 36
Dronke, Ursula 61
Drout, Michael D. C. *J. R. R. Tolkien Encyclopedia: Scholarship and Critical Assessment* 14, 24, 29–30; "Note" 28n13; and Hilary Wynne, "Tom Shippey's *J. R. R. Tolkien: Author of the Century* and a Look Back at Tolkien Criticism Since 1982" 14–16, 38–39
dryad 121
Duggan, Alfred Leo 70n1, 86
Duncan, Miss 52
Dúnedain 302; in fanfiction 317, 321
Dungortheb 183
Dunharrow 207, 315; in fanfiction 318, 323
Dúnhere 271
Dunlendings 146
duty 208, 249, 268, 270, 276
Dwarves 25, 71, 90, 114–15, 125, 147, 189, 198

Eaglestone, Robert. *Reading* The Lord of the Rings 28
Eärendil 113–14, 186, 198, 234
Eärnur 102
earthly paradise 36
Eärwen 155
Easterlings 146
ecofeminism 149
economics and economic power 18, 141
Eddas 61, 193, 224, 231–32, 234, 238, 242, 246, 255; *see also Poetic Edda, Prose Edda,* and individual saga titles
Eddison, E. R. 65–67; *The Worm Ouroboros* 65n30
Eden 158, 196
Edghill, Rosemary 24
Edoras 263, 268–70, 276; *see also* Meduseld
education for women 4, 33–34, 41–67 passim, 137, 285
Edward VII 79
Edwardian literature and culture 73n3, 309
Eilenel 114
Eiríksmál 235
Eisler, Riane. *The Chalice and the Blade* 144–45, 147–49
Elbereth *see* Varda
Eldar 107, 109, 139, 141–43, 146, 160–61, 170n7, 179, 184–85
Eleanor of Aquitaine 263
Elementary Education Act 1870 77, 78n10
Elendil 110
Elfhild (wife of Théoden) in fanfiction 314
Elfstone (brooch; for personal name, see Aragorn) 235
Eliot, George 75, 77
Elizabeth Barrett Browning Junior High School (New York) 92–93
Elizabeth I 33, 284–85, 290–91, 296; as Virgin Queen 290

Elrington and Bosworth Professorship of Anglo-Saxon at Cambridge 63
Elrohir in fanfiction 318
Elrond 101n1, 106–07, 117, 122–23, 125, 147, 198, 252–53, 315; in fanfiction 318; sons 106, 123
Elros 122n3, , 198
Elves 71, 104, 106–07, 118–19, 125–27, 130–31, 133, 138–39, 141, 147, 149, 157–59, 164, 168–69, 174, 184n26, 186, 189–90, 193, 195, 198, 202, 238, 254, 259, 301; creation of 34
Elvish languages 123
Elwë Singollo *see* Thingol
Elwing 113–14, 186
Emeldir 143
enantiodromia 112, 116–17, 147
English literature and culture 45; 16th and 17th centuries 283–85; 20th century 285–86
English Place Name Society 60
Enright, Nancy. "Tolkien's Females and the Defining of Power" 4–5, 31, 118–34
Ents 71, 115, 146, 149, 259
Entwives 27, 146, 149
envy 103, 109
Eöl 109, 113, 147
Éomer 110, 131, 143, 210n12, 213, 215n24, 216, 243, 246, 248, 250, 267, 271, 276; in fanfiction 314–15, 321
Éomund 267, 275
Éowyn 3, 5–6, 18, 25, 27, 29–33, 37, 64–65, 99, 109–11, 116, 118, 120–21, 131–33, 143, 204–16, 224n5, 225–28, 230, 243–51, 253–55, 258–78, 289–90, 297–300, 303, 317; as Dernhelm 27, 33, 110, 245–46, 249, 255, 265, 273–75, 297, 299–300; hair 246–47, 265, 271, 298; in fanfiction 315, 318, 323–24; white clothing 246, 264, 277, 297
epessë (secondary name) 161
epic genre 30, 70
Epstein, Rebecca 14
Equal Rights Amendment 286
Ered Gorgoroth 170
Eredluin (Ered Luin) 154
Eregion 154
Erendis 29, 111n3, 146
Eressea 154
Eru *see* Ilúvatar
essentialism 20, 30, 137–38, 146, 288
Estë 105, 139, 192n3, 194–95
etymology 44n6, 52
eucatastrophe 123–24, 130, 132, 134, 175, 254–55
Eve 33, 139–40, 158
evil 24, 37, 73, 86, 88–91, 100, 102, 104, 108–09, 113, 124–25, 129–30, 133, 146–48, 162, 182–85, 196, 224, 238, 240–41, 254, 281, 286, 300–02
Excalibur 18
exile 154–55, 208, 269
eyes and eye symbolism 107–08, 112, 232, 241–43, 247, 251, 259, 264–65

Fáfnismál 225n8
fairies 32
Fairy queen figure 32, 164
fairy story genre 72, 130, 254, 286
Fall, The 139, 196
The Fall of Arthur 260
fandom and fan studies 15, 38–39
fanfiction 6–7, 309–25; female characters 310–17; male authors 324; scholarship about 311
fantasy genre 16, 66, 115–16, 119–20, 136, 148, 272, 282–83, 310
fanzines 13, 15–16
Far Harad 309
Faramir 6, 18, 27, 31–32, 101n1, 102–03, 110, 118, 132–34, 148, 199, 204, 207, 209, 211–15, 250–51, 253, 275, 277–78, 289, 300, 317; in fanfiction 312–13, 316–18, 321, 323–324
Farmer Maggot 37
fate 171–72, 184–86
fathers 44n5, 147–48, 169, 173n12
Faulkner, Mrs. 46–47
Fëanor 105–07, 111–12, 127, 139–41, 148, 155–57, 160–61, 165–66, 197; Oath of Fëanor 156
fëar 186n30
Feast of Fools (Twelfth Night) 282, 287
Felagund *see* Finrod Felagund
Fellowship, The 41, 90–92, 104, 118, 121, 125, 127, 164, 234–36, 247–49, 263, 289, 300–02; in fanfiction 321–22
The Fellowship of the Ring. Film dir. Peter Jackson 310
female authority figures 20–21
female power 6–7, 25, 86, 121, 125, 133–34, 138, 140, 143–44, 183, 222–23, 239, 286

feminine principle 4, 17–18, 99–117, 139, 147, 185n28, 222–23, 246, 281n2
femininity 21, 31, 190, 241, 244, 267, 290–91, 300
feminism and feminist perspectives 1, 13, 15, 19, 24–26, 29–30, 34–35, 38, 87, 136–37, 144, 145n1, 149, 216, 222, 227
feminist criticism 13, 15n7, 18–20, 24–25, 28–29, 31, 38, 119
Fenwick, Mac. "Breastplates of Silk: Homeric Women in *The Lord of the Rings*" 20, 222, 224, 240
"Fibber McGee and Molly" 205
Field of Cormallen 212n19
Fife, Ernelle. "Wise Warriors in Tolkien, Lewis, and Rowling" 27
Fili 105
La Fille du comte de Pontieu 264
film studies 7, 13–15, 26–27
Fimi, Dimitra. *Tolkien, Race and Cultural History* 24, 38
Finarfin 156–58, 161
Finduilas (Elf) 167
Finduilas (mother of Faramir) 103; in fanfiction 312–13
Fingolfin 106, 141, 158n6, 168
Finrod Felagund 106, 156, 158n6, 161n8, 168, 173–75, 186
Finwë 29, 158n6, 161, 198
fire as masculine symbol 107
Fíriel 320
First Merseberg Charm 242
Fisher, Jason. "Galadriel" 29
Flieger, Verlyn. *Interrupted Music* 189; *Splintered Light* 145–46, 173nn12–13, 184n27
folklore 83, 272
fools 282
forests and woodlands 32; as symbolic space 169–73, 177, 183, 185
forgiveness 133, 200
Forster 1870 Education Act *see* Elementary Education Act 1870
Fôs' Almir 193
Foucault, Michel 119; concept of heterotopia 170n5
France 207–09
fratricide 158
Fredrick, Candice, and Sam McBride. "Battling the Woman Warrior: Females and Combat in Tolkien and Lewis" 30; *Women Among the Inklings* 31, 119, 132, 168n2, 221n1, 300n13
free will 273, 277
freedom 109, 147, 169, 180, 186n30, 245, 249, 292, 303, 318
French (language) 43
Freud, Sigmund 79, 80n12. Works: *On the Interpretation of Dreams* 80n12; *eros/thanatos* concept 145n1; Freudian analysis 17–20, 25, 38
Freya 194
Frigg 194
Frodo Baggins 18n10, 20, 25, 32, 91–92, 99, 101n1, 103–04, 108, 119, 121–26, 129, 148, 154–55, 159, 162–64, 169n4, 199–201, 233–34, 237–38, 241–42, 251–52, 258, 266, 289–90, 301–02; in fanfiction 314, 321, 324
Froude, James Anthony 75
Fuller, Ruth Wolfe. *The Experiences of a War Bride* 205–11
functional grammar 37

Galadriel 4–6, 17, 19–20, 24–27, 29–33, 36–37, 90n21, 99, 101n1, 104, 107, 114, 120–22, 125–31, 133, 141, 144, 148, 153–67, 168, 184nn26–27, 222, 224–28, 230–40, 246–47, 251–52, 254–55, 259, 264, 281n2, 290, 297, 300–03; as a Marian figure 25, 33, 37, 120, 127–29, 153, 163–64, 200, 222; as a penitent 127–28, 153, 162–67; as a rebel 25, 31, 107, 127, 153, 155, 160; ban on return to West 154–55, 157–60, 165–66; golden hair 161–62, 231–32, 235; laughter 162–63; Mirror of 73, 104, 108, 237, 302; mother-name Nerwen 107, 141, 160, 162n10; other names 162, 229–30; parallels to Ayesha 73, 83, 86–87, 90–92; pardon 127, 153, 155, 157, 159–60; Phial of 37, 129, 200, 233–34, 302; physical prowess and athleticism 107, 141, 161–62, 234; pride 159–60; redemption 32, 153–55, 163–64; swan boat 231; temptation 162–65; white clothing 231–32, 264
game studies 7, 15
Gandalf 99, 101n1, 105, 120–21, 125–26, 131, 134, 148, 199–200, 210n12, 243, 247, 249, 263–66, 273, 276–77, 298, 302; as Olórin 105, 200

Gardner, Helen 62–63
gender (social construction) and gender theory 4–5, 16, 20, 30, 33, 36, 39, 85, 99–100, 137, 221–22, 227, 246, 281–303 passim
gender relations 4, 30, 87, 90, 92
gender studies 15, 26, 38
genre and genre studies 4, 35, 38, 85
geology 44
geometry 44
Germanic languages 43, 44n6, 49n14
Germanic myths, legends, and literature 6, 18, 20, 36, 223–55 passim
Germany and Germans 146
giants and giantesses 76, 239
Giddings, Robert. *J. R. R. Tolkien: This Far Land* 18n10
Gift of Men 186, 193
gift-giving 127, 161n9, 228, 233–36, 244, 249, 251–52, 300, 302
Gilbert, Sandra, and Susan Gubar. *The Madwoman in the Attic: The Woman Writer and the Nineteenth-Century Literary Imagination* 25, 272
Gildor Inglorion 104
Gil-galad 106
Gillespie, Vincent 64
Gilman, Greer Ilene 24
Gilraen 21
Gimbutas, Marij 145n1
Gimilkhad 113
Gimli 90–91, 125, 127, 161n9, 232, 235, 237, 263, 301; in fanfiction 321
girls 21, 64–65, 77, 79, 81, 92–93, 119, 136
glass ceiling 61
Glóin 125
Glorfindel 106
God (Judeo-Christian) 138
Goddess 138–39, 145; as Crone 139; as Death 202; as Earth Mother 139; as Maiden 139; as Queen of Heaven 138
gold and gold imagery 233–34, 246–47, 264
Goldberry 19, 29, 33–34, 37, 121–22, 146, 149, 227
Golden Hall, The *see* Meduseld
gold-sickness 105
Gollins, Annie 47
Gollum 99, 101n1, 102, 108, 148, 199
Gondolin 106, 108–09, 157
Gondor 103, 143, 204, 212, 215–16, 252, 272, 274, 276, 289, 299, 319–20; in fanfiction 311–12, 321, 323; Stewards 103, 204, 215n25, 277, 289, 320
Gordon, E. V. 54, 60; knighthood 60; *see also* Tolkien, J. R. R., and E. V. Gordon. *Sir Gawaine and the Green Knight*
Gordon, George 53, 54n18
Gorlim 114
Goselin, Peter Damien. "Two Faces of Eve: Galadriel and Shelob as Anima Figures" 16–17, 222
Gothic language 49n14
Gothic literature 312
government 140
grace 128–30, 154, 164n12, 196, 296
Grant, Cary 205
Gray, Douglas 64
Great Britain 206; post-WWI gender constructions 36
Great Mother archetype 106
Greek language 49n14, 83–84
Greek mythology 193
Grey Havens 252
grief and grieving 190–92, 198, 201–02, 208, 238, 254, 294; *see also* mourning
Griffiths, Elaine 54n18, 58, 61
Grove, Jennie 51, 210n14
guns 116

Hades 139
Haggard, H. Rider 4, 70–91 passim. Works: "About Fiction" 77, 88; *Allan Quatermain* 78–79, 82; *Ayesha: The Return of She* 80; *King Solomon's Mines* 72, 74n5, 78, 80–81, 83n17, 84–85, 92; *The Days of My Life* 80, 87; *She: A History of an Adventure* 4, 70, 72–73, 74n6, 78n10, 80–93; and Andrew Lang, *The World's Desire* 73. Characters: Allan Quatermain 74n5, 78–79; Amahagger people 87; Amenartas 84; Ayesha (She, She-Who-Must-Be-Obeyed) 4, 73, 81, 83–92; Billali 87; Horace Holly 81, 84, 87–90, 92; Job 87; Kallikrates 84, 89; Leo Vincey 84, 86–90; Ustane 86, 88. Objects: Greek Sherd of Amenartas 83–84
Haines, Helen E. *What's in a Novel* 66
Hákonarmál 243n26
Halbarad 252
Halberstam, Judith—theory of female masculinity 37

Haldir 125
Haleth 142–43
Half-elven 122n3, 125, 252
Halliday, M. A. K. 37
Háma 244, 267, 298
Hammond, Wayne 48–49n13, 53
hands and hand symbol 107–08, 112
handwriting 44n6
Hardy, Thomas. *A Pair of Blue Eyes* 82
Harrowdale 271
Hatcher, Melissa McCrory. "Finding Woman's Role in *The Lord of the Rings*" 31
healing and healers 6, 100–01, 105–06, 111, 124–25, 131–34, 139, 148, 169, 175–77, 181–83, 185–86, 194–97, 204, 245, 249, 251, 263, 277–78, 316; in fanfiction 316–17, 320–21, 324
hearth as feminine symbol 106, 117, 149
heaven 193
Heidrek's saga 226n9, 243
Hel 193
Helcaraxë 155–56
Helgi Lays (*Helgakviða Hundingsbana* I and II, *Helgakviða Hjörvarðssonar*) 225n8, 229, 231–34, 241, 242, 243n26, 245. Characters: Helgi 233, 234; Hrímgerth 229, 241; Sigrún 226, 228, 233–34, 238, 245, 250n30, 253; Sváva 226, 228, 233, 253
hell 193
Helm 315
Helm's Deep 244, 266, 269, 271, 302
helmets *see* armor
Henneth Annûn (mailing list) 310
heresy 284
heroes and heroism 123, 148, 202, 254–55, 260, 290; heroism and masculinity 31, 228, 289; in fanfiction 323
heroic literature 6, 25, 30, 38, 70, 223, 225n8
Hervör's saga 225n8. Characters: Hervör or Herför 226, 228, 242n25, 243, 245
Hesser, Katherine. "Éowyn" 29–30; "Goldberry" 29; "Melian" 29
Hethlin (fanfiction character) 317–18, 322
Heyer, Georgette 315n6
hierarchical stuctures 24, 33, 142, 145–46, 282, 288, 309
higher education for women 4, 15n7, 20, 34, 41–67
Hild in fanfiction 315
Hildegard of Bingen 44n7
Hillard, Steve. *Mirkwood* 324
Hírilorn 173
history 319
The History of Middle-earth 31, 153, 158, 168n1; "The Annals of Aman" 156n2, 197; "Laws and Customs among the Eldar" 198; "The Shibboleth of Fëanor" 155, 158–62, 165–66, 168
The Hobbit 51, 54, 56, 58, 61, 66, 99, 118, 120, 136; audience 72, 78; publication history 58; textual history 199; troll scene 58
The Hobbit. Film trilogy dir. Peter Jackson 26; *see also* Tauriel
Hobbits 19, 37, 70n1, 71, 121–22, 133, 145, 149, 189, 199, 226n9, 289, 318; in fanfiction 321, 324
Hollander, Nicole. *Ma, Can I Be a Feminist and Still Like Men?* 136
Holy Spirit 201
Homer. *Odyssey*—influence on Tolkien 20. Characters: Calypso 20, 222; Circe 20, 222; Odysseus 20
homosexuality 120n2, 169n4, 207n7
homosociality 18n10
Honegger, Thomas *see* Weinreich, Frank, and Thomas Honegger
honor 208, 210, 235, 263, 270–71, 274, 300
hope 130, 190, 200, 249–50, 252, 254
Hopkins, Lisa. "Female Authority Figures in the Works of Tolkien, C. S. Lewis and Charles Williams" 20–21, 190, 202
horses 309, 321–22
hospitality 125
Houghton, John Wm. "Ungoliant" 29
House of Eorl 143, 209n11, 244, 267, 270, 272, 276, 298–99
Houses of Healing 111, 210n12, 215n24, 277–78, 300; in fanfiction 311, 319, 322; Warden 278
Howard, Robert E. Characters: Conan the Barbarian 116
Hrafnsmál 232
Huan 174n15, 175–77
Hudson, Anne 64n29
Hughes, Richard 71
humanities 14, 15n7
humility 124, 129, 163–64, 200, 267, 291n9
huorns 115
Húrin 114

I Was a Male War Bride 205
Icelandic language, literature, and mythology 58, 224
Idril Celebrindal 21, 104, 106–07, 167
Illyria 287
Ilúvatar 103, 105, 107, 114, 137–40, 142, 145, 168, 179, 184, 186–87, 189, 193, 196, 198, 200, 202
Imloth Melui 314
immortality 73, 87, 91, 122n3, 123–24, 131, 185, 199, 224, 238, 253
Imperishable Flame 103, 107, 137, 201
impotence 100–01, 108–110, 180
Imrahil in fanfiction 317–18
Incledon, May (née Suffield) 43n4; daughters Marjorie and Mary 43n4
Indis 161
Indo-European cultures 145
Industrial Revolution 142
Inklings 21, 119, 221n1, 285
interdisciplinary studies 14
interlace structure 258, 260–61, 274–75, 278
internet 52
intuition 101–02, 106
invisibility 106, 258, 272–73
Inzilbêth 113, 147
Ioreth 227; in fanfiction 313–14
Iowa 286
irony 131, 293–94, 299
Isengard 200
Isis 138
Islamic religion 139
Ithilien 215n25, 251, 277; in fanfiction 317, 321–22

J. R. R. Tolkien Professorship of English Language and Literature 42, 64
Jackson, Peter *see The Fellowship of the Ring*; *The Hobbit*; *The Lord of the Rings*
James I 293
James, Henry 77. Works: "The Future of the Novel" 85n18
Japan and Japanese culture 211
jewelry 231–34
Joan of Arc 261–63, 276
Johns, C. A. *Flowers of the Field* 93
Johnson, Janice. "The Celeblain of Celeborn and Galadriel" 17
The Journal of Tolkien Research 15
journals, peer-reviewed 13, 15–16
joy 19
Judeo-Christian religions 138
Judith 225n8, 232–33
Julian of Norwich 44n7
Juliana 29, 225n8, 230, 233
Jung, Carl 16, 79, 112, 185n28; Jungian analysis 16–17, 30, 222
The Juniper Tree (fairy tale) 84–85
just war theory 27
justice 101, 200, 202

Kalafarski, Laura 14
Keays-Young, Julia Maud 56
Kementári *see* Yavanna
Kendall, May 75
kenosis 123
Kilbride, K. M. (Katharine) 54
Kili 105
Kindle Worlds 311n4
King Edward's Foundation Bath Row School 44
King Edward's School 41, 43, 44n6, 45, 47n11
kings and kingship 112, 123, 138, 144, 244, 247–48, 250, 255, 263, 265–66, 272, 287–88, 315, 318, 320
King's Peace 316
Kingston, W. H. G. 78n10
Kinslaying 141, 148, 155–56, 158, 160, 198
knights and knighthood 60, 75–76, 263, 272–73, 298; female knights 6, 260–63, 267, 271–78; in fanfiction 317–18
Knox, John. *First Blast of the Trumpet against the Monstrous Regiment of Women* 284
Kocher, Paul. *Master of Middle-earth* 102
Kowalik, Barbara. "Elbereth the Star-Queen Seen in the Light of Medieval Marian Devotion" 36–37; ed., *'O, What a Tangled Web': Tolkien and Medieval Literature, a View from Poland* 36
Kurvinen, Auvo 61n23. Works: *Sir Gawain and the Carl of Carlisle* 61n23

Lake-men 106
Lakowski, Romuald I. "The Fall and Repentance of Galadriel" 5, 31–32, 153–67; "'Perilously Fair': Titania, Galadriel, and the Fairy Queen of Medieval Romance" 32
Lang, Andrew 70, 72–76, 79–80, 82–83,

85, 93. Works: *The Olive Fairy Book* 93; "Realism and Romance" 76; *The Red Romance Book* 75; and H. Rider Haggard, *The World's Desire* 73
language 44n6, 49n14, 84–85, 215n23
Last, M. G. 56
Latin language 43
L'Atre Périlleux 60n22
Laurelin 161
law 101, 106
Lawlor, John 54–55
Lawrence, D. H. 80
Lay of Lúthien 122
Lays of Beleriand. Lay of Leithian 168, 171–72, 174n15, 178n19, 180
Lee, Stuart D., ed. *A Companion to J. R. R. Tolkien* 2
Leeds University 49n14, 53–55, 57, 60
Legolas 91, 108, 263, 302; in fanfiction 321
Leibeger, Carol. "Women in Tolkien's Work" 29–30
Lent 42
The Letters of J. R. R. Tolkien 25, 31–33, 45–46, 53, 124, 127, 141, 153, 161, 164n12, 165, 196, 199, 263, 316; from Mother M. Agnes (unpublished) 54; from Mary Renault 58; to Ruth Austin 153; to Joanna de Bortadano 238n21; to Lord Halsbury 127; to Fr. Robert Murray 128–29, 164n12, 200; to Jane Neave 45n8; to Charlotte and Denis Plimmer 44n6; to Dick Plotz 159; to Mr. Rang 154; to Christopher Tolkien 26, 146; to Michael Tolkien 59–62; to Miss R. Turnbull (unpublished) 51; to Rayner Unwin 71; to Milton Waldman 189, 196; to Elizabeth Mary Wright 48–49
Lewis, C. S. 16, 20–21, 27, 30, 54n18, 71, 76, 80, 82, 119; academic career 49n14, 62; attitude toward women 42, 65–67, 211, 285; death of mother 46; The Kilns 49; letters exchanged with E. R. Eddison 42n3, 65–67; portrayal of female characters 16, 20–21, 221n1, 286, 302; Professor of Medieval and Renaissance Literature at Cambridge 62–63; tutorials 49, 54. Works: *The Dark Tower* 67; "The Shoddy Lands" 67; *Surprised by Joy* 46; *That Hideous Strength* 66; ed., *Essays Presented to Charles Williams* 53n17. Characters: Fairy Hardcastle 21; Father Christmas 30; Jadis (White Witch) 21, 73; Jane Studdock 21, 67; Lady of Perelandra (Tinidril) 21; Lady of the Green Kirtle 21; Lucy Pevensie 21, 30; Mark Studdock 67; Susan Pevensie 21, 30
libraries and librarianship 66, 74, 76, 81–82, 309
light, imagery and symbolism 19, 25, 36–37, 100, 102, 112, 133, 145–46, 173n13, 183–84, 200, 225, 230–34, 240, 242, 251, 264, 277–78, 301–02; *see also* radiance
liminal space 239
literary canon 38
The Little Mermaid (film) 286
LiveJournal 310
Lobelia Sackville-Baggins 226n9, 227
Loki 193
London 206
Longman's Magazine 80
The Lord of the Rings 54; "Lament of Galadriel" 153–55, 159, 164, 239. As myth 72; binary oppositions 24–25; genre 26, 70–94 passim; influence of Haggard's *She* 73; loss as "real theme" 238–39; style 37–38, 71; textual history 38, 153, 159, 202, 207n6
The Lord of the Rings. Film trilogy dir. Peter Jackson 13–14, 26–27, 29, 161n7; *see also The Fellowship of the Ring*
Loreto College (St. Albans) 61
Lórien (Vala; *for the land, see* Lóthlorien) 191n2, 192n3, 194–95, 200
Lóriniel (fanfiction character) 312
Losgar 155–56
loss 123–25, 196, 202, 225, 227, 229, 238–39, 249, 253
Lothíriel in fancition 314–15
Lóthlorien 1, 37, 90n21, 92, 122, 125–26, 129, 144, 153–54, 157, 159, 164, 232, 234–36, 238–40, 254, 300–02; in fanfiction 318
love 5, 18, 31, 86–90, 101, 110, 118, 121, 123–24, 126, 129–30, 132–34, 183, 196, 246, 250–51, 253–54, 268–69, 288, 291, 295
Lucifer 25; *see also* Satan
Lúthien Tinúviel 3, 5, 21, 26, 29, 35, 105, 114, 116–17, 122–24, 143–44, 147–48, 156, 167, 168–87, 198, 253; cloak of hair

144, 173–78, 180–81, 183–84; power of voice, song, and dance 105, 144, 170–71, 176–81, 184–85; rebellion 185; sexuality 5, 168–73, 177, 179n20, 185–86

Mablung in fanfiction 318
MacDonald, George 82
"Macho Man" 100
MacLeish, Archibald 93
MacSherry, Mrs. 47
Maeglin 106, 109
magic 119, 144, 184n26
Maglor 184, 198
Magoun, Francis 54n18
Maher, Michael W. "'A Land without Stain': Medieval Images of Mary and Their Use in the Characterization of Galadriel" 25–26, 37, 129
Maiar 114, 140, 144, 156, 168, 189, 192n3, 200
Makar 192n2
male authors 24–25, 33–34, 72
male critics 70–71, 74, 82
male gaze 266
male power 90, 118, 125–26, 131, 134, 144, 267
Mallorn 15–16, 23, 33
Malone, Kemp 54n18
Malory, Thomas. *Morte d'Arthur* 70, 85–86, 92, 260–63, 266. Characters: Alisaunder 262; Alys, Lady 262; female characters in general 260; lady of the lake 262; Lancelot 86, 261; Morgan Le Fey 30; Tristram 86, 261; *see also* Arthurian legends
Mandos 183, 189–95, 198, 202; Curse/Doom of (on Noldorian rebels) 155–57, 160; Halls of 114, 139, 184, 186, 190, 192–93, 195, 202
Mann, Jill 64n28
Manwë 100, 103–04, 115, 127, 138, 140, 157, 165, 185, 191, 193–95, 197
maps 83n17, 287
marginalization 7, 120, 133, 299, 310, 315, 324–25
Maria Assumpta Teacher Training College 61
marketing 15, 71–72, 77–78, 93
Marquette University Special Collections and University Archives 17
marriage 18, 32, 87, 170, 172, 204–16, 253, 278, 292–93; forced 109, 113, 147, 278; prevention of 173n12
Marryat, Captain 78n10
Marxism 15n7, 264
Mary (mother of Jesus) and Marian imagery 5, 25, 33, 37, 120, 127–29, 138, 153, 163–64, 200–01, 222, 240; Annunciation 129, 201; devotional prayers to 201; Loreto Litany 25, 129; Magnificat 129, 163
Mary Sue characters 322
masculine principle 4, 99–100, 102, 107, 111, 116, 139, 147, 222–23, 246, 281n2
masculinity 36, 116–17, 291, 310; in fanfiction 323
Mason College (Birmingham) 44
masquerade 6, 33, 281–303 passim; *see also* disguises and cross-dressing
matriarchy 145
matrilineal descent 141
McCarthy witch hunts 66
McKillip, Patricia 24
Meásse 192n2
media studies 26
medieval literature and culture 6, 16, 25, 28, 32, 35–38, 76, 221–55 passim, 262–63, 267, 274, 278, 282, 288, 301; female characters 224–26, 243, 258, 260–61, 276–77, 286, 290, 303
medieval studies 38–39, 258
medievalism 25
Meduseld 247, 273; in fanfiction 315; *see also* Edoras
Melian 21, 29, 104–05, 114, 156, 157n5, 167, 168, 170, 173; Girdle of 114, 170, 183
Melkor 34, 103–05, 109, 112, 116, 137–38, 140, 142, 144, 146–48, 154, 156, 160, 169, 176–86, 190, 191n2, 193–96, 198; Iron Crown 3
Men (race in Middle-earth) 71, 123, 139, 143, 146, 149, 184, 186, 193, 198, 202; creation of 34
men's roles 283–84, 291, 301
Menegroth 183n24
mercy 5, 101, 193, 198–202
Meredith, George. *The Egoist* 75n7
Merry Brandybuck 27, 115, 121, 143, 246–49, 255, 271, 273–75, 299; in fanfiction 314
Merton Professorship of English Literature at Oxford 63
Michael, Mother Mary 51, 52n16

Michel, Laura. "Politically Incorrect: Tolkien, Women, and Feminism" 1–2, 29
Middle Ages 76
Middle English literature and language 29, 54, 59n21
A Middle-English Vocabulary 52
military, women in 137
Mills, Stella 53–54, 61; trans., *The Saga of Hrolf Kraki* 54
Milton, John 24
Mîm 198
Minas Tirith 110–11, 125, 132–33, 209, 227, 253n31, 273–74, 276; formerly Minas Anor 111; in fanfiction 311, 313, 317–18, 321
Minas Tirith Evening-Star 17
Míriel 29, 105, 112, 140, 198
misogyny 2, 35, 80n14, 216, 221
Mitchison, Naomi 71
mithril 252
Modern Language Association International Bibliography 14nn5–6, 15, 26, 36
modernity 25
monsters 176, 238, 241, 243; female monsters 20, 25, 239, 243, 284
moral education 77–78
Moral Majority 286
morale 209
morality and moral power 31, 118, 126, 129, 226, 232, 240, 255
Mordor 108, 302; in fanfiction 314, 324
Morgan, Father Francis 41, 44n5, 47, 213n20
Morgoth *see* Melkor
Moria 25, 101n1
Mornië 193
Morris, William—influence on J. R. R. Tolkien 51
mortality 122–24, 185–86, 199, 202, 224, 226, 238, 253; *see also* death
Morwen 21, 114
mourning 5, 190–92, 194, 196–98, 202, 294; *see also* grief and grieving
Muir, Edwin. "A Boy's World" 41n1, 70–71, 85–86, 92; "The Ring" 71; "Strange Epic" 71
Muller, Max 50; theory of mythology as a disease of language 50
Murray, Gilbert 80
music 103, 105–06
Music (Creation of Arda) 34, 104–05, 116, 137, 180, 186–87, 189–90, 193, 196–97
Myers, Doris T. "Brave New World: The Status of Women According to Tolkien, Lewis, and Williams" 1, 16, 19–21
mysticism, Christian 44n7
myth 85, 148
Mythlore 14–17, 19–20, 23, 30, 35
Mythopoeic Society 16n9

names and naming 161–62, 170–71, 174, 178–79
Nargothrond 156–58, 175
narrative technique 35
Narrator (fanfiction character) 319–20, 322
Nathan, Robert 66
Native Americans 215n22
naturalistic style 88n20
nature, nature themes and imagery 25, 38, 105, 115, 121–22, 126, 146, 168–71
Nazgûl 108, 118, 125, 131–32, 143, 199, 210n17, 241, 246, 274–75, 277, 302
Neave, Jane (née Suffield) 42–45; move to Chelmsford 44n7
Neldoreth 122
Nenya 91, 125, 127, 163, 233, 301
Neolithic cultures 144–45
Nerdanel 112, 140
Nessa 105, 139, 191, 192n3
Neville, Jennifer. "Women" 28–29
New Zealand 209, 216
Nienna 5, 105, 139, 189–202; other names 192; textual history 190–95, 202
Nienor Níniel 167, 193
nineteenth century literature and society 71–78, 85, 92, 142; in America 77, 142
Noldor 106–07, 112, 127, 141–42, 154–58, 160, 165, 198; Rebellion of 107, 127–28, 141, 154–57, 160, 165
norns 236–37
Norse language, literature, and mythology 6, 38, 120, 191, 193–94, 224–45 passim, 250, 260
North Pole expeditions 41
Northern Waste 141
Númenor and Númenóreans 108, 111n3, 113, 137, 143–44, 146–47, 215, 309, 312, 320

Odin 227, 229, 235, 237–38, 243
Old English language and literature 28–29, 52, 56–57, 224, 225n8, 228,

230–34, 239–43, 245, 247; *see also* Anglo-Saxon literature and culture
Old Forest 121
Old Man Willow 115, 121
Old Mill (Birmingham) 41
Oliphant, Margaret 79–81. *A Beleaguered City* 75
Olórin *see* Gandalf
Olsen, Stefanie 14
Olszewska, E. 56
Olwë 155–56
"On Fairy-stories" 19, 72, 77, 83–85, 93, 128, 130, 223n4, 254n32
Ondoher 320
Ónen 191n2
Onions, C. T. 54
online communities 310
orcs 71, 125, 142, 147, 181, 199, 241, 301, 309
Ormulum 60
Oromë 105, 139, 192, 195
Ossë 140, 191n2, 192n3
Owen, Wilfred 204n1
Oxford Christian authors 16
Oxford English Dictionary 49n14, 52, 54, 57, 60, 205–06
Oxford High School for Girls 50
Oxford Poetry 53
Oxford University 41–65 passim; allows women members 53; allows women professors 61n23; Bodleian Library 58; English School 42; J. R. R. Tolkien Professorship of English Language and Literature 42, 64; statutes relating to professors 49n14. Clubs: English Club 58; Viking Society 58. Colleges: Balliol 56; Exeter 64; Linacre 61; Magdalen College 49; Merton 63–64; Pembroke 64; St. Edmund Hall 56. Women's colleges 34; Lady Margaret Hall 42, 48, 52, 56, 64; Society of Home-Students 50, 52, 56, 58–59; Somerville 52, 56; St. Anne's 50, 59, 61, 64; St. Hilda's 52, 57, 63n26, 64; St. Hugh's 52, 56–58

Paar, Kathryn 14
palantíri 112, 312
paradise 36, 118
parody 282
Partridge, Brenda. "No Sex Please—We're Hobbits: The Construction of Female Sexuality in *The Lord of the Rings*" 17–19, 25, 281n1
passivity 2, 5–6, 28, 46, 101, 106, 130, 191, 210n12, 211, 258, 264, 268, 277, 284, 286
Paston, Margaret 263
Paths of the Dead 207–08, 210, 248, 269, 271, 276
patriarchy 25, 28, 32–33, 112–13, 119, 132, 138, 140, 142, 145, 221, 269, 281, 284–86, 290, 293, 318
patrilineal descent 140, 267
Paul, St. 123–24
peace 18, 31, 132–33, 234–35
Pearl 36, 45n8
Peary, Robert Edwin 41
Pelargir 321
Pelendur 320
Perrault, Charles. "Sleeping Beauty" 286
Persephone 139
Petrarch 292–93
phallic symbolism 25, 110, 116
philology 48–50, 58
physical prowess 225, 228, 234, 241, 243–44, 261, 275
physiology 44
Pippin Took 91, 115, 121
pity 103, 105, 190, 194, 197–202
player-king figures 289
plot 74
Plotz, Dick 159
Poetic Edda 225n8, 234n17, 242n25, 250n30; Characters: Herföðr 242n25; *see also Eddas*
Poland 36
politics, political participation, and political power 137, 140–44, 245, 262, 271, 302
Popular and American Culture Association, Tolkien Studies Area 15
pornography 311
postmodernism 39
post-traumatic stress disorder in fanfiction 323; *see also* war trauma
power and power relations 4–7, 19–20, 31, 118–34 passim, 136–149 passim, 162–63, 169, 175–76, 180–81, 183, 185, 222, 244, 254, 281–303 passim
power as masculine attribute 100–01, 284
prayer 37

Pretorius, David. "Binary Issues and Feminist Issues in *LOTR*" 24–25, 37
pride 5, 25, 31, 118, 121, 126, 155, 158, 160, 162, 224
priest-kings 144
primary education 77
princesses 75, 120, 247, 266
prophecy 32, 143, 225, 227, 229, 236–38, 246, 252, 275
Prose Edda 225n8. Characters: Skuld 237; *see also Eddas*
Prose Merlin 262, 276. Characters: Avenable 261–62, 276–77; *see also* Arthur, King *and* Arthurian legends
psychoanalysis, feminist 20n11
public schools 48
purgatory 154, 193
Pym, Barbara 57–58

queens 28, 37, 86, 91, 104, 122, 126, 133, 144, 154, 163, 190, 192, 230, 240, 248, 265–66, 272, 276, 315, 320
queer theory and perspectives 37, 310, 313–14; in fanfiction 322
quests and quest romance genre 6, 73, 85, 92, 173, 236, 259–62, 266, 273, 278

race 15n7, 39, 309
radiance 228, 230–32, 247, 251, 255; *see also* light
Ragnarök 237
Rangers 289; in fanfiction 317, 319n7
rape 35, 147, 169n3, 175, 177n17, 179, 270, 276; in fanfiction 319–20
Rapunzel 144
Rawlinson and Bosworth Chair of English (Oxford) 62, 63n27
Rawls, Melanie A. "The Feminine Principle in Tolkien" 4, 17–20, 99–117, 139–40, 146–47, 222–23, 240, 281n2
Ray, Stella M. "Constructions of Gender and Sexualities in J. R. R. Tolkien's *The Silmarillion* and *The Lord of the Rings*" 36
Rea, Jason 14
Recovery (element of fairy-stories) 254
Red Cross 208
Reid, Robin Anne. "Light (noun,1) or Light (adjective, 14b)?: Female Bodies and Femininities in Tolkien's *The Lord of the Rings*" 27n12, 37
reincarnation 192
religion 18, 140
Renaissance literature and culture 6, 16, 32–33, 283–86, 290–91
Renault, Mary 57–58. Works: *The King Must Die* 57; *The Bull from the Sea* 57
reparative reading 309–25
Resnik, Henry. Interview with J. R. R. Tolkien 72, 74, 82–84, 92
Resurrection 130
Richardson, Maurice 71
Ring (the One Ring) 32, 73, 88, 91, 102–05, 107n2, 108, 119, 124–27, 132, 148–49, 153–54, 159–60, 162–65, 199–201, 233, 237–38, 241, 266, 289; in fanfiction 324; other rings of power 125; *see also* Nenya
Ringel, Faye. "Women Fantasists: In the Shadow of the Ring" 24
Ringwraiths *see* Nazgûl
Ripley, Aline. "Feminist Readings of Tolkien" 29–30
Rivendell 106, 122–23, 208n10, 251–52; in fanfiction 321
road as symbol 107n2
Roberts, Adam. "Women" 2
Robertson, Pat 286
Rohan and the Rohirrim 28, 111, 131, 143, 210n13, 214–15, 245–51, 260, 264–69, 272–74, 276, 298; in fanfiction 318, 321
role reversal 33, 282–83, 287–90
Romaine, Suzanne 63
Le Roman de Silence 261. Characters: Silence 261–62, 276–77
Roman marriages 205n2
Roman mythology 193
romance genre 4, 6, 24, 38, 70, 72–76, 78, 85–86, 258, 260–62, 264–65, 272, 274, 276–78, 290, 297–98, 301, 303
Rosie Cotton 227, 259; in fanfiction 324
Rowanna (fanfiction character) 321–22
Rowling, J. K. 27; Harry Potter fanfiction 322
Ryan, J. S. "Another Warrior Woman Who Gave Up Thoughts of Battle and Heroism: Greta the Strong" 17–19

sacrifice 31, 79, 124–25, 129, 131, 225, 238, 249, 254, 259, 272
sagas 38, 224

Sam Gamgee 18n10, 25, 27, 37, 91, 103, 125, 127, 148, 169n4, 184n27, 227, 234–35, 237, 255, 259, 290, 302; in fanfiction 324

sanctuary 19, 37

Saruman 99, 108n2, 110, 134, 199–200, 260, 263, 276, 298, 302

Sassoon, Siegfried. "Glory of Women" 207n7; "Their Frailty" 210n16

Satan 130, 180n23; *see also* Lucifer

Sauron 3, 91, 99, 102, 104–05, 107–09, 116, 125–26, 129, 132–33, 142–44, 146–48, 154, 162–63, 165, 169, 175–79, 181, 185, 200, 210n17, 237, 241, 263, 289, 301, 316; physical form 176–77

Sayers, Dorothy L. 53

Scandinavia 60, 230

science 119

science fiction 115–16

Scotland 212, 214

Scott, Robert Falcon 41

Scott, Sir Walter 78n10. Works: *Ivanhoe* 77, 78n10

Scull, Christina 53, 61n23

Scylla and Charybdis 222

"The Seafarer" 239n23

Seaman, Gerald. "Lúthien" 29

secondary characters 259

sewing 228, 236, 242, 248, 252

sex (biological classification) 4, 99–100

sexism 18, 28, 34, 36, 119, 120

sexual agency and desire 5, 87–88, 90–91, 168–73, 179–80

sexual harassment 318n7

sexuality, female 17–18, 168–73, 179n20, 184–86; in fanfiction 314

Shackleton, Ernest 41

shadow (Jungian analysis) 16

Shadowlands 46

Shakespeare, William 6, 32–33, 36, 281–303; accusations of sexism and misogyny 281; comedies 296–97; female characters in general 281n2, 291, 298. Works: *As You Like It* 170n5; *A Midsummer Night's Dream* 32; *Much Ado About Nothing* 289; "My Mistress' Eyes are Nothing like the Sun" 295; *Romeo and Juliet* 292–93; *The Tempest* 289; *Twelfth Night* 6, 33, 281 303 passim. Characters: Andrew Aguecheek 288; Don Pedro 289; Juliet 293; Malvolio 288–89; Maria 289; Olivia 282, 288–89, 291, 293–96, 300–01, 303; Orlando 170n5; Orsino 288–89, 292–95; Prospero 289; Romeo 292–93; Rosalind (*As You Like It*) 170n5; Rosalind (*Romeo and Juliet*) 292; Sebastian 289, 291n9, 295–96; Titania 32; Toby Belch 288, 296; Valentine 294; Viola 289, 291–96, 298–300, 303; Viola as Cesario 294, 296

shape-shifting 169, 184

Shelob 6, 17, 18n10, 20, 25, 30, 36–38, 102, 115, 120, 184nn26–27, 222, 224n5, 225, 227–30, 234, 239–43, 254–55, 259

Sherman, Delia 24

shieldmaidens 3, 5, 110–11, 132, 143, 204, 215, 243–46, 248, 250–51, 254, 263, 266, 270, 272–74, 277–78

Shippey, Tom 38. Works: *The Road to Middle-earth* 166–67, 215n22; "Tolkien's Sources: The True Tradition" 224

The Shire 33, 91, 121, 226n9, 227

Sickle (constellation) 176

Sigrdrífomál 225n8, 234n17. Characters: Sigrdrífa 226, 234n17, 250n30, 253

Sigurðarkviða en skamma 225n8, 231, 236–37

silence 6, 30, 258–78 passim, 286, 297, 312–13

The Silmarillion. "The Ainulindalë" 105, 196; "The Akallâbeth" 113; "The Mariner's Wife" 111n3; "Valaquenta" 190, 195–97, 200. Textual history 21, 153–67 passim, 168n1, 189–90, 193–95, 259

Silmarillion Writers' Guild 310

Silmarils 3, 112–14, 144, 161, 168, 175, 177, 180–83, 186, 197

simbelmynë 264

Sinclair, May. *Mary Olivier* 325

Sindarin Elves 106, 154, 165

Sir Gawain and the Green Knight 16, 48, 52, 54; scholarship by Elizabeth Mary Wright 48–49; *see also* Tolkien, J. R. R., and E. V. Gordon

Sirens 222

Sirion 198

Sisters of Mercy 51

slang 71

Sleeping Beauty (film) 286; Maleficent 286n5

Sleeping Beauty 286; *see also* Perrault, Charles

Sly, Debbie. "Weaving Nets of Gloom: 'Darkness Profound' in Tolkien and Milton" 24
Smaug 105
Smith, A. H. (Hugh) 54n18, 55, 60
Smith, Helen (née Tomlinson) 55
Smith, Melissa A. "At Home and Abroad: Éowyn's Two-fold Figuring as War Bride in *The Lord of the Rings*" 5–6, 32, 204–16
Smol, Anna. "Gender in Tolkien's Works" 29–30
Snow White and the Seven Dwarfs (film) 286
Snow White 286
Sobol, Donald. *Greta the Strong* 18
social media 310
Solopova, Elizabeth 64n29
song 37, 101, 105–07, 121, 169–70, 172n11, 176, 179–81, 183–85, 189–90, 196, 198, 239, 302
Songs for the Philologists 55
Southrons 146
The Spectator 89
speech and speech acts 6–7, 229, 258, 260, 268, 274, 277–78; female speech and voice 272, 303, 313
Spenser, Edmund 45n8. Works: *The Faerie Queene* 70, 85
spiders 183, 184n26, 239, 241–43
spirituality and spiritual power 4–5, 19, 25, 31, 118, 126, 129–31, 133, 139–41, 144, 234
sports and athletes 107, 141, 160–61
St. Joseph's Catholic Primary School 61
St. Philip's School 43
stars, starlight, and star imagery 36, 113–14, 122, 138, 172n10, 176, 178n19, 191, 193, 197, 231–34, 239, 251–53, 264
Startzman, L. Eugene. "Goldberry and Galadriel: The Quality of Joy" 17, 19–20
Stein, Gertrude 31
stereotypes 1, 6, 28, 118–20, 134, 190, 221, 228, 281, 288–91, 293
Sterne, Lawrence. *A Sentimental Journey* 45n8
Stevenson, Robert Louis 70, 72, 76, 79, 80n15, 82, 93. Works: *Kidnapped* 70, 74; *Treasure Island* 70, 74, 78, 92
Stoker, Bram. *Dracula* 73n3
Strohm, Paul 64
subcreation 26–27, 117, 137–38, 146, 173, 189, 201
submission 31, 129, 267, 286
Suffield, Beatrice 46; destruction of Mabel's papers 46n9
Suffield, Jane *see* Neave, Jane
Suffield, John (brother of Jane, Mabel, and May) 45n8
Suffield, John (father of Jane, Mabel, and May) 43n4, 44n5
Suffield, Mabel *see* Tolkien, Mabel
Suffield, May *see* Incledon, May
suicide 313
sun and sun imagery 111, 231–33, 247, 259, 263; and moon, creation of 195
swan imagery 231
Swann, Donald. *The Road Goes Ever On* 153–54
Swinburne, Algernon Charles 65
Switzerland 45
swords and sword symbolism 25, 110, 116, 148–49, 233, 235n18, 244, 262, 266–68, 271, 286n5, 298–99

Taniquetil (Mount Everwhite) 191, 239
Tar-Míriel 108–09, 147
Tar-Palantir 113
Tauriel 26; *see also The Hobbit*. Film trilogy dir. Peter Jackson
Taur-nu-Fuin 177n18
Taylor, Taryne Jade. "Investigating the Role and Origin of Goldberry in Tolkien's Mythology" 34
TCBS (Tea Club and Barrovian Society) 213n20
technology 101, 115, 146
Teleri 155, 157, 160, 162, 165–66
Telperion 161
Tennyson, Alfred Lord. "Come Down, O Maid" 45
Terrible Mother archetype 184n27
Þe Liflade ant te Passiun of Seinte Iulienen 59
Théoden 109–10, 131, 143, 199, 213, 215n24, 244–50, 260, 264–67, 269, 271–74, 276–77, 289, 297–99, 302; in fanfiction 314–18
Théodred in fanfiction 315
Théodwyn 215n24
Thingol 106, 114, 147, 156, 168, 170, 173–76, 186
Thomas, Paul 66

Thompson, Kristin. "Gollum Talks to Himself: Problems and Solutions in Peter Jackson's Film Adaptation of *The Lord of the Rings*" 26
Thompson, Meredith 60–61
Thompson, Stith 173n12
Thomsen, Morgan 62n24
Thomson, Graham R. (Rosamund Marriott Watson) 75
Þorbjarnardóttir, Arndís 42
Thorbjörg 245
Thorin 105
Thum, Maureen. "Hidden in Plain View: Strategizing Unconventionality in Shakespeare's and Tolkien's Portraits of Women" 6, 32–33, 281–303; "The 'Sub-Subcreation' of Galadriel, Arwen, and Éowyn: Women of Power in Tolkien's and Jackson's *The Lord of the Rings*" 27
Thuringwethil 177–78
time 38, 85, 105, 164; *see also* antiquity
Timmons, Daniel 38; *see also* Clark, George, and Daniel Timmons
tobacco 48
Tol Sirion 174–76, 181
tolerance 125
Tolkien Estate 324
Tolkien Society of America 159
Tolkien, Arthur 44n5
Tolkien, Christopher 17, 26, 53, 158–60, 165, 193, 195; World War II service in South Africa 146
Tolkien, Edith (née Bratt) 26, 41–42, 47, 51, 53, 55, 226; happiness at Leeds 55; World War I experiences 207, 209–11, 213n20
Tolkien, Hilary 41, 44, 46
Tolkien, John (son) 51, 210
Tolkien, John Benjamin (grandfather) 44n5
Tolkien, J. R. R. Personal life: as paterfamilias 42; attitudes toward feminism 2; attitudes toward women 164n12; biographical material 18; childhood homes 41; childhood reading preferences 72, 82–83, 92–93; executor of Joseph Wright's estate 49; female family and associates 4, 29, 41–67 passim; grandchildren 41–42; male friendships 18n10, 41, 47n11, 213n20; marriage to Edith 207; religious beliefs 119, 127–28, 149, 153, 164n12, 201, 226; World War I experiences 18n10, 41, 51–52, 205, 207n8, 209–11, 216. Professional life: academic career in general 62; as philologist 50; as student and professor at Oxford 20, 31, 41–67 passim; attitudes toward female students 52–65; essay for Clark-Hall translation of *Beowulf* 58; grading exams 49n14; interest in languages 44n6, 84; lectures on *Beowulf* 57; professor at Leeds 49n14, 53–57; supervising theses 56–57; tutoring 54–56; tutoring women students 49, 52–53, 56, 60–62; work on the *Oxford English Dictionary* 49n14, 52, 205. Works in general: aesthetic elements 24; American criticism 18n10; bibliography of scholarship about 14–15, 38; ecological concerns 149; female characters in general 2, 13–39, 41, 86, 92, 118, 120, 133–34, 136, 202, 221–27, 230, 240, 251, 254, 260, 262, 291; future of scholarship about 7, 39; history of scholarship about 1–3, 7, 13–39, 85; influences on his work 82–83; invented languages 247–48n29, 287; knowledge of Shakespeare 281; legendarium—style 38; legendarium—textual history 189–98, 201–02; male characters in general 71, 299–300; media adaptations 7; perfectionism 166; popularity of books 74; portrayal of gender 72–73, 92, 119, 131, 146, 191; racist interpretations 146, 309; religious and theological elements 24–25, 128–29; sexist and misogynistic interpretations 28, 34, 36, 120, 167, 216, 221, 281n1; source study about 223; techniques of characterization 37–38; use of symbolism 36; women readers 64–65, 309–10. Works: *listed independently by title*
Tolkien, J. R. R., and E. V. Gordon. *Sir Gawaine and the Green Knight* 48n13
Tolkien, Mabel (née Suffield) 41, 43, 44n6, 226; death 46; destruction of papers 46n9
Tolkien, Michael 52n16, 59
Tolkien, Priscilla 41–42, 46, 53–54, 58, 64
Tolstoy, Leo 93
Tom Bombadil 121, 146, 149

Tooks (Hobbit family) 103
"Total Woman" 100
tourism studies 15, 26
Treebeard 115, 146, 259–60
trees 146
Tubbs, Patricia. "*Juliana*" 29
Tulkas 105, 191n2, 192n3
Tuor 105–06
Turgon 106, 108–09, 113
Túrin Turambar 193, 198
Turville-Petre, Gabriel 61
Tuve, R. 56
Twain, Mark 93
twentieth century literature and culture 15, 32, 39, 71, 85, 120, 204, 285–86
Two Trees 105, 112, 114, 161, 180, 184, 190–92, 195–98; *see also* Laurelin *and* Telperion

ubi sunt poetic motifs 239
Uinen 140, 192n3
Ulmo 113, 191n2, 194
Underhill, Evelyn 44n7
understanding as feminine characteristic 100–04, 106, 125
Unfinished Tales 107, 136. "The History of Galadriel and Celeborn" 153, 158–60, 165–66; "The Mariner's Wife" 111n3. Textual history 158, 160, 165
Ungoliant 24, 29, 36, 109, 170n6, 183–84, 190, 197
United States armed forces 205, 213
University College London 60
University of Helsinki 61n23
University of Liege 59
University of St. Andrew's 44–45
university presses 15
Unwin, Rayner 71
Uruk-hai 199
Urwen 191

Vaccaro, Christopher, ed. *The Body in Tolkien's Legendarium: Essays on Middle-earth Corporeality* 37–38
Vairë 105, 139, 192, 194–95, 202
Valar 103, 105, 114, 127–28, 153, 155–57, 159–60, 166, 186, 189–95, 198, 200–02; Aratar 193; Fëanturi 194; gender, power of gender, and gender pairings 24, 99–100, 114, 138–40, 144, 167, 191, 194, 202; textual history 189, 191–93, 195–98
"Valedictory Address" 49n14, 52
Valhalla 234
Valinor 100, 101n1, 105, 111, 137, 145, 155, 157–61, 165–66, 175, 179–80, 198
valkyries 6, 184n27, 225–55 passim, 260, 281n2, 300, 302; origin of word 229–30
Valmar (Valimar) 190, 239
Vaná 139, 191–92, 194–96
Vanyar 161n8
Varda 24, 36–37, 100, 103–04, 114, 127, 138, 140, 149, 167, 189–91, 200, 202, 239; as a Marian figure 37, 127, 128n5, 138, 200; in fanfiction 315; textual history 191, 195, 197
Venetian Republic 287n6
vengeance and vengefulness 226, 229
Verne, Jules 78n10
Victorian literature and culture 25, 73, 75, 78n10, 92, 112, 309
Victorian scholarship 28, 75
Vingilot 114
violence against women 147, 276
Virgil. *Aeneid*—influence on Tolkien 20
virginity 261, 276
Void 180, 184
Völsunga saga 225n8, 226n9, 234n17, 236, 250n30, 251. Characters: Brynhild 226, 228, 231, 234n17, 236, 238, 243–45, 250n30, 251, 253; Signy 236; Sigurd 236
Völundarkviða 225n8, 231, 236
Völuspá 225n8, 242n25

Wainriders 143, 146
"The Wanderer" 239n23
war and battle 18n10, 32, 41, 75, 102, 106, 110, 118, 142, 144, 208–09, 215–16, 227, 229–30, 237–38, 251, 260–62, 266, 269–71, 299–300, 315
war brides 5–6, 32, 204–16; Japanese 211
War of the Ring 103, 310, 312, 314, 317, 319–21
war poets and poetry 204n1
war trauma 319–20; *see also* post-traumatic stress disorder
Ward, Mrs. Humphrey 77
waste lands 37
water imagery and symbolism 34, 38, 106, 237
water nymphs 121
Watson, William 74, 79

Weathertop 122
weaving 101, 105, 169, 178n19, 183–85, 195, 236, 242, 248, 252
Weinreich, Frank, and Thomas Honegger, eds. *Tolkien and Modernity 1* 29
Wentworth, Marion Craig. "War Brides" 205–06, 211n18
West, Richard C. "Real-World Myth in a Secondary World: Mythological Aspects in the Story of Beren and Lúthien" 25–26, 171n8; *Tolkien Criticism: An Annotated Bibliography* 14
Whitaker, Lynn. "Corrupting Beauty: Rape Narrative in *The Silmarillion*" 35, 169n3, 174, 177n17, 179n20, 180
White Council 126, 302
Whitelock, Dorothy 63
White Tree 216, 252
Who's Who 56
widows 267, 294n11
Williams, Charles 16, 20–21, 82, 119, 221n1. Works: *The Place of the Lion* 20, 66. Characters: Damaris Tighe 20, 66
Williamson, James T. "Emblematic Bodies: Tolkien and the Depiction of Female Physical Presence" 37–38
Wilson, Edmund. "Oo, Those Awful Orcs!" 70
wine 235, 247
Winfrith (fanfiction character) 314–16
wisdom 17, 90, 125, 127, 129, 146, 148, 162, 195, 228
Wiseman, Christopher 47
witches and witchcraft 33, 284–87, 302
Witch-king of Angmar 3, 33, 65, 246, 249–50, 255, 258, 299, 302; *see also* Nazgûl
wives 113, 267, 277–78
wizards 71, 120, 310, 324
Woledge, Brian 60
women authors 24
women in higher education 44–45, 284
women readers 64, 72, 79–81, 136, 309–10, 324–25
women scholars and critics 27n12, 31
women studies programs 15, 221
women warriors 18, 27, 30, 142–43, 243–50, 263, 299–300
women's rights and suffrage 15, 16, 29, 33, 50, 285
women's roles 24, 29, 31, 119, 132, 142, 202, 226, 243n27, 246, 261, 270–71, 281–303 passim
The Wonders of the East 242–43
Wood-elves 148
Woolf, Virginia 31, 42, 50. Works: *The Years* 50; *The Diary of Virginia Woolf* 50n15; *A Room of One's Own* 285
Worcestershire 45
World War I 5–6, 18n10, 32, 34, 36, 41, 51, 204–16 passim; Armistice 51; contemporary pop culture 204
World War II 31, 83, 146, 204–16 passim, 285, 319; contemporary pop culture 204–05; post-war literature and culture 226–27
Wormtongue 33, 110, 199, 209n11, 249, 260, 263–64, 271, 273, 276–77, 289, 298, 302
Woses 146
Wrenn, C. L. 54n18, 63n27
Wright, Elizabeth Mary 48–50, 53. Works: essays on *Beowulf* and *Sir Gawain* 48–49; *The Life of Joseph Wright* 50, 60; *Old Northumbrian Grammar* 48; *Rustic Speech and Folk-lore* 48; "The Word 'Abloy' in 'Sir Gawayne and the Green Knight,' 1.1174" 48n13; *see also* Wright, Joseph
Wright, Joseph 42, 48–51; attitude toward female students 42, 49–51, 60; grading exams and tutoring 49; influence on Tolkien 42, 49–51. Works co-authored with Elizabeth Mary Wright: *An Old English Grammar* 48; *An Elementary Historical New English Grammar* 48; *An Elementary Middle English Grammar* 48
Wulfstan. *Sermo Lupi ad Anglos* 57
Wynne, Hilary 14–15, 38–39
Wyss, Johann David. *Swiss Family Robinson* 78n10

Yavanna 105, 114–15, 139, 189–92, 195–97; alternate name Palúrien 191
Yeskov, Kirill. *The Last Ringbearer* 324
Yorkshire 53
Yugoslavia 287n6

Zettersten, Arne. "*Ancrene Wisse*" 29

Made in the USA
Middletown, DE
13 July 2019